Top UK Companies
of the Future

The Corporate Research Foundation (CRF) is an independent organization that initiates and co-ordinates international research projects in business. The CRF aims to contribute to a better awareness and understanding of corporate culture, effective human resource management, and the strategies of successful enterprise, by researching the key factors behind their success and publishing its findings.

The CRF represents a combined initiative of business journalists, analysts, trade associations, researchers and international publishers, and has been active since 1991 in Australia, Belgium, Germany, Holland, South Africa, Sweden and the United Kingdom.

Other titles in the CRF series in the UK include:

Britain's Top Employers
Top Marketing & Media Companies in the UK
Top ICT Companies in the UK

Corporate Research Foundation
55 Queen Anne Street
London W1G 9JR
Tel: 020 7486 2603
Fax: 020 7486 6245
e-mail: CRF@dial.pipex.com

Top UK Companies of the Future

Corporate Research Foundation
Editor Guy Clapperton

HarperCollinsBusiness
An Imprint of HarperCollins*Publishers*

HarperCollinsBusiness
An Imprint of HarperCollins*Publishers*
77–85 Fulham Palace Road,
Hammersmith, London W6 8JB

www.**fire**and**water**.com/business

Published by HarperCollinsBusiness 2001
1 3 5 7 9 8 6 4 2

Copyright © Corporate Research Foundation 2001

The Corporate Research Foundation asserts the moral right to
be identified as the author of this work

A catalogue record for this book is
available from the British Library

ISBN 0 00 7110294

Set in Meridien by
Rowland Phototypesetting Ltd,
Bury St Edmunds, Suffolk

Printed and bound in Great Britain by
Clays Ltd, St Ives plc

Contents

Editor's Foreword

Anyone who hasn't been exiled on another planet over the last few years will know that there has been a lot of interest or even hype over the so-called new economy. This has in turn been fuelled by new business rules for new media companies, which is overall rather ironic because actually there is nothing new about these businesses. Not that we're saying anything clever there – the crash of so many dot-coms shortly before this book was completed made that abundantly clear. So what are all these new companies doing alongside the more traditional businesses in this volume? This would be a fair question to ask. The answer is prosaic in the extreme; the Corporate Research Foundation believes that the new economy is the same as the old economy, and will ultimately operate within the same rules and parameters. There have been new industries before and there will be again, but none of them has ever truly altered the laws of supply and demand or the need to add value to a service to distinguish it from the competition. So in this volume the new companies queue up to tell their stories alongside the old, and the criteria by which the reader must judge them remain the same.

Not that there aren't new concepts in here. Internet service organizations such as eTribes plus incubator organizations like GorillaPark are represented in here because we're talking about future companies; their business models appear sound but have yet to be tested over a period of time. It will be interesting to watch their progress. There are also organizations sticking with a traditional means of trading; they also believe they have a solid future.

It's likely that both are right. Their stories are told in this volume and hopefully other managers will find much to enlighten and influence them about the strategies that will take these organizations ahead.

Guy Clapperton
Editor

Introduction

Irreverence – An Essential Leadership Quality for Businesses of the Future

You can be forgiven for being jaundiced about the subject of leadership – it has been done to death. Worse, it is still unclear what part leadership plays in building successful businesses, for although it is an everyday concept, it has many definitions. Try to pin it down and it evaporates. So what is the elusive ingredient that new economy leaders must possess to create future successful companies? Let us start with what we do know.

One thing we can be sure of is that leadership is not to do with heroes. They have a short shelf life in business. It is not much to do with charisma either. Many CEOs who preside over highly successful corporations just do not fit the description. They are as likely to be unassuming introverts as magnetic personalities. We also know leadership is about vision, and that the best visions are simple ones. But visions can be short-lived, and are sometimes nothing short of disastrous when the world moves on. Think of British Airways' brilliant strapline: 'the world's favourite airline'. What a vision to be stuck with when things are not going your way.

Leadership is also about business transformation. Jack Welch's turn around of GE's fortunes must be the most oft-quoted example in business history. All well and good when transformation means new ways of doing business and very different models of organizing; not so good when it means corporate anorexia. And do not be fooled into believing that 'leadership as transformation' can be pinned down to creating the fabled learning organization. Judging from the rapidly accelerating pace with which FTSE 100 index and Fortune 500 businesses come and go, organizational learning remains elusive. Amazon and Yahoo! are already best described as old-fashioned dotcoms – five years from now they probably won't exist.

So what we know is that leadership is about vision, change and learning, but that this is not the whole story. What, then, is missing? If you have attended one of the recent rash of 'Leadership for the Third Millennium/New Economy' conferences looking for the answer, the chances are you were disappointed. You will have heard some more about vision, change and learning, standard messages laced with exhortations to leverage knowledge, embrace the e-volution, and become a networked organization. But that is merely the name of the game – a picture of what is already happening, and a timely warning to get up to speed. The missing ingredient in all of this is a healthy *irreverence* for the building blocks of business and organizing that have been with us for nigh on two hundred years.

The reason that Cisco Systems, ABB, Dell, IKEA, Priceline, and other spectacularly successful enterprises are so interesting, is that they have pioneered new business and organizational models. That is why they are so fêted by management gurus. And there are many more you will never hear about, often not even stand-alone businesses, but little pockets of alternative enterprise immersed within conventional corporate structures. Their achievements are possible because there is an ability to question fundamentally what most of us not only take for granted, but hold in high esteem.

Irreverence is the ability to extract oneself from the clutches of a mentality that saturates attention and obliterates alternatives. Acquiring knowledge is not synonymous with thinking differently because if it were, leaders would act on it more often than they do. Anyway, new economy leaders are fully aware that the business environment is fundamentally changing; they know about patterns of globalization, the technological revolution, the organizational migration towards virtual and networked forms. But it is precisely with this awareness that the problem kicks in, and it happens as soon as new insights do not accord with the old truths.

That elegantly simple vision of a business in symbiotic relationship with its customers and suppliers and at one with the new economic order, will be stillborn so long as reverence prevails. Leaders may know, for example, that businesses function better as self-regulating internal markets. But this understanding will not help them to realize a new vision for organizing *their* business so long as they continue to believe that centrally planned economic rationality is the only means of value creation. Only irreverence for the myths of corporate unity and internal political neutrality will achieve that. Similarly, it is irreverence for old ideas about competition and boundary control that allows them to build a vision based on truly interdependent relationships with customers, suppliers and rivals, to excel only in what they are good at and jettison great swathes of their business. And it is irreverence for the simplistic goal of economic growth that will lead them to

think and act on behalf of the many stakeholders in their business –
the people who work there, for example.

Today, then, irreverence makes for good business leadership. Consider all those examples of novel organization in high-tech industries
– it is no coincidence. They have had a natural advantage in side-
stepping the conventions of business practice. Youth, expertise and
total confidence in the power of technology. It is a heady cocktail
when it comes to irreverence but it has probably run its course. We
should not expect high-tech companies to provide a never-ending
supply of new business models, and indeed, the big ones have acquired
some classic symptoms of corporate inertia. But we can learn from
these great examples, or from anywhere else that irreverent leaders
are to be found. That probably includes every industry there is.

Not surprisingly, irreverence does not feature in the competence
list of business leadership. There are too many negative connotations.
But irreverence is what it takes to comprehend the power of a mindset
to constrain and inhibit vision, and so needs to be used well. If it is
not, people misunderstand and they either value or revile it. There is
no middle ground. So what is the difference between constructive
irreverence and the 'in your face' variety? It is a good question. The
answer is that, in today's business world, constructive irreverence is a
watchword for mature leadership. It does not define leadership but it
does add something crucial.

David Butcher, senior lecturer in management development and director of general management programmes, Cranfield School of Management.

Research Team

Editor:

Guy Clapperton

Contributors:

Frank Booty
Paul Bray
Jim Dow
Wendy Grossman
Mike Hardwidge
Dennis Jarrett
Jon Lamb
Rachelle Thackray
Roger Trapp
Dom Panucci
Bryan Betts
Candice Goodwin
Richard Jolley

Top UK Companies
of the Future

@stake^{SM}

@stake works where business and technology intersect, because that is where security is most powerful. The firm integrates technical and business expertise to build security solutions that look beyond the network to the security of applications and data, and future business goals.

@stake couples vertical industry expertise in three areas – financial services, communication service providers and e-markets – with pioneering research, to design and build strategic security solutions that enable the electronic business initiatives of its Global 2000 clients. Amidst other providers for whom security services are a way to sell products or drive the sale of broader service offerings, @stake stands out with its dedicated focus on security consulting services and the unmatched calibre of its people.

Scorecard:

Innovation	★★★★★
Flexibility	★★★★
Human resources	★★★★
Growth markets	★★★
Quality of management	★★★★★
International orientation	★★★

Biggest plus:
You have become part of the upper echelon of online security experts.

Biggest minus:
You can't go down the pub and tell your friends about your work.

@stake
52 Throwley Way, Sutton
Surrey SM1 4BF
Tel: 020 8395 4980
website: www.atstake.com

@stake

The Business

Founded on January 6, 2000, with initial funding of $10 million from Battery Ventures, @stake has grown to meet increasing market demand for security consulting services, opening offices in Raleigh, North Carolina, as well as New York, Denver, Seattle, San Francisco, and London. @stake works with a range of innovative companies, including ATG, Bertelsmann mediaSystems, Blackstone Technology Group, Exodus and Predictive Networks, to create strategic security solutions that enable their business initiatives.

In December 2000, @stake secured a second round of financing totalling $26 million. This round was led by Madison Dearborn Capital Partners III, L.P., and also included original investor Battery Ventures. In addition, the round included private equity investments from high-profile industry executives such as: Bruce Claflin, president and COO of 3Com Corporation; Paul Sagan, president of Akamai Technologies; William Cadogan, chairman, president and CEO of ADC Telecom; Bob Palmer, former chairman, president and CEO of Digital Equipment Corporation; Eckhard Pfeiffer, chairman of Intershop and former CEO of Compaq Computer Corporation; Morgan O'Brien, co-founder of Nextel Communications, Inc and Robert J. Davis, president and CEO of Lycos.

Innovation

@stake's greatest claim to innovation involves its unique and honest approach to the whole issue of e-business security. It is made clear in @stake's publicity material that truthfulness is essential when it comes to security and it states clearly that no network can be made 100 per cent secure. So the company's primary goal is to educate user organizations about the need to only apply the necessary security measures without impeding accessibility to the online services. This awareness building will focus on risk management and not just on fortifying the perimeters around e-business networks. For instance, one of the company's slogans is 'Not everything in your online business is worth protecting' – a message that represents a serious departure from the typical online security sales pitch. @stake will simulate intrusions to an e-business network, to help customers develop a real world view of their security situation so they can perform a more holistic security audit.

The analogy used by @stake takes in a shift from the medieval citadel concept to that of an airport. In a well-managed airport people can have free access to most parts of the building, except in sensitive areas that can then be properly secured without any impediment to business traffic. Within this model, the integrity of the perimeter is maintained and methods like encryption and virtual private networks are used to link with business partners and other trusted third parties. @stake is vendor neutral and makes unbiased recommendations to customers when it comes to selecting security systems.

Keeping up to speed is crucial for @stake and the company has a pioneering research and development team of top professionals dedicated purely to this area of the business. The company is also active in the emerging science of computer forensics, where intruders are tracked by their tell tale 'data trails'. @stake has also established innovators on its board, in particular chief technology officer, Dan Geer, who invented the popular Kerberos security system.

Flexibility

As a new company @stake is still on a fairly steep evolutionary curve, including the second round of venture funding mentioned earlier. Yet the company reckons that scalability and shape-shifting are principles upon which it has been founded anyway. The research and development department effectively drives the way the company will go forward. Examples here include how to apply robust and open security to emerging markets such as wireless or mobile commerce.

Depth and breadth of experience is needed at a company like @stake, but the skills set also needs to be mixed around to ensure that customer projects have the correct resources. To this extent, @stake intends to be a transnational company with a difference – people working for the company are going to be almost fanatically immersed in online security work and will accept a changeable brief.

Europe is also being tackled early on by @stake, with a UK office already up and running. The company accepts that the European market has quite a different dynamic to the US, so @stake is working hard to understand local issues and remain flexible to market needs. As part of this focus on Europe, @stake acquired a company called Cerberus, which had its headquarters in the UK.

In terms of its overall approach to the online security market, @stake has to remain flexible and alert to new developments in both the type and pattern of intrusions, as well as to new techniques to offer flexible protection. If successful, the company will, in turn, help its customers to develop more flexible online businesses where security is nimble and authorized access as open as possible. After all, the company's goal is to secure all digital relationships in the e-business era.

Human Resources

@stake is by no means an average employer. In effect, its potential recruitment pool is limited to barely 1,800 individuals – people who are recognized authorities and talents in the network security community. Added to this demanding requirement is the need to prove vertical market expertise in keeping with @stake's strategic goals.

Word of mouth is key to @stake's assessment of a potential employee and 60 per cent of appointments result from a personal referral. Head-hunters will be used for some executive posts and certain areas of sales. Yet @stake's staff selection process is rigorous. Firstly, any candidate is vetted for security clearance to the highest level and no face-to-face evaluation will take place before these checks are completed. After this the candidate can expect to attend as many as eleven separate interviews before a decision is made. It is not therefore surprising to note that @stake designates its corporate values as integrity, drive, teamwork and growth in expertise.

Growth Markets

There is clearly plenty of potential in the online security market for companies with the winning strategies. The Gartner Group analyst firm reckons that the security services market totalled $7.5 billion in 2000.

Three growth markets have been identified by @stake. One is what the company describes as application infrastructure providers, which is the evolutionary path for the telecommunications industry. Included here are the large Internet Service Providers. Second is the lucrative financial services sector, where online e-business is rapidly taking hold. Third is the digital e-market phenomenon, an area of massive potential. E-markets are online trading environments that bring buyers and sellers together to do business –which clearly have to be secure given the high value of transactions taking place. It is not beyond the realms of possibility that @stake could form separate companies to focus on the three vertical markets.

While Europe is more reactive than the US to online security issues, @stake still sees a quarter of its total revenue coming from places like the UK, France, Germany, Spain, the Netherlands and the Middle East. @stake already has customers with international operations and needs to cover the international reach of these companies. Such enterprises will be found among the Global 2000.

Quality of Management

There is a reported shortage of executive talent for the new breed of online businesses, given the proliferation of dot-coms coinciding with a demographic shortfall of suitable personnel. It is therefore a testament to @stake's potential, that its board consists of high quality and senior people from both the security and commercial sectors.

Dan Geer, the CTO has already been mentioned. Another notable appointee is James Mobley, executive vice-president for professional services, who was formerly a vice-president for sales in a comparable role for Compaq in North America. John Rando, formerly senior vice-president and group general manager at Compaq, is @stake's chairman. Other members of the @stake board have come across from less well known companies that have been innovative in the IT security sector. All this makes for an impressive blend of business and technical talent all the way to the top of the company's hierarchy.

Apart from the senior industry types actually running @stake, the private investors also reveal the respect that this new company's management team has engendered. Among these private funders are Bruce Claflin, president and chief operating officer of 3Com; Bob Palmer, former CEO of Digital Equipment and Eckhard Pfeiffer, a former CEO at Compaq.

In fact, the combination of the @stake management team and these notable supporters has helped the start-up get the regular funding it needs to go to market. The financing will support @stake's planned aggressive growth, research and marketing programmes. Recently, Madison Dearborn Partners publicly stated that a new round of funding had been granted to @stake on the basis of the strength of its management team. @stake is therefore confident enough to describe itself as the only 'pure play' Internet security company on the block.

International Orientation

@stake is taking a flexible approach to international growth, recognizing that its reach has to match that of its customers. The UK office is the first to be opened outside the US and other countries will be covered over time. These include Switzerland, Germany and other Western European states, as well as the Middle East, Latin America and Australia. Basically, @stake will go to the clients whenever necessary. As the company is founded primarily on intellectual capital, its 'assets' can be sent anywhere and with a lower overhead than other types of IT company.

However, due to the nature of its business – oriented solely to Internet security – @stake is also capable of fulfilling its project commitments remotely. This means the work being done in the US.

Over the next year or so, @stake will also have built up a set of alliances to extend its global reach, which means that it might not have to set up an office in every country. @stake reckons that it will be a truly global company within the next three years.

08004homes.com

Property Internet plc owns the website 08004homes.com, the UK's most comprehensive website for house-buyers and estate agents, including the UK's first property news service. Already a public company, and backed by a major bank, it is in a strong position to dominate the online house-buying sector in the UK.

Scorecard:

Innovation	★★★★★
Flexibility	★★★★
Human resources	★★★
Growth markets	★★★★
Quality of management	★★★★★
International orientation	★★★

Biggest plus:
The leading company in its field, with a committed backer and a strong and comprehensive product.

Biggest minus:
Serious competition is looming in the rear-view mirror.

Property Internet plc
157–168 Blackfriars Road
London SE1 8EZ
Tel: 020 7401 7182
Fax: 020 7401 7255
website: 08004homes.com

Property Internet plc

The Business

Property Internet plc runs the UK's most comprehensive Internet site for home buyers, 08004homes.com, and was the first such company to go public. Its core offering consists of listings of properties for sale, drawn from thousands of estate agents throughout England and Wales. Other features include maps, area guides, a list of new homes, mortgages, insurance, a legal section, an interiors magazine, home shopping and property news.

The company was initially self-funded. The flotation on the Alternative Investment Market (AIM) in September 1999 netted £1.6m, and in May 2000 the Commonwealth Bank of Australia bought a 23.5 per cent stake for £6m; the bank is a key active partner, selling mortgage products via the site. Other partners include Legal & General (with 1,400 affiliated estate agents), Cendant (which runs a network for 500 independent estate agents) and Freeserve (which has chosen 08004homes to be a key partner for its own Property Channel).

Innovation

The key value proposition of 08004homes is its rich content. Alan Frame, managing director of Property Internet, says: 'We believe there's no point just having listings, because it doesn't differentiate you – you've got to have content. We're not going to win this game by going down the standard route.'

The site must attract both house-buyers and estate agents. 'People only move house once every seven years on average, so it's hard to build a business on this,' says Frame. 'But people do a lot to their houses after they've moved, and the house-buying process is a trigger to review all their needs. For example, they might make a new will and upgrade their life insurance.'

So the site has a legal section, and an interiors section with feature articles and a directory of more than 1,500 up-market suppliers, of everything from Victorian fireplaces to antique floorboards. There are virtual tours of new houses, and maps showing local amenities to assist people's buying choices.

The company employs five full-time journalists who produce daily property news, weekly features, and comprehensive area guides. The property news is an industry first, says Frame, and the content is syndicated to portal sites including MSN and Excite. There are also sellers' unbiased reviews of estate agents.

Estate agents are a crucial element of the site, so Property Internet offers them a unique package. Properties are listed free of charge. But the company also offers website design and domain name registration, mapping services, and sales of computer hardware and software. These services are charged for, but in return Property Internet sells syndicated advertising on agents' websites, on which the agents receive 65 per cent commission.

Frame's ultimate objective is to improve the whole house-buying process, making it more efficient for buyers and agents. An 'extranet' (like a private Internet, password-protected and accessible only to the parties involved) will enable buyers to track the whole process online – searches, surveys, mortgage approvals etc. This data will be updated by the professionals involved, who will have to field fewer telephone enquiries from their customers. In fact, Property Internet is such a powerhouse of new ideas that it is almost falling over itself to get them to market. Several new projects in 2000 missed their launch deadlines simply because of pressure of work.

Flexibility

'The Internet is constantly changing, and we couldn't exist if we didn't have flexibility,' says Frame. 'We have a three-year plan, but it gets changed every three months. We're already on our third website, and that's not because we like spending money! There's no place here for anybody who can't adapt.'

Property Internet was among the first property websites to realize that, because of increasing competition, estate agents should not be made to pay for having their properties listed. The rest of the market soon followed suit.

The website has even changed its name. It was originally called Home-to-Home.co.uk, but was unable to register the Web address Home-to-Home.com because a conveyancing firm got there first. So the website was relaunched in April 2000 as 08004homes.com.

The company takes a pragmatic approach to getting the right technology. It bought a software development company, Arachnid Systems, which specialized in estate agency systems, and now forms the basis of its in-house IT department. All website content is originated in-house, but the design and hosting of the site have been outsourced to a Swiss company.

Human Resources

Property Internet is largely a young company with an average age for employees of around 28–30. 'That's great,' says Frame, 'because they're not bogged down with old habits.' Most of the 35 staff work in London, with a nine-person IT department in Nottingham. They are adaptable, hard-working people who enjoy their job. 'I get in at 8.15 and I'm not the first,' says Frame.

Nearly all recruits are graduates – and are usually people with existing experience rather than trainees. However, the company has a policy of employing young Americans, mostly recent graduates, on six-month placements; they provide a fresh perspective, and often have highly-developed Internet skills.

Remuneration is adequate rather than generous, with a share options scheme but few other benefits. 'We've had to keep salaries pretty lean, starting at about £20,000,' says Frame.

Growth Markets

Around 1.6 million homes are sold in the UK each year with around 400,000 on the market at any one time. Frame reckons that to achieve critical mass 08004homes needs to list 300,000 of them; he expects to have more than 200,000 by summer 2001. The site is aimed at all house buyers – easier to achieve on the Internet than in the high street, says Frame – with a mid-market editorial content.

Revenues have been minimal during set-up. But once running at full steam, the firm expects revenue to come primarily from agent services and commission from financial services sales, with additional income from areas like advertising and content syndication.

For the future, the company has its eye on retirement homes (over-65s are increasingly using the Internet), student accommodation (banks etc are keen to 'catch 'em young'), and perhaps warranty schemes or even garden products.

Competition is hotting up, however. Several competitors are already trading (although Frame says none has such a full range of content as 08004homes). And Move.com, the strong American market-leader, will be a major challenger with its UK site this year. Frame believes there will be consolidation.

'We want to dominate, but I don't think we can do it on our own,' he says. 'In less than three years we'll be the company that dominates the market, or else a significant part of that company.'

Quality of Management

Unusually for a dot-com start-up, Property Internet is already a plc, and has a board of directors to match; they include Andrew Simon, OBE (a director of Severn Trent and Associated British Ports), and two directors from the Commonwealth Bank of Australia – a demonstration that the bank's commitment goes well beyond its £6m cash investment.

Co-founders Alan Frame and Neil Mackwood were both senior journalists (Frame had been executive editor of the *Daily Express*). Neither had experience in property (Frame has only bought two houses in his life!). But they realized the potential for a property site that would mix listings with services and magazine-style content, and they have recruited an experienced team, including at least three former estate agents.

Frame characterizes the company as comfortably off, but careful. 'We have sufficient cash in the bank not to have to go to the market for at least two years,' he says. 'And having been self-financed at the start, we've shown that we can achieve an efficient use of funds.'

Frame's management style is relaxed, but he is determined to get results. 'I try to be completely open about everything, and encourage everyone to do their own thing and tell me about it later,' he says. 'I want them to think it's their company. But I got rid of one head of department who wasn't performing well and didn't seem to have a strategy, and I wouldn't hesitate to do it again.'

If the company had a weakness, it was its technology, which had to be redesigned from scratch (in August 2000) to allow greater flexibility. 'We were behind one or two of our competitors here,' says Frame, 'but I am confident we have now caught up.'

International Orientation

The American online housing market is already dominated by indigenous players; and Europe is very fragmented, with major national variations in the property-buying process – even Scotland has a different system from England – and often a greater reliance on the rented sector. So international expansion is not at the top of Property Internet's wish list.

'We would like to go into Europe, but we've got to fight the battle on the home front first,' explains Frame. 'Where I do see a real opportunity is in European holiday properties.' So the company is partnering with ImmoStreet.com, a French-based firm with pan-European interests, in the holiday property market. This partnership should come to fruition during 2001.

1st Software is the UK's leading developer and vendor of software for financial advisers. Based in the Midlands, the company has grown very rapidly since its foundation in 1996, a tribute to the quality of its product and customer service. Its software is feature-rich and highly Internet-enabled, which should enable it to increase its share of this fast-growing market.

Scorecard:

Innovation	★★★★
Flexibility	★★★
Human resources	★★★
Growth markets	★★★★★
Quality of management	★★★★
International orientation	★★★

Biggest plus:
The leading vendor in a fast-growing market, with plenty of good ideas up its sleeve.

Biggest minus:
Must ensure that the necessary step-changes in growth do not dilute its strong entrepreneurial and service ethos.

1st Software
The Innovation Centre
Warwick Technology Park
Gallows Hill
Warwick CV34 6UW
Tel: 01926 623230
Fax: 01926 623338
website: www.1st-software.co.uk

1st Software

The Business

Independent Specialist Technology (UK) Ltd, trading as 1st Software, develops and markets software for financial advisers. Founded in 1996, by two entrepreneurs, it has grown rapidly – making £1m in profit on £3.35m turnover in 2000. Between 1996 and 1999, 1st Software was the seventh fastest growing technology company in the UK. Based in Warwick, the company has a branch office in Glasgow and a nation-wide network of trainers and sales people. The total head count is around 50, and growing.

By the end of 2000, the company's software was in use by around 850 companies in the UK, ranging from blue-chip organizations like AON Consulting, Deloitte & Touche and HSBC, to mid-range directly-authorized financial advisers. This makes the company the leading software vendor in its field, with over 18 per cent of the market.

Innovation

1st Software was founded with two main aims – to provide financial advisers with better 'back office' facilities, and to enable them to expand their services onto the Internet.

Rory Curran, co-founder and managing director, says: 'We felt there wasn't a system on the market that would deliver effective e-commerce (electronic commerce), and we wanted to allow financial advisers to squeeze costs out of their business, and concentrate on doing what they're good at, which is giving unbiased advice.'

Although a dozen rival packages are available, Curran believes that none has the same depth and breadth of functions as 1st Software, whose features include pensions projections, capital gains tax forecasts, discretionary portfolio management, and integrated commission and fee accounting. Financial advisers are facing several challenges, from increasing regulation to falling fees, and top-hole software will be essential to help them maintain their income.

A key weapon will be effective use of the Internet. Online services from financial product vendors pose a real threat, but 1st Software wants to help advisers use e-commerce to fight back.

Advisers will be able to provide added-value services to clients, such as personal home pages where they can check their unused pension allowance or the current value of their portfolio. And e-commerce will cut costs by enabling client data to be imported from vendors such as pension companies, without having to be rekeyed.

'We're using the Internet to make advisers more omnipresent to their clients,' says Curran. 'We want to make the financial adviser indispensable. It will change the landscape of the whole market.'

The company's other major innovation has been to rent out its software – instead of selling licences outright. The minimum contract is eighteen months, with subsequent renewals in six-month blocks, which makes 1st Software more attractive than rival products, where the whole cost must be paid up-front. This has enabled 1st Software to establish considerable market share very quickly, and without having to offer discounts – a slippery slope Curran does not want to descend. 'The rental model has been very successful,' says Curran. 'Our clients like it because they feel that, if things go wrong, they can stop paying us. And it drives us to deliver good service so that things don't go wrong!'

Flexibility

Any company which grows 3,000 per cent in five years has got to be pretty flexible, and 1st Software was designed to cope with rapid growth and change. 'There's change around every corner in our market,' says Curran. 'You have to be very flexible to go from a standing start to where we are now, especially if you want to deliver a high standard of service. So we've tried to establish an organizational structure that will let us monitor our growing pains and sort them out. We're not complacent, and we know there are always weak points in the system, but these are always changing over time.'

When they founded the company, Curran's partner, Mik Cons, wrote the software and Curran sold it. Now both are senior managers, and have had to relinquish the tiller to other hands. This has required clear procedures, and the right kind of people. 'We've always tried to take on people who can get on with a job and come back to us if they have a problem,' says Curran.

Human Resources

Staff turnover in the IT industry is high, so a company like 1st Software which has a turnover rate of less than 10 per cent must be doing something right. Curran explains its philosophy: 'From the moment we hire someone, we want them to reach their personal potential, because that's how the company will benefit. We recruit people who want to keep moving on and learning more.'

The company's rapid growth offers plenty of opportunity for career advancement. 'We're conscious that we're breeding talented people, and we have to give them room to grow,' says Curran. The company is now large enough to have a permanent, rolling recruitment programme. The company prefers all recruits to have industry experience,

1st Software is in the process of implementing a big new training programme for staff. Because the company receives regular revenues from renting out its software, it can afford to be more generous in salaries than other software developers. Benefits include pension, personal health insurance, life and critical illness insurance cover, and up to 25 days' holiday, dependent on service.

Growth Markets

As the financial services market becomes more complex, and the population becomes more affluent, increasing numbers of people will require professional financial advice, so 1st Software's potential market is growing all the time. The company already holds a dominant position, with its 18 per cent market share, but expects to increase this still further. 'We think it's realistic to go for 30 per cent,' says Curran. 'Our target is to make the company worth over £100 million pounds within five years.'

Curran believes the company is now poised for growth. 'Doubling the size of our client base would add a lot to our bottom line, because most of our costs, such as the initial development of our software, are already paid for,' he says. 'And with a client base as big as ours, we can start selling additional services, such as e-commerce and document management.'

Curran would like to expand into other financial services, such as employee benefits, and especially investment management, which remains old-fashioned and could benefit from a fresh approach like 1st Software's. But the company is aware that its current growth rate cannot be sustained by organic growth alone, and is also looking to diversify by acquiring complementary companies, in fields like e-commerce and website design. 'We've identified businesses we want to take stakes in,' says Curran.

Quality of Management

The founders of 1st Software, Rory Curran (managing director) and Mik Cons (commercial director), have worked in the financial services software market since the 1980s. Initial funding was provided by a firm of independent financial advisers, Financial Options, which also provided 1st with a ready-made initial customer base. Financial Options was bought in 1999 by IT giant Misys, which retains a 30 per cent share holding in 1st but takes no active part in running the company.

Curran and Cons built up the business – in which they still own the majority share holding – carefully, making sure they hit all the targets in their business plan. They are looking at future funding, but are determined to maintain the entrepreneurial outlook of the business.

Their management style is open. 'We believe in transparency throughout the business, and our staff feel they have access to the people in charge,' says Curran. 'And we try to encourage initiative and new ideas'.

There are monthly management reports to monitor key statistics such as sales, support calls and installations, and the management team agrees clear quarterly objectives. To assist with the latter, a business coach – Norman McQueen, from consultancy Results International – comes every quarter to act as a facilitator in internal discussions. 'This has brought about a lot of positive changes in ourselves, as people and as a management team,' says Curran. 'We can talk to each other and sort out problems, and we're very "non-political".'

Customer service is a key driver, which seems to pay off since the drop-out rate among customers is less than 2 per cent, and a third of new business comes from referrals. 'We always put our head over the parapet with clients, and attend user-group meetings,' says Curran. 'I think a lot of our clients would like to invest in us.'

Asked to sum up 1st Software's strengths, Curran says: 'It's a solid technology business that has sustainable earnings, and knows how to make money out of the Internet and its chosen market. We've got good, sustainable growth ahead of us in a market that's growing rapidly.'

International Orientation

Financial advisers do much the same job the world over, although compliance requirements differ. So one of 1st Software's longer-term aims is to produce a global investment management system. The company already has a few clients in Europe and the Far East who advise British expatriates, but the company needs to do some more work on the way the software handles languages and multiple currencies. It is also beginning to talk to potential foreign sales partners.

Overseas sales could be helped by supplying software on an ASP (application service provider) basis, where the software and data are stored on 1st Software's own computers. This would be especially suitable for smaller financial advisers – at home and abroad –who lack the capacity and expertise to run their own systems. 1st hopes to have an ASP service running by the end of 2001.

Known the world over as 3M, The Minnesota Mining and Manufacturing Company was founded in 1902 and, in 1904, it produced the world's first sandpaper. From video tape to synthetic running tracks, Scotch™ adhesive tape to optical disks, and surgical masks and fibre optics to the ubiquitous Post-it™Note, 3M's history is a near century of innovation in fields whose diversity seems bewildering. Today's 3M uses over a hundred different technologies in forty business units in the industrial, commercial, healthcare and consumer markets.

Scorecard:

Innovation	★★★★★
Flexibility	★★★★
Growth markets	★★★★
Human resources	★★★★
Quality of management	★★★★
International orientation	★★★★★

Biggest plus:
'It's stable, polite and caring and it's a standard bearer for best practice and innovation.'

Biggest minus:
'Practices tend to be deeply entrenched and changes take time.'

3M United Kingdom Plc
3M House
Market Place
Bracknell
Berkshire
RG12 1JU
Tel: 01344 858000
website: www.3m.com

3M

The Business

3M uses over a hundred different technologies in over forty business units in the industrial, commercial, healthcare and consumer markets. Year 2000 figures revealed that the company has 70,000 employees and revenues of $16.7 billion world-wide. In the UK, 3M employs 4,000 people in fifteen locations. The company describes itself as '42 small businesses in one large operation'. 3M is a powerful brand – but a multi-billion dollar organization listed high in the global Fortune 500 must necessarily pay attention to its laurels and 3M is seeking to strengthen customer loyalty by working ever more closely with its customers, and by building on what the company calls 'supply chain excellence'.

Innovation

3M invented sandpaper and the rather more convenient waterproof sandpaper; and is still producing and researching better abrasives. 3M invented the first commercially viable audio and videotape; Scotch™ cellophane tape and Scotchguard™ protection; optical disks and fibre optic cable; the first man-made thing on the Moon – Neil Armstrong's footprint – was made by a 3M sole. A comprehensive list of 3M innovations would run to many pages but what sets 3M apart is not only the sheer volume of invention but the ways in which it has been achieved. 'The more I practise', the golfer Arnold Palmer once remarked, 'the luckier I seem to get'.

There was the man who sang with his local choir and was tired of losing his place when the bits of paper he was using as markers slipped out of his hymn book. A 3M experimental adhesive that didn't stick too well seemed a possibility so Art Fry pasted some on strips of yellow scrap paper. The book marks stayed in place, but could be removed without damaging the pages. This was not an overnight global success – the market for self adhesive book marks is limited – but he persevered and offered small pads of his invention to his colleagues – who found them handy for scribbling notes which could be stuck to things. The Post-it®Note had arrived.

Certainly not all 3M inventions have been the results of happy accident but it is worth noting that the company pioneered the notion that research staff should be encouraged to spend fifteen per cent of their working hours, as UK and Ireland technical director John Howells puts it, 'just doing their own thing'. Research and development is a 3M priority and is not regarded as a candidate for expenditure cuts for the purpose of balancing budgets. Around 7 per cent of 3M revenue is invested in research and development and, says Howells, 'this happens through thick and thin, regardless of the economic climate – it has to – inventiveness is our lifeblood'.

Flexibility

'3M', says Chairman of the board and CEO Livio DeSimone, 'is a unique and dynamic company – one that continually reinvents itself. Our businesses share leading-edge technology platforms, world class manufacturing operations, extensive marketing channels and powerful brands. Our businesses hold leading marketing positions around the globe. We operate companies in many countries and generate more than half our sales outside the United States. Our people are dedicated, experienced and entrepreneurial, and I'm confident in our ability to grow consistently in a world where the pace of change increases day by day.'

E-business has become an integral strategic component in all 3M's many business units; use of the Internet to provide product information, strengthen customer relationships, streamline business processes and reduce costs is full blooded.

Innovation was and is the driving force of 3M culture and growth, and incentive schemes specifically encourage the promotion of newly developed products. What is not flexible is the company's commitment to research and development – currently running at more than $1 billion a year – but the 3M attitude to the results of its R and D – 'what in all this innovation can we take to the bank?' – is that of a company which thinks very much on its feet.

Human Resources

3M encourages the pursuit of long-term careers and emphasis on promotion from within is strong – 'secure and happy employees,' says DeSimone, 'are more likely to be productive at work'.

The company's human resource department is therefore particularly interested in recruiting and developing individuals and helping those individuals to maximize their contributions and potential, and development is seen as partnership involving the individual, the supervisor and the company. Personal development is built into the performance management process – this includes 360 degree feedback – and salary reviews and personal action plans are directly impacted by the process.

Recruitment is accorded great importance and those wishing to move from one part of 3M to another are not discouraged. 3M is not averse to taking calculated risks when putting people into different jobs but, says Human Resource director Paul Davies, 'there is an awareness that today's jobs are ever more demanding and that care is necessary'. Human Resources also supports people in coping with inevitable change and with the need to behave differently when going into something new.

Those likely to flourish, says Davies, 'will most likely be extrovert and gregarious' although those with what he calls 'a dot-com mindset' would find it frustrating. '3M', says Davies, 'means steering a very large moving ship – this is not a start-up'.

Growth Markets

3M describes itself as '42 small businesses in one large operation'. 3M is a powerful brand but a multi-billion dollar organization listed high in the global Fortune 500 must necessarily pay attention to its laurels and 3M is seeking to strengthen customer loyalty by working ever more closely with its customers, and by building on what the company calls 'supply chain excellence'.

The company is embracing many challenges in the global markets in which it operates. The explosion of e-commerce together with the growing demand for shorter product cycles and for fewer but more sophisticated suppliers means ever increasing pressure on the logistics of research, manufacture and distribution. In the mid 1990s the company introduced its 'Pacing Plus' initiative which prioritizes and accelerates the development of 'new products we've identified as winners'.

3M is an organization which has proved itself no slouch at marketing but innovation is still regarded as the trump card. 'Invention', concludes technical director John Howells, 'is one of the main things we're about – there's no point in having a pipeline if there's nothing to put in it.'

Quality of Management

It has been said that, if 3M were a person, it would be 'a middle-aged man with a smart suit and a friendly face'. This may well be true but it is merely part of the story. There is a certain avuncularity but, during the near-century the company's been around, it is estimated to have come up with 'over fifty thousand inventions'.

Some flew, some didn't, but one essential part of 3M management is its attitude to decision making and risk taking – 'it's better to ask for forgiveness than permission – everyone's banging on about empowerment these days but we started implementing it years ago'. William McKnight was 3M chief executive in 1944, which was the year he said 'put fences around people and you get sheep'.

A second 3M essential is its unusually successful blending of the two factions so commonly seen at loggerheads one with the other – research and development versus sales and marketing. 3M operates what it calls a 'dual ladder' which means 'scientists can get up to the same levels as marketeers but, additionally and probably more importantly, there is a cross fertilization'.

As John Howells puts it – 'our boffins can wear suits and entertain audiences, and our salesmen have been known to invent things. Just because I'm the technical director it doesn't mean I sit in an ivory tower. I want to know about commercial viability, I want people to buy our products, I want them to do that because the products are good, and there are times when I get a bit frustrated that the world doesn't yet know just how good some of them are.'

International Orientation

3M operates in nearly 200 countries and more than half its revenues come from outside its native US. There are opportunities for those who wish to be mobile and, says Paul Davies, 'a great many 3M people have made their careers away from their home turf'.

The European market contributes some 24 per cent of 3M sales. The company believes that the euro will 'over time, increase price competition for the company's products across Europe due to cross-border price transparency'. 3M's EMU (European Monetary Union) steering committee was created in early 1997. The committee's brief included:

(1) assessing the euro's impact on the company's business and pricing strategies for customers and supplies, and

(2) ensuring that the company's business processes and IT systems can produce transactions in euros and local currencies during the transition period and achieve the conversion of all relevant local currency data to the euro by December 2001.

ACTINIC

Actinic is the company that developed the first packaged software that enabled people to set up a 'shop' on the Internet, Actinic Catalog. This is basic e-commerce software that can be added to most professionally-hosted websites – Actinic products generally don't work with free websites; however, the vast majority of UK ISPs can support the products on their paid commercial Web space. Publicly listed on the London Stock Exchange, the company was founded in 1996.

Scorecard:

Innovation	★★★★★
Flexibility	★★★★
Human resources	★★★★
Growth markets	★★★★★
Quality of management	★★★★
International orientation	★★★★

Biggest plus:
The atmosphere within the company – people are regarded as important and although Actinic is as businesslike as they come, there is an air of supportiveness.

Biggest minus:
The share price was hit by the tumble taken by the e-commerce sector in late 2000; this has had an inevitable effect on staff morale given that most of them have shares or options.

Actinic
Locke King House
2 Balfour Road
Weybridge
Surrey KT13 8HD
Tel: 01932 871000
website: www.actinic.co.uk

Actinic

The Business

Actinic started trading in 1996, aiming to serve the small-to-medium enterprise market which was at the time just becoming aware of the Internet and its potential as a sales medium. At that stage the only way to trade on the Net was to hire a Web developer who specialized in e-commerce and get them to design a site from the ground up. Actinic launched its Catalog offering as a shrink-wrapped online shop. It was listed in 2000 and has an annual turnover of £2 million; it operates in over 33 countries, mostly through partnerships but in some instances it has a direct presence. It was heading towards a 90-strong UK employee team as this publication went to press, with further personnel based in the US, Hungary and France.

Innovation

Actinic's products were ahead of most of the market in two ways. First they anticipated the need for easy-to-use and install electronic commerce packages without the absolute need for a professional designer, and second it set its focus very firmly on the small-to-medium enterprise (SME). It is comparatively simple to forget that the current vogue for e-business and selling into SMEs had barely started in the middle of the last decade; the area has grown to the extent that there are now 3.7 million of these companies in the UK alone, many of whom want to be able to sell their products online. Actinic's Catalog product enables them to do it for under £500 for the set-up software, and over 10,000 companies have done so.

At that stage all of the elements that made up e-commerce were available – you could have a Web server, database and other pieces of the jigsaw, but it was all painfully slow. Some of the parts didn't interact with each other, for example Excel didn't work in HTML. Actinic's task was to take all these separate threads and unite them into one package. That said, the company is proud of not offering quite the latest technology in its products – it prefers to offer tried and tested solutions.

Actinic takes a number of approaches that differentiate it from its competitors, and the first thing a customer will notice is the quality of the technical support. Although the product is designed to look and feel simple to use, the security needed in e-commerce products means they are far from simple in implementation. Normally the only problems will be if the customer is trying to use free webspace that doesn't allow for online forms, for example; Actinic maintains a list of ISPs that support it and indeed a number of prominent ISPs sell the product as their recommended e-commerce solution.

More recently there have been extra functions added that will help customers integrate their e-shops with their accounting systems by developing interfaces with Quickbooks and Sage's accounting systems. Sales are 100 per cent indirect, either through value-added resellers, ISPs or Web developers – although the product works straight out of the box as long as the ISP has the right systems installed, it can be tailored a lot more to appear like part of the customer's original website if a Web developer is involved.

In the summer of 2000, Actinic went a step further when it introduced Actinic Business. This was an out-of-the-box solution for higher end consumer sites and business-to-business websites, which tried to keep the simplicity of earlier products combined with advanced features. At the other end of the price scale there's Actinic PortalBuilder that provides everything a developer needs to create and run an online community or shopping mall.

Flexibility

Clearly the company has grown rapidly and flexibility has been necessary to manage this change – there were only 30 employees when it floated, and this is heading into three figures now. Managerial strengths have helped in this sort of growth; Barling's background at Reuters meant he was accustomed to larger environments.

It has tried to contain any staff discontentment first by ensuring that the employees are in the right job, and second by sticking to four tenets by which the company lives: first, that employees' families come first – Barling certainly works from home a great deal and is horrified at the number of companies that consider themselves more important than their employees' rights to their private lives. Second, don't lie – if an employee hasn't had time to make a phone call or to do something else, an honest approach is more welcome than a cover story. Third, the company believes in having fun – tying in with the first somewhat, the organization is genuinely interested in promoting a good quality of life for its employees. Fourth, the organization loves its customers – in the way that it will listen to their needs and complaints, and respect them.

Human Resources

Assuming the prospective employee can assimilate and conform to all of the above, there is no reason not to expect a long association with Actinic. The company selects its people carefully and makes extensive use of psychometric testing to avoid ending up with inappropriately-placed individuals.

It has very strong views on structure and reporting, and has drawn up a matrix to show how ideas can cross-fertilize with each other to build up a coherent whole. It makes extensive use of the conferencing system Nextra (formerly known as Cix) for staff discussion boards, customer feedback and customer support. Comments from customers are taken very seriously and 'wish-list' requests for functions are added to company wish-lists as appropriate – then nine times out of ten if a request for a given function is unattainable due to cost or other considerations, the customer who requested it is told why this is the case.

The end result is a company strong on people and low on hierarchy. Employees get a good salary and benefits package including shares and share options depending on their position.

Growth Markets

As has been well documented in this book and elsewhere, the gloss has fallen off the technology market as far as the Stock Exchange is concerned; disillusioning though this is for employee shareholders, however, it is not reflected in Actinic's trading history or record of growth.

It will grow in two ways over the coming years. First the UK market remains its most lucrative and is likely to continue doing so for the foreseeable future; the 3.7 million SMEs are not all selling online yet and that leaves plenty of room for expansion. However, not all companies will be targeted, explains Grumball; he regards the Internet as ideal for niche products people won't be able to get elsewhere but remains unconvinced by mainstream sellers of goods who lack the size of an Amazon.com or a major high street presence to back them up. He points to the example of a customer who owns a Beatles rarities specialist shop; a business that wouldn't attract enough attention with just a high street presence but with a world-wide audience it does extremely well.

The second strand to the company's growth is in the international market; it operates in France, America and Hungary. It has translated the product into French and was poised to introduce Spanish and German versions as well as this book went to press.

Quality of Management

The list of management techniques applied by the company reads a little like a guide on how to implement good practice at all levels; psychometrics, key performance indicators and efforts to keep employees informed about changes to the business at all stages are considered vital, and the dedication to the staff as individuals rather than work-producing units is evident in the 'family first' policy the company operates.

It always looks for people who are a good fit; the marketing people are almost always people with experience of indirect channel marketing, or people who have an understanding of that means of selling. A strong commitment to ethics backs this up

Grumball comments that the average life of a listed company is 20–30 years, although some have been running for more than 300 years – he has every intention, through implementing annual appraisals both of the staff and of the company, of ensuring that Actinic joins them – although he concedes that the company's status in 300 years' time won't actually be much of his business!

International Orientation

Actinic has been successful in France and continues to grow in Europe; this is very much a market in which it is interested. By Grumball's own admission, the company has barely scratched the surface of the American market, and conquering this market remains very much a target with its 15 million small businesses as potential customers.

The main growth for the moment will be in the UK, however, and the 3.7 million companies out there will provide sufficient fodder for excellent expansion. As long as the company sticks to taking its customer feedback seriously and ensures its staff continue to be well treated and motivated, there is every reason to be confident about its future.

Actional

Actional is a Canadian company that has gone international and moved through a number of incarnations to get to its current name and status. Its business is in making links between new technology and old, so that older computers such as mainframes can take their place in an e-business environment. It is privately owned and has completed two successful rounds of funding.

Scorecard:

Innovation	★★★★★
Flexibility	★★★★★
Human resources	★★★
Growth markets	★★★
Quality of management	★★★★
International orientation	★★★★★

Biggest plus:
The uniqueness of the product – it is the only thing specifically designed to integrate e-business applications directly with ERP, legacy and middleware.

Biggest minus:
There are never enough hours in the day!

Actional
1 Liverpool Street
London EC2M 7QD
Tel 020 7956 2006
Fax 020 7956 2206
website: www.actional.com

Actional

The Business

Actional's business is difficult to understand unless you are already in computing. Possibly the easiest way for the non-technical mind to assimilate it is to imagine that all the corporates had bought lots of Betamax and Philips 2000 standard videos and now needed to play them on their VHS video machines; and to add that they had stored all their customer details and financials on Betamax whereas all their customers want to trade via digital TV. It's a mixed metaphor that masks a lot of complexity, but the essence of it is the core of Actional's business; linking old (and in IT terms 'old' can be as recent as the early 1990s) systems with state-of-the-art e-commerce environments. The company is privately owned and has 170 employees world-wide, 70 of whom are in research and development.

Innovation

In some ways it is irrelevant to talk about innovation where Actional is concerned, as it owes its existence to ensuring older technology is not rendered obsolete. There are good reasons for doing this; very few companies can afford to simply jettison everything that is held on a system – even if it was installed 30 years ago, and few of them want to. Also, the older computers are often still fully operational and there is therefore no reason to be rid of them prematurely.

The company therefore pushes itself aggressively towards the Global 2000 style of company that will have the sort of information that will need to be accessed routinely stored on technology that won't in itself support company intranets, which are based on internet technology.

It does this through a set of what it calls Actional Control Brokers (ACBs). These are built for interaction-based IT connectivity – in other words people-to-system functions – and automatic system to system processes; they add no latency to any of the requests or round trips, and this speeds up the delivery of the information requested.

Given the service's usefulness to so many corporate customers it may be wondered why the name isn't better known. This is because Actional was launched last June, having previously been called Visual Edge for 15 years where the earlier versions of the product had been sold via resellers. Actional sells in two ways – directly, and through Original Equipment Manufacturer (OEMs). This stands for and refers to someone who builds the Actional system into their own offering and then sells it on. So someone might think their BEA or Siemens system is excellent at retrieving aged information, and indeed it probably would be – in this instance this would be because of the Actional technology built into it.

The company also sells on referral from other partners including KPMG, with which it has a particularly close relationship.

Flexibility

Actional has to be extremely flexible in what it does – it might be asked to integrate any set of old systems with any new e-commerce application. It has also had to react to very rapid growth and to an incredible increase in the development of new technology. The ACBs themselves are designed to provide the broadest and most diverse system support of any vendor. They need to span messaging, trans-action, mainframe and component technology, while they encompass connecting customer relationship management, e-commerce, enter-prise resource planning, legacy, mainframe and middleware applica-tion. Ease of use is achieved through basing the technology on open technical standards so that customers can work with the new systems within days rather than months.

In corporate terms the UK was set up very swiftly, leaving vice-president and general manager for Europe, Paul Brennan, with 40 people to hire in a very short time. Managerial control and motivation of the staff was clearly an essential point of this and customers needed to be supported throughout; Brennan therefore opted for as flat a management structure as the small number of employees allowed. For the moment at least this means a lot of interchangeability of roles, benefiting customers who might want service at any time.

Human Resources

As mentioned above, the company has as flat a structure as it can in the UK and everyone reports directly to Paul Brennan, who in turn reports to management in Canada. The company philosophy is straightforward and based on an ethical approach. It is completely customer-centric.

This has implications for the sort of person who will perform well within the company. Inflexible people will founder rapidly; those too fond of roles and hierarchies will find the structures are wrong for them. The brief at the UK office is to be pan-European, and the atmos-phere is dynamic. Contact between the various European offices is frequent and lively, and applicants for employment will need to be ready to deal with large companies – organizations like Dresdner Bank and Prudential are among the client lists.

The remuneration is competitive and the right person should have every reason to look forward to a long and successful career with the company.

Growth Markets

It might be imagined that Actional's market is fairly stunted because it focuses on people who still use older technology (actually, this is not strictly true as Actional focuses on any company with an e-business mandate whether the systems are new or old); to examine the computing press you might imagine everyone is using Intranets and other new technology. This is to underestimate the sheer number of organizations still dependent on historical data archived in older systems.

Broadly speaking, long-established companies with any corporate data will be interested in the sorts of service on offer from Actional since their employees will increasingly be used to looking at information through a Web setting – they'll have it at home. The sorts of company that buy the technology at the moment – Lockheed Martin, Siemens, Rockwell, Swisscom, Austria Mobilkom and Deutsche Telekom – are typical of the sort of company that still needs the services Actional offers. For all of these companies, return on investment is often the most important factor. Actional's products have an excellent, proven track record of return on investment. For example, Deutsche Telekom saved 50 per cent of its implementation budget. In real terms, this amounted to a saving of 1.2 million Deutschmarks. Actional enabled Swisscom to go to market with its Commerce One marketplace 6 months early.

The company's existing customer base is also likely to be a source of continuing growth as new e-business applications emerge and older data needs to be connected to them. For example, a few years ago nobody would have imagined the importance of, say, Geographical Information Systems, so they would not have wanted to link them into older data. The continuing evolution of new applications will ensure Actional's growth for a long time to come.

Quality of Management

Actional has been able to attract financial backing from serious players – NeoCarta Venture, New Enterprise Associates and International Capital Partners have all put money in – at least partly because of the calibre of its management team. This includes chief executive officer, John Orcutt, who was previously president and CEO of Augeo Software and ConsenSys Software, and has experience of working with Unisys/Convergent and Hewlett-Packard. Chairman and founder, Michael Foody, evaluated technology investment opportunities for TechCapital Ltd, and it is his vision that led to Actional taking off.

Chief technical officer, Dan Foody, has a solid background in product development and systems integration for products including SAP/R3, DCOM, CORBA and Java – he was one of the primary authors of part of the OMG standard for COM/CORBA.

Other executives on the main board have had similar high-ranking positions at major IT companies.

International Orientation

Actional is an international company. Based in Canada it has chosen to expand into Europe through the UK but is setting up a number of offices in other countries so that customers can be supported by some-one close by who speaks the language – fluency in a second language is one thing, fluency in technospeak in a second language is another! The type and size of many of its customers means that its international orientation is dictated for it whether it wants it or not.

And it does want it. The company is a new business addressing a simple need – to extract vital data from systems that have been super-seded by newer technologies. It could be argued that building up com-puter systems in the 1980s and earlier only to wipe the slate clean and use different technologies completely in the 1990s was crazy; however, that's the environment in which we live and Actional's products will ensure we can continue to trade in it.

adeptra

Adeptra, formerly known as RealCall, provides alerting solutions that enable its clients to deliver personalized information to users in a range of formats: voice, text, graphics or multimedia. The solutions are delivered using an Application Service Provider model from data centres in the US and UK. The company is 30 per cent owned by venture capitalists who have put around $52 million into the company in two rounds of funding. UK-owned, the company employs 75 people and has offices in London and Stamford, Connecticut.

Scorecard:

Innovation	★★★★
Flexibility	★★★
Human resources	★★★
Growth markets	★★★★
Quality of management	★★★★
International orientation	★★★

Biggest plus:
Fun, friendly atmosphere.

Biggest minus:
Trying to keep track of the name changes.

Adeptra
Vigilant House
120 Wilton Road
London SW1
Tel: 020 7233 9733
Fax: 020 7233 9744
website: www.adeptra.com

Adeptra

The Business

The idea behind Adeptra was born in 1996 when co-founder Eric van der Kleij, tried to order some flowers for his wife over the Internet, and was frustrated by not being able to call the site directly to check delivery times. The result was the RealCall button, technology which can be built into websites to let users set up a phone connection with a human operator. RealCall, now called CustomerAlert, is now used by over 15,000 companies. In September 2000, the company extended its offering with the InfoAlert product range, which enables corporate clients to deliver personalized information to users in a range of formats: voice, text, graphics or multimedia. Major clients include KPMG, Compuserve, Barclays Bank, Honda, Excite.com and BBC Radio Online.

The company has been through two name changes since its birth in 1996: from Answer Communications to RealCall in September 1999, when it got its first $12 million of venture capital and opened its US office; and from RealCall to Adeptra the following year, when its second round of funding netted a further $40 million. The company currently employs 75 people and has offices in London and Stamford, Connecticut, though it will soon be moving its UK office to Basingstoke. It is 30 per cent owned by its investors, with the rest of its stock held by employees.

Innovation

Mobile alerting services are ten a penny, but what Adeptra brings to the table is the element of interactivity, plus valuable feedback to its clients on who is using the service, for what information and with what result. Its clients' customers can not only request information to be sent to them using their own choice of parameters and delivery methods, but can then choose to act on the alert in a variety of ways.

Info Alert +Connect lets them act on an alert by connecting directly to a human operator by phone; +Commerce lets them receive product information then order the product if they wish; and +Content enables them to get headline data and then proceed to requesting more detailed information.

The technology to do all this takes the form of an integrated computer-telephony system that Adeptra has called AlertXChange Server. Another of Adeptra's innovations has been to make this available on an Application Service Provider basis, from data centres operated by Exodus from three locations (two in the US and one in the UK), The

ASP approach gives clients who want to offer the service a low cost of entry; they are charged an initial set-up fee then pay a usage charge as they go along. By offering low entry costs Adeptra is able to widen its potential market. Clients then have the option of absorbing the charges or passing them on to their customers.

In future the company is looking to keep its alerting service ahead of the pack by taking advantage of emerging technologies such as location detection, speech recognition and the new possibilities, such as multimedia alerts, opened up by higher bandwidth mobile networks.

Adeptra provides a 'white label' service to its clients, who incorporate its technology into their own branded offerings. The company does not therefore need to invest heavily in building a consumer brand of its own. It spends around 10 per cent of its budget on marketing and focuses on making direct contacts with potential corporate clients in its chosen vertical markets. Its relationships with major technology partners such as Oracle, Cisco Systems and Sun are another source of business contacts.

Flexibility

So far, it's been hard to fault Adeptra's ability to detect and adapt to changing business conditions. Over four years, the company has changed its name twice as its product line has evolved and grown; expanding from a two-man start-up to a company of 75 staff and rising; and it has set up US offices to follow the emerging business opportunities across the Atlantic.

The name changes have now stopped, enabling Adeptra to establish a settled identity in the e-commerce market. The company is now focusing on its four key vertical markets – while continuing to keep an eye on emerging opportunities elsewhere. It has so far managed to bring out leading-edge alerting technology ahead of the rest of the pack, and its heavy investment in research and development, which accounts for a significant chunk of its latest $40 million funding injection, is intended to ensure that it maintains that leading position.

Adeptra's use of an ASP approach to offering its service provides added flexibility. It can add new customers without adding hugely to its technical support costs, since the actual application is hosted centrally. Though its intended market is large corporates, its scalable technical architecture, based on Sun hardware and the Oracle database, enables it to cater for wide variations in levels of demand, from just a few hundred alerts for premium customers to thousands a week.

The company's early move into America is an example of its continuing willingness to react quickly to market trends, in this case capitalizing on latent demand for voice alerts in the US, where unlike Europe text messaging has not become universal among mobile phone users.

Human Resources

Adeptra's workforce has grown rapidly from eight people a year ago to 75 today. The company is about to move into new premises in Basingstoke to accommodate its burgeoning workforce, which is expected to continue to grow to around 200 before stabilizing towards the end of 2002. So far the company has had a small, almost family atmosphere in which founder Eric van der Kleij has been able to exert a direct motivating influence throughout the company. As the workforce grows, this will inevitably have to change, but the company is hoping to maintain something of the commitment, fun and enthusiasm of working for a start-up as it moves into the next, more mature phase of its growth.

Currently staff are split roughly 50–50 between its offices in London and Connecticut. Around half its workforce are in development and technical support, and the challenge of producing innovative technology continues to provide an element of excitement for both the developers who build the products and the sales and marketing people who sell them.

Growth Markets

As more companies start to take advantage of electronic media to sell their products and services, new growth opportunities for Adeptra are opening up all the time. Consultancy Analysys has estimated that the interactive alerting market will grow to over $3 billion by 2005, up from around $91 million today. Adeptra is focusing on four vertical markets which the company believes have the highest growth potential for alerting services: finance, media, travel and retail. Adeptra can offer clients in these sectors the ability to alert their customers with offers personalized to their own specification, and let them respond interactively to the alert while it's still fresh in their minds.

In parallel with the general expansion of e-commerce, the emergence of higher-bandwidth mobile networks and of new technologies such as location detection and speech recognition are also creating opportunities for Adeptra to offer new services, and the company is investing in development to make sure it takes advantage of them. For example, speech recognition could enable clients to ask for additional information over a phone line using natural language; and location detection will make it possible to send out alerts personalized to a customer's actual whereabouts.

Quality of Management

Adeptra is a technology company rather than a dot-com, and is led by an experienced management team with long track records in IT, telecoms and general business. Eric van der Kleij, its founder, chief operating officer and its main driving force, spent 19 years working in communications, computer-telephony integration and software development before setting up the company. His chief executive officer, Stephen Voller, formerly managing director of Netscape UK, South Africa and Ireland, has 20 years experience in IT and is a member of the UK Parliamentary IT Committee. The company's chairman, Sir Colin Southgate, has worked in the IT industry since 1960 and founded Software Sciences, which later became part of Thorn EMI.

Perhaps the greatest tribute to van der Kleij and his management team is that they succeeded in putting together a business plan that convinced European venture capitalists – notoriously wary of technology investments – to put $40 million into the company at a time when technology stocks were falling all around them. The team is targeting this investment cannily, using it to develop the technology which provides its competitive edge and to attack the large, but historically hard to crack, US market.

Though the company is not yet quoting any actual sales figures or giving firm estimates of when it will be moving into profit, the fact that 40 per cent of its sales are already coming from the US provides some early indication that the strategy is paying off.

International Orientation

Adeptra believes that its biggest opportunities lie in Europe and North America where Web commerce is most mature. As of the start of 2001, roughly 60 per cent of its business was coming from the UK and Europe and 40 per cent from the US, with a few clients in the Far East too. The company expects this to change round over the next year or so, with around 70 per cent of its business ultimately coming from the US.

Conscious of the problems many European technology companies have had in gaining acceptance across the Atlantic, it opened a US office in Stamford, Connecticut back in 1999. Half its staff and around 75 per cent of its development team, including the chief technology officer, are now based over there, giving the company the general air of an indigenous US company to prospective US buyers. It also has small sales offices in Santa Clara and Philadelphia. It also plans to open offices in strategic locations around Europe over the next few months.

ADMIRAL

Admiral is a direct insurance company – customers pay for their insurance but do not pay commission to insurance agents. Founded in 1992 the company is relatively new, is privately owned, and is the ninth largest vehicle insurance company in the UK. The company sold its first policy in January 1993. Admiral has grown, and is still growing. Based in Cardiff, Admiral today has 1,300 staff and, in the year 2000, reported turnover of £214 million.

Scorecard:

Innovation	★★★★★
Flexibility	★★★★
Growth markets	★★★
Human resources	★★★★
Quality of management	★★★★★
International orientation	★

Biggest plus:
'You can have ideas, you can voice them, and people will listen.'

Biggest minus:
'We're in a tough industry – you not only have to get ahead but you have to stay ahead.'

Admiral plc
Capital Tower
Grey Friars Road
Cardiff CF10 3AZ
Tel: 0870 243 2431
Fax: 0870 013 2172
website: www.admiral.com

Admiral plc

The Business

Admiral started on Saturday, January 2, 1993 with one brand, 57 employees and no customers. The brand was direct car insurance – you pay the premium but you don't pay commission to agents. By the beginning of 2001 there were six brands under the Admiral Group umbrella. The main holding company is Admiral Group Ltd (AGL) which was incorporated during a 1999 management buyout and owns the following companies:

Admiral Insurance Services Ltd (AISL) generates premiums on behalf of the insurance companies who underwrite Admiral business – Syndicate 2004, Great Lakes and Hibernian. AISL trades as Admiral Insurance, Bell Direct, Diamond Insurance and elephant.co.uk. AISL also owns ABLE Insurance Service Ltd, which trades as Gladiator Motor and Gladiator Commercial Insurance; Elephant Insurance Services Ltd; the currently non-trading Rosyglow Ltd; and the entertainingly named Confused.com Ltd which, unsurprisingly, is to be found on the Internet at www.confused.com.

Innovation

Insurance can be a dull business – 'they take your money and everything's fine until you want to make a claim, at which point everything gets awkward.' Admiral was not the first insurance company to go public with the statement that it desired to help rather than impede its customers, but it was the first to broaden its scope from what the industry traditionally regarded as 'safe' risks. Chief executive, Henry Engelhardt, was born in Chicago, lives in Cardiff and is the driving force behind Admiral. 'Insurance companies,' says Engelhardt, 'are in business to make money – you balance the risks so that your premiums more than cover them. Having said that I see no reason why the people in any insurance company should forget it's the customers who pay their salaries, and the customers are entitled to the best service you can possibly give them.'

Admiral's first innovative move was to go outside the conventionally accepted 'safe risk circle'. 'Effectively, Admiral went into the next circle outside the conventionally safe one – just because you don't happen to be 50 years old and living in Surrey it doesn't necessarily make you a bad risk and we take the view that there are no bad risks – there are merely badly calculated premiums.' Admiral targeted younger people – 'maybe city dwellers with bigger cars' – who had been treated with wariness, if not shunned, by more conventional insurance companies.

As Engelhardt explains: 'In effect, there was less competition. Your marketing costs are similar no matter what your chosen section of the market and, with no intermediaries taking a percentage cut, you are able to offer a superior price.'

In 1994 Gladiator was launched, this intermediary being set up to help high risk drivers whom Admiral itself was unable to insure. 1998 saw the institution of Gladiator Commercial after Admiral had observed a demand for commercial vehicle insurance. In 1996 Admiral was first to offer a 'bonus accelerator' policy whereby if the customer made no claims, the no claims bonus became effective after ten months rather than the traditional year. The year 2000 saw Admiral – one of the first insurance companies on the then fledgling Internet in 1995 – consolidate its e-commerce position by becoming the first insurer, via its company elephant.co.uk, to offer an 'all Internet' insurance service.

Flexibility

'We have to be flexible', says Engelhardt, 'because we cannot afford to be slow.' Admiral is in what is generally regarded as a slow industry but, says Engelhardt, 'I do not consider it enough to be better – that's just another way of saying you're not quite as bad as the rest. I want Admiral to be the best and one of the ways to achieve that is to listen to what your people have to say – if someone comes up with a good idea then we'll put it into practice and then ask our customers what they think of it.'

The 1999 management buyout was a potential watershed but the company handled this by being open – 'MBO's can introduce all manner of pitfalls and we took pains to ensure that all our staff were kept informed, whether it sounded like good news or bad news, at every step along the way.' This, Engelhardt expounds, is desirable because it's honest but in any case represents sound common sense: 'there are few things more dangerous than badly informed grapevines.'

Human Resources

The well-being of Admiral employees is of paramount importance and the company takes pains to recognize and reward contributions from individuals. Those who flourish will need 'high energy and a good attitude' and Admiral is keen that its employees will not be afraid to try new ideas: 'If it fails, it fails – that's better than not trying and the successes certainly outweigh the failures.' Those unlikely to flourish? 'People who want to do the whole thing on their own – those with the John Wayne syndrome, if you like.'

Rules on dress and appearance are relaxed: 'you don't tell people what to wear to a wedding so why tell them what to wear to work?' and bureaucracy and red tape are deliberately kept to a minimum. Admiral's values are described as 'having fun and making money' with the qualification that there has to be honesty, trust, compassion and no hypocrisy. Admiral has no mission statement as, in the considered opinion of CEO Henry Engelhardt, 'setting stuff like that in concrete is tantamount to inviting management by hypocrisy. It is', he emphasizes, 'preferable to have values which we live rather than values which are made up and then scribbled down somewhere.'

Admiral seeks to be active in the local community where initiatives include the sponsoring of Cardiff's buses on New Year's Eve. In 1999 Admiral was named Welsh Company of the Year.

Growth Markets

The United Kingdom insurance market has changed and is still changing – 'you could say, that, in world insurance terms, the UK is in the vanguard of change and that competition is far more aggressive than it used to be.'

Admiral today is specifically UK based, but it is eyeing markets in continental Europe and, whilst nothing is certain, Germany, France and Italy may be future candidates for an Admiral invasion. There is, however, opportunity for growth on home turf – 'at the moment, we've got about 4 per cent of the UK market so there's plenty of work to be done here,' concludes Engelhardt.

Quality of Management

Admiral measures itself relentlessly against any data it can find. Customers are asked to rate the company's performance against various criteria and the responses are analysed and acted upon. The well being of Admiral employees is of paramount importance and the company takes pains to recognize and reward contributions from individuals.

The company prides itself on operating as a collection of small organizations rather than as one amorphous mass – the common sense approach once more prevailing in that this is a natural way to generate energy and enthusiasm. All new starters see the CEO personally before their first week's employment is up and everyone in the company knows, on a day to day basis, how their particular department is doing.

The Admiral Group employs a total of 1,300 people. Virtually all jobs are advertised internally and those advertised externally 'usually go in the local papers'. Employee referral is encouraged and those who have recommended friends whose employment is successful receive a £300 bonus. Admiral runs two call centres – one in Cardiff, the other in Swansea – and Admiral is at pains to emphasize that the company attitude to call centre employees is 'not the battery chicken treatment that gets call centres a bad name'.

People can, and do, rejoin the company after leaving and, although shift work may be involved, there is no bar to flexible part time working. Staff turnover at an average of 28 per cent compares favourably with the 35–50 per cent which is common in call centre based businesses.

International Orientation

'At the moment – none; but don't think we're not looking.'
   Henry Engelhardt
   Chief executive officer, Admiral plc

ARM

ARM designs chips that power numerous devices other than computers. It supplies fast processors for items including mobile phones and personal organizers, set-top boxes, MP3 devices and many other innovative products such as printers, digital cameras, automotive electronics and hard disk drives. Its origins date back to the beginning of the BBC Micro computer in 1982. It now supplies some of the most advanced and smallest RISC-based chips available. Floated on the London Stock Exchange and Nasdaq, it employs 660 people.

Scorecard:

Innovation	★★★★★
Flexibility	★★★★
Human resources	★★★★★
Growth markets	★★★★★
Quality of management	★★★★★
International orientation	★★★★★

Biggest plus:
The people and the culture that emphasizes the positive.

Biggest minus:
The sheer breadth of the technical challenge will exhaust some people.

ARM Holdings plc
110 Fulbourn Road
Cambridge CB1 9NJ
Tel: 01223 400400
Fax: 01223 400404
website: www.arm.com

ARM Holdings plc

The Business

ARM is a microprocessor developer, which can lead less informed people to consider it a second fiddle to Intel. In fact it is no such thing. It aims at an entirely different market – that of the embedded system. Embedded chips are those found in mobile phones and many other consumer electronic products but also in more demanding applications such as automotive and industrial areas. 5 per cent of its shares are traded in the US and the remainder in the UK. Its products sell internationally which explains why sections of its website are in Japanese.

Innovation

ARM has a history of innovation that can be traced back to the early 1980s when a group of engineers at Acorn spotted the importance of the then obscure RISC computing architecture – RISC standing for Reduced Instruction Set Computing. It's important to remember that mobile phones weren't big business at the time and neither were PDAs; the pocket calculator was the nearest most people came to portable personal electronics outside the toy industry. The idea of a small, low-cost processor was therefore useful in theory but had fewer applications than are immediately apparent now.

The company's origins lie within Acorn which introduced the RISC PC in 1987, a fully-functioning computer for around £700 – a stunning price at the time, before the IBM PC had taken over as the de facto standard. It was a high-performance system for its time and offered good graphics, video, sound and an operating system in read-only memory (ROM) – so reinstallation and cleaning of computer files was less painful than even modern reloads.

This was the Acorn computer, and the marketing was less successful than the design. It was for this reason that the company decided to sell its Acorn RISC Machines or ARM chips to other companies. This changed to Advanced RISCisc Machines in 1990 when the company was spun out of Acorn, and quickly found Apple interested in the chips for its Newton, one of the first hand-held organizers.

February 1991 was a milestone for the company because Robin Saxby joined as chief executive officer. He did some analysis on the sale of chips to Apple and worked out that ARM would be more profitable if it simply licensed the technology and left the manufacturing to others. The company therefore moved entirely into research and development.

This strategy has been a success. The company was listed on the

London Stock Exchange and Nasdaq in 1998. It focuses on eight end-markets including: secure, wireless applications; mass storage; industrial; consumer entertainment; automotive and imaging areas. One of the latest products to include the technology is the Orange Videophone – which includes: videophone; ordinary phone; digital camera; audio player and PDA in one unit.

Flexibility

In terms of the nature of its business, ARM has altered more than many companies and has survived each transition well. Starting as a design company, its main source of income was from contract design work for Apple and Acorn. As the company grew, so did licensing, royalties and design consulting – development systems and application software followed. ARM is now primarily focused on research and development, specifically the design of chips and development tools, making its money from licensing and royalties.

The fact that the company is listed on the stock market actually helps a lot in this respect, since this means sticking to a rigid quarterly reporting regime so that the state of the business is understood fully at board level at any given time. This helps when the market is changing so rapidly – only half a decade ago, for example, few people would have predicted how widespread mobile phones were to become, and the mobile Internet was not even imagined.

The organization works on rolling five-year plans, and although there is clear flexibility in these in case the market changes it does give the company a framework within which to operate. It evaluates every change and every part of its business periodically and will introduce amendments as necessary. Chief operating officer, Warren East, describes how in 1996 he investigated the sale of development tools that went with the microprocessors, and found that as much money was being spent on developing these as was being made by selling them – so they were effectively being given away. Remedial action was taken including a more concentrated focus on the tools side of the business.

This led to a more analytical culture throughout the company, and subsequently questions of the 'can we do this?' variety are not answered simply with technological information – a tempting trap for an organization whose primary function is design to fall into, but with cost examinations built in as well.

Human Resources

The human resources culture within ARM is very collegiate – there is little room for mavericks while capable team players are welcomed. Like any organization that earns its money by licensing anything it is aware that its main asset is its intellectual property, which equates to its people, and it ensures that employees are motivated the whole time. On entering the company's Cambridge premises you are struck not only by the hive of offices but also by the efforts that have clearly gone into catering and relaxation areas – this is an organization that expects dedication and rewards it with a good working environment as well as competitive remuneration.

The hierarchy is relatively flat, and the people at its upper levels aim to be approachable at all times. Feedback is welcomed from the staff, both formally and informally, at question and answer sessions – ten of which had been run over the two years prior to the publication of this book.

Growth Markets

The markets opening themselves up to ARM are largely dictated not by the consumer, but by what the manufacturers licensing the technology plan to do with it in the coming years. For this reason the explosion in combined mobile phone and organizer products, spearheaded by companies like Nokia, should open up a lot of business for ARM.

The sales force has it as part of its brief to watch for changes in the company's markets and to continue pushing elements such as development tools towards people already buying the basic products. It will continue to exploit its existing markets of automotive (including the emerging global positioning systems), consumer entertainment, digital imaging (including scanners and printers), industrial, networking, security, storage and wireless systems – each of which is growing independently of any efforts by ARM.

Related to these areas the company hopes to make more of itself as a brand name – in the same way that Intel has made 'Intel Inside' an asset in the PC world, ARM hopes to ensure that consumers will be increasingly aware of its brand in the products they buy.

Quality of Management

Robin Saxby, chief executive of ARM, has received numerous awards for his work with the company. Under his leadership the company has moved from being a vehicle for promoting processors from an essentially dead computing platform in the shape of the Acorn to an organization with a market capitalization of around £3 billion. It controls around 75 per cent of the world's market share for 32-bit embedded chips; Saxby was reported in *Time* magazine in 2000 as having visions of developing chips that would work in the human body to restore lost motor functions.

Further along the lines of management, the already-mentioned five-year plans are among the tenets by which the company runs, and, as has already been established, its communication with and motivation of the staff are elements it holds to be vitally important. Targets and plans are revisited every quarter to ensure that the company is on track and that moves in the market haven't made existing plans redundant – the collegiate approach works throughout this process.

The company is ISO 9000 accredited.

International Orientation

The market for embedded chips is world-wide – very few companies would want to manufacture the sort of goods into which ARM-designed chips go only for the UK market. It is for this reason that the company's approach is totally global, from the design centre in Texas complementing operations in the UK, to the balance of where its business happens – only 5 per cent of its transactions are British-based.

ARM does a lot of business in the Far East and is working with many emerging economies, which it is hoping will become increasingly mature over the next five to ten years. Assuming they do, the company plans to continue its leadership by licensing its technologies to chunks of that market.

If it continues along its current policy of valuing its intellectual property by looking after those who create it, there is no reason to predict anything but continued success for this company.

www.ask.co.uk

AskJeeves UK is a branch of the American search engine of the same name. Part-owned by the US company, its other shareholders include Carlton Communications and Granada, both massive media specialists. It is in the search engine business and its main selling point is that you can enter questions in proper English rather than keywords and mathematical symbols. The UK office was established in February 2000.

Scorecard:

Innovation	★★★★★
Flexibility	★★★★
Human resources	★★★★
Growth markets	★★★★
Quality of management	★★★★★
International orientation	★★★★

Biggest plus:
The variety – no two days are ever the same. Also the speed with which the company has acquired 3.1 million users in the UK.

Biggest minus:
Having to keep up with the pace without unlimited resources!

AskJeeves
53 Parker Street
London WC2B 5PT
Tel: 020 7400 2222
Fax: 020 7400 2221
website: www.ask.co.uk

AskJeeves

The Business

AskJeeves' business is set up on a blissfully simple premise – people who want to find things out on the Internet don't want to spend time using keywords and plus signs, and they don't necessarily want to know what 'Boolean' means. They wish simply to ask a question in plain English, like: 'Where can I find cheap flights?' and to be taken to the answer. When the founders worked out an algorithm to cope with this in the US they realized they had a powerful search tool. They founded the company in the US and floated in 1999; the UK version set up with one employee in early 2000 and just over a year later employed over 80 people.

Innovation

The main innovation the company offers is clearly the chance to ask questions rather than enter keywords into search engines. This isn't suitable every time someone wants to know something but it's invaluable for the novice. That's a piece of technology in action – the clever stuff, however, is the way in which the company turns this into a profit. Numerous search engines and portals have failed to make any money out of apparently infallible models, and AskJeeves is a refreshing exception.

It is supported by advertising but it sells this in an interesting manner. It is important to understand that the answers people get to their questions are editorialized to an extent; the system detects keywords and sends a set of possible answers in three ways: similar questions to those editorially built within the company's database, popularity-based sites to which people are directed (using technology that detects how long other people have stayed on the site and by extension whether they found it useful – from a company AskJeeves purchased last year, DirectHit), and results from other search engines and directories. Every question gets around ten answers on average.

Each of the answers directs the customer to a website, and companies offering relevant services to the customer can precisely target their visit via keyword search, categories and channels by using a wide range of commercial spaces such as conventional advertising banners and buttons. For a premium they can opt to have their ad site placed more prominently on the answers page presented to a customer – this is known as a Dynamic Response Anchor Tenancy (DRAT) – the company gets a motivated customer who is obviously ready to spend their money, and the customer quickly gets to the service they require.

AskJeeves regulates this very firmly, though – it will not promote companies it wouldn't have suggested in its answers already, thereby ensuring that answers returned are always relevant. Companies can also pay to be promoted up the list of relevant answer options returned.

Less well-known is its offering of the search technology to other businesses. Companies including Dell have licensed the technology and use it so that their customers in turn can ask their sites plain English questions and get taken to areas in which there is a sensible answer.

Flexibility

Unusually, the model under which AskJeeves operates means that it does not expect visitors to stay on its site for long unlike many of the early dot-coms, which sold their services to advertisers on the length of time that customers stayed on their website. AskJeeves accepts willingly that its users will quickly move off and go to other sites as soon as they find what they are looking for.

That said, it has not shied away from adding services through its channels, including a shopping area for customers who want it which it operates with QM4 and which searches for the best deals on whichever products the customer asks for. There is also an auction area which runs in conjunction with eBay.

The popularity of AskJeeves meant that the organization has had to face a number of alterations both to its structure – when it launched in the UK it had just one employee and it is now an 80-person company. Director of corporate communications, Nick Mason Pearson, confirms that the growth plan in terms of personnel was far more aggressive when the organization first started up, and that it shrank when the gloss fell off the dot-com market. He concedes that growth with double the headcount would have been easier and more fun initially but stresses that the conservative growth plan that replaced it meant that in the UK AskJeeves did not suffer the redundancies seen by so much of its competition.

The idea of selling the search engine software to corporate clients such as Dell, Compaq, Nike and Ford is also comparatively new, and it enables visitors on all of these sites to see the answers to their queries more clearly than would otherwise have been possible as well as offering an additional revenue stream to AskJeeves.

Human Resources

In spite of its youth the company has a mature attitude to human resources – staff must be motivated and they are all offered share options and standard benefits depending on their length of service and the position they hold. Although market conditions in the early

twenty-first century do not favour a flotation, the company understands clearly that if these options are to be worth anything then a
listing will be essential once the climate is right.

Prospective employees should expect a lively environment, and a
company proud of the amount of brand recognition it has achieved in
a comparatively short time. It's fast but there is a 'chill-out room' in
which staff are encouraged to relax for a short while, and in which
business meetings are banned!

Growth Markets

The aforementioned business-to-business proposition, in which Ask-
Jeeves sells its search technology for other corporates to use on their
sites, is a relatively hard sell – until they've seen it, they don't know
they want it – but it remains an area in which the organization foresees
a lot of growth in the medium term.

Aside from that, the focus is very much on continuing to improve
the online experience for existing and new customers in the UK, and
to search for new ways to get income from the site as long as this does
not interfere with the running of it. It's worth mentioning that the
organization went straight through its sales targets for 2000 and it
proposes to do so again. This, it believes, is as much due to a realistic
assessment of potential growth and a consequent setting of realistic
targets rather than falling for more fanciful figures; this is something
it plans to continue.

Quality of Management

As was mentioned at the outset, AskJeeves in the UK is part owned
by Carlton and Granada. This allows it access to shareholder board
members who are part of two of the largest media companies in the
UK, so although it may be perceived as 'new media' its parentage is
solidly traditional media.

This adds to the managerial strength but it would be wrong to
assume that all of the company's depth comes from outside as it was
the core management team that helped shape the company's business
plan, and who scaled down the targets and growth plans to within
more conservative and realistic estimates during 2000. Expertise from
the parent company in the US is also on site in the shape of George
Lichter, president of AskJeeves International and CEO in the UK.
Senior vice-president Adrian Cox is also present and his responsibility
is for sales, marketing and branding; his previous experience was at
St Ivel where he headed up the marketing of the Utterly Butterly
brand. Before that he was at Cadbury Schweppes where his track
record included the launch of the Boost, Twirl and Timeout bars.

It is worth noting that whereas in the beginning the UK operation took a lot of advice from the US, the US is now coming to the UK for advice as the business matures.

International Orientation

The business retains its headquarters in the US and as well as the UK it has an Australian site. The business-to-business model has also been applied in Japan.

The company also owns Pregunta.com – Pregunta is Spanish for 'ask'. This is a Spanish-language version of the site primarily aimed at the Hispanic population in the US, but which clearly also allows the business a foothold in Central and South America as well as Spain. The plan is to roll out more languages as it becomes manageable, although no timescale was available as this book went to press.

As long as any linguistic difficulties can be overcome, there is every reason to predict that the company will succeed both in its home territory and elsewhere. In spite of all the gloss, the best selling point remains the simplicity – ask a proper question in natural language rather than a series of keywords and codes and you get a sensible answer. The appeal is likely to be universal and the competition is bafflingly small.

asserta home

Asserta Home is widely regarded as one of the UK's leading property portals. Partnered with over 4,500 estate agents nation-wide, it has 160,000–200,000 unique visitors each month, who view an average of 19 pages per visit. The site is owned by CGNU, the UK's largest insurance firm.

Scorecard:

Innovation	★★★
Flexibility	★★★★
Human resources	★★★★
Growth markets	★★★★★
Quality of management	★★★★★
International orientation	★★★★

Biggest plus:
Massive user base and extensive partnerships.

Biggest minus:
Shifting priorities as dictated by the market won't suit everyone.

Asserta Home
Union House
182–194 Union Street
London SE1 0LH
Tel: 020 7922 5061
Fax: 020 7922 5041
website: www.assertahome.com

Asserta Home

The Business

Asserta Home was launched in May 2000 as a subsidiary of CGNU. The giant insurance company saw an online property portal as an excellent tool for understanding net-literate consumers at a key time of financial decision-making. Already in its short lifespan Asserta Home can lay claim to being the leading property portal in what is a very congested marketplace. As well as the home sites of estate agents there are dozens of national and local sites on the Web. Given £40 million in funds, the business is expected to move into profit during 2003.

Innovation

In order to maximize the revenue it generates, Asserta Home is focused on driving large volumes of good quality traffic to the site. In achieving this, strategy has been built around three key elements. The first is building the largest independent property database in the UK. Updated every 24 hours, it gives details of around 200,000 properties for sale or rent nation-wide within any price range – representing more than half the total market. The database is serviced by a powerful search engine which offers the user a choice of 16 search criteria, as well as keyword entries.

Alongside this, Asserta Home aims to provide the best customer experience of all the property sites. There is a high quality threshold for featured homes – around one in ten submitted are rejected due to insufficient detail – and plans to introduce technology that will enable virtual tours are underway. Other content includes: help finding the right estate agent, solicitor or removal firm; a stage-by-stage guide to the home-buying process; a property folder in which users can leave their requirements in order to be updated via an SMS message or e-mail when suitable properties become available; and a humorous weekly bulletin containing regular features on celebrity homes and great building disasters.

Finally, Asserta Home has successfully striven to become the dominant online market presence. It has done this by striking deals with leading ISPs, including AOL and Freeserve, to occupy the number one spot on their UK property search lists and by recognizing the potential of digital TV by securing deals with Telewest and Open. It has also spent heavily (£8 million in its first year) on marketing itself. Brand awareness strategy was split into two: after its launch, there was a high-profile TV advertising campaign featuring Dennis, a boy being reluctantly dragged around by his parents, who are home-hunting in the traditional way. Subsequently, the company adopted a more targeted approach by sponsoring the Channel Four property series *Location, location, location*.

The combination of strengths has helped propel Asserta Home to the head of the home portal queue: the site was ranked number one in the UK in surveys by *FT connectis*, the Net magazine, *Metro* newspaper and HouseAbout.

Flexibility

Business growth has been achieved through a combination of organic and non-organic growth. The launch pad for the site was the acquisition of UK Property Gold; this brought access to a database and functionality, as well as management knowledge and expertise in a new market. From that position the business was able to aggressively penetrate the Estate Agency market and secure the necessary critical mass for market leadership at launch. Specializing in new developments, the UKPG site currently co-exists with its parent but will eventually be fully integrated. The purchase of a second property site, Smove, in late 2000 helped enrich Asserta's editorial content and strengthen non-core services. Smove employed Mark Edmonds, ex-property editor of the *Daily Telegraph*, and offered a humorous slant on the moving process as well as a comprehensive range of post-move services.

Asserta Home took an early decision to transfer IT development outside London when it decided the wealth of opportunities in the capital might endanger its long-term ability to retain staff. Though Sapient initially built the site, redevelopment work is now carried out in-house and the company wants to ensure the training given to programmers is used in the business's interest. A development centre was therefore established in Cheltenham, where employment patterns are more stable and living costs are lower. The other key acquisition was GMW, a software house (see Growth Markets).

Human Resources

According to Asserta Home's managing director, Andrew Doyle, the work environment is demanding and requires a lot of adaptability from employees. Doyle, who does not have his own office, observes: 'People here tend to be intelligent, flexible and able to think out of the box. They are comfortable with uncertainty.'

The reason for the constant change is the highly competitive market in which Asserta operates. Needless to say, external events dictate that the individual business teams must remain closely aligned. From a managerial point-of-view, the main challenge is in ensuring a balance is struck between the occasionally competing interests. Apart from IT development, which is carefully structured, every area must, in theory, bend to accommodate the business priority of the moment.

Employing over 80 people in total, Asserta Home is a highly sociable environment, with an event organized for all London employees to attend each month. Pay levels are competitive, there is a good pension scheme and bonuses are awarded to exceptional performers.

Growth Markets

Though Asserta Home does not charge partner estate agents for the exposure it gives their properties, a chargeable business model is likely to be introduced in the future. For now, however, the company's primary revenue streams are from the sale of software and advertising revenues.

It is estimated that one third of estate agents in the UK are still without an Internet presence while others are using relatively unsophisticated applications. Asserta Home is determined to grab as large a share of this market as possible. To develop this side of the business, it acquired GMW, a back-office solutions provider for around 1,600 estate agents.

Many estate agents have been persuaded of the merits of a tool which allows them to market their properties much more powerfully. But the company is in a race with at least four other key suppliers and so has recruited a contract sales team to accelerate its speed of reach. Potential customers are offered a free older version of the software as a tryout, which they can then pay to upgrade. After installation, further revenue can be generated by maintenance work carried out by Asserta Home.

By attracting the most traffic to its site and achieving a dominant market presence Asserta Home also aims to bump up advertising revenues. And in the longer term it will seek to increase business-to-consumer revenue through a mix of tenancy fees, lead generation fees and product conversion fees which are paid to Asserta by a range of quality partners.

Quality of Management

In establishing the business, CGNU recognized that start-up skills are quite different to operational capabilities. Accordingly, MD Andrew Doyle was not appointed until after the launch. Formerly deputy finance director at Norwich Union Long Term Savings, he was closely involved in its recent flotation. He also has a background in change management. Along with finance director Stephen Harry, a former strategic consultant with PWC, he reports to a relatively 'hands-off' board of senior Norwich Union personnel.

As a well-funded venture backed by a large institution, Asserta Home poses a different challenge than that faced by the head of a typical start-up. Rather than fend off larger competitors, Doyle must decide which of the many approaches from companies keen to be acquired have any strategic value. He lists an ability to walk away from deals quickly and to respond both to press comment and to a quickly changing market as the main skills he has so far developed.

Asserta Home's acquisitions mean the management team also includes entrepreneurs. Jim and Nancy Cruikshank founded Smove and head up marketing and business development respectively. Likewise Philip Caterer and Ian Davis (ex-UK Property Gold) manage the estate agency relationships and IT sections. Simon Phipps, head of customer proposition and previously CGNU strategy and planning associate, Group Strategy, looks after the overall development of the site and ensures the IT function remains aware of commercial realities.

International Orientation

As the sixth biggest insurance company in the world, CGNU has customer databases in a large number of countries. With this in mind, McKinsey & Co was commissioned to research the European property market and assess the viability of transferring functionality to areas of cultural similarity. Following the research, however, it was decided that Asserta Home's interests would be better served by targeting its resources on the market in England and Wales – where the home-buying process is widely viewed as especially inefficient – and perfecting the customer proposition. The wisdom of a 'land grab' approach to e-business has been revised in the light of difficulties experienced by a number of operators.

autobytel.co.uk

The company launched its website www.autobytel.co.uk in April 1999, which allowed motorists in Britain to buy a full range of UK-based, new and used cars using the Internet for the first time. Based in Milton Keynes, this UK company is constructed on the model of autobytel.com, which is one of the largest generators of car sales in North America. Autobytel.co.uk has yet to make a profit, but the latest figures have revealed that the site had received more than 55,000 individual car purchase requests since launch and that it had attracted more than 3.5 million unique visitors, generating more than 280 million hits and more than 90 million page impressions. At present it has 34 members of staff – all of which work from the company's Milton Keynes head-quarters.

Scorecard:

Innovation	★★★★★
Flexibility	★★★★
Human resources	★★★★
Growth markets	★★★★★
Quality of management	★★★★★
International orientation	★★★★

Biggest plus:
Autobytel.co.uk is a prime mover in the car e-tailing business.

Biggest minus:
Fortunes are linked to a new industry, whose success is based on projections.

Autobytel.co.uk
Medina House
324/326 Silbury Boulevard
Milton Keynes MK9 2AE
Tel: 0870 6070909
website: www.autobytel.co.uk

Autobytel.co.uk

The Business

Autobytel.co.uk is a wholly owned subsidiary of Inchcape plc, which secured the licence from Autobytel.com to launch a copycat site in the UK in 1999. Inchcape plc has a small stake in Autobytel.com, which has sold more than half a million cars since its launch in 1995, and is expected to go into profit by the third quarter of 2001. On top of its interest in Autobytel.com, Inchcape plc is a shareholder of Autobytel Europe, the company set up to build the Autobytel brand across Europe, through launching country-specific sites across the Continent. It has set up sites in Sweden, the Netherlands and Spain so far, with plans for more sites in France, Norway, Denmark, Finland, Belgium and Germany.

Innovation

Autobytel.co.uk was the first website in Britain to offer motorists the opportunity to buy new or used vehicles using the Internet. Owners Inchcape plc spotted early on how the Internet would provide another avenue for retailing so the e-tailer was created with the philosophy that Autobytel.co.uk would appear as a virtual shop window on the world of UK cars. The site is supported by more than 150 car dealers across the UK, 55 of which are owned by Inchcape plc, and it's these dealers who provide the new and used cars. Autobytel.co.uk has recently increased the number of services available through the site, to include an in-house customer service centre, a sell your car programme, which is not conditional on any trade-in or part exchange, and a home delivery service to maximize customer convenience. As well as these new features, site visitors can also get car financing and insurance deals. The company says the site's new features are part of its policy of building customer freedom. Kevin Turnbull, chief executive of Autobytel.co.uk explains: 'We are committed to a policy of customer freedom, which means liberating the online customer from the straitjacket of the traditional car buying process.' Turnbull goes on to say that this means making the buying experience as convenient for the customer as possible. As part of this policy, the site does not offer cars from outside the UK, as it claims the administrative problems involved with bringing cars into the country would jeopardize its commitment to convenience. With the e-commerce industry being so new, much of the business's cash, which totalled £8 million in 2000, is ploughed into research and development, as the company studies the needs and desires of Internet users. Much of its advertising to date has been done in the form of print media and sponsorship. The company has little faith in online banner advertising. To boost its brand, the company is currently in negotiations with other site owners over partnering deals, whereby partners' sites will have their own car buying section powered by Autobytel.co.uk.

Flexibility

According to Turnbull people's view of what the Internet is for has changed, and is still changing, as the technology becomes more mainstream. 'Not that long ago if we were talking about what people would buy online, we would be talking about books and CDs,' says Turnbull. 'But one reason why we recently upgraded our website is because these perceptions are changing and people want to buy other things online, including cars.'

Turnbull admits that, to some extent, buying a car over the Internet still falls into the unusual category, but as the level of security for making purchases online improves and people become more comfortable with the whole concept outside of books and CDs, the practice will become more commonplace. Turnbull adds that this is evident in the feedback the company received prior to its site overhaul last year. 'We got a lot of responses from people during the site's early stages saying we came online to buy a car and have been passed on to a dealer, yet we came online because we wanted to buy on the Internet.'

Of course, e-commerce nowadays has spawned a number of spin-offs such as m-commerce for mobile Internet services and t-commerce for interactive television services. But Autobytel.co.uk is not going to be jumping on any bandwagons, instead the company will wait for the technology to be proven workable and popular among customers. 'We never really got into WAP technology because from our point of view it never promised the level of performance we wanted. On top of this, its popularity never matched expectations,' says Turnbull. He says the company is keeping a close eye on the evolution of interactive television but it has no plans to make the leap onto an iTV platform – it would rather hold off until it's more mainstream.

'We had first mover advantage on the Internet and we want to continue building our brand in this area,' he says.

Human Resources

Autobytel.co.uk currently has 34 employees but this figure is expected to double during 2001. Being fun-loving and flexible are the two attributes common to each member of staff, both of which fit in with the spirit of entrepreneurship. Reflecting the pioneering nature of e-commerce right now, the company is keen for workers' in-put both on current practices and future developments. It seeks out these views during informal get togethers (such the regular company outings, which can include go-karting) and formal meetings. If it's not fun, then it's not worth doing, is the catchphrase that Turnbull sticks to, and which, he believes, is the mantra running throughout the business. He's keen to point out that the basic principle of the new economy is to do things differently, and this principle can be seen throughout the business. It's all pervasive, from the informal workwear among staff to the willingness of managers to listen to employees' concerns, which may include the need for a new sofa in a rest area.

Growth Markets

As a UK-based and UK-focused new business, the company aims to grow solely within this country. Its projections are that it will be in profit by 2003, following the increasing popularity of buying online. The site was given a new look in October, with a raft of services added to the existing offering. And it's the addition of further services for the customer, making the site pretty much a one-stop-shop for motoring needs, that lies at the heart of the company's plans for the future. Customer relationship management (CRM) is a phrase that is currently being bandied about the place. Turnbull explains why it is important for Autobytel.co.uk: 'We want to build up a relationship with our customers so that ours is the site they immediately turn to if they want to buy a car.' A key area in the expansion of the business over the next twelve months is going to be its programme of affiliate partnerships. With its prime mover status and strong brand recognition the company is looking to strike deals with sites which would want their own car e-tailing section. The company has begun talks with site owners but is yet to announce any deals at this time.

Quality of Management

In keeping with the fast-moving pace of e-commerce, the business has departmental meetings every two weeks, where staff can discuss their individual workloads, the firm's core objectives and put forward ideas. As Turnbull explains the input of the employees is key for the business to evolve: 'these are the people who are at the sharp end – so to have their input in the development of such a new business is crucial'.

He goes on to say these meetings can be 'free for alls' where, owing to the looseness of their agenda, the meetings can raise a multitude of issues from working practices, to site service, to office conditions.

But as he says, the looseness also gives a sense of inclusiveness, whereby whatever the concern of an employee they will be listened to. On top of these meetings, the company holds formal strategic sessions where the development of the company is discussed. A session was held just after Christmas 2000, when staff were told of the strategic direction of the company over the next twelve months. This session tied in with the launch of the new-look Autobytel.co.uk site kicked-off in October 2000. Part of the reason for the session was to get feedback from staff on the overhauled site, which through its additional services had revised the company's business model. Turnbull re-emphasizes the point that the firm's employees are the most important part of the company. 'While the business's model may be sound, unless you have a committed team behind it, it's not going to work, and as an e-tailer in a new industry this is even more important.'

International Orientation

As previously mentioned, the company is UK-focused, and it plans to grow solely within this country. However, through its parent company, Inchcape plc, it still has an interest in the development of the Autobytel brand across Europe. It is a shareholder in Autobytel Europe Holdings which will make it a pan-European brand. However, part of the ethos of the Autobytel marque is that it offers a localized service, hence its UK operation is run by people who know the UK market, and the Dutch operation is run by people from the Netherlands.

'Unless you're an expert in every localized European market, you couldn't hope to build the brand across the continent because it goes against what it's all about,' says Turnbull.

'Our strategic investment plans are both here in the UK and in Europe because we want to be a key e-commerce player in the European automotive industry.'

Autonomy

Autonomy is a technology infrastructure company with head-quarters in both Cambridge, UK, and San Francisco. It specializes in pattern recognition technology that enables vast volumes of 'unstructured' information (office documents, e-mails, intranet and Web content, amongst others) to be automatically managed and processed on the basis of the concepts the information contains. Autonomy was founded in 1996 and is traded on the London Stock Exchange, EASDAQ and Nasdaq.

Scorecard:

Innovation	★★★★★
Flexibility	★★★★
Human resources	★★★★
Growth markets	★★★
Quality of management	★★★★
International orientation	★★★★★

Biggest plus:
Massive customer base, technology that genuinely makes people's lives easier.

Biggest minus:
Some fool only put 24 hours in every day.

Autonomy
Cambridge Business Park
Cowley Road
Cambridge CB4 0WZ
Tel: 01223 448000
Fax: 01223 448001
website: www.autonomy.com

Autonomy

The Business

Autonomy was founded in 1996 just when the Internet was about to take off. This is significant because while a number of commentators were hyping the potential of this new communications medium, Autonomy was more interested in just how all of this data could be organized. It has grown to the extent that it is listed on the London Stock Exchange, EASDAQ and Nasdaq. It has 425 blue-chip customers, with 100 partners and 40 original equipment manufacturers (OEMs) – companies that buy or license the Autonomy offering and label it as their own to sell to their customers.

Innovation

Autonomy's business innovates from two angles – first its own products, and second the fact that it feeds off other technological innovation. Its task, put simply, is to take the mass of unmanaged information that arrives on people's computers every day, analyse it and enable it to be processed automatically. This might involve categorizing it in a relevant directory, or sending the information to a particular person, or linking the information to other resources that address the same issues. This isn't a simple undertaking – it means the system has to 'read' every e-mail, internal Web page, external Web page and office document and automate the actions performed upon it. A major corporate will typically process thousands of these pieces of information in a day.

Perhaps oddly for such a radical concept, the technology is based on the work of an eighteenth-century presbyterian minister, Rev. Thomas Bayes, who was a mathematical genius in his spare time. He evolved Bayes' Theorem, which concerns pattern recognition and which enables Autonomy to process unstructured digital information, to identify concepts and to establish relationships between different pieces of information. It is language-independent and can be implemented on its own or it can be used as an element of an existing corporate application.

The end result is that the individuals using the company's products can focus on their core tasks, while the Autonomy system does the sifting and redirecting of the information that will make them more effective. Autonomy calls the process 'automated intelligence'. It is scalable and is sold by 100 partners and 40 OEMs, which effectively means manufacturers who incorporate the software into their own systems to add value, and then sell the resulting combination as their own.

Flexibility

The nature of the Autonomy product offering is that it needs to be completely flexible in terms of product development since it has to decipher everything the market chooses to throw at it. Fortunately the pattern recognition technology works across any computing platform and in over 200 data formats – including the industry-favoured XML – and is therefore likely to be adaptable to all of these demands.

The company itself has needed flexibility and managerial depth to sustain extremely rapid growth. It launched in only 1996 and is based on the work of founder Dr. Michael Lynch at Cambridge Neuro-dynamics, which in turn took the work on probabilistic modelling undertaken by Dr. Lynch at Cambridge University and turned it into what would ultimately become the Autonomy product range (Auton-omy now owns all rights to the technology). It managed its growth into a global player by a number of means – primarily the injection of $15 million from venture capitalists willing to trust to Neurodynam-ics' track record and the market potential.

One area in which the company shows no inclination towards flexibility, however, is in its commitment to the indirect sales channel, which is absolute. It sticks to this because it enables partners to build in good margins and therefore motivates them to form a thousands-strong sales force on behalf of Autonomy, something the company could not otherwise manage.

Human Resources

As might be expected from a company that specializes in information distributed electronically, Autonomy has an excellent section on career opportunities on its website. Without wishing to appear negative, this makes it clear that the total number of employees is unlikely to change radically in the near future – this being another advantage of the indirect sales model, the sales force can increase without building on the staff head count.

The technology does evolve, though, so there is a need for fresh expertise from time to time. Candidates for employment should expect excellent compensation and benefits in return for hard work and the right skills to take the company forward. Autonomy is an equal oppor-tunities employer.

Growth Markets

One of the best things about Autonomy is that its market is growing, unprompted, by itself. Anybody working in a corporate environment will confirm that the sheer amount of information arriving in an unstructured manner is too much for people to deal with manually, particularly given that these people all have other, more 'core' tasks they are expected to perform. It is therefore difficult to limit which markets exactly the company will expand into, particularly since most of these will be targeted through the VARs and systems integrators with which Autonomy works.

However, it is exploiting the new content delivery channels as they emerge – witness its focus on e-commerce and the I-WAP product, designed to manage messages and e-mails as delivered to the Wireless Application Protocol devices. Witness also its newly-developed voice technology, Voice Suite, which treats voice as another source of unstructured information, and its support for i-Mode, the Asian equivalent of WAP. More will follow as new delivery technologies emerge.

Dr. Mike Lynch, founder and Group CEO of Autonomy, comments: 'Going forward, we are excited about our future and we will continue to execute our strategy of leveraging our indirect distribution channels to drive forward our business into new markets and our technology into new areas.'

Quality of Management

Founding managing director, Dr. Michael Lynch, has been with the company since day one and its sustained growth, plus its ability to raise $15 million in venture capital clearly shows how highly the management is regarded in international markets.

Other than Lynch, the board includes board and finance director Ralph Harms, who has had senior positions in Philips Semiconductor, Intel, Rockwell International and Xerox; Richard Gaunt was technical director of Neurodynamics, from which Autonomy came, and has been responsible for Autonomy's underlying technology. Marketing falls to Dominic Johnson, who joined in February 1997 and became a board member with responsibility for marketing the following year; his previous experience includes head of marketing at News International's multimedia division as well as marketing manager for Channel 4 Learning and general manager at Granada Education Publishing. Director Barry Ariko joined the board early in 2000 after leaving a position as senior vice president at America Online, where he headed the Netscape Enterprise Group.

John McMonigall is on the remuneration committee and audit committee of the company, having started out as a director in 1996; he had previously held positions on the management board of BT and he also serves on the boards of Dialog Demiconductor GmbH, JazzTel plc and TelDaFax GmbH. Senator Richard Perle has been a director for over a year and has been a resident fellow of the American Enterprise

Institute for Public Policy Research since 1987, as well as being CEO and chairman of the board at Hollinger Digital Inc. Director Richard Wilson has been on the board since April 1999 after working his way through the company which he joined in 1995. He is also a director of JazzTel plc, Nholdings Ltd and Efita OSS Solutions Inc.

As readers will gather, there are no lightweights on the board – the company is multinational already but has secured the managerial depth to allow for further growth.

International Orientation

As has been established already, Autonomy is a multinational company whose dual head offices extend across two continents. A glance at the directors' biographies will confirm that this commitment to expand the company internationally extends to the recruitment of key personnel.

Overall the company appears to have taken note of a distinct corporate malaise of the early twenty-first century and done something about it. This should logically assure not only a good future for Autonomy but it should ease the growth of its clients and allow them to focus on their core tasks rather than get overwhelmed with disorganized data. Not only is this of benefit to business but it stands a chance of improving the quality of the employees' lives; more people than just the shareholders therefore stand to benefit as long as Autonomy continues its growth.

BALTIMORE™

www.baltimore.com

Baltimore Technologies is a global leader in a vitally important area of technology for electronic commerce: security. As such, it has been one of the most visible and earliest successes of the Internet era. The company has several offices world-wide and has headquarters in: Dublin, Ireland; London, UK; Boston, US and Sydney, Australia. In the UK, Baltimore has offices in Basingstoke, Theale, Uxbridge, and Hemel Hempstead. For the year end 2000, about 47 per cent of Baltimore's revenues came from EMEA (Europe, Middle East, India, Africa); 22 per cent came from the US and the remainder from the Asia Pacific (31 per cent).

Scorecard:

Innovation	★★★★
Flexibility	★★★★
Human resources	★★★
Growth markets	★★★★
Quality of management	★★★
International orientation	★★★★

Biggest plus:
Dynamic, challenging environment of constant change in a relatively young but already substantial company with global ambitions.

Biggest minus:
Technology could veer in a different direction at any time.

Baltimore Technologies
Parkgate Street,
Dublin 8,
Ireland
Tel: 353 1 881 6000
website: www.baltimore.com
e-mail: info@baltimore.com

Baltimore Technologies

The Business

Baltimore Technologies, a global leader in e-security, develops and markets security products and services to enable companies to develop trusted, secure systems for e-business, the Internet and mobile commerce. Founded in 1976 in Ireland, Baltimore was acquired by its current CEO, Fran Rooney, and private investors in 1996. In 1999, it merged with the UK cryptography specialist Zergo Holdings, adopting the Baltimore name. Baltimore Technologies employs over 1200 people world-wide and operates in over 30 cities, with headquarters in Dublin, Ireland; London, UK; Boston, US and Sydney, Australia. Baltimore Technologies is a public company with dual listings on Nasdaq (BALT) and the London Stock Exchange (BLM).

Innovation

Baltimore's products include a wide range of Public Key Infrastructure (PKI) products and services, access control and authorization products, wireless e-security solutions, cryptographic toolkits, content security products, security applications and hardware cryptographic devices.

For many decades, cryptography was the sole province of governments, in part because of the computing power required; most countries thought of it as a military weapon. The new technique known as public-key cryptography was developed in 1978, and opened the way for the spontaneous exchange of secured data between strangers, changing the entire field. The advent of the Internet has turned cryptography into a necessary enabling technology moving into widespread use to protect sensitive information as it traverses the public Internet – everything from credit card details entered into an e-commerce site by customers, to drafts of company reports sent between divisions by e-mail. Cryptography software encrypts this data, scrambling it so that even if it's intercepted it can't be read by unauthorized people.

Baltimore spotted the opportunity posed by the opening emergence of the market for cryptography products, both hardware and software, earlier than most. Zergo Holdings, while it was still a separate company, did cryptography development work for, among others, the British government. Meanwhile, much debate raged between privacy advocates, technical experts, and software companies, who all wanted fewer restrictions on the use, deployment, and export of strong cryptography, which continued to be regarded as a military weapon. Baltimore boasts that it developed the first Java-based cryptography and developed the entire idea of public key infrastructure (PKI) and invented many of the security products now used in e-business. The mathematical algorithm underlying Baltimore's products, as Paddy Holahan, executive vice-president, admits, has been available for nearly 25 years, but to build it into usable business products was another matter entirely.

Flexibility

'It was very challenging to set up a software company in Ireland at the time,' says Paddy Holahan. 'It was impossible to get capital.' The company therefore had to be profitable early in its life; it's only in the last few years that Ireland has changed to become more like the funding environment in the US.

As a direct result, Baltimore adopted three strategies for growth: create and build more new products, partner with other companies, and acquire other companies. It uses all three of these, evaluating market opportunities as they come along and selecting the strategy it believes is most appropriate. Unlike many organizations, which assemble an acquisitions team in advance of a merger that disbands as soon as it's over, Baltimore maintains teams in all these areas at all times, making it ready to move in any direction when necessary. Baltimore's role model in this area is Cisco Systems, which has built itself up into a huge company by pursuing a relentless strategy of acquiring start-ups that have enabled the company to develop the next bit of new technology that it needs.

'We do a lot of work on the structure and management before we acquire a company,' says Holahan, 'so when we acquire it everything is in place and we can just execute.'

Baltimore Technologies has had to change and adapt in many ways over the years. Just four years ago, it had seven employees and over 90 per cent of its revenues came from EMEA. Now, it has 1,200 employees and its revenues are split into roughly: 47 per cent EMEA, 22 per cent US, and 31 per cent Asia-Pacific. It acquired five companies in the year 2000. To manage that amount of change, the company has to be very flexible. 'If we're not changing we're in trouble, because the industry is changing.'

Human Resources

Baltimore boasts a low staff turnover. 'Fundamentally, we're a software company,' says Holahan, 'so the people are the only thing that matter. We have no plant or machinery, just people and computers, so we recognize right away that our staff are the most important thing.' People with 'the right attitude,' he says, thrive at the company if they work hard and execute well; you do need to be adaptable and forward-looking. The company is not the right place for people who want predictable, repetitive work.

Culturally, because of its high-tech nature, the company is 'somewhere between California and Boston'. Open-plan seating prevails. The focus on the ongoing growth of the business also means that people with the right skills and abilities may assume responsibility very quickly without regard to age or experience. The company lists job openings on its website (www.baltimore.com/corporate/jobs/index.html), and solicits CVs by e-mail to the address listed with each job. Shareholding goes right through the company, and staff also get healthy bonuses.

'The people that thrive are prepared to look to the future, get on with it, and accommodate change,' says Holahan.

Growth Markets

'We want to be number one,' says Holahan boldly. And he doesn't mean number one in Ireland or even number one in Europe – he means number one in the world. 'We believe there is a $16 billion market out there, and we want the biggest piece. We are going to go for that. We are not going to say, 'Oh, we can't beat these guys.'

In picking this line of business, at the outset, Baltimore Technologies didn't have the assets of competitors like RSA Data Security, which had a steady stream of licence fees from its patent on the most commonly used cryptography algorithm, or the ready access to capital of the new US-based security companies such as Entrust and Network Associates. Although the financial press tends to finger Verisign, a US-based authentication service based on cryptographic technology spun off from RSA, as Baltimore's main competitor, the company says in fact it doesn't compete in terms of sales. RSA is a customer; other licensees and partners include IBM, EDS, Accenture, Hewlett-Packard, Logica, PricewaterhouseCoopers (PWC) Cisco Systems, CheckPoint and many others.

The partnership programme is a key plank in Baltimore's growth plans. 'Our approach was that the security market was going to explode, and there was no way to grow fast enough to keep up,' says Holahan.

Quality of Management

Senior managers at Baltimore tend to be entrepreneurial types, typically people who have run their own companies at some stage in their careers. Fran Rooney, the CEO, has been with the company since his original investment in 1996. Aidan Gallagher, the executive vice-president of global business development, was formerly managing director of Visibility International. Holahan was co-founder and CEO of East Coast Software, which developed utility software for PCs. This is, in other words, a high-tech company whose upper ranks are populated with experienced managers, many with an entrepreneurial spirit.

Although the company's share price has fluctuated along with the rest of the high-tech market this year, Baltimore tends to be well-liked among financial analysts, who generally speak favourably of its management and aggressive outlook. The company has been in and out of the FTSE 100 index several times in 2000–2001, but analysts have remained positive, especially as the company's customer base broadens beyond e-commerce to include authentication – an important function when you're dealing with strangers across electronic networks – as well as security.

'We could have gone down the cul-de-sacs of key escrow or SET,' says Holahan, referring to two directions in security that were hot in the mid 1990s, 'and we wouldn't be here now if we had.'

'Management's ability to cope with the task or function assigned to them is what matters,' says Holahan, noting that the company's organizational structure means that there is a mix of regional and global management. Matrix reporting is common; that is, employees may report to more than one manager, such as both a regional manager and a global manager, and the company believes this practice helps keep the culture relatively free of internal politics.

Because of the company's aggressive acquisition strategy, senior managers also have to be able to accommodate new senior management.

International Orientation

Electronic commerce is an inherently international business, just as the Internet is an inherently international medium. Baltimore's target market, therefore, is any company world-wide that seeks to do business electronically, whether this means selling products to consumers or to other businesses, or jointly creating intellectual property. Accordingly, the company is resolutely international in orientation, helped by its many acquisitions in countries from Canada (where it bought Nevex in 2000) to Dubai, where it opened an office in November 2000.

The company has research labs in Dublin, London, Sydney, Boston, and Tokyo, and sales offices in many more countries. The Dubai office is intended to spearhead its expansion into the Middle East by building a series of partnerships. International expansion is so important to the company's ambitions to be number one in its market that it deliberately chose to accept a couple of years of financial losses in order to implement it. Just as it has done elsewhere, it intends to build an extensive series of partnerships throughout the Middle East to help it expand more rapidly than it can on its own.

bol.com®

BOL is part of the massive and privately owned Bertlesmann company. The BOL parent enterprise is to be found among the top four media companies world-wide and boasts nearly 700 separate operations. BOL came into being in February 1999, and has its headquarters in London. Currently BOL operates in 16 countries and claims to be the most international media and entertainment e-commerce company.

Scorecard:

Innovation	★★★★
Flexibility	★★★★
Human resources	★★★
Growth markets	★★★★
Quality of management	★★★★
International orientation	★★★★

Biggest plus:
'BOL' is a fast moving, innovative and fun company to work for, and the fact that we are backed by Bertelsmann provides far greater security than most dot-coms.'

Biggest minus:
You will be working in a highly competitive, unpredictable marketplace.

Bol
Greater London House
Hampstead Road
London N1 9TZ
Tel: 020 7760 6900
Fax: 020 7760 6901
website: www.bol.com

BOL

The Business

BOL is part of a private company, Bertlesmann, which has revenues of £10 billion and has been in profit since 1945. The management at BOL claim this is an important differentiator during the currently troubled market conditions facing online commerce operations. In Europe BOL has operations in the UK, France, Germany, Switzerland, the Netherlands, Spain and Italy, as well as Denmark, Norway, Sweden and Finland. The company also has a strong presence in the Far East, including Japan, China, Malaysia, Singapore and Hong Kong. Each country is served by an online store specific to that nationality. BOL sells a wide range of products, ranging from books to music to DVDs and videos and games and software, as well as gifts. Around 70 people work for BOL in the UK.

Innovation

The areas where BOL claims to be most innovative involve the quality of the customer experience and consequently fuelling enthusiasm for the products offered. The company positions its websites as efficient warehouses to create a superior customer experience.

Apart from the choice provided – BOL says it has 1.4 million books alone in stock – this also means humanizing the online shopping scenario. Facilities offered include customer chat rooms and the ability to directly contact BOL staff, even during transactions. The personalization of the sites goes as far as the provision of customer portals, so that specific interests can be catered for. Photos of the company's employees are also displayed to enhance the 'human face' look and feel that BOL is striving for.

Another value proposition claimed by BOL is its focus on fast problem resolution for customers. It is now established that online shoppers will shy away from sites where they had difficulty fulfilling a transaction. Customer retention is a cornerstone of BOL's business strategy. The company also operates a service called BOL TV, where customers can watch authors discussing a variety of topics.

To further its goal of delivering a warm and enjoyable shopping experience, BOL has also focused on providing superior digital content. The company reveals that it holds around 1.5 million clips of different kinds, ranging from songs to videos and more – allowing more latitude to the consumer. For instance, a prospective customer can listen to a soundtrack for up to 10 days before deciding whether or not to buy. BOL is also taking a multichannel route to market and is already making sales via digital TV, as well as via PC-based access. Other access media to be catered for in the future include mobile devices enabled with WAP or I-Mode – two sets of technology to help cell phones connect to the Web.

Flexibility

BOL claims that there was not a formal blueprint for the company at first, with very small staff numbers involved at the beginning – essentially a group of enthusiastic people. Once initial staff numbers reached between 20–30, a clear structure and management reporting system fell into place. BOL also needed to add multiple skill sets and specialists in several areas, such as music, books and video.

The concern at the company was initially whether or not these divergent groups would gel into a homogenous organization, but it seems that such fears have proved mostly unfounded. Two reasons for this are the open-door management policy that has been instituted at BOL and the establishment of a formal company structure allowing everyone to find their own place. Yet with such a range of specialists on board, BOL had to work hard to eradicate the sense of any division within the organization.

Even so, BOL does not have the typical start-up profile and this has almost certainly helped in what appears to be a smoother corporate evolution than most. Clearly the Bertlesmann parent company will not fund ventures that do not promise returns over time, while allowing enough time for a particular group to grow and test its market capability. In the case of BOL, clear progress has been made – the primary evidence for this being its continued international expansion.

Flexibility is expected of BOL employees in terms of the hours worked, as the company is not, in any respect, a nine-to-five operation. When night-shifts or weekends are worked, then staff are expected to regain the extra hours spent at work from other rosters. The management does get concerned, however, when too many people turn up for weekend duties.

Human Resources

There is a youthful quality to the BOL operation, without everyone necessarily being young in years. Most people are in their late 20s or early 30s. These are people who have already developed careers in areas relevant to BOL, such as the media and film. The management claims, and there is clear evidence of this, that an open and accessible culture prevails. Two examples show the camaraderie and togetherness that can be found within the company. One is the existence of a company football team, another is the unofficial and refreshingly honest 'Bolaholics' club. The Bolaholics are the people who regularly get together at local hostelries after work.

BOL claims to be open to different personalities and sets few barriers in terms of age and style of working. The type of people who thrive at BOL are open minded and enjoy their work. Only one person has left BOL in the UK since 1999 – quite an achievement for a recently formed company.

Growth Markets

BOL sees its future in providing what it calls an online virtual warehouse service, where media and entertainment wholesalers are aggregated through the company's site to provide direct shopping to customers with a 24-hour turnaround on delivery. This will inevitably involve multiple channels, ranging from the PC, to interactive TV and mobile phones over the next few years, according to BOL management.

Additional products and product combinations are also being considered to further engage the customer and boost revenue. This could involve selling tickets of various kinds – such as for music shows and films – or even travel tickets to various locations that a customer has already shown interest in. For instance, if someone has bought a book about Italy why not offer the means to visit the place and see everything contained in the book for real, or offer the same customer a chance to sample Italian wine. This exemplifies the kind of thinking going on at BOL.

Overall the evolution of growth markets for BOL depends on how well it serves the lifestyle needs of its customers, as opposed to just selling different categories of product.

Quality of Management

At BOL, the management is keen to stress that its profile does not fit in with the typical stereotype of a dot-com organization. The BOL managers are all people previously experienced in the areas of business covered by the company, coming mostly from bricks-and-mortar company backgrounds. This means that underneath the surface, BOL is run very much according to a more traditional business model than may appear at first glance – which has been adapted to demands of the digital economy.

So there is a good level of previous management experience in retail, publishing and the entertainment industries, among others. Younger managers can be fitted in with more recent knowledge and are given the opportunity to develop new areas of expertise. Therefore BOL considers itself to have a healthy balance to its management teams, which remain open to positive suggestions from among the employee ranks. Equally, senior managers have a fairly high level of freedom to act independently, so long as they are hitting the numbers. In turn, this kind of freedom in decision making cascades down the organizational structure – so long as the results are right.

However, no company can be run on completely democratic lines. So there is often the need to choose between 'necessities' as one request, say for extra sales staff, might have an unwanted effect on more critical situations elsewhere. To offset such outcomes, the management has regular meetings where all relevant dynamic trends get discussed. Communication is encouraged across the board, but in particular at the senior levels.

International Orientation

Over time BOL intends to be completely international in its operations, with the ultimate aspiration being to evolve into a truly global operation. It has to be said that the company has already achieved a broad multinational reach, but there is clearly room for further expansion.

Where the emphasis has been predominantly on Europe, Scandinavia and key Far Eastern markets up till now, other geographies will be catered for over time. The next most likely region to be developed by BOL is South America. A move into this market will take place over a period of time, as BOL does not seem to rush the implementation of a national site until all the elements are there to provide a good service – plus, of course, the existence of a decent market opportunity.

To this extent, BOL does not see Eastern Europe or Africa as potential markets at the stage of development that can sustain a dedicated operation in the near future.

brightstation™

technology born for business

Bright Station plc provides Internet-based solutions, primarily based on proprietary knowledge management and information retrieval technologies (its Web Solutions division) and e-commerce. A third group, Internet Ventures, provides risk capital and incubator services. The company lost £16.8 million on revenues of £8.5 million in the year ending December 2000 – although this was in line with expectations. During the year, Bright Station disposed of its high-value Information Services Division to The Thomson Corporation, and invested substantially in future business.

Scorecard:

Innovation	★★★★
Flexibility	★★★
Human resources	★★★
Growth markets	★★★★
Quality of management	★★★★
International orientation	★★★★

Biggest plus:
Bright Station is keen, focused, cash-rich and entrepreneurial, making for a great working atmosphere.

Biggest minus:
Although there is more than one way to realize value from small, high-growth companies, the business's strategic aim of floating individual operations to realize their value naturally depends on the attitude of the stock market to high-tech shares.

Bright Station plc
The Communications Building
48 Leicester Square
London WC2H 7DB
Tel: 020 7930 6900
website: www.brightstation.com

Bright Station

The Business

Bright Station began life as MAID plc in 1985 and subsequently became The Dialog Corporation, both of them specialized information services operations. In May 2000 the company sold that business for $275 million, paid off its debts, changed its name, and invested substantially in some of the key elements that it retained.

They include search-and-sort technologies, primarily the WebTop search tool and the SmartLogik knowledge management suite, and e-commerce systems. The Sparza hosted online retailing solution (also known as e-commerce ASP) has recently gone live with its second customer. Sparza's first customer, OfficeShopper is the fourth of Bright Station's subsidiaries. It is an online business supplies company that generated sales of £1.6 million last year and is expected to deliver around £4 million of sales during 2001. Bright Station Ventures was launched last year to invest in promising new technology start-ups and to assist the Bright Station subsidiaries with corporate financing. At least one new subsidiary is expected to be launched this year.

SmartLogik delivered sales of more than £4 million in 2000, nearly half of Bright Station's total revenues of £8.5 million (SmartLogik employs 126 of the 250 staff and has over 100 blue-chip clients).

The group's operating loss of £16.8 million for 2000 can reasonably be attributed to investment in the infrastructure and technology assets of the group's businesses, but there was more than £16 million in the bank at the year-end. Bright Station is run by and closely identified with entrepreneur Dan Wagner, now chief executive, but it is publicly quoted in London and New York and has a number of institutional shareholders.

Innovation

There are serious competitors for all of Bright Station's operating divisions, but the group does own some world-class technologies in leading-edge markets. WebTop is an Internet search engine that combines proprietary 'concept-based' retrieval technology with a powerful indexing system; it has catalogued and organized more than 500 million Web pages (it is second only to Google among search engines). A more spectacular business in commercial terms is the SmartLogik knowledge management suite of products. SmartLogik is designed for collecting and organizing data from internal and external sources (including, for instance, the Dialog databases). This is due to be the first Bright Station spin-off, and it has been valued by analysts at up to £300 million (against the Bright Station group's current market capitalization of less than £62 million). The Sparza suite, also based on proprietary technology, effectively outsources a company's e-commerce investment; the recent acquisition at a knock-down price of the key software behind failed online retailer boo.com provided more leading-edge technology that Bright Station should be able to optimize in providing hosted services to retailers.

Flexibility

Bright Station has changed dramatically in the last eighteen months, turning a heavily indebted information management provider into a cash-rich multi-division group with significant e-commerce and information retrieval technologies. It wasn't a complete U-turn, since most of the proprietary technologies were already on board; but the cultural shift to becoming a self-styled 'originator of change' – complete with an in-house incubator function – has been spectacular.

Human Resources

Bright Station is heavily oriented towards product development at present, with over 140 programmers in its total of 250 employees. (Around 50 programmers were recruited from the high-calibre boo.com team.)

The bulk of Bright Station's people work in the SmartLogik operation, which now numbers 126 staff based in offices in Central London, on the East and West coasts of the US, in Denmark and in an R&D facility in Cambridge.

Bright Station aims to build businesses in-house and eventually to float them off as independent operations (with the parent group probably retaining a significant stake). One result of this policy is an entrepreneurial culture, with staff encouraged to offer ideas. Another effect: the operating divisions have developed their own internal culture, with SmartLogik for instance more focused and more structured than the younger and less well developed Sparza teams.

Overall it seems that Bright Station does encourage proactive employees who are willing to take the initiative – and to take pride in their work. As with many new-technology companies with emergent products and young teams, career paths are emerging on an ad hoc basis. There is no profit-sharing scheme as yet, however there is a SAYE share saving scheme and a share option scheme for executive level management.

Growth Markets

Bright Station operates in a number of high-potential markets, especially for its enterprise-class products (Sparza and SmartLogik). This field is proving more immediately profitable than the more direct offerings – knowledge management, which is SmartLogik's field, is widely tipped as one of the killer applications for the current decade, and market analysts Ovum have forecast market growth from $515 million in 1999 to $3.5 billion in 2004. But even the OfficeShopper business-to-business catalogue and the WebTop search engine are reasonably safe bets and could be well positioned for future developments in online marketing. Bright Station has announced a series of technology and marketing agreements with heavy hitters – among them Intel Corporation, for the joint development and marketing of SmartLogik solutions on Intel servers – that will provide mutual assistance. SmartLogik client list topped the 100 mark during 2000 with big names like BBC, Yellow Pages, Fujitsu, Bank of England, and Shell. OfficeShopper more than doubled its own customer base during the year to over 900: and Sparza – which is just coming out of development – was chosen as the exclusive solutions partner for a new 'e-tail alliance' formed by Deutsche Post Fulfilment GmbH, Egremont and Lakewest Consulting.

Quality of Management

Bright Station is an unusual business: although it is a long-established public company with stock market quotations in London and New York, the dramatic change in direction caused by the sale last year of its major operations means that, in effect, it starts from scratch with no debts and a substantial cash hoard. Crucially though, it has been able to draw on ongoing technology and product developments.

The latter half of 2000 was spent largely in building a management team that could maximize revenues and deploy resources while holding down costs – all at a tricky time for high-tech enterprises. The group appears to have successfully recruited some high-calibre management to head up the subsidiary businesses. These appointments are particularly important because of their appeal to the City; the intention is that the operating divisions will be floated as soon as possible to realize their value as separate businesses.

Bright Station has shown itself to be alive to opportunity, for instance in the acquisition for a bargain-basement price of the assets of boo.com – principally some technology for online retailing that was probably ahead of its time and which cost around £30 million to develop. These assets represent overkill for a single retailer but will be valuable for a multiple-client operation – particularly at the knockdown price of just $375,000. Bright Station has also been able to employ around 50 of the boo.com programming team, and since it was planning to recruit that many programmers on the open market anyway the savings of around £1 million on recruitment consultants make the deal look even better.

International Orientation

Bright Station already has a Nasdaq listing, a legacy of its Dialog days, and the company clearly sees a commercial and corporate future outside the UK. In particular, SmartLogik – the best developed of the subsidiary businesses – has offices on the East and West coasts of the US and in Denmark. Agencies and resellers are being appointed throughout Europe, and SmartLogik already has a Danish presence.

Bulmers

Bulmers is an international alcoholic drinks manufacturer, is the world's largest cider maker and is the runaway leader in the UK cider market. It is also a company with a base in more than a century of family tradition, but one with the agility of mind to adapt to changing markets and conditions. As outgoing chairman Esmond Bulmer said in 2000, 'in the forty years I have been with the business, we have seen the company grow from a small family business into a public company which is a leader in its field.'

Scorecard:

Innovation	★★★
Flexibility	★★★
Growth markets	★★★★
Human resources	★★★★
Quality of management	★★★★
International orientation	★★★

Biggest plus:
'A highly unusual combination of traditional values with modern buzz, energy and vitality.'

Biggest minus:
'When they get here they tend to love it but, initially, it's not always easy to attract the best talent to Hereford.'

HP Bulmer Limited
The Cider Mills
Plough Lane
Hereford HR4 0LE
Tel: 01432 352000
Fax: 01432 352084
website: www.bulmers.com

HP Bulmer Limited

The Business

HP Bulmer (Bulmers) is a British company. It is based in Hereford, where it was founded in 1887, and is synonymous with cider manufacture and the traditional values associated with such an enterprise. The traditional values remain but today's Bulmers is a thriving international business with production facilities in seven countries, sales in over 60, and a growing share of the world-wide LAD (long alcoholic drinks) market. Results for the year ended April 2000 showed turnover up 6 per cent to £335.1 million, pre-tax profits up 14 per cent to £28.4 million and net dividends per ordinary share up 10 per cent to 17.6 pence. Members of the Bulmer family now own slightly less than 50 per cent of the company's shares.

Innovation

Bulmers states its intentions clearly: 'our vision – a world class, innovative, consumer focused, international long alcoholic drinks company'.

The company is no stranger to innovation and, in May 2000, it embraced e-commerce with the launch of its 'Pubservecom' website. Bulmers had acquired leading UK drinks distributor The Beer Seller – with a UK national network of 18 depots and a range of over 3000 lines, and subsequent alliances with non competing partners brought in catering suppliers Brake Bros and leading non food product supplier King UK.

Pubserve, in short, is set up to supply 'absolutely everything a good pub needs' through the Internet; or, to quote Bulmers UK managing director Tim Furse, 'this structure, where major non-competitive suppliers have come together to service a single industry via the Internet, is unique in the licensed trade and provides a new route making business-to-business e-commerce viable'. Pubserve's natural market is 'free houses' and, surprisingly, nearly 100,000 of the UK's 134,288 licensed premises are independent. Additional major partners to the scheme are Cadbury Scheweppes (soft drinks and confectionery) and Walkers (snacks) and its 24 additional sponsors include Bass, Fullers, Anhauser Busch, Interbrew, Scotco, Guinness, UDV and Coca-Cola.

Bulmers' philosophy has always been that 'innovation is not solely the province of managers but resides in everybody' and, in 1998, the company set up an 'innovation unit' whose specific role is to act as a catalyst in seeking out new information and suggesting ways in which the company should act on it. This does not usurp the place of the company's traditional thirst for innovative ideas from its employees at all levels but complements as a way in which 'randomly scattered ideas' can be gathered.

Flexibility

In an industry perceived as traditional Bulmers' management style is anything but, and managers are encouraged to pursue innovative methods to engage people to the notion that there are different ways of doing things. 'Breakthrough' was a culture change programme introduced in the late 1990s and, according to Rob Garner, 'it is a common sense approach to changing the way we work. It is', he says, 'about everyone owning one vision – to make Bulmers a world class, innovative business that is responsive to the needs of its customers, consumers, employees, shareholders and suppliers.'

Bulmers is nevertheless in a market whose participants are very susceptible to exterior and uncontrollable forces. This puts a premium on responsiveness and flexibility and diversity. In addition to its cider interests – these include the company's Strongbow, Woodpecker and Scrumpy Jack brands and its year 2000 acquisition of the American Hard Cider Company and the Green Mountain Cidery – Bulmers' portfolio includes exclusive UK distribution of Amstel, DAB, Red Stripe and San Miguel lagers and, from a standing start in December 2000, the company's 'Sidekick' range is on target for sales of an exceedingly respectable 800,000 cases in its first 12 months.

Bulmers, in short, is always on the lookout for opportunities. 'We are', concludes Rob Garner, 'relatively small but we're also very nimble – pace, agility and flexibility are important attributes in today's business world.'

Human Resources

Bulmers enjoys an open and strong relationship with its staff. Obviously one of Hereford's major employers, many staff have significant length of service – Bulmers' year 2000 annual report lists by name 87 employees who have been with the company for thirty years or more and mentions that a further 104 have completed 25 years' service. Personnel policies focus on reskilling, developing positive attitudes to change, a more international approach, and continuing to build a culture appropriate for a creative, entrepreneurial and consumer focused business.

Equal opportunity is pursued in the widest sense of the expression and, supported by the Employee Council and the company's recognized Trade Union, a rigorous equal opportunities policy is pursued. The company operates an extensive health and fitness centre, a learning centre and a heavily subsidized staff restaurant, which are open to all employees.

Bulmers displays few trappings of a previous and more formal era when status was proclaimed by size of office and location of car parking space. The style is open plan and informal, many of what would previously have been 'proper' meetings are now simply conducted via informal 'huddles' and – although delegation means decisions on a particular brand are taken by the respective brand manager – anyone can talk to the CEO.

The traditional values of integrity, fairness and caring, however, are strongly in evidence and Bulmers takes an active role in its local community – it is no ordinary lip-serving paternalism that causes a company openly to canvass its staff with figures on everything from world poverty to local heroin addiction and the question 'is there more that Bulmers can do than just make money?'

Growth Markets

Bulmers describes its priority growth market as the USA where, as the company's year 2000 annual report sanguinely expresses it, 'cider is still just a dot on the radar'. With equal sanguineness, however, the report points out that, with sustained double digit growth, cider is the fastest expanding US drinks category. Thanks to determined marketing – year 2000 advertising ran to $2 million – plus its acquisitions of the American Hard Cider Company and the Green Mountain Cidery, the company has already gained more than 50 per cent of a currently small but fast growing and thus potentially lucrative market.

Bulmers owns 65 per cent of the Chinese Sankong Brewery and has dedicated sales teams in Beijing and Shanghai. After the UK, South Africa is the world's second largest cider market and Bulmers has formed a packaging and distribution joint venture with the second largest South African brewery Bavaria Brau.

In the UK growth will continue to come through the development of Strongbow and other cider and beer brands, whilst The Beer Seller and Pubserve provide everything a good pub could possibly need.

Quality of Management

Bulmers is active in sports sponsorship – Leeds United football club, for example, is sponsored by the Strongbow brand. Rob Garner employs the body's immune system analogously – 'what you've got', he says, 'is a system which will deal effectively and more or less automatically with the odd boil or splinter but there's the feedback loop of pain if something gets seriously out of kilter. That's what we believe a business needs – a system – call it the much over-used "empowerment" if you like – that's self organizing and can, and will, deal with day-to-day ups and downs. All this takes place within a framework of focus, with appropriate measurement systems and tolerance levels – so that support can quickly be available whenever it's needed'.

The company is still changing ways of being and ways of behaviour and must, says Garner, go further down its chosen road of confidence, enablement and delegation within a framework:'what we want to achieve is the ability to make speedy decisions, but to make sure they're wise decisions'.

International Orientation

Bulmers' international business is growing and it is intended that international growth will continue. There are wholly owned subsidiaries in Australia, Belgium, New Zealand the US and majority holdings in businesses in China and South Africa. 20 per cent of year 2000 profit came from outside the UK and, by 2005, it is the company's intention that this will have grown to 50 per cent.

CAPITA

Capita Group is one of the unseen powerhouses of the service revolution. Phone the BBC or the Criminal Records Bureau, and the chances are that you will be speaking to one of Capita's employees, offering a very high level of service. With over 14,000 staff, more than 100 sites, and a turnover of £453m, Capita is one of the UK's leading providers of professional support services, and much of its work involves re-engineering and improving its clients' businesses.

Scorecard:

Innovation	★★★★
Flexibility	★★★★
Human resources	★★★
Growth markets	★★★★★
Quality of management	★★★★
International orientation	★★

Biggest plus:
Already a dominant player in its markets, but with plenty of good ideas and lots of headroom for growth.

Biggest minus:
Tends to be rather 'invisible', so needs to work hard at building its own brand.

The Capita Group plc
71 Victoria Street
London SW1H 0XA
Tel: 020 7799 1525
Fax: 020 7799 1526
website: www.capita.co.uk

The Capita Group plc

The Business

The Capita Group is one of the UK's leading white-collar outsourcing companies, providing professional support services to a wide range of public and private sector organizations. It specializes in long-term contracts in areas requiring substantial business change and improvements in service quality.

Capita is one of the fastest-growing companies in Britain. From a standing start in 1984, it was floated on the USM in 1989, received a full stock market listing in 1991, joined the All Share 250 in 1997, and made the FTSE 100 index in March 2000.

The company provides a very wide range of services: customer and administration services, human resources, IT, software services, commercial and strategic consultancy and support services, and property consultancy. Its clients include several government departments, many blue-chip companies including Abbey National, the BBC, British Airways and Railtrack, 23,000 schools, and virtually every local authority in the country.

Innovation

Innovation is key to what Capita offers its clients, and it simply would not be in business if it was not able to prove that it could do a job better, more efficiently than an in-house department. 'Our function is to lead and innovate, not follow and replicate,' says Rod Aldridge, Capita's founder and executive chairman.

The company sees itself as one of the leaders in the outsourcing market. 'We shaped the business process outsourcing industry, especially in the public sector but also increasingly in the private sector,' says Aldridge. 'All through our life and development we've had to be ahead of what the market requires.' For example, Capita was the first provider of multi-service-oriented contracts, including functions such as IT, benefits, payroll, pensions and human resources (HR); and it was the first company to provide complete HR outsourcing to a local authority.

It also sees itself as a key shaper of the companies it works for. 'Our style is to be interactive and help people take their organizations in new directions,' says Aldridge. 'A lot of our clients have to modernize, and we are the catalyst for them to change.' The company has specialized in setting up greenfield sites for central government, including the new Criminal Records Bureau and the Individual Learning Accounts scheme. Private sector achievements include new service delivery models for Abbey National, which will enable the bank to greatly extend the range of its general insurance business.

Success, believes Aldridge, comes from knowing each business from the inside. 'It comes from having a deep understanding of the business,' he says. 'A lot of our people have worked in these environments. We're also very strong on technology and how it can be used to innovate. And improving customer service is a major contractual and cultural aim for us.'

Flexibility

An outsourcing company has to be a bit of a chameleon. It must often take on the outward form of its many clients – after all, nobody who phones Abbey National or the BBC wants to know that their call is actually being handled by Capita. And it must cope with regular influxes of hundreds of new staff who join when their in-house oper-ation is taken over – 2,500 people in the first three months of 2001 alone.

Shona Nichols, Capita's group marketing director, describes the company as 'amoebic'. 'It's continually going through change, because we change with each new service we deliver and each contract we take on,' she says.

A critical factor is Capita's flexible infrastructure, which enables it to respond very quickly. Instead of a single, monolithic company, it has ten regional business centres which can put people on the ground quickly to handle bids and set up new operations. 'We think of our-selves as a small business that's doing very well, not as a large organiz-ation,' says Nichols. 'We don't have a great strategic plan. It wouldn't be appropriate in the business we're in.'

The company's phenomenal growth has been mostly organic, but about a third is due to acquisitions, including Eastgate (making the group the largest provider of outsourced insurance services), share registration specialist IRG, and School Information Management Systems (SIMS), which formed the basis of Capita's highly successful education business. Rod Aldridge is particularly proud of the last, which has seen education grow to a sixth of the group's turnover in just four years. The group is now number one in providing support services to local education authorities (LEAs) and schools, and provides management information systems to 23,000 schools and 120 LEAs. Its latest initiative is an education 'portal' on the Internet to support education managers, and to provide a gateway for parents to find out about their children's performance, homework requirements and attendance records.

Human Resources

Human resources can be a delicate issue for outsourcing companies, which generally acquire most of their staff in situ with new contracts. 'We've got to welcome them and make them feel special, because 60 per cent of them haven't chosen to join Capita,' says Aldridge. 'We have to remotivate them and empower them to flourish in their jobs.'

In practice, this is not difficult, because in-house support departments are often grudgingly under-funded adjuncts to the main organization, whereas at Capita they form part of the company's main business. 'People here feel they're part of something that's growing and successful, and where they're well rewarded,' says Aldridge.

Capita also recruits directly – graduates and school-leavers, as well as experienced people such as project managers – and being a provider of HR services, it knows how to do it properly. But the company also likes to fill vacancies from within, and a lot of people move from the organizations they were 'acquired' to join other projects and businesses within the group.

Growth Markets

Despite having already become a big company – more than 14,000 people and a turnover of £453m – Capita continues to double in size every two-and-a-half years, and sees no risk of this tailing off. Moreover, its business model generates regular cash revenues, which can easily be used to finance expansion. 'We've certainly got plenty of headroom to grow the business as we have been, but we want to do it safely and keep delivering to our customers and shareholders,' says Aldridge. 'We already have the management structure to cope with being several times bigger.'

The UK white-collar outsourcing market is potentially worth £25–30bn per year, says Aldridge. Only 18 per cent of local authorities have, so far, outsourced white-collar staff; central government outsourcing is mostly restricted to IT at present; the education market is wide open; and business process outsourcing in the private sector is still very new. The only real competition comes from existing in-house departments, since other outsourcing companies tend to be much more narrowly specialist than Capita.

All this means that Capita can virtually choose the contracts it wants to bid for. 'We don't say we want X per cent of our business to come from a particular sector,' says Aldridge. 'We bid for the contracts where we see the best opportunities and can use our skills best.'

Capita's major challenge now is to increase recognition of its own brand – a perennial problem for outsourcing companies, which always operate in the name of their clients. This will be especially important as the company seeks to expand its portfolio in the private sector.

Quality of Management

Anyone who thinks outsourcing companies are full of dead-beat ex-civil servants would soon change their tune if they knew Capita. 'Some of our best people are from the public sector,' says Aldridge. 'Pulling together the best of both public and private sectors has been the foundation of what we've achieved.'

The group operates a flat management structure and an open-door style, and works hard at being non-bureaucratic and at treating staff as individuals. 'You're never put in a silo,' says Nichols. There are a lot of 'virtual' teams to facilitate innovation, and a 'Think Thank' programme to reward people who come up with good new ideas.

Management is very hands-on, with many of the group's senior people still actively involved in running client projects, and all managers are expected to be financially literate. The group is keen to develop its senior managers, and last year devised a special programme with Cranfield School of Management to enhance their all-round skills. In 2001 the next level of managers will attend a similar course.

Through courses and staff mobility, Capita has built up a strong networking culture. 'If you don't know about something, you always know someone who does, and they'll always give you time,' says Nichols. The company also prides itself on having a social conscience. It actively supports charities like the Prince's Trust and the NSPCC, and encourages staff to get involved with charities at a local level.

Asked to encapsulate Capita's position, Aldridge says: 'The business is underpinned by long-term contracts, and is highly financially driven, by earnings-per-share growth rather than top-line growth. We are leading and shaping our markets, and have a very good track record in managing growth and development, along with a very open management style. And our shareholders obviously trust us – nobody came to our AGM last year!'

International Orientation

All Capita's operations are in the UK, and the group does not feel that it needs to expand internationally in the near future. 'Our model is capable of being replicated elsewhere, but international operations are not for us,' says Aldridge. 'We would have to acquire other businesses, and that would put unnecessary pressures on our management. Currently there are no constraints on our growth within the UK.'

CPP Card Protection Plan

CPP handles more insurance for credit and payment card customers than any other company. An international concern based in the UK, it has been running for 18 years and pioneered the concept of its product in this country. It employs some 1100 people in London, Spain, Lisbon, Milan and most recently in Frankfurt. It is part of a joint venture in Brazil. It remains in private hands but when market conditions are right it will float.

Scorecard:

Innovation	★★★★★
Flexibility	★★★★
Human resources	★★★
Growth markets	★★★★
Quality of management	★★★★
International orientation	★★★★★

Biggest plus:
The sheer number of contacts, the customer base and the channel partners.

Biggest minus:
The tendency to allow all those things listed under 'biggest plus' to foster a sense of complacency about the business.

Card Protection Plan Limited
Holgate Park
Poppleton Road
YORK YO26 4GA
Tel: 01904 544 500
Fax: 01904 544 686
website: www.cpp.co.uk

Card Protection Plan Limited

The Business

Card Protection Plan's (CPP) proposition to the card issuers in 1982 was very simple: people who lost their credit and payment cards often had no service to fall back on for an easy replacement, and customers would welcome an insurance – possibly as a branded service with the same name as the credit/payment card, possibly from an independent source – that would take the worry away when such a loss happened, whether through accident or theft.

Since this time it has moved into most of the card issuers' offerings as one of the standard parts of the package, and signing up to one of its policies is as simple as ticking a box on a credit or payment card application form. The company remains in private hands and the founding CEO stepped into a non-executive position in only 1999 to allow for a more growth-oriented style of manager.

Innovation

At least in the UK, the concept of credit and payment card protection was brand new and in itself an innovation when the company introduced it. The product, however, became commoditized over time. What one insurer can do another can mimic, so CPP has set about building extra value into its services to the end customers over the years. It was CPP, for example, that expanded the service to include all documents. In this way if a traveller is overseas, for example, and loses their passport, driving licence and airline tickets as well as their credit and payment cards, CPP will provide assistance to replace them all and endeavour to trace any lost luggage, replace keys and so forth.

It's worth mentioning as well that as part of this service the company trains its helpline staff extensively to be as calm and businesslike as possible, and to respond quickly when the phone rings – the customer's material wellbeing is not CPP's only concern at these times of stress, it wants the customers to feel reassured.

Other elements the company has brought in include the charge-free telephone line for lost or stolen credit and payment cards, which is available seven days a week and 24 hours a day; it has also introduced mobile phone insurance as mobiles are now as frequently lost and stolen as cards. This not only handles the replacement phone but CPP will arrange for call barring on the old SIM card. It also introduced the annual rather than one-off travel insurance product. It was in the process of buying a company in the debt management business as this book went to press.

Flexibility

One area the current group chief executive, Alan Blank, has been keen to build is the flexibility of its staff and the company overall. He is acutely aware that immediately an insurance product is commoditized it can be duplicated by other companies, and as a result has encouraged as many innovations as possible to distinguish the company from its competitors. The difficulty was that once relationships had been set up with all of the key card issuers, the temptation to start taking these for granted and not move them on was considerable. Also the fact that so much of the business was self-generating was a serious problem in that it allowed the staff to avoid proactivity.

Blank therefore set about replacing some of the management with people more receptive to change, and he is the first to admit that the process was not without an element of pain. He restructured the entire management team, leaving only one of the original managers in place – the company had become too set in the CPP way of doing things, he says, and companies that try to fit their customers' changing requirements into an existing product-set rather than looking for ways of innovating have a dubious future. The company now focuses on constantly re-evaluating its products and examining its pricing period-ically, and on rolling out new products and innovations as described above.

The other transition Blank sought to make was away from a com-pany led by a founder and towards a more professional, detached approach. This is not to criticize someone who brought the company forward from nothing to turning over £40 million, but an acceptance that increased growth both financially and in manpower requires more delegation than the original entrepreneur could handle by himself.

The new management introduced a number of innovations, not least of which was the Internet side of the business. Internet was an area very few card issuers wanted even to acknowledge in the late 1990s; CPP ensured that when the inevitable change in attitude hap-pened, it was ready with a tailored offering.

Seasonal changes affect the demand for this sort of service – it doesn't take a great detective to work out that holiday times and Christmas are likely to see peaks of demand. CPP therefore has a policy of outsourcing helpdesk seats and other functions where necessary.

Human Resources

The call centre employees are crucial to the business since they are the people who customers contact in a crisis. Training them to deal with stressed people is therefore a priority, and keeping them motivated is vital. Attention is therefore paid to the environment in which they work, particularly where the contact centre is concerned. Something that isn't apparent to the end customer is that CPP also does virtually all of the selling and customer service to the consumer, sometimes as a branded or co-branded call. So when someone gets a call from their card issuer about card protection the chances are it's a CPP employee on the phone – speaking with the full backing of the issuer and taking the company into a business area that it would otherwise be unable to address.

Staff retention is improving, partly because of Blank and his team's commitment to the self-worth of every individual. The remuneration package is competitive for the work on offer, and creative ideas are welcomed from staff at all levels. Possibly more importantly there is a flexible benefit package that allows staff to tailor benefits to their own needs.

Growth Markets

There are still plenty of people in the UK who have yet to avail them-selves of credit /payment cards. However, the growth for CPP appears to be away from the card market as such for the moment. The emergence of the packaged cover market as mentioned already will represent significant growth for some time to come, as will the mobile phone insurance area.

Another area that is likely to emerge as a consequence, although nobody is talking about it yet so this has to be taken as speculation, is the whole mobile office market. If the mobile phone can be insured then so should the PDA – Personal Digital Assistant/organizer – that many executives carry with it; indeed, some of these are combined units. It isn't unreasonable to suggest that the mobile phone insurance idea is likely to open up demand for cover for many other portable items.

Quality of Management

One of the first things Blank did during his restructure was to bring in some heavyweight management to back up his growth plans. People from Booker PLC, Compaq and Andersen Consulting took their places on the board, for example.

The management approach is very much the collegial style. Rapport between both the managers and the staff is regarded as an essential element of the business, and as a result the managers always try to make themselves accessible. Personal evaluations take place period-ically and are detailed exercises so that personal objectives are always aligned with those of the business. Every effort is made to establish that these evaluations are not confrontational but perceived as ways of overcoming difficulties, both actual and potential.

Blank notes that in business the least experienced managers tend to finish up managing the most people, so he and the board prioritize smooth communications with middle management the whole time. In reality any problems that come up tend to be with middle managers not buying into change. The board therefore tries to communicate the changes it wants as exciting opportunities, and above all, to ensure that their enthusiasm translates into execution. The way this is achieved is to target the information going out very carefully – in an organization the size of CPP, action can be delayed substantially by being relayed to *almost* the right person.

International Orientation

The company operates in the UK, Spain, Portugal, Italy and through a joint venture in Brazil. The international operations tend to be grown almost as new businesses– certainly the Spanish manager grew the office from nothing and hopes to grow it as the market matures.

To a large extent the company's international ambitions are dictated by the state of the credit and payment card markets in the various territories in which it operates. The German presence is not the largest – not because of the size of the population but because the Germans resist borrowing in this way. The company is constantly evaluating other territories but publicly at least, remains content with the huge growth opportunities in the UK and elsewhere.

Career Legal is a recruitment consultancy group that has broadened its early specialization in placing legal secretaries to encompass temporary and permanent positions at most levels in the legal sector. A subsidiary, Hudson York Farrell, was set up in 1995 to handle placements in banking. The group, which retains its original founders and has grown to 52 staff, reported turnover to March 2000 of around £12.6m – up from £8.3m in 1999, and a dramatic gain on the £1.6m sales in 1996. Since that represents less than 1 per cent of the total market, the management sees considerable potential for organic growth.

Scorecard:

Innovation	★★★★
Flexibility	★★★★
Human resources	★★★★★
Growth markets	★★★★★
Quality of management	★★★★
International orientation	★★★

Biggest plus:
Career Legal carries an impressive reputation among clients, and the company has a highly professional but stimulating approach to its business and its employees.

Biggest minus:
It is approaching a transition stage in terms of business size, where changes in working style may be needed to sustain growth.

Career Legal Limited
Broad Street House
55 Old Broad Street
London EC2M 1RX
Tel: 020 7628 7117
website: www.careerlegal.co.uk

Career Legal

The Business

Career Legal was established in 1991 with three working directors (all still involved in the company) to supply legal secretaries. The business survived the recession and the Bishopsgate bombing to become the fastest-growing non-IT recruitment consultancy in the UK.

Today Career Legal places secretaries, financial staff and now lawyers. Another arm, Hudson York Farrell specializes in banking secretaries, desktop publishing, graphics, facilities and administrative services. HYF now contributes about half of the group's turnover.

In a competitive business Career Legal has always emphasized the value of long-term relationships, seeking to ensure a continuing status as preferred supplier to what is an inherently risk-averse clientele. Career Legal takes considerable pride in never having lost a client; its 500-plus customer base currently includes 69 of the top 75 law firms in the UK.

The year to March 2000 saw net profits of just over £1m on sales of £12.6m, and for the current financial year the company is forecasting £16.6m turnover and £2.1m earnings.

Innovation

The recruitment business, and especially that part of it which specializes in temporary staff, has a reputation for high staff turnover, pushy sales consultants, and a business model that emphasizes the short-term. Career Legal's innovative contribution was to emphasize longer-term relationships and to build a business based on preferred-supplier status. The group expected that expansion would come from maximizing service to the client base, with new specialisms and new recruitment divisions being established to provide additional routes into those clients.

That is exactly how Career Legal has developed. Staff tend to stay with the company and so build rapport with clients: and the clients stay with Career Legal too. The initial emphasis on placing legal secretaries from inception (early 1991) was supplemented by 1995 by temporary as well as permanent staff, and finance and accountancy vacancies as well as secretarial. Subsequently, in 1997, the group added Career Legal Professional, a fee-earners arm (for placing lawyers): and Hudson York Farrell, the corporate services division (for office services and facilities management). All of these could address the same core client base.

Also in 1995 a separately branded operation was established under the name Hudson York Farrell to attack the banking market.

A recruitment agency obviously needs a large and detailed database in order to be able to offer the right candidate for a post. Career Legal, which currently has over 20,000 candidates on file, has invested substantially in IT – notably via a 50-screen Profile 2000 system from Microdec, one of the leading specialist suppliers of systems for recruitment services. In practice this system can automate most back-office operations and contributes to core business procedures from prospect identification to administering and delivering the entire recruitment process.

Career Legal operates websites at www.careerlegal.co.uk and www.hyf.co.uk for corporate information and vacancies. The jobs on offer are updated daily and candidates can request a regular e-mail update – a reasonable but fairly basic approach to the job seeker. The present sites look good and work well enough, but a redesign with more interactivity is planned.

Flexibility

Career Legal has demonstrated the capability to respond quickly and successfully to adversity – the IRA's Bishopsgate bomb in the early 1990s destroyed the fledgling company's offices and, more importantly, its vital database of candidates.

Career Legal has also proved willing to react to customer demand and market opportunity without compromising its core business. New activities and new divisions have been added in a logical and organic pattern – from permanent legal secretarial vacancies to temps, from legal secretaries to other law firm positions (eventually including fee-earners), from top-flight law firms to City financial institutions.

Human Resources

As a matter of policy, Career Legal works hard at keeping its own staff (and especially its consultants) to ensure continuity for the clients. The business culture emphasizes personal responsibility, and Career Legal avoids setting sales targets for consultants – 'target-setting in our business is for management that cannot maintain local control'. It cultivates a relaxed and informal atmosphere in the office, believing that extreme pressure impairs performance. And there is considerable on- and off-site training, especially for the system administrators who maintain the crucial candidate database records.

In a business sector where job-hopping is common, the policy has ensured low staff turnover; Career Legal's experience is that its people stay with the group for four years or more.

Growth Markets

The markets in which Career Legal operates have been independently estimated as being worth £2bn this year, and the management sees its target clientele as comprising 400 law firms and 400 financial institutions. Given a turnover of £16.6m and a client base of some 500 companies, there is obviously a good deal of mileage in continuing to grow organically.

Although Career Legal competes for new business, there is an emphasis on retaining and developing existing clients. This practice has produced growth by reacting to customer demand, using its reputation and relationships to provide more and different types of job placements in the same core group of clients – particularly among fee-earners and financial management.

The business has developed organically, with new divisions providing multiple options for servicing the core clients. The essence of the business – indeed, of any employment service – lies in understanding the client's needs and work culture so well that no inappropriate candidate will be put forward. The newer business venture, providing staff for banks, represents a logical development. There are similar requirements for probity and competence in job candidates, and reputation and relationships in client dealings.

Quality of Management

Career Legal has a clean, simple and fairly flat management structure that provides clear lines of reporting and responsibility but also allows a good deal of flexibility.

The company prides itself on an 'open door' policy (fostered by working in largely open-plan offices) which ensures ease of access between staff and management.

There are seven separate workgroups individually managed by hands-on recruiters, the managers reporting straight to the three founder Directors – all of whom came from the recruitment business and are still actively involved. Michael Swaby is the MD, Joe Neilson manages PR and advertising, Denis Simpson looks after the permanent legal secretary division and takes primary responsibility for the line managers.

The other two directors are non-executive. They were appointed for their overall experience in recruitment management but also add specific skills in IT and training to the board.

This commitment and experience is reflected in the corporate culture – the emphasis on client relationships and Career Legal's position on preferred-supplier lists, the precedence of on-the-job responsibility over crude sales targets, the pride in low staff – and client –turnover.

Each recruitment sector within Career Legal is handled by a small team of consultants working under a manager. Managers tend to be grow into the job, and Career Legal has not as yet had to appoint from outside. This clearly provides a focused approach to sales and reporting, and the recently upgraded IT system automates and documents a lot of the practicalities of management.

International Orientation

Career Legal has no offices outside the UK and there are no plans to diversify overseas. The company has a tightly targeted business, aimed primarily at the top UK legal firms, and secondarily at the London offices of the major banks – that has necessitated no international expansion. Career Legal can, and has, placed staff beyond the M25, however, and emphasizes that it reacts to customer demand: if one of its established clients required personnel for an office outside the UK, Career Legal would try to put up candidates.

Chrysalis

Chrysalis Group is one of the UK's leading independent media companies, with interests in radio, music, TV production, publishing and the Internet. The group has completely reinvented itself over the last decade, building up several successful businesses through a mixture of vision and opportunism. It employs about 1,000 people, and in 1999–2000 group turnover was £162 million.

Scorecard:

Innovation	★★★★★
Flexibility	★★★★
Human resources	★★★
Growth markets	★★★★
Quality of management	★★★★
International orientation	★★★

Biggest plus:
A leading independent in the media business, combining the creativity of a smaller company and the professionalism of a plc.

Biggest minus:
The diverse portfolio could make it difficult to focus on key growth areas.

Chrysalis Group plc
The Chrysalis Building
13 Bramley Road
London W10 6SP
Tel: 020 7221 2213
Fax: 020 7221 6455
website: www.chrysalis.com

Chrysalis Group plc

The Business

Media group Chrysalis is hardly a household name, yet its products are familiar to millions – from its Galaxy and Heart local radio stations to TV programmes like *The Midsomer Murders* and Formula One racing. Founded in 1969 by media entrepreneurs Chris Wright and Terry Ellis, and floated in 1985, Chrysalis is now a £162 million turnover plc, making it a strong mid-market media business. Wright still owns around 28 per cent of the shares; the other major shareholder is Schroders, with 15 per cent.

The group's five – rather diverse – divisions are: Radio, including up-and-coming regional stations Heart and Galaxy with nearly five million listeners; Music, including the Echo and Papillon record labels and a strong music publishing business; Visual Entertainment, which mostly makes drama, sport and entertainment programmes for the BBC and commercial broadcasters; Media Products, originally an export business but now expanded to include non-fiction illustrated book publishing; and a fledgling New Media (mostly Internet) division.

Innovation

Being a medium-sized player in an increasingly corporate market gives Chrysalis unique strengths, says group chief executive, Richard Huntingford: 'As one of the leading independents in radio, music and TV, we combine a high reputation for managing creativity, with the financial security and muscle of a larger group. As global consolidation increases, we can work closely with the creative talents we sign, while taking a longer-term commercial view of how best to use them.'

The group's flagship Radio division had secured 7.8 per cent of the UK commercial radio market by 2000 from a standing start. 'Building two significant brands from scratch shows that we can enter a virtually monopolistic market and, through a mixture of research-led product and innovative marketing, create leading brand positions,' says Phil Riley, chief executive of Chrysalis Radio. Heart and Galaxy targeted gaps in the market – Galaxy is aimed at twenty-somethings, Heart at people in their 30s – and between them have nearly 5 million listeners a week. Chrysalis is now developing a third radio brand, Arrow, to play adult rock.

Chrysalis Radio's studios and infrastructure have been digital since its inception in the mid-90s, which will be a big advantage when the company begins digital broadcasting in summer 2001. Chrysalis has won several regional digital licences, which it sees as key platforms for the future. Its digital partners include Ford – to encourage the provision of digital radios in cars – and mobile computer company Psion, which is installing digital radios in schools for downloading educational data. The New Media division aims to build on Chrysalis's 'old media' strengths, so it focuses on music, radio and sport. Its brands include Rivals.net, a website aggregating sport content from independent supporters' sites, and Puremix, which does the same for music. Both are clever concepts, because being based on 'unofficial' websites they do not need deals with clubs or artists. Rivals.net received 27 million page impressions in its first seven months.

The group is also innovative financially. In March 2001, Chrysalis Music raised £60 million through a securitization of its music publishing catalogue – by creating a borrowing facility against the value of its catalogue. This was an innovative way of getting some of the company's intangible assets onto the balance sheet, and providing investment resources without drawing on the funds of the main group.

Flexibility

As might be expected from a company whose very name implies a state of transition, Chrysalis is no stranger to change. The group reinvented itself in 1992, selling its music recording business to Thorn EMI, and diversifying into radio, TV production and publishing. Now it is changing again, having recently added a New Media division – a logical progression for a forward-looking media company.

Chrysalis prides itself on both its artistic and commercial flexibility. 'The Chrysalis brand has a very high reputation for its ability to maintain creativity and provide the right environment for creative people to flourish,' says Huntingford. 'Our culture allows people to be innovative and have a chance to shine.'

The diversification process was somewhat 'finger-in-the-air', as the company divided its eggs between several baskets. In the event, all the new divisions have been relatively successful, leaving the group with a rather eclectic portfolio which some analysts believe it should rationalize. The obvious area to sell off would be Media Products – which has been greatly strengthened by opportunistically snapping up several unprofitable small publishers and turning them round – and Visual Entertainment (TV production).

The TV production business was a strong idea. 'The strategy was that, with a multiplicity of new channels appearing in the early 1990s, there would be increasing demand for new programmes,' says Huntingford. But despite being Chrysalis's largest division (at £57 million), it is now under-performing – making only a 3 per cent margin compared with an industry average of 5 per cent. So in late 2000 the division was restructured, with a more focused approach – concentrating on the three core areas of entertainment, drama and sport – with a harder-nosed, more centralized approach to budgeting and negotiation.

Human Resources

Chrysalis Group employs about 1,000 permanent staff, plus up to several hundred freelances. The average age is late 20s/early 30s, and although most recruits are graduates, a degree is not essential – Huntingford himself is not a graduate, and firmly believes ability and experience are more important than paper qualifications.

The group has recently beefed up its personnel management, with a more formal emphasis on training, personal development and career appraisals. 'We like to feel that we can offer a lot of career opportunities to our staff,' says Huntingford.

The aim is to pay competitive salaries, mostly with a performance-related element, and in 2001 the company introduced a share-save scheme for all staff – an unusual innovation for a medium-sized media company, but one which the board felt was important for rewarding staff and building loyalty.

Growth Markets

Radio, which is rapidly becoming Chrysalis's core business, is a burgeoning industry. 'Radio is on a long-term upward trend, and will continue to increase its share of the advertising market,' says Riley. 'We have a very strong position in a consolidating sector, with considerable potential for profit growth.'

But Chrysalis Radio faces a critical period in 2001–2. The impending relaxation of government regulations will allow its larger competitors to increase their market share (which is effectively capped under current rules). Analysts believe this leaves medium-sized players like Chrysalis with a 'window of opportunity' before the gloves come off.

Chrysalis Radio's flagship stations, Galaxy and Heart, are still young, and growing as more listeners start tuning in (Galaxy's audience grew by more than 11 per cent in 2000); and winning several new regional digital licences will ultimately help the company reach a wider audience. But ideally it needs to acquire other stations, and quickly – yet without paying over the odds in an overheated market – a risk that the management is well aware of.

The Music division has strong potential, particularly since it owns the rights to much of the material it publishes and distributes. 'More and more media are opening up, and they all need music,' says Huntingford, who believes the value of the music business could double within five years.

The book publishing business also has great ambitions. Already highly profitable (generating over £2 million in profit on a turnover of £13 million in 1999–2000), it now aims to reach a turnover of £50 million delivering 12 per cent operating margins. The recent acquisition of illustrated book publisher Collins & Brown should bring it up to around £40 million.

Quality of Management

As a good-sized business which stops short of being a corporate behemoth, Chrysalis works hard to achieve the best of both worlds. 'We seek to capitalize on being an independent, but also a public company with a duty of accountability,' says Huntingford.

The company is financially cautious. It refuses to capitalize investments, preferring to write them off (the main reason why the group was in the red after its mid-1990s restructuring, until returning to profit in 1999–2000). And it is keen to keep its five divisions separate, with little cross-funding or joint development work – probably a healthy attitude, given the group's diversity.

Huntingford's management philosophy is one of empowerment tempered by accountability, so that divisional chief executives are left to run their own ships, within an overall group strategic direction. Staff at all levels are encouraged to participate. 'We recognize that good ideas are not the prerogative of management, and we want to ensure that people aren't afraid to put forward suggestions,' says Huntingford.

'I like to think we're a very good people organization, because a lot of what we do is about people,' he continues. 'We're good at providing the right framework to create very good teams. My door is always open, and on Friday afternoons I just wander round the building and talk to people.'

International Orientation

During the last few years, Chrysalis Music has set up subsidiaries in eight countries outside the UK, including the US, France, Germany, Spain and Scandinavia. In 2002 these will take over the sub-publishing of Chrysalis's copyrights (currently contracted out to EMI).

This is an important strategy, says Huntingford: 'It allows us to punch above our weight, because we're able to identify new talent in each territory and add them to our overall portfolio. It will also allow us to ensure that our catalogue is fully exploited in other territories.'

The group is always looking for other opportunities to expand abroad. It has a large TV production joint venture in the Netherlands with Dutch publisher VNU, and a share of a TV joint venture in Spain, as well as a small TV production operation in New Zealand. Radio operations are entirely UK-based at present.

CISCO SYSTEMS ®

Cisco's international headquarters is in San Jose, where the company was founded in 1984 by a small group of Stanford University computer scientists 'seeking an easier way to connect different types of computer systems'. The first product was shipped in 1986 and, in the year 2000, Cisco reported revenues of $18.3 billion. The company says it serves as the best example of a business that has changed itself by using the Internet. It also says it is a phenomenon. It could be right.

Scorecard:

Innovation	★★★★★
Flexibility	★★★★★
Growth markets	★★★★★
Human resources	★★★★★
Quality of management	★★★★★
International orientation	★★★★★

Biggest plus:
'Definitely the people – bright, challenging, achievement orientated – and great fun.'

Biggest minus:
'The rate of change – there are times when you wish it'd just slow down for a bit; and the way we keep outgrowing our space can be frustrating.'

Cisco Systems
3 The Square
Stockley Park
Uxbridge UB11 1BN
Tel: 020 8756 8000
Fax: 020 8756 8010
website: www.cisco.com

Cisco Systems

The Business

Cisco describes what it does as 'enabling the Internet business generation' and it has been one of the fastest growing and most profitable
companies in the history of the computer industry. From its 1984
establishment by a small group of computer scientists, Cisco has grown
to a multinational operation with over 43,000 employees and more
than two hundred offices spread across 55 countries.

The company floated on the Nasdaq in 1990 and its year 2000
revenues of $18.3 billion was a 55 per cent increase on the preceding
twelve months although recent diluted earnings per share growth –
sixteen cents per share in 1995 to 62 cents in 1999 – is respectable
rather than astronomical.

Innovation

Cisco is a company where innovation is regarded as the norm and it
comes across as an organization with a clear belief in practising what
it preaches. Research and development expenses in 2000 were $2.7
billion – 62 per cent up on the $1.66 billion spent in 1999. Expressed
as a proportion of the company's net sales, 1999 research and development spend was 13.7 per cent and this was up to 14.3 per cent in the
year 2000.

The Cisco Internet Business Solutions Group, whose mission is
described as 'to provide business strategy consulting and help move
our relationships with customers from that of a vendor to that of a
strategic partner', has been consulted by executives in more than half
the US Fortune 500 companies – 45 per cent of the top companies in
Europe, the middle East, Africa and Asia; and 65 per cent of the world's
leading service providers.

'Cisco Systems', says the company, 'has been responsible for creating
and enhancing the frontiers of IP Internetworking technology over the
past decade. The traditional limitation of merely providing connections
and lower level transport services is giving way as service providers
are called on to play a larger role in supporting network infrastructures
for companies and individuals alike. This means hosting Internet applications, providing integrated data and voice systems, and offering new
Internet access options ranging from dial to broadband throughout the
public network infrastructure.'

Flexibility

Company statement:

> Cisco often serves as the best example of a business that has changed itself using the Internet. We have always believed technology could help us do things that our competition could not. Customer service was the first application to go online. This was quickly followed by applications in manufacturing, commerce, finance, recruiting, marketing, training and sales. It has given us a competitive advantage in our industry. It has allowed us to remain agile and responsive, and it is based on employee and customer empowerment through the Internet. We provide this same expertise to our customers, helping them create Internet solutions for their own organizations.

Employees are encouraged to contribute to their own advancement. According to Janet Huckvale, human resources leader, 'E-learning accounts for 80 per cent of Cisco instruction and employees can expect to spend at least 20 days a year in training – in a business that moves as fast as ours you could be unemployable in two years if you don't invest in your own development.' The Cisco Learning Network is a system designed to train employees around the world, while also providing accountability by tracking results. The company's Networking Academy Program (CNAP) is an alliance between Cisco and education, business, government, and community organizations around the world. By the year 2000 CNAP had enrolled 81,000 students from 83 countries providing, as Cisco puts it, 'networking skills to a broad range of students, including those in high school community colleges, homeless shelters, and juvenile centres and outgoing military personnel'.

Cisco is a company which expects work to be enjoyable but nevertheless takes what it perceives to be its responsibilities as seriously as it takes its business. As Huckvale summarizes: 'You must be up for the challenge and it's no place for a quiet life'.

Human Resources

Janet Huckvale is quick to point out that many conventional functions 'simply don't exist at Cisco – we're an Internet company and there just aren't jobs that involve processing and holding on to pieces of paper – expense claims, for example, go straight into the system and they usually get cleared the same day.' Human resources considers its major occupation to be pro-active in helping to manage 'the company's most precious asset – its people'.

Much of the company's recruitment – all jobs are advertised both internally and externally – is done via the Internet although 'all ways of recruiting are considered' and Cisco has its own internal head hunters. Graduates are naturally welcome but there is no bar for non-graduates – 'what interests us most', says Huckvale, 'is the attitude'. Those who have left the Cisco fold, however, are not encouraged to rejoin.

Growth Markets

Cisco lists its 3-year goals bluntly:

- Customer partner status – success, satisfaction and trust
- The Internet experts – the global Internet company
- The leader in New World data, voice, video solutions
- The IP technology leader recognized for leadership, integrity, trust and teamwork
- Leadership in financial performance – new business models, eco-systems, and empowerment.
- Number one or two position in systems, software, markets, functions
- $50 billion plus in revenue – profitability leadership.

President and chief executive officer, John Chambers, goes on to say:

In our opinion, the radical business transformations taking place around the world will accelerate, making the opportunities ahead of Cisco far greater than ever before. We believe that Cisco has the potential to be the most influential and generous company in history. We are in the fortunate position to be at the centre of the Internet economy and we recognize that, although this position gives us confidence, we must balance this confidence with healthy paranoia.

We are proud of our accomplishments and want to thank our shareholders, customers, employees, partners and suppliers for their continued commitment and confidence in our ability to execute. Together, we are only beginning to explore all that's possible on the Internet.

Quality of Management

Every Cisco employee has a credit card replica upon which the Cisco culture is summarized, it reads:
'Quality team; no technology religion; stretch goals;
Teamwork; empowerment; trust/fair/integrity;
Drive change; frugality; market transitions; open communication'
and it ends with: 'customer success'.

The environment is openly entrepreneurial and those likely to succeed will be those prepared to attempt things which are 'unprecedented – there's no objection to anything just because it's never been done before'. Goals are described as 'challenging – it can look frightening at the beginning of the year' but with the qualification that teamwork is critical and is the basis for 'extraordinary results being achieved by ordinary people'.

Wanting to come to work because it's fun is important, but so are ethical business standards, and so is giving back to the community – 'there is a passion about Cisco', says human resources leader, Janet Huckvale, 'we intend to get there but part of the passion is that it does matter how we get there'. Dedicated nine-to-fivers are unlikely to flourish but both UK and international staff turnover approximate to a low annual 3 per cent. It isn't anarchy but 'it's certainly not "silo" culture – there are no taboos, no real hierarchy and, if you want to phone the CEO in the States and question something then no-one will try to stop you'.

Cisco is, in short, something of a rarity. Yes, people come across as enthusiastic and pushy but certainly not in the messianic nor crass manner most commonly associated with such words. Most of all, people come across as being happy – you can, as they say, feel the buzz.

International Orientation

That Cisco, in geographical terms, is an international organization is beyond dispute. But the organization goes further and, in its own words:

The Internet is driving a global Internet economy that is creating unprecedented opportunities for people, companies and countries around the world.

The communications landscape is changing dramatically. Advances in technology have made online experiences much more consistent, accessible, richer in content and, above all, easier to use than ever before. As a result, a tremendous technological transformation is under way. By any measure, it's a New World in networking for service providers and their customers.

Cisco is leading the migration to the New World in ways that vendors, whose roots are in the old world of circuit-oriented networks could not easily provide, Unlike traditional telecommunications suppliers, Cisco is poised to help service providers not only to build intelligent networks, but also to create new business opportunities through value-added services.

It is estimated that one in five potential Internet users lives in China and Cisco consultants are currently working with China Telecom.

CityReach International

CityReach International was founded in 1999 with the aim of constructing a network of quality standard-setting data centres across Europe with the very high levels of resiliency and redundancy required to enable corporates to outsource their core business applications to the Internet. Building on their network of facilities, CityReach's strategy is to become the preferred foundation for business Internet applications in Europe, copying the best features of corporate data centre environments into their managed facilities, but making them more scalable, flexible and cost-effective than ever before.

Scorecard:

Innovation	★★★★★
Flexibility	★★★★
Human resources	★★★★
Growth markets	★★★★★
Quality of management	★★★★
International Orientation	★★★★★

Biggest plus:
The energy and enthusiasm of the personnel, and being the first into the market.

Biggest minus:
At this early stage the company still has a 'best effort' culture, while the managers want a total commitment to results.

CityReach International, Ltd.
5 Greenwich View Place
Millharbour
London E14 9NN
Tel: 020 7515 1720
website: www.city-reach.com

CityReach International Limited

The Business

CityReach International was founded in September 1999, backed by significant venture capital and with an aim of serving the co-location market. It built data centres in key European cities in approximately half the time and for half the cost of the competition, but rapidly decided this was not sufficiently unique. Several rounds of funding later the owners came to realize that the real money in Web services was going to be in offering the technology that enables the replication of the best features of corporate data centre environments in outsourced facilities as companies migrate their mission-critical business applications to the Internet. Consequently, CityReach has developed a series of value added services such as server management, data storage, mainframes and private networks which are designed to be more scaleable, flexible and cost effective than corporate operations. It now employs 350 people throughout Europe focusing on this business.

Innovation

CityReach's main claim to being an innovator stems from the simple fact that it is the only company providing the exact service it offers at the moment. There are plenty of co-location organization- and application-hosting specialists but the technology that underpins these providers is available from only a very few companies. The reliability of the solution has to be absolute, as anyone who has ever had something as simple as an e-mail system fall down on them will confirm.

CityReach's facilities are designed to serve a diverse community of customers, including ISPs, ASPs, bandwidth providers, Web-hosters, content providers and corporate outsourcing customers. This business-enabling marketplace provides each customer with access to a range of other Internet-focused businesses, providing valuable support services and new business opportunities.

CityReach's route to its consumer base is therefore carefully mapped through indirect channels. It works with service providers and system integrators such as BT Ignite and others of similar stature and these companies do the selling to their customers – CityReach only appears to the end customer at the request of the partnering company, which has the option to put its own name on the service if it wishes to do so. 'These people take the applications to the Web and we provide the platform,' explains CityReach chief executive Sanjaya Addanki.

CityReach expect the bulk of future spend on the Internet to come from large and medium corporates taking their business to the Web –

embracing applications such as supply chain management, enterprise resource planning, customer relationship management and e-procurement.

Addanki believes that as businesses now move the delivery of the their core business applications to the Internet they have a different focus: they must ensure security, reliability, manageability and scalability. 'If your supply chain system fails for several minutes causing a production line to shut down, it has a significant impact on profitability. The CityReach platform delivers non-stop operation.'

Contrary to what might be expected, however, the technical nature of the customers' requirements doesn't make the sale cycle any shorter as the technical due diligence on the part of the service providers is time consuming.

The success of the strategy can be seen in the company's footprint across Europe with eight operational data centres. Each is more robust and scalable than is normal in a corporate setting, and more will follow as the market matures. Once cash flow becomes positive a high proportion of revenue will go into research and development to keep the offerings current.

Flexibility

The company's flexibility is considerable and can be exemplified in the two changes of focus it has undergone since its establishment, plus the rapid growth in which over 330 staff were added to a core team of 11 within the space of 15 months.

Initially the company offered co-location services. The first move away from this business model came when it added services, such as first line maintenance, power options and fire suppression. Although this required the recruitment of extra personnel, Addanki suggests the transition was smooth because the only real change was in adding extra value to the existing core service.

The second change in focus was further reaching and resulted from updating the business Internet-platform provision model the company operates. The skill sets required from the staff were different in that more people with an IT services background were required. Although Addanki suggests this was a longer-term change it's noticeable that it only took two months to accomplish, and all the staff have now bought into it – as have the equity analysts and industry analysts who follow the company.

Solid management inevitably played its part in this transition, so the change was not problematic for customers.

Human Resources

The first thing to note on the personnel side is that every employee is a shareholder to some degree, depending on their salary and position – and that's where the importance of the hierarchy all but stops. Prospective employees can expect a competitive salary and a benefits package, which includes health insurance and a good pension. Share ownership will be of value to staff only if the company floats or sells, of course; current plans are to float when the market turns in favour of the IT sector.

There are three basic tenets in the company culture, some of which were still evolving as this book went to press. The first is that the business is committed to targets and results and does not have the 'best efforts' attitude typical of many small companies. The second tenet is that there is no room for turf wars; if the chief executive suddenly has to become sales director that's OK, and vice versa. Addanki notes that when companies' staff numbers move from 11 people to 100, staff often start drawing up organizational charts to establish where they are in the business; this isn't an appropriate thing to do in CityReach. The third tenet is technical excellence – whether someone is in engineering or sales, they have to excel in their core competency.

Growth Markets

CityReach prides itself on its absolute focus on the indirect market and will continue to regard Web-integrators, Web-hosts, Systems Integrators, ISPs, ASPs and whichever other SPs evolve over time as its market. An area that is likely to grow in the short and medium term is the GSM mobile phone operator. 'They are going to have to become ISPs in their own right and they don't yet know how to do this,' comments Addanki, which is exactly the skill set offered by CityReach.

Quality of Management

Addanki looks for a number of things in a manager, the first of which is 'Can he or she replace me?' If the answer is yes, preferably today, that person might be right for CityReach; yes, maybe tomorrow is also acceptable. This has to do with leadership, and the company always seeks to recruit doers rather than talkers in this respect. The second and probably most important thing is that the person should be a team player. An ex-IBM employee, Addanki has taken the words of IBM CEO Lou Gerstner to heart, when he said he drew an X axis and a Y axis, X being revenue and Y being the ability to work in a team. The ideal manager's performance will be in the top right hand corner; if the sales are bad then that can be for a number of reasons so someone can have another chance, but if the team playing is bad then the person should look for another job. People wanting to value their personal performance above what they can do for CityReach are not welcomed.

The third element of course is competence. The managers are all good at what they do, and there's no hiding – they are listed by name on the company website with links to comprehensive professional biographies for most of them. The sum of these biographies reads like a Who's Who of major companies in technology, telecommunications, venture capital and other areas of business – there are no lightweights on board.

International Orientation

CityReach has its headquarters in London and has facilities in Amsterdam, Berlin, Budapest, Dublin, London, Munich, Stockholm and Paris.

America is another key market but the company will take a slightly different tack and work alongside partners, since the co-location market is longer established with several key differences to Europe.

This appears a sensible strategy to take when the market is as mature as it is over there as compared to here, and this decision is typical of the flexible approach that has led the company to grow as quickly as it has. It employed only 11 people in January 2000 and as this book went to press in mid-2001 it had 350 people on board. It has managed its growth well and shows every sign of pulling into operating profit by the end of 2001; as long as it retains its ability to react to whatever changes the market dictates it should continue to enjoy strong performance.

Civista

Civista is a software company launched in 2000 which operates in the wireless world. Its services basically amount to connecting any repository of information that isn't based on proprietary standards to any wireless device – so if information was stored in an HTML form, LDAP or SAP format, Civista's products would read it and output it as XML, then broadcast it to a mobile phone, PDA or whichever wireless device was required by the customer.

Scorecard:

Innovation	★★★★★
Flexibility	★★★★★
Human resources	★★★★
Growth markets	★★★★
Quality of management	★★★★★
International orientation	★★★★★

Biggest plus:
Getting into an emerging market so early – if it fulfils its potential it should be an exciting ride.

Biggest minus:
The newness of the company means it can't guarantee results – either for the market as a whole or for its share of it as it grows.

Civista
7th Floor Tolworth Tower North
Ewell Road
Tolworth KT6 7EL
Tel: 020 8408 6370
website: civista.com

Civista

The Business

Civista is a multinational company which opened simultaneously in the UK and Spain, and which opened an office in Rome a few months later. Privately-owned, it aims to unite content held on established technologies with wireless, frequently mobile, output devices. It launched in May 2000 and now has two offices in Spain and one in the UK. Eventually, when it has been established for a few years, and assuming fair market conditions, it will float on the stock exchange. For the moment it is concerned with its potential for high growth in Europe.

Innovation

The company is focused very carefully on companies that want to use innovative products in the wireless area but which have yet to find a means of linking their existing information into the new display devices – whether these are WAP phones, PDAs or other wireless technology. The field is starting to become significant in the US with companies like Ethereal Systems doing well, but in Europe few businesses specialize in this field. So the product area itself marks Civista out as doing something a little different, as does the fact that it's actually delivering product – there is a lot of what the computer industry calls 'vapourware' out there at the moment, in other words companies are talking about delivering more often than they are actually selling goods. Civista's 'Civista Anywhere' product is real and selling now.

In terms of getting to the market the company is talking to a number of partners and potential partners, recognizing that its 100-strong staff won't be able to service the entire potential market itself. It has agreements with a number of Web integrators and systems integrators and is also talking to partners such as Computacenter and BT Cellnet to get into markets in which it would require more credibility than any start-up could have.

It recognizes that the technology behind its products is the whole of its value and although it doesn't break its turnover down for public consumption, it is happy to confirm that almost half of its staff is focused on research and development.

Young though the company is it has scored a number of major contracts; it is thanks to its technology that Reed Elsevier and the PPA websites are WAP-enabled. It has strong alliances with a number of the established computer hardware sellers including IBM, Sun and Storage Networks.

Flexibility

In spite of the organization's youth it has already had one major refocus in its business – when it decided not to operate as an application service provider (ASP). ASPs host computing applications for their customers, who can then dial into them through an Internet or direct dial-up connection from their own computer. It became apparent quite swiftly that this was not a suitable area for the business to operate in. 'A lot of people are now claiming to be wireless ASPs,' comments marketing manager Rob Coleman; Civista won't be among them for a number of reasons – it doesn't want to compete in an overcrowded market and it has recognized that its strength is in product development.

The resulting changeover meant that different people had to be recruited from those already on board because a different set of skills was suddenly needed for product development rather than ASP work. Reallocation of resources was not an entirely painless process but the company felt it couldn't compete in an area away from its strengths; the website still says it will work as an ASP but in practice this will be achieved through a series of partnerships with other organizations.

The market has also changed, demanding alterations in emphasis from Civista and any other participants. The launch of WAP in 2000 was basically botched by a number of organizations and left customers highly disillusioned by the sudden acquisition of this text-only service when they had been promised the Internet in the palm of their hands. The business community is now taking WAP seriously so companies are having to develop for it again. In any industry that moves as quickly as that of wireless technology it is essential that a company should be nimble, and Civista has proven itself so.

Human Resources

Every one of the 100 members of staff is a shareholder in Civista, which takes employee participation very seriously. It plans to move into a more comfortable UK headquarters as soon as this becomes affordable, for example, and there is a full complement of benefits available in the competitive remuneration package.

That said, although the company isn't cheap, it doesn't hire people on price alone – staff who chase only after money will be looking for the next job within a couple of months. It sells itself to its prospective employees as much on its culture; the majority of its staff are ex-corporate employees at various levels and the excitement of working in a start-up for the first time is challenging and stimulating (and frustrating – when an employee is used to services such as the easy availability of business cards, for example, it can be quite a shock when there's nobody there to source the things).

The ideal employee would be motivated, excited by the prospect of joining a new market at ground level and will be very flexible.

Growth Markets

Just about any company with any data it wants to put onto a small computer will fit into Civista's picture of who it wants to sell to; the growth of the wireless market is universally forecast to be colossal until at least 2003. However, due to only being able to do one thing at a time the company will be focusing on the media industry for the moment before moving on (this can be a good idea not only from the solid business point of view but also in terms of attracting publicity – if journalists use it they will probably mention it sometime).

It has a number of alliances in order to get talking to some of the other industries in which it is interested, particularly the banks – it will be working with Computacenter, BT Internet and Grey Interactive to get to this market.

Quality of Management

At first glance the company looks overmanaged, almost comically so – it has 100 staff, nine of whom are vice-presidents. There are reasons for this, however; the company anticipates continuing its rapid growth and therefore needs the people at the top with some weight in advance so that it can grow smoothly and keep trading in the meantime. There is no plan to recruit any more senior management so once the staff has expanded to 1000 the number of directors will appear more reasonable. The other reason for having so many is, of course, that venture capitalists and backers like VPs.

And they are VPs with impressive pedigrees in the corporate world: senior personnel from within IBM, One2One and other major mobile and IT companies are involved, planning to build the company into a leader in its field in Europe.

On an individual basis the company negotiates individual objectives with the staff and has quarterly reviews to see how close these are to being achieved.

International Orientation

For such a young company Civista has an impressive array of overseas offices already including two in Spain and one in Rome. More will follow as the company wants to become the de facto supplier of this sort of technology in Europe. It has no plans to open an office in the US, however, as there is already established competition, the competitive culture is different and frankly there is plenty of room for growth in Europe.

Its growth plans are aggressive and its decision to put its management structure of vice-presidents in place in advance of market share or even a particularly large market – the wireless market is attracting a lot of interest at the moment and that's about it – shows a certain optimism about just how much the company can grow in a relatively short time. Its early international expansion is impressive as are the curriculum vitae of the aforementioned vice-presidents; assuming the wireless arena grows as the analysts believe it will then there is no reason Civista shouldn't become one of the leading players.

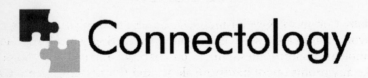 Connectology

Connectology is a leading supplier of network computing and Internet solutions for business. It sells equipment from well-known suppliers, but the major element of its service is the ability to understand the customer's requirements and design a complete solution for them. For a relatively small company – it has 28 employees, and turnover this year is around £3.2 million – it has been able to compete with some much larger players to win significant business from blue-chip enterprises.

Scorecard:

Innovation	★★★★
Flexibility	★★★★
Human resources	★★★★
Growth markets	★★★★
Quality of management	★★★★
International orientation	★★★★

Biggest plus:
Connectology is a recognized leader in what are arguably the most exciting areas of the high-potential high-tech marketplace.

Biggest minus:
But it is still a small company, and there must be a danger that it does not yet have the strength to resist being squeezed out by much larger competitors.

Connectology Limited
1 St. Andrews Court
Wellington Street
Thame
Oxfordshire OX9 3WT
Tel: 01844 218383
website: www.connectology.com

Connectology Limited

The Business

Initially Connectology's business was based on supplying cabling and network hardware, with the company reacting quickly to new-technology opportunities. But it has become increasingly tough to make any profits out of hardware alone, and Connectology has moved quite deliberately towards a service model. Today Connectology sees itself more as a strategic consultancy, emphasizing its problem-solving knowledge and very close relationships with customers – the hardware only features as part of the solution that it might offer a client.

Founded in 1994 by its present management (and still privately funded) Connectology has expanded quickly. The last published turnover figure of £3.7 million relates to 1999, when the company showed a profit of £298,000. Back in 1995 Connectology's sales were just £358,000.

But both 1999 results were down on the year before, and for financial year 2000 Connectology expects to report a 'small' loss on turnover of £3.2 million. Clearly Connectology is having to pause to draw breath, to invest in company structures and forward strategies. In recent months extra key management appointments have been made to handle this.

The current year should see some real growth again, with a predicted turnover 'in excess of' £4.5 million. The next few months should see the company's first acquisitions.

The company has five operating divisions – Sales and Consulting/Engineering earn the money, Internal Systems, Finance, and Administration run the organization. Each of these functions has a single responsible manager and these people form Connectology's management team.

Connectology employs 28 full-time staff.

Innovation

Connectology was quick to recognize the potential of the Internet, and it has a strong position in providing e-business solutions to the UK's medium- and large-sized enterprises.

Its own Web presence is an impressive piece of work following heavy investment in 1999. The site at www.connectology.com has three main components: an online product catalogue and price list; a public information area and a password-protected extranet that provides individual customers with personalized information and online ordering facilities.

This is by far the most active element – customers can set up meetings with individual Connectology consultants there, for instance, and online ordering has cut both the time and the overheads of sales processing. Clients can also see up-to-date diagrams of their in-progress network solutions, which means they can get a project update whenever they want it.

More generally, the company claims to have the most skilled, experienced, committed and innovative team of designers, implementers and support engineers working in the UK today on local and wide area networks. These days those networks are no longer simply moving computer data between corporate offices – the traffic could include video and voice as well, and the network will certainly include external links to suppliers, customers, and the Internet. Connectology has become a major centre of competence on these fledgling networks.

As a matter of policy, Connectology does not use advertising – it simply doesn't see the need. Marketing consists of small-scale direct marketing, seminars on specific issues for key prospects, and PR (press comment on Connectology is almost always favourable).

Flexibility

Connectology has been well placed to use technology in its business, and the impressive Web operation has clearly contributed to a lean, nimble-footed business that can react quickly to customer demand. It gives customers and staff immediate access to the kind of information that might otherwise need a large back-office bureaucracy to provide.

That augurs well, and illustrates the care with which the company has progressed from its very modest beginnings.

Rapid growth has been achieved without damaging the core culture of the business and its essential emphasis on customer service. The way it has made money has evolved logically, with early insights into the profitability problems of dealing in only hardware and it has developed real ways to add value to its basic offer.

So far so good. Connectology is aware though that some real tests lie ahead – particularly in managing the transition from a smallish £4m company to a medium-sized (perhaps international) player with sales of £10m and up. The directors seem to be positioning Connectology quite sensibly for that growth – by looking for strategic acquisitions that will add to the mix, for instance. They are prepared to dilute their own shareholdings to attract the external capital that will be needed.

Human Resources

In general Connectology employs people with specific technical skills but it also looks for a practical appreciation of business services.

The company values personal responsibility and the individual's contribution to the organization. In return staff are paid 'the going rate'. Probably more important is the freedom, respect and professional development they receive. Connectology emphasizes its flexibility in dealing with staff – by varying sales targets to suit personal circumstances, for example. The company believes that well-motivated people will take personal responsibility for their work, which minimizes the need for oppressive management. Incentives also matter – Connectology claims to throw great parties, and there are twice-yearly hotel getaway weekends for everyone (with so many staff working on customer sites, these parties are the only time when the whole company gets together in one place).

Connectology has a handful of people working full-time at client sites, and this trend will continue as the company expands its strategic involvement with customers.

Growth Markets

Connectology's business is split more or less equally between very large (often global) corporations and much smaller enterprises. The larger firms typically use Connectology to handle rapid changes – relocations, consolidation, new technology – while the smaller ones are generally having to cope with fast growth (an area Connectology understands, if only because 'we are our own best case study').

Both sectors will continue to provide growth opportunities for Connectology. The appeal of outsourcing business services like network design and management is only going to increase, and as new technology becomes available the kind of people who understand all the issues will be at a premium. Connectology is well placed to capitalize on this.

Connectology also intends to start acquiring complementary businesses to fill gaps in its own portfolio and to provide new market opportunities. We can expect the first such takeovers in 2001.

Quality of Management

Connectology's business is based on key service-company principles: new business is less cost-effective than repeat business, knowledge and advice are more profitable than selling hardware, close long-term relationships with clients are built on customer satisfaction and particularly the ability to take ownership of the customer's problem.

Close relationships were always part of the game plan, but in the early days the business relied on reselling branded hardware. Connectology is still associated with some of the biggest brands in its field – it is a leading reseller of Cisco, BICC, IBM, and Compaq – but by the late 1990s fierce competition and falling prices were driving down margins in that business. Connectology saw the trend early and it decided to lessen its dependence on hardware and to become more service-oriented, with consultants recruited as much for their business services skills as their technical competence. The supply of network hardware then becomes only part of the solution, and not the most profitable part at that.

This insight was hardly unique, but many of Connectology's competitors have found themselves unable to adapt as quickly and as effectively to the new business landscape. As a result, this small Oxfordshire-based company is able to compete on equal terms with big-name giants of the IT world such as Siemens and Arthur Anderson.

A classic problem with growing companies is a skills gap at management level – entrepreneurs don't always do so well at day-to-day management, and such detailed attention is increasingly required when the organization starts to grow larger. Connectology recognizes this problem, and a new managing director recently joined the company to look after UK operations. This has freed founder-director Jonathan Wagstaffe for more strategic corporate issues such as forward planning.

International Orientation

Connectology already does between 15 and 20 per cent of its business outside the UK, but this generally happens because a UK-based client is implementing an international network which will be ordered and operated from Britain. Connectology staff will be exported as and when required for this kind of job.

The company recognizes that a more permanent presence in mainland Europe and possibly the USA may be required, if only to service the needs of larger corporations who have local operations. But such plans are embryonic at present, and Connectology will react to user demand rather than speculate on an international operation.

countrybookshop
This is your local shop ————— .co.uk

Country Bookshop is an online and offline book retailer, that also has a wholesale business. The UK's second most popular book e-tailer, it employs 19 people and had a turnover of £1m in 1999. The 3,000 ft physical shop includes a dedicated children's section and an Internet café.

Scorecard:

Innovation	★★★
Flexibility	★★★★★
Human resources	★★★★
Growth markets	★★★★
Quality of management	★★★★★
International orientation	★★

Biggest plus:
The popularity and impact that the company has made in a short time.

Biggest minus:
The downturn of the e-business economy will have devalued the company for its shareholdrs although it was trading strongly.

Country Bookshop
Hassop Station
Bakewell
Derbyshire DE45 1NW
Tel: 01629 813444
Fax: 01629 814355
website: www.countrybookshop.co.uk

Country Bookshop

The Business

Country Bookshop began life in 1987 as a wholesale operation exclusively geared to the tourist and heritage market. Its location in the Peak District made it ideally situated to do this and it is a market it continues to serve. Four years later, retail operations commenced, with stock comprised of remainder titles and bargain books.

In 1996, the business was acquired as a limited company by husband and wife team, Geraldine Rose and Sridhar Gowda, who became its directors. From that time on, retail operations began to assume prominence within the business. Against a backdrop of increasing pressure on independent operators from the major chains, the store began to stock all types of book and organized author events to generate more local interest.

Gowda, an engineer by trade, helped launch an online facility a year later, though the website proper was not launched until March 1999. Within months it was receiving between 500–1,000 orders per week.

Innovation

By the end of 2000, Country Bookshop was bested only by Amazon for the number of visitors to its website, according to Internet traffic monitor Alexa. For a small, independent bookseller this is quite an achievement. With limited resources at its disposal, it has shown the way to better-funded competitors through the application of a smart business strategy and by drawing on Geraldine Rose's well-established knowledge and contacts within the bookselling industry.

Marketing policy has centred on the building of online strategic alliances. The offspring of a specialist bookshop, the website targets specific interest groups, such as ramblers and gardening enthusiasts. Partners join its associate programme which offers referral fees of between 5–10 per cent of transactional costs. There are also links from credit card sites and customers can purchase items with the Web currency Beenz.

The shop itself continues to thrive as a business and serves as an effective vehicle for publicising the website. Country Bookshop is keen to become a focal point for local cultural activity and nearby Chatsworth House has long been a landmark on the Peak District tourist trail. Media coverage is generated through sponsorship of the annual Peak District Book of the Year competition and through book-signings from regional celebrities such as Dickie Bird and Richard Whitely.

High levels of repeat business have been presaged on ease of use of the site, lower prices than rivals and efficient product delivery. The availability of all titles is displayed and those in stock will be delivered free of charge to UK customers within 24 hours. Those books that are not in stock can be obtained quickly – usually within two or three days, and never more than a week. This is made possible because the company deals direct with the publishers, only using wholesalers as backup. The relationships long predate Country Bookshop's online activities and allow for better margins as well as adding value through extras like an out-of-print service and discounting of up to 75 per cent on selected titles.

Flexibility

One of the UK's first true 'bricks-and-clicks' businesses, Country Book-shop changed its business model to adapt and survive in the market in which it operates. Though already successful and growing in size prior to its reinvention as an Internet bookseller, the owners had observed other independent retailers fail and decided to pre-empt any future downturn they might themselves experience.

From the outset, there was a determination to retain control of all aspects of the Web operations. So whereas many book retailers either bought in new media expertise or outsourced platform and content functionality, the Country Bookshop site was built entirely in-house. This do-it-yourself approach saved money on tenancy fees and has enabled the company to react more quickly both to its customers' requirements and to the needs of the business. As demand has grown this has become more important – and more of a challenge!

For the first two years, Country Bookshop only offered a selection of titles. But the directors quickly realized that the profile of online customer was different to that of the store visitor and expanded the offering to one million titles – that is, every UK book in print as listed by Whitakers book catalogue.

Even though it was relatively quick off the mark, the company immediately faced tremendous competition from other retailers with much greater brand presence. But ironically, its determinedly un-hip name has proved an asset. The site is registered with all the major search engines, and its URL means that surfers seeking to make a book purchase are likely to find it figures prominently on a list of search results.

As a traditional business Country Bookshop always portrayed itself as belonging to its customers and the same ethos applies to the website. Customers are encouraged to vote for their favourite authors or books and give feedback about their shopping experience. The expanding customer service team, secure ordering and an online order tracking system have earned the site accreditation from Bizrate.com, which rates e-tailers for service delivery.

Human Resources

Country Bookshop is unlike the average small or medium-sized business. There can be few businesses that combine a cutting-edge technological environment with the opportunity to sell books to passing ramblers – but that is exactly the kind of place it is. The shop is open seven days a week and is busiest at the weekends. If front-of-house staff are stretched, the Web programmers may join them to help out.

There is some pride that the business has made such an impact on the Web without abandoning its roots. Finding the right people has not been a problem. Graduates from nearby Derby and Sheffield universities have typically been recruited; young people attracted by the idea of working in a dot-com environment, without having to move to find it.

Growth Markets

The company has big ambitions. Currently with a significant slice of the UK online bookselling market it wants to achieve a quarter share of the market by 2004; this would firmly establish it as the second biggest book e-tailer, behind Amazon. In doing so, however, it will not diversify into other areas. The company's knowledge is in bookselling and it is reluctant to expand its product portfolio and lose focus as a consequence.

Though Country Bookshop is a fundamentally consumer-oriented concept, the expertise it has developed in the construction of its online business has become an additional revenue stream. With book publishers, in the US, as well as the UK, approaching them for advice on platform construction and site design, the directors set up a separate Web design company, Inamaste. With around 20,000 publishing houses in this country alone, business-to-business activity is set to become an increasingly important part of the job.

At the beginning of 2001, the three constituent parts of the business contributed in equal share to its profitability – although new media turnover vastly exceeded the others. As custom through the website has grown, the focus becomes the need to keep pace with technological developments in the wider marketplace. Having launched a WAP site in September 2000, the company sees digital TV as the next logical step and has established a relationship with leading supplier ONDigital.

Quality of Management

The move into digital TV and expanding on-site warehouse capacity mean for the first time Country Bookshop requires outside capital. At the moment between 10 to 15 per cent of profits are reinvested for the business's development. But around £3 million is sought to really take it forward, although Sridhar Gowda insists, 'it's not a necessary thing – it will just give us a quantum leap.'

Potential investors will no doubt be reminded that growth thus far has been achieved without any significant injection of finance and that the strait-jacket on spending has helped the business stay in the black, unlike all its major competitors. They may also take heart from the accolades that have come its way. The site came second in the DTI e-commerce awards in 2000, and was ranked fourteenth in the *Sunday Times* e-league of Europe's top 100 businesses.

International Orientation

Just as they are adamant they will not diversify into product streams, so the directors are wary of operating outside the UK book market which they know so well. There is little prospect that they will ever stock non-English language books and, fearing loss of control, they have no plans to expand into other countries.

Ironically, when it first launched the site received 65 per cent of its orders from overseas customers – from Europe, the US, Canada and even Asia. Over time, however, the proportions have reversed, now 80 per cent of its customers are UK-based.

DIAGEO

Diageo plc is a world-leading premium drinks company, an £18 billion business that was formed in 1997 by the merger of Guinness and Grand Metropolitan. Diageo also owns the Burger King fast food chain and packaged foods enterprise Pillsbury, though both are to be separated from Diageo as the company refocuses on its core business. Diageo is a UK company with operations in over 200 countries; it employs some 70,000 people world-wide.

Scorecard:

Innovation	★★★
Flexibility	★★★
Human resources	★★★★
Growth markets	★★★★
Quality of management	★★★★
International orientation	★★★★

Biggest plus:
Diageo is a leading British blue-chip company with all the pride and power that market leadership and instant brand recognition can provide.

Biggest minus:
The stock market has sometimes been less than enthusiastic, however, probably because of the plethora of brands and the possible diffusion of the group's focus (both of which appear to be addressed in the current strategy).

Diageo
8 Henrietta Place
London W1M 9AG
Tel: 020 7518 5200
website: www.diageo.co.uk

Diageo plc

The Business

Diageo plc is a leading international premium drinks company formed from the merger of Guinness and Grand Metropolitan in 1997. Diageo's brand portfolio combines the world's number one seller of spirits with one of the oldest names in beer. The company is responsible for a wide portfolio of brands – including Johnnie Walker, and J&B whiskies, Guinness, Smirnoff, Malibu, Baileys, and Tanqueray – in some 200 countries around the world. Diageo also owns a third of French champagne and cognac producer Moët Hennessy, and it has a 45 per cent stake of top tequila house Jose Cuervo SA. At the end of 2000 Diageo and Pernod-Ricard paid over $8 billion for the drinks operations of Seagram.

For its last full year, to June 2000, Diageo reported revenues of £18 billion and net income of £1.9 billion. The half-year results to December 2000 showed operating profits 9.4 per cent higher at £1.2 billion on sales that rose 4 per cent to £6.8 billion. The group employs 72,400 people around the world.

Innovation

Diageo isn't a business that constantly invents new products – but it is a business that has to stay right on top of its market, and that translates into a deep understanding of consumers and a focus on brands. Some of Diageo's marketing has been imaginative and innovative, for instance, the Guinness TV ads regularly win plaudits from the industry and consumers alike.

Within the group itself there is much emphasis on business process re-engineering to ensure that the company stays ahead of the game in terms of the operation of the business. It is also large enough to influence the way suppliers deal with it; and while business requirements will drive new technology implementations, there is a willingness to adopt potential technology improvements that open up ways of working which were not possible before.

Flexibility

Diageo is coming out of the first three years of a fairly traumatic birth, with cost savings from the merger of two very well established companies being offset by the inevitable operational hiccups and many issues of policy to be decided. During this period the group faltered slightly in terms of maintaining growth in sales and profits, and it's clear that Diageo has changed tack quite dramatically during 2000. The return to core products and core markets suggests that the company has been able to react to changing conditions without any major long-term impact on its financial results or on its share price.

Human Resources

Diageo is a huge and diverse organization, but it does emphasize its overriding concern to recruit and keep the best people. It has certainly invested considerably in employee development principles and pro-grammes, including 'a framework of processes and behaviours that commit us to winning through people' called The Diageo Way of Building Talent.

For top managers Diageo operates a bonus system based on three-year targets for profit improvement; each manager's annual bonuses are 'banked', to be paid out over a number of years – a process which ensures that performance is sustained. For its most senior executives, Diageo also has a long-term incentive programme that compares the company's performance against a peer group of 19 other businesses.

It's also worth noting that Diageo has established the Diageo Foundation, a world-wide effort to help local communities by providing charitable donations and long-term social investment. Tomorrow's People, one of the UK's leading charities helping the unemployed, is among the recipients.

Growth Markets

Diageo is a marketing-led company in a brand-dominated business. Research and development typically equates to just 0.6 per cent of sales, and while new products are fed into the mix the group's growth will come from increased focus on high margin brands in their most important markets. Heavy marketing, based on in-depth understanding of the consumer (and especially high-spend consumer occasions), is the watchword, and for the six months to December 2000 Diageo increased the marketing spend on premium drinks by 9 per cent.

This policy appears to be paying off. Half-year operating profits for wines and spirits were up 14 per cent; for beer the increase was 13 per cent. These results were far better than income for the packaged food business and quick service restaurants, both of which are to be sold off.

These figures also look good against a background of low overall growth for the alcoholic drinks industry across Europe and to a lesser extent the US. Retail patterns are changing too, with much competition for shelf space and distribution opportunities. Diageo clearly understands that it needs extremely strong brands which can outperform the market, and current strategies are geared to this. The decision to integrate Guinness with its spirits brands, for instance, marks a policy of presenting Guinness as a 'ready to drink' beverage alongside Malibu, Pimms, and Smirnoff Ice – and a reflection of the way consumers are increasingly selecting a wider range of drinks for any given drinking occasion.

Quality of Management

Diageo has had a hectic three years since the merger. The inevitable convulsions of amalgamating two substantial enterprises appear to have resulted in the headline strategic decisions that emerged during 2000, at the start of which Paul Walsh became chief executive designate (he got the full title in September). By the summer Diageo had announced its intention to concentrate on drinks, with full integration of its spirits unit UDV with the beer business of Guinness. At the end of the year Diageo in partnership with French drinks group Pernod-Ricard had won the $8.2 billion auction for the drinks arm of Canadian group Seagram; the two will be dividing Seagram's assets between them (the portfolio includes Chivas Regal, Martell and Captain Morgan).

This policy makes sense to observers, who feel that a plethora of different brands and different businesses has produced lower profitability than might be expected. And sales of around $235,000 per employee in 2000 are actually lower than achieved by Diageo's big European competitors, Pernod-Ricard ($283,000 per employee) and Allied Domecq ($270,000). The new Diageo strategy of focusing on the top brands in its core business has been well received, and a clear-out over the past twelve months has seen the sale of many of the smaller properties to concentrate on nine 'global priority brands' (including Johnnie Walker, Smirnoff and Baileys).

Seagram looks a canny deal, too. It's not just the wine and spirits business that will add to Diageo's income – the purchase also prevents the Seagram brands from being acquired by Diageo's most immediate competitor, Allied Domecq. For Allied, Seagram looked a once-in-a-lifetime chance to match the merger that created Diageo.

Diageo's non-drinks businesses are to go, and Pillsbury is already being transferred to General Mills with Diageo retaining a 33 per cent stake. Burger King, which is currently turning in disappointing results, is being readied for disposal probably through a staged flotation in which Diageo will gradually withdraw from the investment – the plan is that Burger King will be totally floated by 2003, though the timetable has been upset by stock market conditions. The renowned reference publisher, Guinness World Records, is also for sale.

The speedy departure of Burger King (restaurant sales down 6 per cent in 2000, operating profits 7 per cent lower) and Pillsbury (only just returned to profitable growth, with turnover up 2 per cent and operating profits up 11 per cent in 2000) will help the bottom line.

Underlying financial statements also suggest that the right management decisions are being taken. On the figures for the year to June 2000, the company had reduced inventory turnover considerably – on average it had 93 days of expensive stock on hand, against 122 days' worth the year before. And accounts receivable were equivalent to 50 days of sales, another improvement over 1999 when money owed was worth 65 days of sales.

International Orientation

Diageo has an international perspective: it operates in over 200 countries; and though the key markets for alcoholic beverages are the UK, the US, Ireland and Spain, Diageo sees new global opportunities for its premium brands. At present, North America accounts for over 47 per cent of total sales, though this will change when the group divests itself of the US-oriented Burger King and Pillsbury.

Direct Digital, established in 1993, supplies digital photocopiers – typically where the equipment is used as a high-volume high-quality online reprographics centre for users on a corporate network. Direct Digital can offer financing arrangements for the purchase of the equipment (this is enabled by arrangements with two major finance houses which allow Direct Digital to offer an own-branded service) and also expects customers to sign up to an efficient maintenance contract as part of the deal.

Scorecard:

Innovation	★★★★
Flexibility	★★★★
Human resources	★★★★
Growth markets	★★★★
Quality of management	★★★★
International orientation	★★★

Biggest plus:
Digital Direct operates in a sales-oriented goal-driven business, but its approach to customer service and its ability to back up its proposals with a solid assessment of costs and benefits obviously removes much of the pressure from the sales team.

Biggest minus:
The head office is a functional and glitz-free working environment just over Vauxhall Bridge in London.

Direct Digital Limited
The Riverhouse
4–6 South Lambeth Place
London SW8 1SP
Tel: 020 7735 9992
website: www.directdigital.co.uk

Direct Digital Limited

The Business

The London company was founded in 1993 by Michael Horgan, Brian Seifert and David Esdaile and it is still managed by them.

Direct Digital was an early player in the market for digital photocopiers, which can produce pages more quickly, at significantly lower cost, and with considerably more flexibility than a conventional photocopier. The same solution also competes well against laser printers for high-volume work. So Direct Digital had some good product lines; but equally importantly, it has majored on providing customer service in a business that has had a poor reputation for customer care. This policy has, for instance, led to the establishment of a national service operation, developed to guarantee service levels.

Today the mix of technological competence and user-service continues to see the company prosper against some larger and better-known competitors – notably the market leader Xerox. The product portfolio includes photocopier-based products from Ricoh, Sharp, Canon and Kodak, plus high-volume laser printers from Hewlett-Packard, Kyocera, Lexmark and Ricoh; the customer roster includes blue-chip names like British Gas, News International and WPP Group.

Innovation

Direct Digital owes its existence partly to good timing – the recession of the late 1980s encouraged more large firms to outsource activities such as volume copying, and that coincided with the arrival of the new digital photocopiers. As well as the head-to-head competition with conventional analogue copiers, the digital photocopier can (and has) evolved into a network-connected print station for workgroups, with sophisticated scheduling, load balancing, and overall control of what is printed where, when and why.

Direct Digital specialized in the new-technology products. But in a business which traditionally has had a poor reputation for pushy salespeople and poor service, what has really set Direct Digital apart is the concern to add value to the customer's investment. In practice that has meant putting time and effort into analysis of the customer's needs, presenting a detailed and costed proposal, and working towards a long-term contract and a close relationship with the customer.

That is exemplified by the emphasis on service. The industry average is one engineer per 140 machines; Direct Digital operates with one for 80. Engineers are based on site for clients with more than that. And a programme of regular preventative maintenance minimizes the need for emergency call-outs. This premium-service approach means Direct Digital does not have to compete on price alone.

Similarly, Direct Digital's normal sales approach includes a no-fee, no-commitment analysis of the potential client's requirements – a detailed data-collection exercise that can cover operational procedures, print volumes and varying work patterns in different user departments. This innovative approach has demonstrated the superiority of both digital photocopier technology and Direct Digital's commitment to service.

The emphasis on applying new technology remains. Direct Digital's clients now tend to be IT departments rather than the office manager or the finance director, and its products need to be integrated into network systems.

Digital Direct operates as a people business, which means the main new-business technique is cold calling via the well regarded Dun and Bradstreet prospecting system. There is little supporting marketing; the website at *www.directdigital.co.uk/* is used as an online corporate brochure rather than an order-taking or project-tracking tool.

Flexibility

Keeping the print room up to date is a pressing requirement for many user companies. It's also a job for a specialist supplier, and that's how Direct Digital regards itself. As the market expands and changes, Direct Digital has reacted to add new services – often anticipating the trends.

It can do this partly because the essential business idea is so good: Direct Digital doesn't simply supply up-to-date photocopiers, it can propose the best way to use print and reprographic services within the enterprise: and it can support its proposals with an ongoing relationship that doesn't just extend to emergency call-outs when the equipment breaks down.

This emphasis on service, on adding value to the sales proposition, means that Direct Digital can adapt the detail of its product portfolio to suit different circumstances. For example, it can offer a comprehensive facilities management service for print room outsourcing, where Direct Digital supplies staff as well as hardware. And the same approach works for an IT-based sell, where digital photocopiers are offered as an alternative workgroup print facility to high-volume laser printers.

Direct Digital has also learned from the mistakes of others. At a time when many competitors were subcontracting engineering cover for their clients, Direct Digital's decision to set up its own nation-wide service network might have looked like an expensive gamble. But it has meant that the company can guarantee service levels, including regular preventative maintenance, and that assurance has definitely helped the company win and keep new business.

Human Resources

Direct Digital doesn't deal in corporate image – its offices are smart and efficient enough, but they are inescapably located under a railway line in Vauxhall, opposite the MI6 building on the Thames. Client contact generally takes place away from the office, but the company does have an up-to-the-minute showroom where clients may view products. That air of roll-your-sleeves-up pragmatism, of reluctance to waste money on inessentials, is part of the working culture.

So is account management. The business sales team gets the new business, but once the customer is signed up they become the responsibility of an account manager who maintains the contact.

Direct Digital tends to keep its staff, though there have been some problems in offering salespeople promotion to management roles – a good salesperson doesn't necessarily make a good sales manager, and in practice Direct Digital has recruited its managers from outside the company. To keep the sales teams happy Digital Direct offers competitive salaries and it also provides a working environment that is flexible and enjoyable.

Growth Markets

Direct Digital's market is still in a phase of explosive growth. In 1996 digital products accounted for less than 1 per cent of copier sales throughout Europe. By 2002 the market is expected to be 100 per cent digital.

And it's clear that the essential nature of the reprographics centre within large organizations is continuing to develop. New technology here doesn't just let the user do more printing at lower cost. Modern in-house reprographic systems include networks and control software as well as the print station hardware, and designing and installing them requires the supplier to be constantly on top of their game.

The economics of digital printing are also changing, with Direct Digital's photocopier-based systems increasingly able to displace the high-volume laser printers traditionally supplied by specialist IT vendors.

Direct Digital is well placed to take advantage of these trends, and has for instance invested in acquiring IT knowledge (including a specialist support team) to stand alongside its existing understanding of reprographics.

Acquisitions are a distinct possibility, though primarily as a means of adding to the customer base and buying contracted forward income – Direct Digital sees massive scope for its core business over the middle term and the company is reluctant to diversify.

Quality of Management

Mike Horgan, Brian Seifert and David Esdaile set up Direct Digital in 1993 – Horgan with a background in photocopier sales, the other two with business experience gained by running a reprographics bureau. This combination still provides a good basic mix, and clearly there has been a high level of agreement about the company's goals and culture.

The business decisions certainly appear very sound. Some of the photocopier business's major players in the early 1990s were sitting targets – complacent, cumbersome, fragmented and unable to react quickly to new technology and new opportunities.

With the core business values in place, Direct Digital's progress has been essentially conservative. The sales procedure involves a detailed (and complementary) appraisal with costed recommendations, and this represents a significant cost: but its value is seen in the response of Direct Digital's clients. It invested substantially in a service operation which enables Direct Digital to demonstrate the ratio of engineers to installations (much better than the industry norm) and to guarantee levels of service (one-hour response to emergency call outs, monthly preventative maintenance checks, resident onsite engineers for larger clients).

The returns are good in terms of customer satisfaction as well as sales. And even on the bottom line, the company has minimized its exposure by canny negotiation of discounts (Direct Digital gets better terms than the industry average simply because of the sales volumes it can deliver).

The investment in pre- and post-sales services have affected the company's profits. But management feels that this is the year when the benefits will show through in improved profitability.

International Orientation

The UK market for photocopiers and print services has traditionally been regarded as idiosyncratic, if not unique, and to some extent Direct Digital has found success by making clear the difference between its offerings and its competitors' in this local market. But it's clear that many of the company's sales and support techniques will transfer to other national markets, should Direct Digital choose to make the required investment – which could be substantial, given the need to provide local financing arrangements and especially local maintenance support.

Direct Digital's business remains centred on Britain – but expansion into mainland Europe is on the cards, as UK clients with overseas operations seek to standardize their print and reprographic needs.

Ebookers is a true online travel agency in that it grew from an existing travel agent rather than from an idea thought up by a bunch of Internet whiz kids. Its predecessor, flightbookers, had two premises – one at Gatwick Airport and another in central London, and had been running successfully for 15 years before it launched the website that became ebookers in June 1999. Ebookers subsequently bought flightbookers. It raised $65 million on Nasdaq and the Neumarkt and now operates in 11 locations throughout Europe.

Scorecard:

Innovation	★★★★★
Flexibility	★★★★
Human resources	★★★★
Growth markets	★★★★
Quality of management	★★★★
International orientation	★★★★★

Biggest plus:
The dynamic environment and the pace of the business and the culture, plus the satisfaction of benefiting customers daily.

Biggest minus:
The speed at which the market changes means the company has to keep moving at a breakneck pace.

Ebookers
25 Farringdon Street
London WC1H 0TA
Tel: 020 7489 2222
website: www.ebookers.com

Ebookers

The Business

Ebookers started as the web presence of flightbookers, a successful London travel agent specializing in flights. Once the website was launched the chief executive, who had run the previous company for some 15 years, noted that it was growing much faster than the more traditional side of the business. He therefore spun ebookers off as a company in its own right with its own management and staff, formally incorporating it in June 1999. It opened in France and Germany in November of the same year and now operates in 11 countries in Europe; one notable country where the company is not active is Italy, and the company plans to open there in the future.

Innovation

Although it can no longer be classified as innovative, it is worth mentioning that when ebookers started in its embryonic, pre-incorporation form, the idea of booking a flight on the Internet was still in its infancy – there was a lot of scepticism about the security of the Internet and the launch itself could reasonably be described as a risk. In fact, it was the first interactive flight booking engine in the UK at the time of its launch in 1996.

The main area of innovation at the moment is the sheer breadth of flights on offer from the company. The competition tends to offer one of two categories of journey: the 'distressed' flight as it is known, in other words the unsold or cancelled seat on a flight that sells at the last minute for very little money, or the regular published flight that goes for the full published price. Very few sites sell both types of tickets and ebookers is one of them.

In addition to this, however, it sells a middle ground flight – the one with the ebookers discount. This is a flight at a special price that would appear to be a distressed flight price, but which is available in advance to ebookers' customers. Discounts can be up to 65 per cent, offering extraordinary value for advanced bookings. The company's negotiating skills are such that it does not need to undertake to buy a minimum number of flights to secure these discounts, so there is never any question of pushing flights at customers.

At the launch, the company made a great deal of its standard advertising – press campaigns, radio and other media promotions, and the brand became established very quickly. It swiftly consolidated this with a deal with AOL Europe in which it became the company AOL Europe recommends to its customers of all of its brands – so AOL subscribers as well as CompuServe and NetScape customers are all sent to ebookers whenever they want to buy a flight.

In addition to this the company has a set of affiliates and other partners. There is a tiered system for this; some of its current partnerships are larger than others, but in total there are over 1000 in the UK, delivering customers to the site and taking a small percentage per sale or fee per click-through. Approaches such as this have led to the company becoming the number one or two travel site in the UK, depending on the data source and month you're reading, and ebookers is consistently in the top-10 of all retail domains.

Flexibility

The rapid growth the company has enjoyed points to a marked ability to accept and assimilate change. There are now close to 500 employees, one third of whom are in the UK.

This speedy growth has been underpinned by a number of factors that have enabled the company to continue trading throughout with no adverse effects for the customers, however. Prime among these is the expertise in the travel industry. It cannot be stressed enough that ebookers and those businesses it has purchased are companies that started in travel and came to the Internet as a means of delivery; their knowledge of their field is considerable. Whenever the organization has bought or even considered buying a company in a country in which it wants to operate it is conscious that it needs to be acquiring local expertise rather than simply a customer base.

Acquisitions have been pursued aggressively and the company plans to continue this policy rather than growing greenfield operations in countries in which it lacks a presence – one experiment in doing precisely that, in Switzerland, took longer than was desirable to consolidate its position. The assimilation of companies that are bought in normally takes between three and six months depending on the size and culture of the concern in question.

One thing about which the company is totally inflexible is the quality of service to the customer – no matter what the business is doing internally ebookers tries to ensure that the customer is never troubled by any interruption to the service or site.

Human Resources

As would be the case with any service company, the culture at ebookers is completely centred round the customer. A high proportion of the 500 staff are actually devoted to customer service in spite of the Internet-based nature of the business; this is because travel arrangements can be complex and the company is aware of the need for some hand-holding at times. Flexibility is key to working in the business because the customers may have complex itineraries which will need individual planning, and they will want to speak to a human being rather than plan on the website alone.

It is a young company; the ground staff tend to be in their twenties although the managers are not inexperienced – on average they have ten years in the travel industry apiece. They all have share options and other benefits as would be expected from a company in a competitive field that aims to attract the best people. The rewards are good and the atmosphere either exhilarating or extremely tough, depending on how the individual responds to the stimulus.

If readers considering applying for jobs in ebookers went away from this book with only one impression of ebookers then it should be that it suits people who want to work in the travel industry – its investment in IT and Web infrastructure is considerable.

Growth Markets

The vast majority of ebookers' sales go to private individuals seeking to plan their travel itineraries. This is an area the company will continue to pursue whilst growing its second market, the small business and unmanaged corporate travel area.

Unmanaged in this case means that each individual plans his or her own journey and does not rely on a central corporate buying pool. There are no plans at present to grow into the managed corporate market but the small/medium enterprise (SME)/unmanaged corporate arena may get its own offering soon from the company since it is about to trial such a scheme in France.

Another area of the company's offering is in the packaged holiday market. While the ebookers site is geared toward the leisure traveller planning their own holiday, there is some scope for people who want ebookers to plan a complete holiday package.

Quality of Management

As has been stated already, ebookers is a bricks and clicks travel company rather than a pure dot-com so it is no surprise to note that the majority of the managers have in-depth experience of the travel sector. Few managers have less than ten years experience in the field, and founder Dinesh Dhamija has more than twenty, having started as a manager at Royal Nepal Airlines and taking flightbookers from a start-up to a $60 million company.

Other board members have experience with fast-moving consumer goods companies, including corporates; the overall impression is that the management has its roots firmly at the coalface of the travel industry but the managerial depth and experience to oversee much more growth yet is certainly in place should the company choose to accelerate its plans.

International Orientation

From a UK-only start in 1999 the company now operates in 11 countries throughout Europe, and as this book went to press the French operation had taken its place as one of the top two travel companies in the country. An Italian operation will follow although the company is not publicizing its plans in that area just yet.

One area to which it won't be moving is the US; there are too many good operators out there already and the growth potential in Europe is huge. Figures from Jupiter Research and others point to the European travel market being worth between $18-$20 billion per annum before long, so it can be seen that it is content with its European markets.

Its competition will undoubtedly grow in significance, but ebookers looks well placed to retain an excellent market share and even to expand the market. Its stated ambition is to be number one or two in every territory in which it operates, and it is on the way to achieving this aim in most of them; its approach to marketing and sheer passion for matching people with the right travel arrangements should ensure its continued success.

etribes™

etribes is a company based on a simple yet powerful vision, as seen by chief executive Simon Grice when working on an Internet project in 1990. This was when he was posted to Cern, the research centre in Switzerland, at the inception of what became the World Wide Web. His idea was that the technology should enable massive amounts of collaboration, which simply wasn't happening at the time; setting up Internet communities became a natural extension of this.

Scorecard:

Innovation	★★★★★
Flexibility	★★★★★
Human resources	★★★★
Growth markets	★★★★
Quality of management	★★★★
International orientation	★★★★

Biggest plus:
The company's clear commitment to a particular vision.

Biggest minus:
The concept of what etribes is doing has yet to take off in a major way, although given the speed at which the Net is moving this may change by the time this book is published.

etribes
22 Old Steine
Brighton BN1 1EL
Tel: 01273 648378
website: www.etribes.co.uk

etribes

The Business

etribes is a company that creates online communities for voluntary and commercial organizations – or rather it harnesses communities that are already there and which don't necessarily realize that they are communities as such. More on that under the 'innovation' section. The business is privately owned with chief executive Simon Grice as the majority shareholder. It is a geographically disparate organization that is results-focused rather than geared towards any single narrow product offering.

Innovation

The idea of a Web community is one that has yet to be explored in any depth in the commercial world, but a number of voluntary and corporate clients have already found it to be well worth investigating. The notion is to take the corporate website a stage further by encouraging individuals who log on to become part of the site's 'community', whether through a discussion board or other means.

It's simple to add a discussion board to a site, and etribes use commoditized software to do this – it doesn't make its own. Instead it offers a consultancy service to corporates wanting to extend their Web presence. The approach is phased so that the company's needs are addressed first; a bulletin board approach might not suit the client, or the client may not have a particular objective in mind for its website and a spot of consultancy can help to crystallize this. The overall aim is to get people feeling like part of an online community, whether this is on a company's internal intranet or externally as a customer or supporter.

If this sounds a little theoretical then that's because it's very new; there are examples of it happening, however. One leading travel agency wanted to develop a community for travellers to exchange information about holidays, and etribes set this up. The effect commercially is that customers recommend different holiday deals to each other, while the side benefits include the ability to be proactive if someone raises a negative point that the company would want to address.

etribes works to the same ethos internally. Its team of employees is very much a virtual one, there are no centralized office premises – most of its business happens over the Internet, although Grice is keen to stress that it's wrong to use the Net as a substitute for contact.

The overall objective is to make people feel increasingly part of a company; to increase the said company's trading and awareness, and to create a feeling of stakeholdership as a result.

Flexibility

The aforementioned virtual nature of the working groups means that etribes is one of the most flexible companies in the UK. If it needs to expand its staff by 50 per cent in a year then that's fine, there are no concerns about premises to address; conversely, should it need to reduce its staff, there will be no wasted space. It doesn't count hosting or buying hardware as a core activity so the opportunity to be as light on its feet as possible is considerable – you could argue that at any stage, the company will be all but perfectly structured around the needs of its clients. This also means people can be contacted and active wherever they are. Grice points to a recent occasion where he was out of the country, but was still able to log onto the company's intranet. This meant that he could be as active as if he were in the same office as his colleagues, several of whom didn't know he wasn't in the UK.

This has knock-on effects for the staff, who find they don't have to be in an office for 9.00am on a Monday morning, they simply need to get their work in on time and serve the client's deadline. Clearly this requires self-discipline but overall it works.

Human Resources

As can be gathered from the preceding paragraph, the person who succeeds in etribes will be flexible in the extreme and able to work on their own initiative and unsupervised. They will be goal-driven rather than tied to specific working hours and routines, which might sound like a piece of heaven to a lot of people but which actually requires particular qualities that are not all that common.

Prospective employees should thrive in a start-up environment and will need to buy into the vision that drives the company forward. Those enjoying a rigid hierarchical management structure will not enjoy working for etribes. Those who want to own a part, and be a part of a company with serious vision about how the Internet can operate will do well.

Growth Markets

The business model as applied by etribes could apply to any niche in which people are likely to gather on the Internet. In order to grow initially, however, it has targeted two specific sectors: the corporate travel, retail and publishing industries and voluntary organizations.

Even in the voluntary sector, however, it is sticking with the larger organizations – in order to make the service worthwhile there needs to be a critical mass of potential community members who will be likely to participate. The voluntary sector is a good prospect because its participants are by default motivated to contribute something without any immediate material reward, and will enjoy finding like-minded people electronically.

Other than ad-hoc markets etribes is actively looking at the recruitment sector, in which candidates will certainly be eager to participate and present themselves as suitable employees for companies. Outside this there is going to be a service called communitybuilder™, which is effectively a shrinkwrapped version of the full service. This will be offered as an Application Service Provider service, in which smaller voluntary organizations and companies can hire some time and space on a server and set their own online community up.

Quality of Management

Grice is aware of the need to develop a strong business management ethic and plans to follow the example he set himself in a previous business by employing a business-oriented manager to handle the more commercial side of the organization. He is the first to admit that the person with the initial vision and inspiration to grow a company from nothing is not necessarily the right person to run it once it's established and becomes a more day-to-day affair. Nor does he underestimate the difficulty of finding someone who not only has the right managerial skills but who will readily accept the decentralized, premises-less foundation on which the company has been built.

Grice's own managerial background should be taken into account when evaluating the company; he has owned and sold two companies previously, one of which was a Web consultancy, and both are running profitably at the moment. Combined with his depth of experience in the Internet at the outset – he worked with the people who invented the World Wide Web – a company in which he plans to make his long-term home should be fascinating to watch.

International Orientation

Much has been made in the past of the international scope of the Internet – anyone can communicate with anyone else for the price of a local call (or less if they're unmetered). However, for the moment etribes proposes to focus its efforts on the UK.

There are a number of reasons for this. First there are the logistics – etribes is a small company and a new one, and has no desire to overstretch itself. Second there are the marketing issues, which also relate to overreaching– from every point of view the single-country model seems the best.

It is also unrealistic, though, to suggest that the corporates served by the company will have operations in only one geographical area, so the chances are very good that end users from elsewhere in Europe already contribute to the communities that have been established. It follows logically that the client companies will want to replicate the etribes model, if successful, elsewhere in their international operations. So regardless of the company's intentions to stay focused on the UK, the pressure to expand will already be growing on the client side – and by the time it becomes unavoidable, Grice will be ready with his business manager to grow etribes in whichever manner is appropriate.

every_
woman.com

Launched in September 1999 by Karen Gill and Maxine Benson, Everywoman.co.uk was the first UK site designed specifically for women, providing information on home and small business issues and discussion forums where women can meet online. Using its established community as a springboard, the company is now moving beyond basic Web publishing to offer flexible work opportunities to women and a range of outsourced services to companies through a new venture called Everywoman Workforce. Based in Richmond, Surrey, the company has a small full-time team and is privately funded.

Scorecard:

Innovation	★★★★
Flexibility	★★★
Human resources	★★★
Growth markets	★★★
Quality of management	★★
International orientation	★

Biggest plus:
Flexible work from home.

Biggest minus:
Working with minimum human contact.

Everywoman Limited
15 Little Green
Richmond
Surrey TW9 1QH
Tel: 020 8407 3746
Fax: 020 8407 3738
website: www.everywoman.com and www.everywoman.co.uk

Everywoman Limited

The Business

Launched in September 1999 by Karen Gill and Maxine Benson, every-woman.co.uk was the first UK site designed specifically with women in mind. Providing content and discussion forums on home and business issues, the site has established a strong community of around 20,000 regular visitors a month, with initial revenues mainly coming from sponsorship. Feedback from the Everywoman community has indicated that opportunities for flexible work were one of women's top requirements, and provided the inspiration for the next phase in the company's evolution – Everywoman Workforce, an outsourcing venture that will draw on the skills of the existing community to carry out Web-related work such as content management, indexing, market intelligence and business research. Currently privately funded, the company is now looking for external investment in order to develop its growth plans.

Innovation

Everywoman's breakthrough has been to spot the potential for transforming its online community into a flexible workforce – a move that could have benefits for both their members, who want flexible work, and customers who want projects delivered quickly and cost-effectively. The community's reaction to a pilot project was highly positive, with 500 members volunteering to get involved in the space of 24 hours.

Innovative technology is, however, the other factor in the equation, providing the tools for transforming its online community into a viable workforce. To carry off the difficult feat of managing a remote and highly distributed workforce, Everywoman plans to use The WorkCenter™ community management software developed in the US by technology partner Ktopia. Ktopia has already launched a virtual workforce of its own in the US but Everywoman has an exclusive licence to use WorkCenter™ in the UK, which it hopes will provide a competitive edge when it launches its outsourcing service later this year.

Everywoman has to-date spent little on marketing. To market the outsourcing service, the directors want to direct business connections and contacts made through partnerships and alliances – such as those with IBM and Egg, its online banking partner – rather than by a heavy marketing spend. IBM is one of Everywoman's sponsors and the alliance has already proved fruitful in raising the profile of the site.

For example, the two companies have co-hosted a conference where the directors spoke on issues to do with working women.

Flexibility

With the launch of Everywoman Workforce in the spring, the company is poised to make a radical change in the way it operates, from content provider to service provider. Technology is the enabling factor that will make this possible. Its online discussion groups enabled it to build up a community of around 20,000 regular visitors, and by tracking visitors' behaviour on the site and listening to online discussions, the directors have been able to build up a clear picture of their interests and capabilities.

In adapting to change, the company is also helped by the fact that it currently has a very small permanent team. Other activities are contracted out to partner organizations, making it easy to ramp capacity up and down as needs change. For example, its website development is carried out by Red Square Fusion, whose premises Everywoman operates out of and which is a shareholder of the company.

Being a small company can, however, also have its downsides when bidding for large projects. To help it move into new markets, Everywoman is seeking strategic partners, possibly from the content management, online categorization, or outsourcing arena.

Human Resources

With a small core team, Everywoman has not, until now, had to deal with much in the way of human resources issues. This will change as its outsourcing venture gets underway. Its founders will face the tricky task of managing a large virtual team of home workers, most of whom they will probably never meet.

The company's technology platform will enable it to keep track of how quickly, efficiently and accurately its remote workforce is performing, but the founders are also acutely aware of the need to provide positive motivation and a sense of belonging to the company. In addition to monitoring performance, the founders intend to provide incentives and community-based recreational activities as well as integrated community tools, such as virtual help desks, bulletin and chat boards. The company also has two years experience of running a successful electronic community, and this community will provide members of the virtual team with a channel for feedback.

The long-term plan is to extend the virtual workforce to include other groups of people with a strong requirement for flexible working, such as the older/retired and student community. As the workforce grows, Everywoman intends to build sub-groups of people with specific vertical market skills.

Growth Markets

With even major Internet companies facing problems selling ad space, it's timely that Everywoman has decided to move away from an ad- and sponsorship-based revenue model towards using the Web to sell services. Once its pilots have been completed, Everywoman's next step will be to go out and look for full-scale projects for community members to take on.

Market estimates suggest that there should be plenty of work out there. The electronic content space already accounts for 20 per cent, and growing, of an outsourcing market worth around £13bn.

In competing for work in this area, speed and quality will be Everywoman's main differentiator. Having access to a large virtual workforce should enable it to use volume to tackle major projects quickly and give it spare capacity to apply stringent quality controls.

Meanwhile the founders are also looking to grow the Everywoman community by expanding into other groups with a need for flexible work from home, giving the company the critical mass to take on seriously large projects.

Quality of Management

Founders and joint managing directors Karen Gill and Maxine Benson came to the Web with a strong general business background. Gill spent 15 years in sales and marketing with Inter-Continental Hotels and Resorts while Benson worked for several years in the airline industry before moving into film casting. They are backed up by non-executive director John Trewhitt, a former investment banker with Prudential Securities in New York and London and CEO of Dutch ISP EuroNet Internet, now part of France Telecom's Wanadoo operation.

The directors' business background combined with common sense have encouraged them to take a slow but steady approach to growing their company, keeping advertising spend to a minimum and listening carefully to feedback from their members in deciding on their next step. Outsourcing key operations to business partners has enabled them to keep fixed costs to a minimum.

Everywoman's new business direction shows that the directors have also been keeping a careful eye on trends in the market: the decision to pursue a business model based on services rather than ad and sponsorship revenue is timely with market research showing many Internet companies struggling to fill their ad space. If it takes off, the services business should provide higher profit margins and reduced competition.

The directors recognize, however, that to compete effectively in the outsourcing area, they will need to take on additional staff to deal with client management and this is one of the areas that would be addressed by additional funding.

International Orientation

Currently the company's focus is in the UK where around 80 per cent of the existing Everywoman community comes from. But because the company is building up a virtual workforce that can take on projects through the Internet, the directors intend to look for work throughout Europe and beyond. This would probably happen through partner organizations in the local countries, who would provide knowledge of the local business community and, of course, the language.

Expedia:co.uk
Hands on travel for hands on people.

Expedia is one of the top five travel agents in the world, on or offline. Currently with a presence in the US, Canada, UK and Germany, Expedia was launched by Microsoft in October 1996, representing the first foray into the online travel arena by a major technology player. A specially-tailored site for the UK market – Expedia.co.uk – was introduced by Microsoft's consumer Internet service MSN in November 1998 and is now the number one online travel agent in the UK. Expedia.co.uk gives customers the choice and control to easily plan their travel by allowing them access to the same information as a high street travel agent.

Scorecard:

Innovation	★★★★★
Flexibility	★★★★
Human resources	★★★★
Growth markets	★★★★
Quality of management	★★★★
International orientation	★★★★

Biggest plus:
Hitting the right market at the right time with the right products appropriate to customer needs.

Biggest minus:
Being two years behind the US parent's technology, having to bide time until the local market catches up.

Expedia.co.uk
Microsoft House
10 Great Pulteney Street
London W1R 3DG
Tel: 020 7434 6500
website: www.expedia.co.uk

Expedia.co.uk

The Business

Expedia.co.uk is the number one online travel agent in the UK. Born on 12 November 1998, the site's specially-tailored service was introduced by Microsoft's consumer Internet service MSN after several years of development. Expedia debuted on the Internet with its US-based site Expedia.com on 22 October 1996. Expedia.co.uk gives customers the choice and control to plan their travel by allowing access to the same information as a high street travel agent. Globally, Expedia is one of the top ten travel agents, on or offline. In the financial year ending June 2000, Expedia Inc achieved gross bookings of $1.325 billion for its four sites in the US, Canada, UK and Germany.

Innovation

Expedia.co.uk's managing director James Vaile says, 'In modern travel history, there have been three defining moments: the development of the jet engine, which triggered the mass movement of people; worldwide computerized booking engines, allowing the rapid exchange of information; and the Internet, which puts ordinary people in control of their travel arrangements for the first time.'

Analysts maintain that the UK – one of the key European travel markets – is ready to embrace travel e-commerce with 63 per cent of consumers believing the Internet will become the dominant technology for booking holidays within five years (source: PhoCusWright: *The European Online Travel Marketplace 2000–2002*). 'In this environment we've established ourselves as the number one full service online travel company in the UK,' says Vaile. According to analysts at Gartner Group, the online bookings market was worth $280 million in 1999 and is expected to reach $3.35 billion by 2003.

'We give customers access to the site without having to register,' says Vaile. 'Research by Jupiter Communications showed 40 per cent of online users were put off by site registration. We led the online travel industry in removing the need for customers to input their personal details before browsing the site.' Users have the choice of booking from 450 airlines, over 81,000 accommodation options with more than 4 million hotel rooms, the top 20 UK tour operators' package deals, specialist skiing, golf and adventure holidays or car rental from all the major agencies. The company's market position enables Expedia to negotiate significant exclusive discounts on accommodation and travel.

'We provide more than just tickets,' says Vaile. 'The site includes related services such as photo processing, insurance and travel goods, in-depth destination guides and maps, travel information service with free online newsletter, plus thousands of links to relevant websites.'

Flexibility

Expedia.co.uk has built up a reputation for excellence of technology and consumer service, as a sizeable tally of awards testifies, eg it was the winner of best travel site, *Future* Internet Publishing Awards 2000; best travel information service, *Telegraph* Travel Awards ceremony October 2000; and best online travel site, *New Media Age* Awards 1999 and 2000. It had already been voted Europe's best travel site in Forrester Research's 'The best of Europe's e-commerce' analysis in August 1999.

'Last December we became the first UK full service online travel company to launch an integrated wireless travel information product for both Personal Digital Assistants – PDAs – and WAP phones, with the announcement of Expedia To Go,' says Vaile.

Capital for development and marketing has roots in Microsoft spinning off some 17 per cent of Expedia Inc – Expedia.co.uk's parent group – for £78.2 million. Expedia Inc was floated on the Nasdaq stock exchange on 10 November 1999. 'Our marketing strategy is to embrace advertising, PR, sponsorship and online marketing,' says Vaile. The company became the first online travel company to be promoted on UK television when it launched a £4 million integrated advertising campaign covering press, online advertising and PR (the theme being 'hands on travel for hands on people').

'In January 2001, our second TV and poster brand campaign rolled out across TV, outdoor sites, press and online,' says Vaile. 'The result (within days) was record sales and visits to the site. With the strapline "When it comes to travel we've thought of everything – have you?" the campaign communicates how we take care of every element of an individual's travel arrangements including flights, hotel and car hire bookings, and valuable information about the destination. That's every element of travel arrangements in one place to enable the customer to design the trip of their choice.'

Human Resources

Since 1998, Expedia.co.uk has grown from three to twenty-five staff. 'The key challenge was to ensure the cultural aspects of Microsoft as a good employer were transmitted across to Expedia. We wanted the best qualities plus we wanted to create a new culture,' says Vaile. 'Instead of management telling the workers our vision, we wanted buy-in from everyone.' Workshops produced a list of seven values that relate what Expedia means internally and how its look-and-feel is purveyed externally: smart, fun, passion, customers, innovation, people and technology (in no priority). 'The values feed the vision which is delivering the world to our customers,' says Vaile. 'That vision is communicated, referred to and identified as critical for every decision or roadblock that any staff come across.'

Microsoft's tough recruitment process – an earmarked best practice – has been grafted into Expedia.co.uk. A third-party recruitment company filters personnel prior to seven one-hour interviews. 'It's paramount that the skill-set and cultural fit is right – we're living history in the making,' says Vaile. To date no full-time employee has left the company.

Growth Markets

Movements in Europe can be expected. 'The most important strategy for us to follow is that we have to make sure we enter the right markets at the right time with the right and relevant products,' says Vaile. 'A competitor blanket-marketed to 11 countries in Europe and is nowhere near being ready to operate. That's not the way we do things.'

'Having our Microsoft heritage, we need to ratify USPs within each market. We delayed launching in the UK for two years to address market-specific functions – that is, the integration of published air fares and those fares distributed to travel agencies,' says Vaile. 'There was much to do. It was a complex operation but our strengths were our technology base and Microsoft parentage.'

Three parameters control the next market roll-out: Internet penetration, online consumers willing to purchase online, and strong travel habits. 'We need all three to be met, not just one,' says Vaile. 'The next markets we're looking at are the Nordic block and France, with Spain and Italy following.'

By 2003 Vaile believes European markets as a collective will be larger than the US over three different platforms: web, wireless and interactive digital TV. The latter is seen as a perfect vehicle for package holidays (some 50 per cent of sales in the UK and similarly across Europe) – and a good mass market medium to reach the package holiday traveller.

Quality of Management

Overall responsibility for the management of the business including marketing, sales, supplier relationships and fulfilment operations devolves to Vaile, who plays a key role in promoting the company's successful e-travel model. 'I believe business needs to be exciting and fun, and online travel should be a product at the cutting edge of today's business world.'

The underlying success and management style within the Expedia organization has much to do with Microsoft's disciplines. Everyone is encouraged to voice an opinion, challenge and debate. There's a flat structure – no management hierarchy as in the old economy. 'The whole empowerment of each employee through ownership speaks volumes through the focus on the success of Expedia.'

Every full-time employee receives a bundle of options taking four to five years to vest at six-monthly periods. Remuneration packages are made up of salary (commensurate with IT industry standards), car allowance, the options package at sign-on and the Employee Stock Purchase Plan (ESPP), which is based on salary sacrifice of one to ten per cent (up to the individual), where the company deducts the percentage from the monthly pay packet and every six months purchases stock in Expedia less 15 per cent of the market value (ie a guaranteed 15 per cent earner). There are twice yearly cash and option bonus allocations. Annual salary reviews and bonuses are performance-based, with employees measured against a strict set of objectives. Rounding off the package are pension, mobile phones, health club membership and private health insurance.

International Orientation

The company is global and will only expand into fresh territory when the market is right, at the right time with the right and relevant products. Independent research (source: MMXI) showed 365,000 unique users accessed Expedia.co.uk from home PCs in January 2001, but with the inclusion of business users, it is calculated that the site has approximately three times the MMXI numbers in unique visitors per month.

Being an Internet company, property is not a key issue. The Seattle HQ has its own building. The German and UK offices are, as subsidiaries of Microsoft (it owns 70 per cent of the business), located in Microsoft properties. As roll-out proceeds across Europe, Expedia will move to its own premises. 'It's a twilight period,' says Vaile. 'Microsoft offers us as much support as possible with its facilities. Everything works well for both of us.' While overall, as the vision goes, the customer gets the world.

EXPOCENTRIC.PLC

Expocentric is a technology-based application service providing commercial 3D interactive exhibition halls that can be accessed 24 hours a day. The business was launched in September 1999 and floated on the London Stock Exchange in November 2000, raising £40 million from investors. It employs 65 people in the UK and US.

Scorecard:

Innovation	★★★★★
Flexibility	★★★★★
Human resources	★★★★
Growth markets	★★★★
Quality of management	★★★★★
International orientation	★★★★

Biggest plus:
Being the first with an innovative service.

Biggest minus:
Initial scepticism of clients.

Expocentric plc
1100 Parkway
Solent Business Park
Whiteley
Fareham
Hampshire PO15 7AB
Tel: 01489 611810
Fax: 01489 611728
website: www.expocentric.com

Expocentric plc

The Business

Expocentric's founder and CEO, Stephen Moore, hit on the idea for virtual exhibitions while running a company responsible for stand design and construction. Struck by the high level of investment needed for a temporary structure, he saw the Internet as a vehicle for reducing costs and improving the quality of business information.

In February 1999, Moore began talking to potential partners about developing technology for the proposition and by July had assembled a core management team. Seed financing of £5 million was raised, chiefly for product development, with some investment from partners like Oracle and Superscape. A further £14 million was raised through a private placement ahead of an IPO which was two and a half times oversubscribed.

Among the virtual exhibitions hosted so far are Live 2000 at Earls Court, Gitex 2000 in Dubai and Broadband Communications Europe in Olympia, London. In addition, the company has recently signed an agreement with the NEC in Birmingham to link its technology with this leading UK venue.

Innovation

A virtual exhibition operates on the same principle as its real-life counterpart, being a demonstration of all that is new in products and services in a given industry sector. But the technology that powers it gives it a number of advantages.

For organizers and exhibitors it is a new and extremely precise marketing tool. Visitor details are collected in the registration process so their movements around the exhibition can be tracked. Whenever a visitor moves onto a stand, the database 'underneath' records every action they take: what products were viewed, for how long and in what detail. And by aggregating data for all those 'e-ttending' an event, Expocentric can run concurrent reports about the volume and profile of visitors to each stand – useful data for the show organiser. Virtual exhibitions can also be marketed relatively inexpensively within the promotional material for their real-life counterparts.

For customers it is a business information marketing tool that improves access to industry information by removing location obstacles and by extending the duration of an event (virtual exhibitions normally run for up to two months rather than the typical three-day trade shows).

Underpinning the proposition's credibility is the technology used to create a realistic approximation of an offline event. Participating exhibitors have two options for stand construction. They can buy a ready-built stand from Expocentric and design a look for it by utilizing its Stand Wizard software. Alternatively, they can purchase stand space on which a stand in a size or shape of their choice will be constructed. Here again, Expocentric will arrange for stand contractors to carry out the task. Stand assistants can serve as an interface between visitors and exhibitor. The planned introduction of voice technology will further enhance this feature.

Flexibility

Expocentric had to be quick to market with its product in order to pre-empt any similar move by exhibition organizers. Prior to launch there was an awareness that venues were exploring ways to harness the Internet – even if many of them had got no further than offering an online registration facility for the exhibitions.

The strength of the proposition was persuasive in itself and licensing agreements with a number of key technology providers were struck. The site's database, tracking tools and search engine capability are all powered by Oracle. Superscape provides high-quality 3D visuals that are relatively quick to download. A multi-user chat facility was created by blaxxun technology (the interaction between visitors it enables is something that has traditionally been confined to the gaming world). Other key partners are Sun Microsystems (hardware) and Exodus (secure data hosting).

Significant angel investment in the start-up afforded a choice between a fast-track and a conservative business plan. Given the strength of the technology at the company's disposal, there was an initial belief that the accelerated route would prevail. However, initial projections were revised after slower than envisaged initial take-up and profitability is not now anticipated until late 2002 or early 2003.

That there was more scepticism among potential clients than anticipated was not due to failings in the technology. Rather it was a reflection of the conservative nature of some sections of the exhibitions industry. Additional sales and marketing support was provided and case studies were made available to demonstrate the platform's functionality. It also built more flexibility into methods of payment. Needless to say, this approach was dictated by the need to build long-lasting business relationships.

Human Resources

While Expocentric is a fast-moving and often demanding place to work, its leaders adhere firmly to the principle that it must remain fun and enjoyable. This has remained the case throughout the short life of the business. Employees are stimulated in their work and there is a strong collegiate atmosphere – forged, in part, by the effort expended in preparing for the IPO. Budding recruits must share their belief in the uniqueness of the product and want to help push it far and wide into the marketplace. The company was notable in the sector in appointing a human resources director within its first months of development.

Naturally, processes have had to be refined as Expocentric has grown from a small private company to medium-size plc. From the outset, there were very formal processes in place for product development and this approach has been extended to further strengthen communication channels between component business areas.

Growth Markets

Income from virtual stand space sold to exhibitors is key revenue to the company and is split with event organizers.

Sponsorship and advertising within the virtual exhibitions are another area of growth. But the number of banner ads and logo placements will always be managed so as not to detract heavily from content.

There are also e-commerce opportunities for the exhibitors, who can retail products directly from their stands and for whom links to company websites can be carried.

Future revenues can be generated from registrations at each show. A nominal fee gives businesses or individuals access for the duration of the event – by giving them a user name and password, they are effectively subscribers. The size of the fee is influenced by the overall quality of exhibition content.

Though conscious that its high-performance technology will not suit every sector, the company has already found some unlikely markets for example, in agriculture. The geographic remoteness of many farmers, and the need to stay close to their business, makes virtual exhibitions the ideal place to order seed and other farm products.

Upcoming product development spend will be targeted at provision of a bolt-on conferencing solution which will function along similar lines.

In addition, the company is piloting a scheme funded by the Department for Education and Employment to encourage students to choose the UK for their university education. The pilot involves paralleling a series of British Council Exhibitions in China – the Web extends the British Council's reach throughout this huge land mass.

Quality of Management

Though its strong technology is one reason why the business has proved attractive to investors, the credibility of the brand arises in large part from its leadership. Many among the top tier of management have a background in the exhibitions industry and their knowledge has served to leverage Expocentric into markets ahead of competitors who may have access to the right technology but have no real understanding of the industry.

Alongside the entrepreneurial skills of Stephen Moore, the team includes COO Hugh Scrimgeour, previously chairman and managing director of Earls Court and Olympia Limited, London's leading exhibition business. Terry Golding, the non-executive chairman, was formerly chief executive of the NEC in Birmingham, while another board member is Robin Hicks, who was a show director at Earls Court Olympia, including the Royal Smithfield Show.

Shortly after flotation and the appointment of a plc board the company announced it had entered into a co-operation agreement to develop virtual shows for exhibitions at the NEC – the UK's largest venue and the seventh largest exhibition area in Europe.

Despite the extra capitalization the IPO brought, operating costs did not rise significantly. Neither the marketing budget or product development were greatly increased and progress towards short, medium and long-term objectives is measured on a quarterly basis.

International Orientation

The strong corporate image Expocentric has built up means that brand recognition in non-domestic markets is on the increase. Key overseas growth areas are the US, the Middle East and the Asia Pacific region. A US subsidiary, Expocentric Inc, was established in New Jersey in November 2000 and comprises a sales and marketing team and a small online team to ensure top-quality digital delivery of shows. Elsewhere there is an agreement with a semi-governmental organization in France to help promote hosted shows to that market.

Because the main route for online exhibition visitors is via the show sites themselves, Expocentric sees little value in building separate sites for foreign markets. Each virtual show is marketed via the organizer and exhibitor and can also be accessed directly from the company's own website.

ɛyɛst⟲rm

www.eyestorm.com

---

eyestorm is an online art forum selling limited edition photography and art by established artists to a global market. Current artists include Damien Hirst, David Hockney and Marc Quinn. Founded by two former gallery owners, the London-based business launched in December 1999, and employs 65 people in the UK and four in New York. The website receives 90,000 unique viewers a month. After eight months trading revenue was into seven figures.

Scorecard:

Innovation	★★★★★
Flexibility	★★★★★
Human resources	★★★★
Growth markets	★★★★
Quality of management	★★★★★
International orientation	★★★★★

Biggest plus:
Strong business continued to attract confidence in spite of the downturn in dot-coms.

Biggest minus:
Selling luxury items may leave the company vulnerable in the face of recession.

eyestorm
8 Apollo Studios
Charlton King's Road
London NW5 2SB
Tel: 020 7485 5888
Fax: 020 7485 5889
website: www.eyestorm.com

eyestorm

The Business

Eyestorm is an online art forum offering limited edition contemporary art work by established artists to a mass audience. Each print is signed by the artist and is available at a fixed price, typically in batches of several hundred. The majority of the works are photographic prints, signed by the artists in editions of 200 – 500, with a price point of around $500. Orders are processed by the company and shipped free of charge.

The concept was created by eyestorm's co-founders, David Grob and Michael Hue-Williams. Both former gallery owners, they feel the insulated and exclusive nature of the traditional art market disadvantages artists and deters many potential customers.

Together with CEO Don Smith, they found $4m backing for their plan through US venture capitalists Arts Alliance and ePartners and launched the website in December 1999. Initially offering work by 35 artists, it generated $40,000 in revenue in its first month.

In April 2000, the business sourced a further $4m from venture capitalists in South-East Asia and in August that year received $14m in third round financing from a consortium of UK and US investors, including NEA and Charles Schwab. With its existing partners increasing their investments, total financing in eyestorm, by the end of 2000, stood at $26m. The company is projected to be in profit in January 2002.

Innovation

Why did eyestorm continue to attract high levels of funding after investors went cool on e-tailers? Fundamentally, because its business model is very strong. By eliminating galleries from the process of buying and selling art, there are higher margins for artist and business alike. And by signing up each artist to exclusive deals, eyestorm ensures customers must visit one place on the Internet to buy their work.

Eyestorm has so far signed up around 80 artists, all attracted by the transparency of the process and the chance to reach a wider audience. With luminaries such as Hirst, Helmut Newton and Jeff Koons on board it can reasonably lay claim to being the premier online art forum.

The artists have been instrumental in eyestorm's own marketing strategy. By publicizing the site in newspaper interviews they have helped drive up sales far quicker than traditional advertising and in the process saved the company money. Overall, $6 million has been allocated for marketing the brand, yet so far less than a quarter of that has been spent.

Ahead of its expansion into the North American market, the company forged an off-line alliance with New York-based *Blind Spot* magazine. The influential art periodical carries eyestorm editorial and is linked to the site.

Eyestorm has also formed a partnership with The Saatchi Gallery to build a bricks and mortar extension to the gallery to house eyestorm prints commissioned from Saatchi artists. The prints will also be shown online on a special eyestorm/Saatchi microsite.

Flexibility

Eyestorm was originally conceived as a business-to-consumer model. At the time first-round financing was being sought this alone was enough for its backers, who were not even concerned that the company hadn't produced a business plan. But faced with increasing caution on the part of investors, the company began to explore new revenue streams as it sought further capitalization.

Today, bottom-line growth is seen as primarily driven by corporate clients and image licensing. In October 2000, the company announced a commercial partnership with Magnum, the world-renowned photographic agency. Under the terms of the three-year agreement, eyestorm will market exclusive editions of Magnum Photos' members' work and eyestorm is planning further initiatives with its partner.

According to Don Smith, eyestorm beat off competition from larger competitors because it was seen as a better cultural fit by the highly image-conscious agency. The move is also consistent with eyestorm's own strategy of marketing photography by established artists.

The company recognizes that there is a huge potential market for corporate art, and the main focus of its marketing has switched from individual purchasers to restaurants, hotels and offices. At the time of the Magnum deal, eyestorm's business-to-business activities accounted for two fifths of its revenue. By the end of 2001, this is expected to have markedly increased.

Human Resources

Eyestorm has grown quickly in a short space of time but there is still a genuinely flat structure in which managers are as accessible as anyone else. However, the 'fun and funky atmosphere', as Don Smith describes it, can be deceptive, as former employees who relaxed just a little too much found out.

He says: 'On the face of it, eyestorm's a very creative, relaxed business, but underneath everyone's pedalling like crazy. They all know what they have to do within the business and they're all a part of the business, even down to having options and shares in it.'

It sounds like a cliché, but there is a real commitment to quality service delivery on the part of employees. There has to be – after all, eyestorm markets itself as a quality brand. The customer service team answers phone calls from around the world and each member aims to respond to e-mails within three to five minutes.

'The place is buzzing from eight till midnight sometimes,' adds Don Smith. 'We'll put wine and beer in the fridge for the evening and order pizza. People don't have to be here, they're here because they want to be.'

Management aims to grow the business to be worth $500m by 2003. But to do this means hiring the right people to take it into new markets. As well having the right skills, it is vital they fit into the culture of the company. This means expansion will not be rushed.

Growth Markets

In the long-term, eyestorm intends to offer an integrated art solution for anyone interested in the art world – meaning there are a myriad of potential opportunities for growth. Consequently, the company must decide which areas are worth pursuing.

When the business launched, the art offered for sale was almost exclusively photographic, because that medium transferred best onto the site. Investment in better technology has meant a greater number of art objects have since featured. Art books, CDs and videos will all be sold in the future. There are also plans to exploit travel and accommodation opportunities surrounding the annual art exhibition calendar. And there is even the possibility of an eyestorm TV channel.

Many such suggestions come from the artists themselves, who feel involved enough with the business to want to redefine its boundaries. Behind them all is a determination to push the brand, while maintaining its association with quality.

According to Don Smith, 'The art world is still very fragmented – there's no one dominant player. But somebody will become one over the next few years and eyestorm's very well positioned because of its funding and also because of its content. We want to be to art what Nike is to sportswear.'

Quality of Management

Leaving aside the underlying strength of the business model, how do eyestorm's founders convince investors they remain the right team to establish it as a leading brand?

'The best way to do it is to execute and deliver,' says Don Smith, 'You say you're going to hit a certain sales target or establish a certain deal – then you deliver it. And back it up. When you're going into new areas as we are, you support it with research and a business plan.'

This principle has been adhered to since the site launch, when the first set of sales targets were exceeded. At each new stage in strategy, money is spent on researching and trialling the facility to see how much revenue it generates. If it meets expectations more funds will be released; if not it will be abandoned.

It is also worth mentioning that the company deliberately targeted investors who were known to have an avowed personal interest in art. Dick Kramlich, co-founder and general partner of NEA, and Charles Schwab fall into this category. Both sit on eyestorm's board, but although US-based they are in no way remote from its day-to-day operations. Very informal lines of communication allow for regular exchanges of information on strategy between the key stakeholders in the business. Ironically, the real challenge to management has been to maintain focus and resist the temptation to be profligate.

International Orientation

From its inception, eyestorm has had a strategy to become a global brand and no better has this been demonstrated in its approach to its own capitalization. After its first round of financing, it looked for venture capitalists in the Far East: Vertex is backed by Singapore Technologies, which has a strong presence in South-East Asia. As well as providing the initial infrastructure for the site planned for early 2001, its local market knowledge will inform eyestorm's decision-making on content, distribution and marketing strategy for that continent.

North America is the first target, however. A New York office has already been established and there is an artist liaison representative in Los Angeles. And because it is well-funded, eyestorm does not need to cut corners. Its research into site content found that whereas European visitors were happy to spend time browsing, Americans wanted something that was much easier to navigate. Such attention to detail is deemed vital for successful foreign market penetration.

Don Smith says, 'We still want to run overall strategy centrally (from the UK), but execution needs to be local. You need local market awareness and so we must have people on the ground.' As an illustration of this, two thirds of site traffic is North American compared to a quarter European, yet those who make purchases online are overwhelmingly European.

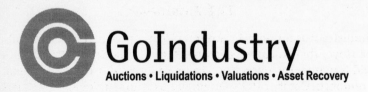

GoIndustry

Auctions • Liquidations • Valuations • Asset Recovery

GoIndustry, an industrial asset recovery service provider for corporations world-wide, provides its clients with valuation, auction and asset disposal services. Through its acquisition strategy and its industry leading online trading platform www.goindustry.com, GoIndustry has merged old and new economies to form a single, powerful organization. The company's estimated turnover for 2001 is £14m, this is an increase from £4.6 m for 2000. In the UK it employs a workforce of 40, and world-wide it has a staff in excess of 100. It is a private business, whose mother company is GoIndustry AG, which has its head office in Munich, Germany.

Scorecard:

Innovation	★★★★★
Flexibility	★★★★★
Human resources	★★★★
Growth markets	★★★★
Quality of management	★★★★
International orientation	★★★★★

Biggest plus:

Its commitment to expansion while at the same time not losing sight of its core values.

Biggest minus:

The challenging targets the company has set itself.

GoIndustry Limited
5 Waterside
44/48 Wharf Road
London N1 7UX
Tel: 020 7766 3900
Fax: 020 7566 3929
website: www.goindustry.com

GoIndustry Limited

The Business

GoIndustry was founded by Andrew Heath, the chief executive officer, Alex Hoye, the executive vice president of product development, and David Nahama, the executive vice president of business development, in London, in October 1999. Originally it set up as a global online market-place for trading industrial equipment, after the founders spotted inefficiencies in the existing market and realized that their company could bring together an unprecedented number of buyers and sellers, regardless of geographical location or language. It is now a leading industrial auctioneer having acquired a number of offline auction houses. At launch, it received an investment of $10 million from venture capitalist Atlas Venture, followed by a successful second round funding from Internet Capital Group (ICG) and Atlas Venture in May 2000.

Innovation

Plugging into the Internet, GoIndustry launched the www.goindustry.-com platform that offers surplus products from the fields of metal working, machine tools, plastics and rubber processing, computers and office automation. On top of this, the platform also offers woodworking materials, materials for handling equipment, construction machinery, food and packaging equipment, filling technology, office equipment and entire plants. This extensive range of products has attracted more than 8,000 registered buyers and sellers to the site. But GoIndustry is now much more than simply an online auctioneer, acquiring bricks and mortar auction houses. With the auction house acquisition strategy and its online trading platform, the company is merging old- and new-economy firms, thus offering its customers a comprehensive service encompassing all the fields of industrial asset purchase. This distinguishes it from its competitors, according to Steve Flavell, executive vice president of international markets.

'When we went to corporations and leasing companies we found they wanted a complete service offering, so this is what we decided to give them,' he says. The complete service, Flavell describes, includes identifying recoverable industrial goods for customers, stock and inventory taking, evaluations, recommendations of sales format, and execution of sale. The business is investing in its customer relationship management (CRM) capabilities, and uses extensive direct marketing, such as telemarketing, direct mail/fax/e-mail, plus trade press advertising, national press and PR. As part of its global expansion, GoIndustry also uses trade fairs. The company has also been featured on television, notably Channel 4, in December 2000, when it was identified as successfully marrying online technologies with old-economy business to create a more efficient business model. Strategic partnerships include working with VR Leasing, the second largest leasing company in Germany, giving it access to massive supply of modern used machines from VR Leasing's VR machinery division.

Flexibility

GoIndustry may have started on the back of the Internet's evolution as a business-to-business medium, where firms could use the technology to boost efficiencies in their transactions but it has refused to stand still. The company has built up its position as Europe's leading industrial auctioneer by setting up operations across the Continent. Spearheading this drive was the company's acquisition of businesses whose markets tied in with GoIndustry's own. In Germany, where the firm is now headquartered, it brought Karner & Co AG, one of Europe's leading old economy industrial asset appraisal and auction companies, into the newly created GoIndustry Group, in October 2000. This was followed by Plohmann, a North German auction house, which was integrated with the group in January 2001, and then Belgian auction house Appelboom. Further to this it has signed an alliance with masActivo, a similar venture serving the Latin American market. In all, the group has offices in the UK, France, Austria, Belgium, Spain, Norway, Turkey and Poland. The expansion of the business has seen it acquire registered buyers and sellers from around the world, and provided it with a workforce of more than 100. In an attempt to maintain its core value of customer focus, the business created country-specific key account managers, and ensured buyers were supported by international industry experts. Unlike purely old-economy businesses, GoIndustry has had the benefit of a new economy heritage which has brought with it a dynamism and flexibility that can be seen in its transition to a company that has successfully merged old and new economies. The company has grown quickly and Flavell recognizes that this has brought challenges with it, such as maintaining the same ethos first created when the company was set up in 1999.

Human Resources

Flavell says there is a common link between all employees at GoIndustry despite them being scattered around the globe, having differing native languages and coming from different backgrounds. The link, he says, is that they all reflect the drive seen in the company's founders.

Colleague Andrea Moretti, vice president of human resources, describes each employee as a valued team member.

'There were more than 26 nationalities represented in the first 100 people the company employed, representing a huge mixture of ages and past experiences,' he says.

'Furthermore, as our service of creating a liquid marketplace is the culmination of everyone's effort, there is a high acceptance that everyone represents a different and vital piece of the puzzle.'

Moretti goes on to say every team member owns stock options for at least 10 per cent of his/her compensation and the company is pragmatic and forward thinking in its work practices, allowing part-time home-based work for mothers.

Growth Markets

For GoIndustry playing a greater part in the flow of surplus business and industrial equipment from Europe to the rest of the world is what it is bidding for. Executive vice president of international markets, Steve Flavell says this year the key strategic areas the company wants to advance into are Central Europe, Africa, India, parts of the Middle East and Asia. But he adds the firm will not be spreading itself too thinly: 'We have decided we will not stretch ourselves too much say in Asia for instance.'

The company is already operating in Poland and India, but Flavell is working towards setting up offices in Russia, Iran, India and Egypt.

'These are all very good markets for us, for flows of equipment that are originally from Europe. Trading surplus equipment to these countries is very attractive to European businesses' he says.

As complete customer focus is a core value of the company, each new office that is opened abroad is strongly linked with its local community. This goes right down to it being staffed with local people, who have developed connections with industry and government in the area.

'It's the case that if you want to the business to work you need good local customer service,' he says.

Quality of Management

The company says that when it was small with a staff of less than 40 it was easy to keep the human touch in its management. But Andrea Moretti, vice president of human resources, says it has had to employ a number of initiatives to maintain this feeling as the firm has grown to employ a workforce of more than 100.

There are now bi-weekly office meetings and question and answer sessions with senior management. There are also pan-European team conference calls and quarterly face-to-face meetings to keep the team bonded together.

On the lighter side, there are annual strategic offsite 'get togethers' for the whole company, and the signs of hierarchy are deliberately downplayed, with minimal use of titles and the same rules on expenses for everyone, including the chief executive.

Moretti says: 'At meetings all participants are encouraged to speak, and by playing down a feeling of hierarchy we encourage team members to make contributions where appropriate.'

Each new member of staff gets an induction programme on their first week at the company, and a point is made of each of them meeting other colleagues so everyone knows who is responsible for what. Thereafter, the firm relies on staff to be proactive in asking for help and training. Highlighting team members' willingness to ask for help, Moretti says a cold calling course was arranged after a suggestion by an employee.

The company has developed an appraisal system where everyone, managers included, self-appraises themselves on 42 relevant skills and on a comparison of actual results versus their original targets. The self appraisal then forms the basis for a one on one review meeting with their superior.

Moretti believes this format provides a structure for a discussion and open feedback from the appraised and the appraiser.

International Orientation

GoIndustry's was founded as a global online marketplace making it as internationally orientated as it is possible to get. But the company has now become both a major online and offline player world-wide, its aim has been to ensure its operations are as closely linked to their local markets as possible. On top of this, it wants the people working from these satellite offices to have the same drive and determination to develop the company as its founders.

'We expect strong growth, because internationally this business is still not very developed but will be in the next few years,' says Flavell.

He points out that used machinery is very helpful for companies in foreign countries whose economies are not as well developed as those in Europe.

The fact that the company operates with an auction-based pricing model also makes it more attractive to the countries where companies have less money to spend.

Goldman Sachs

Goldman Sachs is something of an enigma among world-class finance companies – more than a century old, yet still highly flexible and receptive to new ideas. It combines an enviable brand and truly global reach with an informal structure which allows it to put together the best team for each client project. This has helped it to weather the storms and ride the trade winds better than almost any other investment bank in recent decades, and it should continue to do so in future.

Scorecard:

Innovation	★★★★
Flexibility	★★★★★
Human resources	★★★★
Growth markets	★★★★
Quality of management	★★★★
International orientation	★★★★★

Biggest plus:

A blue-chip reputation and client base, yet still flexible and open to new ideas.

Biggest minus:

It is now reaching a size where its informal, matrix-like structure will require a lot of effort to maintain.

Goldman Sachs International
Peterborough Court
133 Fleet Street
London EC4A 2BB
Tel: 020 7774 1000
Fax: 020 7774 4477
website: www.gs.com

Goldman Sachs International

The Business

Goldman Sachs is one of the world's most successful financial institutions, whose clients range from governments and multinational corporations to start-up businesses and wealthy individuals. Its main operations are investment banking (i.e. the buying and selling of companies), asset management, and trading and principal investing in equity and fixed income stocks.

Founded in New York in 1869, Goldman Sachs now has about 20,000 staff world-wide, of whom 4,300 are in Europe, with 3,500 in London. One of the last major Wall Street institutions to remain a private partnership, the firm went public in the spring of 1999. Around 70–80 per cent of its stock is owned by its own staff.

Innovation

Goldman Sachs describes itself as a 'matrix organization', where teams of experts are brought together to service particular client projects (the groups are disbanded when the project has been completed), and the sharing of knowledge and expertise are part of the culture. This is not at all typical of the traditional 'stuffy' image of a big investment bank – but then, Goldman Sachs is neither traditional nor stuffy, as evidenced by the relative lack of suits and ties at its London headquarters.

'What differentiates us is that we're a client service organization, ensuring that clients benefit from the talents of *all* our staff, not just a narrow selection of them,' says Mark Slaughter, chief operating officer of Goldman Sachs International. 'We have a teamwork culture that's real, and our structure lets us get together the right group of people and give them a free rein to service the client.'

Teams display an unusually wide range of age and seniority, and even the most senior people are very receptive to new ideas. This is helped by the firm's very flat organizational structure, and a 'collegiate' style of working. People have many contacts at Goldman Sachs offices around the world and know they can always ask their advice; failing that, they can send out a general e-mail.

'We have a culture of communication, and there's a moral imperative to respond,' says Slaughter. 'It would be totally irresponsible to have information and not share it.'

The company frequently takes people or teams 'offline' (i.e. away from revenue-earning client projects), so they can come up with innovative ideas. This could be anything from a fresh approach to financing mergers, to a project to produce electronic trading tools at the firm's technology development centre in California's Silicon Valley.

Recent specific innovations have included new ways of using securities to raise capital, better ways of using derivatives, and Financial Workbench, a software tool supplied over the Internet. Such projects often involve some of the firm's top people. 'We're prepared to give it time and give it talent,' says Alison Bott, director for human resources in Europe.

Flexibility

'Maximizing flexibility is the essence of our culture and structure,' says Slaughter. 'We're used to adapting and working quickly, because the markets change so fast that otherwise we'd miss out on business. You can't really predict changes in the financial markets because they're so fluid. All you can do is to be very flexible.'

Part of the key is to hire highly adaptable people. 'Anyone round here could do a multitude of different jobs, and they do,' says Bott. 'You get used to things being reviewed, even things you've been responsible for.'

About 200 people in Europe changed divisions last year, and a further 500 moved into or out of the European operation. Within each division, people change teams and offices frequently, but one advantage of the flexible culture is that the business can be restructured bit by bit rather than by big bang.

'We don't have to launch ourselves into a big "strategy" in order to get people to change, because we're able to change anyway,' says Bott. The most recent upheaval faced by Goldman Sachs was the flotation two years ago. This was not done to raise immediate capital, but for other reasons, such as extending ownership more widely among staff, facilitating acquisitions, and making it easier to raise cash in future, if required. There were some fears that the altered status would damage the firm's fluid culture, but they have proved groundless.

The bigger issue will be how Goldman Sachs can maintain its communicative, collegiate atmosphere during a period of such rapid growth – currently around 20 per cent a year. It is helped by its unusually low staff turnover rate (less than 10 per cent a year), which means that plenty of people 'rise through the ranks' and can pass the culture on. But the firm is also implementing more formal management and induction training to ensure that the culture and contacts are passed on.

Human Resources

The Goldman Sachs approach to human resources is to recruit the best people and provide the right environment for them to do their best work. About half the 700 new recruits in Europe each year come straight from university, the other half being more experienced people. The company prefers to promote people through the organization than bring outsiders into senior positions – doubtless partly because new-comers will not have built up the all-important network of contacts within the firm.

Once in, the careers structure is informal, with more emphasis on developing excellence than building empires. 'You don't have to have hundreds of people reporting to you to be seen as successful,' says Bott. 'You know you're doing well if you get asked to do things.'

Remuneration is largely performance-based, and Goldman Sachs's success allows it to pay very competitive rates – though it draws the line at engaging in 'bidding wars' for particular high-fliers.

Growth Markets

Goldman Sachs has grown rapidly over the last decade or more, and last year saw a 27 per cent increase in net earnings. Growth in Europe last year was significant, and Slaughter believes this growth will con-tinue over time.

Several trends in Europe should be conducive to growth, including the expansion of the European Union, the advent of the single cur-rency, the growth of high-yield bonds, an increase in share ownership and the rate of new issues, and a growing number of mergers and acquisitions. Developments in trading technologies will tend to make the European markets more international, which will play into the hands of a truly international finance house like Goldman Sachs.

The firm is also keen to increase its percentage share of these grow-ing world markets, partly by organic growth, but also by acquisition. Last year it paid more than 8bn dollars for Spear Leeds Kellogg, a New York equities firm which is strong on Nasdaq (the American high-tech stock market) – thus complementing Goldman Sachs's existing strength on Wall Street. Goldman Sachs also bought Hall, another New York equities firm with expertise in options and electronic trading.

Quality of Management

'Our organization may look chaotic from the outside, but it's not,' says Slaughter. 'It's very organic and action-oriented, and not at all authority-driven or hierarchical.'

The company is basically organized into divisions based on its main lines of business – investment banking, equities, asset management, etc – which are then sub-divided on product lines. Geographical organizations cut across these, and teams for particular client projects may be multidisciplinary, which all helps to give the firm its distinctive 'matrix' structure.

Despite being king of the hill compared to its competitors, Goldman Sachs is never complacent. 'We're always looking to improve and we're pretty self-critical,' says Slaughter. 'If you sit a group of us round a table, it won't be long before we start discussing all the things we could be doing better.' There is a general receptiveness to innovation. 'Doors really are open,' says Bott. 'I've never worked in a company where it was so easy to go and see somebody senior with a good idea.'

The firm believes everybody should be accountable, and operates a policy of '360 degree reviews', where managers are reviewed by those they manage, as well as vice versa. 'Management is very much assessed by the managed, and the managed help to promote the managers from within,' says Slaughter. Directors, for example, are nominated by the divisions they work for, and people in other divisions are then asked for a second opinion.

Yet, for all its flexibility and innovative working practices, Goldman Sachs is very protective of its brand, and would rather turn work away than compromise its professional image. This is one reason why it is not keen on brash marketing campaigns.

International Orientation

Goldman Sachs operates in almost every significant country in the world, and has offices in 28 countries, including most of Western Europe, Russia, Japan, China, Hong Kong, South Africa, Australia and the Middle East, as well as North and South America.

It is divided into three regions – the Americas, Europe and Asia – but refuses to be hamstrung by these demarcations, and regards itself as a genuinely global company. If someone in London is selling US shares to a European company, or someone in Tokyo is arranging an acquisition for buyers in America, the deal will straddle more than one region anyway, and it is common for staff to travel half way round the globe to help another region install a new system or implement a new procedure.

So multi-geographical teams are common, there are a lot of global reporting lines, and more than half the company's managing directors have worked in other regions. 'One of our key competitive strengths is that we're "efficiently" global and can provide a truly global service to our clients,' says Slaughter.

GorillaPark
FROM IDEA TO IPO™

GorillaPark invests in very early-stage technology, ideas, and companies, and seeks to develop them until they are ready either to go public or to merge with other, larger companies. The company is optimistic about its prospects despite the dot-com crash that began shortly after its foundation in February 2000 and the shaky results of a number of other companies founded with similar intentions. GorillaPark believes its methods are sufficiently different and better developed to make it a success even in this difficult market. In early 2001, it was particularly interested in technologies such as Bluetooth, XML, second and third generation wireless, biometrics, and P2P.

Scorecard:

Innovation	★★★★
Flexibility	★★★
Human resources	★★★
Growth markets	★★★
Quality of management	★★★
International orientation	★★★

Biggest plus:
The excitement of working with new technology and companies.

Biggest minus:
Very high-risk.

GorillaPark
42–46 Princelet Street
London E1 5LP
Tel: 020 7920 2500
Fax: 020 7920 2501
website: www.gorillapark.com
e-mail: recruitment@gorillapark.com

GorillaPark

The Business

GorillaPark is an Internet accelerator – it doesn't like the term 'incubator'. Itself venture-capital funded, GorillaPark began its programme of investments in February 2000, and expects them to start paying off in February 2002. As of the end of 2000, GorillaPark has 100 employees who focus on the 14 companies in which it's invested, up from the eight employees it started with in October 1999. The company was founded by Jerome Mol, who also founded the Amsterdam-based help desk company Prolin, sold to Hewlett-Packard in 1997, and *Tornado-Insider*, a magazine and events company covering the pan-European new economy.

Innovation

There are by now hundreds of Internet incubators. Mol believes his 'accelerator' is different because of its international and highly intensive approach to the start-ups it invests in. 'The main thing is changing the way businesses in the high-tech sector are created throughout Europe,' he says. 'We see the incubator as part of the financing life cycle. The idea is that for the first phase of the life cycle, an incubator is the best place to go to.' GorillaPark, he argues, takes a start-up from a nascent idea to a company large enough to be of interest to venture capital firms. 'There will be a huge deal flow coming out of our operation and then passed on to venture capital firms.' Prominent among GorillaPark's lineup of investments is the Netherlands-based online department store Hot Orange; Barbadosoft, a software tools development firm specializing in XML; Exaide, which provides architecture for e-business; Moonshake Technologies, which provides technical services to Internet start-ups; Nerve Wireless, which supports collaborative working independent of enterprise, device, or location; Pharmeon, an online healthcare company; and SwapItShop, an online swapping shop for kids. GorillaPark believes its system of developing companies is substantially different from the average Internet incubator. Although the company won't go into details in public, regarding its system as its intellectual property, it has an eight-point process for new companies that Mol likens to a well-designed assembly line. 'If you assemble a BMW or a Mercedes,' he says, 'at some point you need tyres, but you don't need them at the beginning because you don't yet have a wheelbase'. GorillaPark, he says, has figured out what companies need at different points in their development, and this understanding is being constantly updated. 'We are continuously learning what to do for a company at a certain period of time,' he says. Mol expects the company to become profitable in 2002.

Flexibility

GorillaPark has four reasons to be flexible: its own growth from 13 to 107 employees in less than a year, the growth of its babies, its five international offices, and, most important, the reality that the technology industry completely reinvents itself every two years. Staff may also be assigned to the start-ups GorillaPark invests in, either temporarily or permanently. Ideas and business plans come to GorillaPark in three ways: direct, unsolicited submissions; referrals, and research. The company receives approximately 200 business plans a month, the equivalent of the 'slush pile' that flies in over the transom in publishing. Entrepreneurs with ideas are invited to submit them via the company's website, which has full instructions for doing so. The best quality ideas, however, says Mol, tend to be the ones the company finds itself through researching the industry, an enterprise he says is ongoing and pervasive throughout the company. Because the market for dot-com start-ups is so uncertain, GorillaPark itself has to be flexible in planning ahead. Mol says the company has three plans ready for scenarios from bear market to bull market. Even in the worst case, Mol believes the company has good prospects, if only because venture capitalists, through all types of markets, have tended to make a good return for their investors – and he thinks GorillaPark's investment methods are smarter than those of venture capitalists and will ensure a higher rate of success. Nontheless, the company has to plan for the eventuality that a number of its start-ups will fail, though he says even most of these would be acquired 'out of mercy'. The rest, roughly 40 to 50 per cent, the company expects to be successful, though some of these, too, might be acquired (but for a much greater return).

Human Resources

Like the staff at any dot-com start-up, staff at GorillaPark work long, intense hours – a minimum of 60 to 80 hours a week. 'If you have a nine-to-five attitude, it's sure that you won't do well,' says Mol, 'we won't even hire you'. The 100-plus employees GorillaPark had at the end of 2000 were working with 14 start-up companies; in the longer term the optimum is three to five per company. GorillaPark also assists its start-ups with recruiting. 'We recruit people for their skill set, drive, and motivation.' Staff at GorillaPark tend to have entrepreneurial backgrounds, having been previously successful in one or two entrepreneurial environments. The reason for this is that GorillaPark's way of working is to take a company founder with an idea and, as Mol puts it, surround him or her with 'an entire IPO class team.' Over time, as the new company matures, GorillaPark gradually decreases its input.

Growth Markets

GorillaPark's growth depends on the companies it invests in and on the investment climate. Very much like a venture capital firm, GorillaPark's revenues come when the budding company goes public or is sold. Investment, in GorillaPark's terms, includes services such as the nuts and bolts of setting up the company and links to venture capitalists and other funding sources on top of a relatively small amount of money (typically £500,000 to £1,000,000). In return, GorillaPark takes 25 per cent equity. As for GorillaPark's own prospects, Mol believes that incubation itself is a huge market. 'Billions of dollars that used to be spent in research and development in large corporations now mostly go to start-ups. The twenty-first century is the age for smaller companies.' He cites the example of Cisco Systems, which has a constant programme of acquisitions that buys it the new technology it needs to keep moving forward. 'There's a lot of corporate venturing now – people would rather acquire a start-up that has been successful.' Accordingly, he says, Cable and Wireless funds GorillaPark rather than run its own incubator. 'My vision,' says Mol, 'is that 60 to 70 per cent of companies will start through incubators'.

Quality of Management

Mol, the most visible member of GorillaPark's management team, has been involved in one other new venture since leaving Hewlett-Packard. This is the Amsterdam-based monthly magazine *Tornado-Insider*, which covers the European new economy; the magazine also runs a website that's updated daily and a series of events across Europe. Like many dot-com ventures, *Tornado-Insider* had layoffs at the end of 2000; Mol expects that business to become profitable in 2001. GorillaPark's other managers have all run their own companies or been involved in entrepreneurial environments. Robert Spicer, for example, who is in charge of international development, has been involved with Omnisky, Lucent, and Palm, while Richard Farr, the company's chief financial officer, has been involved in both start-ups and turnarounds. Jos de Waard, chief customer services officer, was in charge of customer service at the Netherlands-based Stratus Computer before joining Mol's venture, Prolin, as vice-president of professional services; he was also involved in the early stages at *Tornado-Insider*. Greg Hassett, the chief technology officer, was co-founder of the Internet-based news service Pointcast (and started work at Digital Equipment Corporation at the age of 15). Managers may stay with GorillaPark; equally, they may work for the company for three to six months working with two to four start-ups on a project basis before joining one of them permanently. 'What GorillaPark really is, is a sort of marketplace between talent, capital, great ideas, and alliances,' says Mol. Because of the company's international structure, employees typically report both to managers in their particular country and managers in charge of their particular function – engineering, finance, customer services, marketing, strategy, or research. The company is open to promoting people from within. 'If you grow as fast as we are, there are a tremendous amount of opportunities,' Mol says, adding that employees have to be very flexible: 'We don't want people who hang onto a particular function.'

International Orientation

GorillaPark's sights are resolutely international; it has offices in London, Munich, Paris, Stockholm, and San Francisco, plus its home base in Amsterdam. It expects to expand to ten or twelve offices worldwide in 2001, doubling its personnel. GorillaPark is particularly looking for business plans in the areas of the themes it has identified as the most important for the coming couple of years, and all of these by their nature require an international orientation: Bluetooth, XML, second and third generation wireless, artificial intelligence, biometrics, and P2P. Investments are recommended by the international offices, but the final decision is made centrally. People do swap among the various offices, and those who cover specific areas may work in more than one office. However, GorillaPark tries to keep a balance so that employees capture the international element of the business while staying reasonably close to home. The various offices and companies meet with some regularity.

the technology agency

Gyro is a marketing services agency that has developed a speciality in the IT business-to-business sector. Established in 1991 by the two friends who are now joint managing directors, Gyro currently employs 66 staff and is expecting sales for the current financial year of around £9.5 million – up by more than a quarter on the previous year.

Scorecard:

Innovation	★★★
Flexibility	★★★★★
Human resources	★★★★★
Growth markets	★★★★
Quality of management	★★★★
International orientation	★★★★

Biggest plus:
Gyro has a working culture that combines professionalism and serious management controls with the buzz of working for a young, friendly, fast-growing company with high-tech tools and high-tech clients.

Biggest minus:
The potential danger is that Gyro currently relies on the IT industry, and in particular a group of major players in that business.

Gyro Limited
1/9 Harbour Yard
Chelsea Harbour
London SW10 0XD
Tel: 020 7351 1550
Fax: 020 7351 3318
website: www.gyro.co.uk

Gyro Limited

The Business

This marketing communications agency designs websites, advertisements, video promotions, brochures and the like; it also organizes complete marketing campaigns, including for instance mailshots and product launches.

Gyro describes its business as brand communications – services to help its clients build recognition and strength for their brands. The IT business is still a major focus, and Gyro has invested time and money in understanding this sector. But it won't turn away consumer work, and it has worked for Avia (funky shoes) and Ginzing (Ginseng-based alcopops).

Currently Gyro has six operating divisions: Gyro – the technology agency (brand Communications for the technology industry); Gyro New Media (websites and Internet related activity); Gyro Editions (branded merchandise) and Gyro Productions (corporate video and broadcast graphics): plus overseas offices in California and Geneva.

The first two are the major money-earners. The last reported turnover figure (for the financial year 1998–1999) was £7.4 million, about 20 per cent up on the year before. For the current year Gyro is expecting about £9.5 million, a gain of about 28 per cent; and for 2000–2001 it's projecting nearly £14 million. (Gyro doesn't like to publish profit figures, which isn't unusual for privately owned and privately funded companies.)

Gyro is still owned and run by the two partners who established the company in 1991, Graham Dodridge and Gary Brine. By the end of its first five years Gyro had expanded to 16 people. In the second five it has gone to 70 staff, and the London base has been joined by offices in San Francisco and Geneva.

Innovation

As you would expect from a marketing services agency, Gyro has some very good ideas for marketing itself – professionally made DVD and CD-ROM promotions, a slick website (more of a billboard and brochure than a tool for clients: an extranet is under consideration), Gyro-branded merchandise, and more.

But its reputation is Gyro's main sales tool, supported as it is by the evidence of long-term client relationships and successful projects. And the scope of the group's capabilities also encourages prospective customers: even if Gyro is quoting for a relatively narrow job like a brochure or a website, it gives the client confidence to know that it could provide a much more comprehensive marketing programme.

Flexibility

Gyro has managed the trick of applying an essentially conservative approach to management in an environment that fosters creativity. The underlying corporate structures, including the computerized 'job bag' system for each client project, enable the group to react quickly to new business opportunities.

In its early days the company was able acquire new capabilities in response to client demand. For instance, a client request for a direct mail campaign led Gyro to invest time and effort in building that knowledge; now Gyro can claim response rates of up to 30 per cent for direct marketing programmes it has delivered into the IT sector.

These days Gyro is able to take a more considered approach to developing its skills set and choosing the marketing operations it can offer. A recent example is its video production arm; Gyro regards video as an accessible but under-utilized medium in the business-to-business space.

Human Resources

When founders Graham Dodridge and Gary Brine decided to strike out on their own, they were determined to build a high-morale company that didn't exploit staff – to have fun while making money, in other words. The result is an MTV culture, salaries up to, or ahead of, industry standards, a location in the hip Chelsea Harbour development, whole-company weekend outings – including visits to New York and Prague, and 'legendary' Christmas parties. It's a work-hard play-hard culture that still feels fresh and interesting, even for the company's longest-serving employees.

Gyro has worked hard to keep that culture intact as the group has expanded, and much of its success in that regard is down to the selection of sympathetic staff. Gyro reckons it has the smartest marketers and the most outstanding creatives in its business, but employees also have to fit the company's working environment.

Some staff vacancies are posted on the company's website. But recruitment tends to be by personal contact, with a bounty on offer for recommendations.

Growth Markets

Gyro recognizes that its business is not recession proof. The Internet continues to fuel significant year-on-year growth for IT as a whole, however, and Gyro is riding the wave. And while the IT business-to-business sector isn't necessarily as glamorous as some areas of marketing communications, Gyro has made this world its own. The company is knowledgeable and confident, it is able to attract high-quality staff, and it operates with a degree of professionalism that is not always associated with graphics-based marketing services companies. It appears well placed for continued growth.

To date that growth has come primarily by reinvesting profits. Acquisition has not hitherto been a significant factor, though Gyro has taken over some smaller companies – typically one-man bands where the aim was to recruit the proprietor. It is currently looking at acquiring a more substantial design company, again by using its own resources.

This may be the start of something bigger. Gyro is primed for expansion, feels that it can do well in Europe and the US, and wants to become a major player in its field. The directors recognize that a major leap forward will require external capital and have already considered the implications of this, in terms of diluting their own holdings and seeking alliances.

The nature of the business may also start to change. Gyro began life as a graphic design studio, being commissioned for very specific client jobs. But its experience and expertise is now such that Gyro can be engaged at the highest level to advise on brand strategies for the client as well as implementing the programmes that might result.

Most of its competitors can do one or the other but not both. Gyro also has a network of strategic 'partners' that can be involved for specific skills like PR or list broking.

Gyro terms this a 'holistic' approach to marketing. More prosaically, the multi-service capability and the accumulated knowledge mean that Gyro can effectively become an outsourced marketing department if clients so wish. Already some clients look to Gyro to provide some stability in their marketing planning – an area where job-hopping is not unknown.

There is considerable potential in this, and the arrival of qualified manager-level marketing professionals within the group augurs well for development.

Quality of Management

Gyro's two founders, Graham Dodridge and Gary Brine, are joint managing directors. This isn't necessarily a recipe for success, especially when the group gets large enough to require more layers of management. For now, the partnership works very well, with input from good business advisers and obvious agreement between the MDs about the company's direction and culture.

In practice, Gyro is a surprisingly tight structure, with clear departmental and functional demarcations. At the same time the group is glued together by the work-hard play-hard culture and the emphasis on professionalism – Gyro takes pride in never having missed a deadline or failed to meet a budget, and it is important that the staff sub-scribe to the same goals.

Equally important is the tight management accounting, exemplified by a purpose-built company-wide computerized job-tracking system that can instantly show the progress of any client contract, the resources being used, the contact record, and the cumulative billing status. There is a very high level of technology in Gyro's offices.

Gyro is also good at retaining clients, and works hard at client contact. Indeed, Gyro employs more client-facing staff such as account handlers than it does creative people in the design studios.

Dodridge and Brine run the company with a management team of nine, the heads of the major departments. Operational responsibility lies with these managers, who for instance have hire-and-fire responsi-bility; this group gets an annual four-day retreat away from the office for checkpointing and planning.

International Orientation

Gyro has not rushed into international expansion, instead locating its overseas offices (Geneva and San Francisco) where they can justify their existence in terms of servicing major locally based clients who were signed up in London.

The group has high hopes for the Californian arm of the business, however. This is a good base from which to approach US companies looking for marketing services to cover Europe, and Gyro has a fine track record in this field – after all, most of its clients are ultimately US-owned.

handbag.com, jointly owned by The Boots Company and Hollinger Telegraph New Media, was the first female-focused site to launch in the UK on 6 October, 1999. It is now Europe's most useful site for women online, bringing together a winning combination of edited content for women from recognized experts, using interactive tools and a lively community. Some ten months after launch, over 1 million people had visited the site, there were over 312,000 regular monthly visitors, over 5 million page impressions a month, and a 55 per cent awareness among female Internet users. The company expects to have 500,000 regular users by mid-2001 and break-even should be reached within three years.

Scorecard:

Innovation	★★★★
Flexibility	★★★★
Human resources	★★★★
Growth markets	★★★★
International orientation	★★★★

Biggest plus:
Staff are given huge responsibility – the policy is to delegate responsibility to every level.

Biggest minus:
Because the company is small, there is no clear career path.

handbag.com
151 Oxford Street
London W1R 1TB
Tel: 020 7292 0022
Fax: 020 7292 0021
website: www.handbag.com

handbag.com

The Business

handbag.com was formed in the spring of 1999 and launched on 6 October that year with the vision of becoming the most useful site online for UK women. Joint owners are The Boots Company (90 per cent of women in the UK shop at a Boots store monthly) and Hollinger Telegraph New Media, the new media division of the *Daily Telegraph* newspaper group. Revenue streams derive from advertising and sponsorship (60 per cent) and retail sales (40 per cent). The company had 25 employees at the end of 2000, and this figure was expected to reach 30 by mid-2001. The target customer base is English-speaking people anywhere, but the site is focused on the UK. The audited user base in July 2000, was 312,158 and was expected to pass 500,000 by mid-2001.

Innovation

The handbag.com site is built around partners. 'There are 100 content partners including content companies, freelance writers, experts in particular fields such as cookery and wine, and celebrities,' says managing director Dominic Riley. 'The way we work with our customers is focused and attentive. We have the objective to be the most useful site using three key drivers.' These are the interactivity using the unique properties of the Internet in working with women; utilizing recognized expertise (bringing expertise confers credibility); and the breadth and depth of the content, edited specifically for women.

There are 18 channels of content and information. Channel content is complemented by a range of services including free '@handbag.com' e-mail addresses, discussion groups, horoscopes, Web search, weather, TV and radio guide. 'Discussion boards represent the fastest growing points area of the site,' says Riley. Content partners include Rough Guides, Healthscout, Iglu, Boots, Majestic Wine, Ananova (formerly PA News), Expedia and Autoexpress. Each channel includes a recognized expert who answers up to six user questions a week, and participates in discussion groups and live chats, as well as providing features on their subject.

Customers are typically working women aged 25–45 with access to the Internet, and live in London, the South East or one of the major metropolitan areas. 'Communication and community combine with the core of useful information we provide,' says Riley. 'It's a constantly evolving mix.' Interestingly, 25 per cent of users are male. Customers are interested in traditional areas of female interest such as health, beauty and fashion, but can also be interested in such commercially important content as motoring, property and finance. The largest spend is on marketing, followed by content and personnel. 'Some 5 per cent of our spend goes on R&D,' says Riley.

Flexibility

From inception to the October launch, handbag.com's site was built in 12 weeks, and staff had grown from Riley, the first appointee, to 18 people. 'We had a publishing system built at launch which allowed for change, new content to be published and new partners to be brought on board,' says Riley. 'It had to be flexible. The first challenge was in May 2000 when we restructured and redesigned the site, as a result of feedback from our customers. We closed two channels and amalgamated their content into others, and opened a new channel – on pets. We have become good at implementing ideas.' Channel content includes careers, relationships, sport & fitness, travel, family, money, news and shopping.

'Looking forward, you have to be able to accommodate changing markets,' says Riley. 'You can either run a website or develop the site to become a brand, accessible across a number of platforms, such as PC, TV, telephone and digital radio.' The National Opinion Polls (NOP) organization conducted research into handbag.com – 'the most positive research ever done' – and found it to be 'a strong brand, with great potential and a loyal band of customers'. The handbag.com woman is smart, spirited and intuitive – and visits the site two/three times a month for 10 minutes per visit.

'In July 1999 websites were purely PC accessible,' says Riley. 'By July 2001 we'll offer WAP and broadband access, and by July 2002 there'll be TV and radio. Different platform offerings involve reversioning the service, to accommodate the different capabilities of viewing screens and technology at the back-end.' Broadband allows faster access, and BT's ADSL service 'will allow video and audio on demand' – so expect two-minute videos of cookery, beauty, DIY, etc, plus stock libraries of mending fuses, putting shelves up, etc. Partnering with radio companies will offer digital radio opportunities.

Human Resources

This is a small company where people need to be flexible and willing to turn their hand to do different things. 'There is an open philosophy,' says Riley. 'If there are problems they are *our* problems and *we* have to fix them. We're not frightened to make mistakes. We do, we try, and sometimes we fail. We learn and improve. We don't over-analyse – that's for large corporates.'

The company outsources a lot: hosting of the site; development of website building tools; advertising; PR; media buying; back-end finance; personnel management; and pensions. 'The people we like are people who can manage,' says Riley. 'We place a high value on honesty and integrity. Individuals must be serious players, professional and capable of thriving on managing a range of contacts through using technology, e-mail, phone and meetings.'

There are big company benefits: good basic salary and bonus scheme for all staff; contributory money-purchase pension; five weeks holiday; Boots discount card after three months service. Weekly team meetings encourage communication 'up-down-across', while three annual 'away days' equally encourage contribution of ideas.

Growth Markets

Riley sees growth for handbag.com in Internet, broadband access, mobile, TV and radio markets. 'We'll see 50 per cent of the UK population online by 2003, from the current 33 per cent. It's going to be as important as TV, radio and phone combined, because it supplies interactivity and content on demand. People are now visiting fewer and fewer websites. In the US it's down to nine per month and falling. More people in the UK are online, but on average they spend 6.5 hours a month online and are looking at fewer websites. A hierarchy of leading sites and brands will emerge.' The company believes that there is only room in the UK market for two sites aimed at women: handbag.com and one other. 'It's a – very fast growing – mass market. There's no support for niche business now. Fewer players are in the market. Only a few successful players will emerge,' says Riley. 'We believe in scale'.

Access to the Internet will become faster through the growth of broadband communications, accessed over cable or ADSL services. Mobile presents international opportunities with WAP. There are opportunities to extend the handbag.com brand to existing customers in a new way, or to give it to people who don't currently access the service. BT Genie and Mviva are partners, adding content to their telephones. With TV, the vision is to have a broad access platform, with a TV channel currently being assessed. Digital radio offers enormous potential, with new branded access.

Quality of Management

handbag.com has the driven objective to create value for shareholders. It is the ability of the company to generate profits above the cost of capital employed and Riley is confident the company will at least break even by 2003. This is not an over-ambitious dot-com company like so many others that fell by the wayside because they didn't have rigorous financial planning, were over-staffed and produced complex screen displays that few customers could download. handbag.com approaches the market sensibly and with a clear focus and direction. It is measured by its financial reporting and through monthly board meetings. Financial reports are issued publicly every six months and Boots breaks out handbag.com's financials in its annual report. There is a greater sense of corporate governance than in a private company.

The company is not a Boots-branded product. It is independent, a joint venture between Boots and Hollinger Telegraph New Media, and the company 'sits in Boots at the corporate level'. Indeed Boots learns from handbag.com's experience, for example on flexibility. Boots likes the 70 per cent solution – 'you can't get 100 per cent right before you do something, but if you get 70 per cent right you're well on the way'. There's a close relationship with Boots' website, and Boots sponsors the health & beauty channel. 'We're the biggest driver of traffic to Boots' websites,' says Riley.

Regular meetings are held with the Hollinger Telegraph side too. Two Boots and two Hollinger directors on handbag.com's board represent the interests of shareholders. Riley, as MD, runs the business. His experience stems from work at Kingfisher and the BBC, while the financial director, Anne Lewis, was formerly financial director at Boots Properties plc. Although handbag.com is a small limited company, it has an openness and discipline traditionally associated with large publicly-quoted corporates.

International Orientation

handbag.com is associated with the UK but 'would operate internationally if it was commercially sensible to do so'. It is building an international base of English language-speaking customers, often driven through a 'member-get-member' grapevine approach. The company has partnerships with European operators, such as Cello broadband and WAP content in Scandinavia (syndicating content for the region).

The fastest-growing area – 'the most useful site online' – is the discussion group. 'Handbaggers' meet up to party in locations like Croydon, London, Blackpool, Nottingham, Edinburgh, Newcastle and Dublin.

Property is not a key issue, as it is an Internet company, which has partnerships with suppliers, no stock is carried, so no strategically-placed warehousing/storage is required. All retail partners have to pass the handbag.com shopping promise, including offering transparent delivery charges, detailing how long goods take to arrive, and ensuring a returns policy that can be clearly expressed through phone/e-mail.

As the company says, 'Everything you need is in your handbag.com' – wherever you are.

Hitoori is a service company in the communications area that takes a complex problem and offers a simple answer. The problem is that there are too many communications reaching most people in business – fax, e-mail, voicemail, mobile phone, mobile voicemail, work phone and home phone. The answer – as presented by Hitoori – is to give people a single number and e-mail address so that they can either have their messages forwarded to wherever they are, or they can pick them up from any computer with an Internet connection. It is privately owned and employs some 38 people.

Scorecard:

Innovation	★★★★★
Flexibility	★★★★
Human resources	★★★★
Growth markets	★★★★
Quality of management	★★★★
International orientation	★★★★

Biggest plus:
Being a pioneer in a market with such promise, and making a contribution to people's quality of life by eliminating the difficulty of getting hold of someone.

Biggest minus:
The flipside of the biggest plus is that the pioneers are the people who end up educating the market, and corporate customers in particular can take some winning over!

ABS Telecom House
607 High Road
London N12 0DZ
Tel: 020 8343 9121
website: www.hitoori.com

ABS Telecom House

The Business

Hitoori is a new company, launched in August 2000 as a messaging service, by ABS Telecom with a new version launched in March 2001. Its service is simple; the basic version allows you to register for a Hitoori number and message page on the Web, and then every time someone calls that number they can be routed to you wherever you are, or put through to a voicemail – or it will receive a fax for you. You choose the numbers to which your calls are forwarded. You can then pick up voicemails, e-mails and faxes from a secure customer area on the company's website. It 'sells' – if a charge-free service can be described as sold – primarily to individuals, although business versions were about to launch as this book went to press.

Innovation

There are few, if any, companies doing exactly what Hitoori does at the moment, and those that do offer the same service tend to have purchased it from Hitoori in the first place. Essentially it has no direct competition. Others offer a fax number that then sends a fax to an e-mail address as an attachment; still others offer to send voice messages around the globe and attach those in their turn to e-mails, but thus far only Hitoori will set up a website that operates as your in-box for e-mail, fax and voicemail, and read you the mail out loud if you can't get to a computer and want to hear it over your mobile phone.

The corporate version, due to be launched in 2001, has still more bells and whistles (and customers have to pay for this version; the basic package is free to users (the company makes its money from the higher-rate charges for incoming calls to Hitoori numbers)). It connects to corporate e-mail systems such as Microsoft Outlook, and it offers diary as well as e-mail functions. The diary function as well as e-mails can be read to customers over any phone using text-to-voice technology.

In addition to this, the corporate version allows people to use an existing number as their Hitoori number – so if you want to use your existing business number then you can do so; Hitoori will then forward the call. Group accounts will also be available, so you can offer clients the facility to dial an extension to get to the person in your company they need. Your set-up costs will be slashed since this will work with whatever phone system you already have installed.

The other area the company is examining is the possibility of licensing its technology so that other companies can sell it as part of a larger offering. IBM is among those that have already elected to offer a unified messaging service to its customers using technology from Hitoori – more will follow.

Flexibility

ABS Telecom (the company behind Hitoori) was acquired by the current shareholders in 1998. ABS Telecom was an ailing and loss-making telecom reseller and the main challenge was to refocus its operation to create a unified communications company.

The main rationale behind the acquisition was that ABS Telecom offered a number of advantages. Prime among these was the fact that ABS Telecom was a licensed telecommunications company in the UK and could make short work of setting up the Hitoori phone numbers and the call forwarding service.

So the company had more or less a complete makeover. Chief executive, Ahal Besorai, comments that he keeps staff motivated during such corporate alterations by keeping them completely informed about everything that is going on – staff meetings cover everything from company turnover to sales targets and the business.

As well as corporate flexibility the company adds an open-minded approach to its marketing. It acknowledges that some of the Web-based companies have thrown a lot of money at marketing and have not done well, so it prefers to set up alliances with people like easyEverything to attract new people to the business. There has been a small amount spent on direct mail but the company prefers to look for alternative means of finding new customers.

Its other cultural change has been in the form its sales take. The transition between the consumer's effective impulse buy and the corporate not wanting to spend money until they have examined the pros and cons of every purchase has been achievable but the difference is noticeable.

Human Resources

As has already been stated, the company has a policy of being totally open with its employees – they are all shareholders and at any given time they will know about turnover and profit as well as their own tasks within the organization. The company culture is very much that of ownership. Besorai believes that everyone contributes to the profitability of the company and needs to feel that their contribution is of value.

He adds that this sense of inclusion is more important than financial inducements for a lot of people. Motivating staff isn't as simple as throwing money at them. Nevertheless, the share scheme and the competitiveness of the IT and communications industries will ensure that the Hitoori remuneration package will remain competitive.

Growth Markets

As outlined above, Hitoori is growing in a number of areas including: the individual 'retail' version of its product, which is free to the customer; the corporate version for the small/medium enterprise; and the licensed version, that other companies can buy and customize. Besorai does not comment on which of those is likely to yield the most growth in the short or medium term – each area of the business has its own credible niche.

However, it is possible to speculate that the reluctance of the small/medium enterprise to spend its money until the value of a product is proven will hold Hitoori back in that market until the benefits are better known, and the return on investment is proven many times over, rather than once or twice (there are already customers who can cite increased business and diminishing costs as a result of the service but its profile is not yet high). Initial growth is therefore likely to come from the other two sectors in the short term, until the concept is established, at which stage the corporate version is likely to overtake the others very rapidly indeed.

Quality of Management

To understand why Hitoori is going to last it is important to understand a few things about its management. First it is owned by ABS Telecom, which means that it has a parent company with solid experience of the communications market. ABS Telecom has gone through the licensing loop to become an accredited telecommunications provider and this is not something that should be underestimated. Investors include, among others, individuals who have held senior positions within Goldman Sachs and Morgan Stanley, so there are serious hitters around.

On a day-to-day basis Besorai tries always to measure the success of every individual in terms of the company's performance. This isn't a rigid 'we're in profit or you've failed' approach: he keeps everyone on target sometimes by adjusting the targets on both corporate and individual levels according to changes in the market. The overall effect is that people are made to feel they need to do better but only realistically so, so they continue to be motivated and the company grows.

International Orientation

The company plans to consolidate its European presence first, but the licensing of its technology paves the way for rapid expansion of an international presence in a purely reactive way. For example, approaches have been made from Singapore. Hitoori had no immediate plans to expand into Singapore, but if someone wants to license the technology the door is open for negotiations.

In terms of proactive expansion, Europe remains the company's target. It will focus on the UK initially and other countries will be entered through a mix of all three of the current product offerings.

Overall the product is strong – nobody else can put all of the messages a person might receive in the one place that can be accessed from anywhere, and the de-stressing effect that this can have on a busy professional is considerable. In business terms the Hitoori customer's clients can get to them much more easily if the Hitoori service is in use – this means fewer people hanging up because they're on hold and therefore more prospects turning into actual customers. Demand is therefore likely to be high for the service, and Hitoori's background in the telecommunications arena should ensure that it remains one of the top players in the field.

hotrecruit.co.uk
OOO's of temporary jobs

HotRecruit is part of the Hot Group, a service that has a marketing agency called Hot Factor and a technology provider called Hot Labels as well; HotRecruit forms the majority of the business. Privately owned by the chief executive and a consortium of industry leaders, it offers temporary jobs to students and returning travellers. It employs some 35 staff and was about to move into its new Covent Garden offices as this publication went to press.

Scorecard:

Innovation	★★★★
Flexibility	★★★★★
Human resources	★★★★
Growth markets	★★★★
Quality of management	★★★★
International orientation	★★★

Biggest plus:
The people – it's a creative atmosphere with a lot of young blood around, and the new location can only increase the fun factor.

Biggest minus:
The market is volatile for Internet start-ups, which is likely to affect the value of shareholdings and options until it turns round again.

HotRecruit Limited
37 Shelton Street
Covent Garden
London WC2H 9HN
website: www.hotrecruit.co.uk

HotRecruit

The Business

HotRecruit is a website for job seekers, as long as they aren't looking for a full-time job. It focuses very specifically on students who want summer or part-time employment or travellers returning home who need an income for a while. The company tries to focus on fun by sourcing atypical work for its clients – for example, as this book went to press there were posts for marshals at paintball contests. Founded in August 1999 it employs 35 staff and remains privately owned.

Innovation

HotRecruit isn't just another dot-com or even just a recruitment site, says managing director, Harvey Sinclair, it's as much about lifestyle as anything. This is reflected in the tone of the site and in the nature of the jobs on offer; they are part-time and temporary jobs clearly aimed at the student and traveller community. Typically these people will be young – in the 16–28 age bracket – and will have low expectations of the sorts of job they will be able to attract. HotRecruit sees it as its mission to 'fundamentally change the jobs young people find, and the way employers find staff for part-time vacancies.'

To this end the company takes a deliberately lively approach to its jobs and the site on which they are displayed, always seeking out unusual opportunities (and singling them out as crazy jobs of the week) as well as trying to find appealing ways of presenting the jobs to the target market – for example one campaign had a young man sitting outside a cybercafé holding a placard with words to the effect 'if only I'd known about HotRecruit.co.uk I wouldn't be sitting here'.

The company focuses on a number of niche areas including hospitality, retail and travel and leisure as well as office-based work. It stresses the fun side of working; 'If you want to do bar work it doesn't have to be in a dingy pub, you could be a cocktail mixer at the Pitcher and Piano or somewhere,' says Sinclair.

Crucially, the liveliness of the website and the staff is underpinned by solid technology and a different means of paying for clients. Instead of having to make a booking for a given amount of time, clients can book a certain number of days, but not have to use them all at once – so someone who books 100 days could advertise 50 jobs for two days or one job for 100 days, or indeed one job for five days until it is filled and keep a further 95 days in the bank for later.

Flexibility

The billing and flexibility of the Web offering is one of the company's key selling points, and the immediacy of Internet technology allows it to keep its website changing.

Structurally the company has had to keep mobile because of the rate at which it has grown – it went from three to six people which is easy, then doubled to 12, then moved to 20 and then 30 and has shown no signs of slowing down. This rapid growth has been facilitated with the help of human resources director, Jennifer Semple, ex-acting CEO and one of the original founders of Office Angels. Any business that has had two office moves in as many years is likely to be prone to a certain ruffling of feathers, and Sinclair readily admits there have been growing pains.

The other area that has changed for the company, although not one that affects its day to day running a great deal, is the ability of dot-coms trying to raise capital. Initially it was caught up in the enthusiasm that surrounded such projects but this didn't last. At times the staff feel understandably vulnerable in the dot-com world. The company tries its best to offset this feeling with good training programmes and empowerment of the staff with transferable skills.

Human Resources

In terms of its human resources the company has a very open book policy – the people are where the value is, it's well understood, and keeping them interested and motivated is a major facet of the business. The approach can be flexible: the sales staff will almost certainly be at their phones and going for 8.30 am whereas the technical people are more likely to want a 10.00 start. As long as the jobs get done the company accommodates people.

Every employee has share options allocated after a six-month induction period; the value of these will be realized when the company reaches its goal of selling itself to a larger organization. Even if the market conditions were more favourable Sinclair has no immediate desire to float, since the nature of the business is more suited to a trade sell than an IPO.

It makes full use of technology in managing its human resources function, combining this with a full-blown customer relationship management system.

Growth Markets

In many ways HotRecruit doesn't have to look at any growth markets because its market has already grown. The temporary recruitment industry accounts for some 92 per cent of the total recruitment market, and typically 900,000 people are placed in a temporary job every year compared to half this figure for permanent jobs. The value of the market is £17.5 billion, and the scope for a mould-breaker of some sort to liven this up with the addition of an offbeat approach should be considerable.

And the market is growing. More and more people are going into higher education and grants are things of the past, so these people will have debts to pay during, and after, their education. Gap years are becoming the norm rather than the exception, so the returning travel-ler seeking work is a growing target as well.

Quality of Management

As a young company HotRecruit has identified a number of gaps in its managerial skills and has already started taking steps to put these right – the human resources director is an example of this. More buying in of skill may follow as the company grows, although in principle it wants very much to train its own staff. As a consequence it makes extensive use of the Institute of Directors' courses – every director has been on one.

In terms of day-to-day business, the emphasis is very much on continuing development for every member of staff. Sinclair isn't fond of annual appraisals, preferring to give them every three months and seeking to learn as much as he feeds back in the process.

The management structure itself is fairly flat – there are six people in charge including Sinclair himself, and they cover operations, finance, marketing, sales and technology.

International Orientation

Any company that looks towards the returning traveller as one of its core markets is already aware of the opportunities that exist overseas. HotRecruit definitely has plans to expand outside the UK, and Australia looks set to be the next port of call; a number of reasons dictate this, not least of which is the absence of a language barrier combined with the comparatively unexplored nature of the territory as compared to the US.

South Africa is also on the list of possible territories for expansion, backed like Australia by the commonality of the gap year by now; as the brand grows in the UK it is entirely possible that the company will find its existing audience will be looking for it in different territories anyway.

The chances are good that it will seek to expand into these territories through partnerships rather than by trying to set up on its own, and Sinclair will be actively looking for prospective companies in the near future. For the moment the UK is burgeoning with the right sort of clients looking for the people HotRecruit's award-winning campaigns are attracting; the service has a ready audience and a solid delivery mechanism and there is every reason to predict success in its future.

Ifyoutravel.com is a family of websites catering for the needs of active and adventurous travellers, including ifyouski.com, ifyougolf.com, ifyoudive.com, ifyouexplore.com and waxed.com, an extreme sports site. The company was formed in mid-2000 through the merger of four of Europe's leading ski sites, but the company's ultimate aim is to be Europe's leading online specialist travel provider, covering a range of adventure travel. In April 2000 Ifyoutravel.com raised £3.05 million from Europatweb and is seeking additional investment to fund further growth. Based in West London, it employs 28 people.

Scorecard:

Innovation	★★★
Flexibility	★★★
Human resources	★★★
Growth markets	★★★
Quality of management	★★★★
International orientation	★★★★

Biggest plus:
The chance to earn money finding out more about your favourite sport.

Biggest minus:
Careful cost control means you won't spend all your time going on free trips.

IfYouTravel
27a Pembridge Villas
London W11 3EP
Tel: 020 7565 7575
Fax: 020 7565 7576
website: www.Ifyoutravel.com.

Ifyoutravel.com

The Business

Ifyoutravel.com was launched in mid-2000 as a merger of four of Europe's leading winter sports travel sites, giving the company an immediate foothold in France, Denmark and Germany as well as the UK. Complete-skier.com was set up by former Olympic skier Michael Liebreich, Ifyoutravel.com's founder and present chairman. The company is now trying to move beyond its initial focus on ski by launching other specialist travel sites for golf, diving and adventure travel holidays. Internet investment company Europatweb, which last April put £3.05 million into the company, has a 35 per cent stake; the rest is divided between Liebreich, staff and Aspect Internet, the company's software partner. Ifyoutravel.com.com is based in West London and has a core headcount of around 25, taking on extra staff for special promotions. The company is currently looking for further investment to develop its growth plans.

Innovation

Specialist travel is a potentially lucrative market but one that has proved tricky to exploit, as the demise of several players in the area demonstrates. Ifyoutravel.com believes that the Web is the ideal vehicle for selling specialist travel products and services, making it possible to bundle a wide range of activity holiday offerings, online booking, relevant and authoritative background information and communities of travel enthusiasts into a single one-stop shop.

This ability to offer everything the adventurous traveller needs in a single site is Ifyoutravel.com's key value proposition. Through its formation by the merger of four of Europe's leading ski sites, Ifyoutravel.com immediately gave itself a head start in the ski travel market, and is now seeking to build on this success in other travel sectors.

In-depth, well-researched travel information is one of the magic ingredients. According to group managing director Francesca Ecsery-Merrens, the company aims to provide 'meat, not fluff' and over half its staff – 60 per cent – are involved in content generation. As well as holiday and booking information, sites include features such as interactive resort maps, panoramic 360° images and video equipment reviews; news, forums, and visitor polls. To build customer loyalty, online content is reinforced by a regular e-mail newsletter sent out on request to site visitors.

Once content is generated, it can be reused by a number of different sites; information on Bermuda, say, could be used on both the golf and dive sites. Its interactive gear-finder system, originally developed for ski equipment, is also relevant to those looking for equipment for other activities. Re-purposed content can also provide Ifyoutravel.com with a form of low-cost advertising; editorial supplied to a range of publications and attributed to the company is an important way of bringing in new customers.

But strong content by itself is nothing new. Ifyoutravel.com argues that while many other travel sites offer holiday and booking information, customers have no way of knowing whether the holidays listed are actually available to book. Ifyoutravel.com's ability to take bookings online is the second ingredient in the mix.

A third is wide choice for the customer: Ifyoutravel.com aims to work with a large number of travel partners, both large and small, to ensure its customers get the best possible variety of holiday packages.

Flexibility

Around 50 per cent of Ifyoutravel.com's customers arrive via its distribution partners who incorporate its specialist content on to their sites. Its content management software, built by development partner Aspect, is designed to make it easy to rebadge content to provide the same look and feel as the third-party sites. Distribution partners get a share of the bookings revenue, and have the option of exclusive content too. They include general travel firms such as Thomas Cook, media organizations including Teletext and the BBC, Internet portals such as Yahoo!, Excite, Netscape and AOL.

Managing the shift from its stronghold in ski Web provision to expansion into other specialist travel areas is obviously going to be a major challenge for Ifyoutravel.com. It has recruited specialists to produce content for its golf, scuba-diving and adventure travel sites, but the key challenge will be to set up the distribution and supply partnerships it needs to make these new ventures a success.

In forming new partnerships the company's content management system, developed for it by software house Aspect, is a key strategic tool, enabling it to automatically generate content that has the look and feel of a distribution partner's site while keeping the links back to its booking system intact. So while Ifyoutravel.com provides specialist ski content to companies such as Yahoo! and AOL, visitors will not be aware that they are moving outside the original site – an important selling point in setting up new partnerships.

Content can also be generated in a variety of different languages, making it much easier for the company to move flexibly into new geographic markets. Content can, potentially, be produced for new delivery channels such as WAP or interactive TV.

While having its own content management system is a vital competitive tool for Ifyoutravel.com, other non-key areas are outsourced to partners, making it possible to handle large volumes of business without overloading its own systems. Rather than the company operating its own call centre, for example, customer enquiries are routed seamlessly to the call centre for the partner selling that particular travel product.

Ifyoutravel.com boasts that it is produced for enthusiasts by enthusiasts, and a high proportion of its employees are people with experience of or enthusiasm for travel or for one of its key sports – skiing, skiboarding, golf or scuba-diving. It has six former Olympic skiers on its staff, including Liebreich himself, and three former professional golfers.

Around 60 per cent of the staff are engaged in generating authoritative content, and specialist expertise is obviously important here. But many of its marketing and customer relations staff also come from a travel background and when recruiting, priority is given to people who have a good understanding of the needs of specialist travellers.

A certain amount of international travel goes with the territory, and sales and marketing staff need to make appearances at the major travel shows around the world. But working for Ifyoutravel.com isn't all about jetting off to exotic locations; the company is run as a tight ship with expenses kept to the minimum, so most of the travelling staff do will still probably be in their spare time.

Growth Markets

Ifyoutravel.com.com has two main directions for growth: into new specialist travel areas and new geographic markets. In both cases, acquisitions and further partnerships will be crucial. The company already has a wide range of strong partnerships in the ski area and is now working to build up an equally powerful range of alliances in golf, diving and adventure travel.

In doing this it has two key advantages. Its content management software enables it to offer potential partners co-branded content with their own look and feel. And through its family of interconnected travel sites, it can also provide the opportunity to cross-sell to new groups of prospective customers; people who are into adventure travel are highly likely to also want to go scuba-diving, for example.

Quality of Management

As well as in-depth experience of the ski sector, as a former member of the British Olympic Ski Team, Ifyoutravel.com's chairman Michael Liebreich has solid business experience too. He has an MBA from Harvard Business School, has worked as a management consultant for McKinsey, and was deputy managing director of Associated Press Television.

Group managing director Francesca Ecsery-Merrens is a marketing specialist who has board-level experience with both Thorn EMI, where she was European marketing director, and travel agency Going Places, where she was marketing director, commercial director then business development director. She has also worked in strategic marketing for Thomas Cook.

The two founders are aiming to achieve rapid growth while maintaining their focus and market differentiation. They have given careful thought to competitive positioning, aiming to differentiate themselves from specialist travel companies on one hand and general leisure travel operators on the other by quality of content, a strong community, a wide range of distribution partners and by offering a diverse range of adventure holidays and related non-travel content.

So far the formula seems to be working. While a number of specialist travel competitors are struggling or have gone under, Ifyoutravel.com is still going strong, on track to book 10,000 holidays this year compared with 3,000 in 2000. The founders are aiming to break even in 2003. The newly-launched sites for golf, scuba-diving and adventure travel will be able to complement the existing ski sites not only in terms of general subject matter but through reuse of content, one of Ifyouski's biggest costs.

On the basis of his expansion plans, in April 2000 Liebreich succeeded in raising £3.05 million in cash and equity from Internet investment company Europatweb, facilitating the initial merger that formed Ifyoutravel.com. The founders are now seeking additional funding for further expansion.

International Orientation

Ifyoutravel.com has its headquarters in the UK and so far most of its revenues come from the UK market, seen as the most mature in terms of demand for ski holidays. But by merging the UK's complete-skier with three leading European winter sports sites – Skiin, Skiguide and Skigebiete – the company started out with a firm foothold in France, Denmark and Germany.

The sites have been rebadged under the Ifyouski identity while still retaining their local following and many of their local staff, though to keep costs down the operation is mainly run from out of the UK site.

Part of Ifyoutravel.com's business plan is to set up further overseas sites through partnership and acquisition, assuming it is successful in gaining a second round of funding. In doing this it will be aided by its content management system, which enables it to generate foreign-language versions of the site for little additional cost.

IGLU.COM is an online provider of wintersports holidays. It employs 52 people and operates in the UK, France and Germany. The company has a database containing over 12,000 ski chalets and apartments in over 350 resorts world-wide. Its websites together receive over a quarter of a million visitors per month. There is also a subsidiary, IgluVillas.com, offering summer villas across Europe.

Scorecard:

Innovation	★★★★
Flexibility	★★★★
Human resources	★★★
Growth markets	★★★★
Quality of management	★★★★
International orientation	★★★★★

Biggest plus:
First mover in the market.

Biggest minus:
Competition constantly hotting up.

IGLU.COM Ltd
3rd Floor
165 The Broadway
Wimbledon
London SW19 1NE
Tel: 020 8544 6400
Fax: 020 8542 9223
website: www.iglu.com

IGLU.COM

The Business

Founded in June 1998, IGLU.COM is the brainchild of Richard Downs and Emmanuelle Drouet and offers a one-stop solution for those wanting to book a skiing or snowboarding package holiday.

The venture received seed investment from a consortium of investors, including the London Business School, and its website was launched in October. The following summer the company received £3.1m backing from US venture capitalists Geocapital Partners, which enabled it to expand into France and Germany.

In 2000, second round financing of £2.7m came from Barclays Ventures and Geocapital Partners.

That year the company launched a sister site offering activity holidays in France – giving it an all-year-round business model – and the company relaunched the UK and French sites.

Innovation

IGLU.COM serves as an affordable additional distribution channel for tour operators, many of whom may not be online, and who need only pay a commission fee for each holiday sold through the website.

For wintersports enthusiasts, it is *the* place to visit ahead of each season offering a package to suit all kinds of budget. Every aspect of the holiday can be tailored to suit individual requirements from car hire through to insurance arrangements, it is even the best ski school to visit to hone your technique. Even if you want to arrange your own travel, the site will direct you to a budget airline partner company. With around 15 key ISP partnership agreements – including Yahoo!, Virgin, and ntl – the site is not hard to find.

There a number of features designed to make it the site of choice for skiers. Live Web-cams on the ski slopes at top European resorts enable holidaymakers to check weather conditions before travelling. And having partnered with Internet Pictures Corporation (IPIX), visitors can take a virtual tour of ski resorts and see photos of 360° views of the scenery.

Customers can check the availability and prices of thousands of properties in up to 350 resorts in 21 countries. There is a price guarantee and a special offers section lists the current best deals available from operators, many of which are exclusive to IGLU.COM. Registered users can receive a personalized special offers shortlist and will be sent regular newsletter bulletins.

Online payment is handled by Secure Trading and Barclays

Merchant Services, with the company taking a 2 per cent booking fee per credit card transaction. Last year, it was accorded membership of the Association of British Travel Agents (ABTA) and granted an ATOL licence – the only online ski specialist to achieve membership of both organizations.

Relaunching the website at the 2000 *Daily Mail* Ski Show exhibition, IGLU.COM made its presence felt with an 11 metre stand and gave away a free holiday on each of the ten days of the show

Flexibility

Despite having first-mover advantage, the company faces considerable competition for traffic from online information sites as well as generic holiday providers, however its balanced management with deep knowledge of selling ski holidays and ABTA bonding gives it a distinct competitive edge. In obtaining its second round of financing, it restructured and refocused itself in line with shifting market expectations.

With significant funds committed to improving website functionality and expanding the size of the business, the company set about reducing operational costs. Accordingly, marketing strategy switched from the engagement of a public relations firm to hiring a former Fleet Street editor to co-ordinate a much more targeted approach. Through adept use of media contacts, he secured prominent editorial coverage for the website in national newspapers which resulted in a significant increase in site traffic. The company took out advertising space in titles that appeal to its core ABC1 market. And it moved out of central London to more spacious offices in the suburbs, where rents are considerably cheaper.

Service delivery has also changed to reflect customer preferences. Originally customers were only able to book a holiday online; however, research found that personal contact with the company during the process was highly valued – particularly on the part of those planning more expensive vacations. Now IGLU.COM has a 20-strong customer service team, though it also offers online booking for those who want it.

Human Resources

As the company has expanded, so its structure has necessarily become more hierarchical. Where once there was a degree of homogeneity about the organization, now there are recognized pools of management. This means greater accountability for employees. Though they will get managerial support, there is more pressure on people to make the right decision first time.

The company's aim is to be the leading online provider of snowsports holidays and it wants its customers to experience the best possible service in the process. The result is the strong customer focus ethos that underlies all aspects of operations acts as a unifying force. In the infancy of the business, by contrast, there was sometimes a tendency for people to be too preoccupied with their particular area of responsibility.

IGLU.COM is aimed at an outgoing section of the population, so it is no surprise its own people are lively and enthusiastic. They are also overwhelmingly skiers themselves. Many of the present sales team were hired after visiting the company's stand at last year's Ski Show.

Growth Markets

IGLU.COM's identity is bound up with being a specialist provider of wintersports holidays. As Richard Downs observes, 'In the early years of e-commerce it was considered a disadvantage to have a well-defined market for your business. It was far cooler to have anonymous potential customers because this implied a model that was infinitely scalable. But the view today is that it is important to have a firm understanding of who your customers are and what they want and in that respect we have been very focused from the start.'

But given that in the UK most skiers make bookings for the coming season either early (in February) or from September onwards, this left the core business model relatively inactive for much of the year. Having launched igluactive.com, however, the company had an all-year-round proposition. Enquiries to this site convinced management to focus on villas during summer. Relaunched and rebranded in January 2001, Igluvillas.com has aggregated over 5,000 villas across Europe.

Increasing brand awareness is another key focus. The company has partnered with *Onboard Magazine*, a leading magazine for snowboard enthusiasts published in five European languages. It also part-funded *Snow Odyssey II*, a film which premiered at the Ski Exhibition 2000 and played in cinemas across the UK. And it sponsored a team in the World Boardercross Championships.

Quality of Management

The co-founders each bring different strengths to the business. An alumnus of the London Business School, Downs is a former stockbroker with expertise in raising capital. Drouet, a French national, has experience of working within and alongside the tourist industry in her native country.

Expansion in 2000 brought about managerial changes. Drouet, previously overall managing director, became responsible for European operations, while the company's sales and commercial director was appointed UK managing director. In addition, Peter Dyer, former head of Crystal Holidays – the UK's biggest ski company – was appointed to the Iglu board as a non-executive director with special responsibility to develop the company into a major force in world travel. According to Downs, 'He's this industry's equivalent of Sir Alex Ferguson.'

The connection with tour operators, including Crystal Holidays (now owned by Thomson) is a strong one. As the dot-com is an intermediary between customer and supplier, they are not in direct competition with tour operators.

International Orientation

Although traffic to the French and German sites is not comparable to that of the UK site, which still generates over 60 per cent of overall site traffic, there are content managers based in both countries tailoring the proposition to best appeal to localized custom. The UK market is more lucrative than those on the continent, with the package holiday a less familiar concept to French and German skiers, who tend to book much later in the year, make their own transport arrangements and often prefer hotels to chalet accommodation. And with the average British skier spending £500 per holiday compared to £200 spent by their French counterparts, UK customers clearly represent the larger revenue stream for the company.

Long-term, however, IGLU.COM aims to be the number one website for skiers world-wide. Obviously this makes the US an eventual target; but needless to say capturing a share of that market will require substantial further capitalization of the business.

ihave**m**oved.com

Ihavemoved.com is an online change of address service aimed at simplifying one element of the home moving process. Launched in November 1999, the UK-registered site has around 140,000 users and has partner agreements with over 500 services, including many major utility companies. The business employs 25 people, five of whom are based in a German subsidiary in Hamburg, which launched in August 2000.

Scorecard:

Innovation	★★★★★
Flexibility	★★★★★
Human resources	★★★★
Growth markets	★★★
Quality of management	★★★★★
International orientation	★★★★

Biggest plus:
Strong customer base and partnership scheme.

Biggest minus:
There are never enough hours in the day!

Ihavemoved.com
9 Tufton Street
London SW1P 3QP
Tel: 020 7799 3300
Fax: 020 7691 7307
website: www.ihavemoved.com

Ihavemoved.com

The Business

Ihavemoved.com was founded in July 1999 by David Anstee, Francesco Benincasa, Niko Komninos and Onic Palandijan. A private company, its market is aimed at the estimated 6 million Britons that move home annually, 80 per cent of whom are between the ages of 15 and 44.

A free service, it generates revenue through partner agreements with service providers. Call centre and processing costs mean companies currently spend an average of £3–4 per address change. The online solution from Ihavemoved.com means companies are charged a fraction of this cost and are offered the opportunity to co-sponsor pages on the site. In return, Ihavemoved.com has various levels of presence on the service provider websites from links to complete ASP integration.

Last April, it received a £2.5m investment from financiers sourced by N. M. Rothschild. The UK operations are predicted to be profitable by the second half of 2002.

Innovation

A unique business proposition underpins the company's strategy, and the founders are the first to bring the concept of the online change of address to market in Europe.

Ihavemoved.com was created to simplify a process which is laborious and time-consuming for home movers, and inefficient and unsatisfactory for their suppliers. For the former group, it provides a one-stop solution by circulating the change of address details they enter onto the website free of charge to all the companies with which they have a commercial relationship.

On the supplier side, it benefits companies that mailshoot, by providing more up-to-date information. In addition, those companies who oblige calling customers to wait in a phone queue system are not best placed to cross-sell products when their operatives do finally make contact. Ihavemoved.com complies fully with the provisions of the 1998 Data Protection Act, therefore the privacy of individuals is respected. However, the site can help client companies build up aggregate profiles of their customer base to help them improve their marketing strategy.

And because the site charges companies to, in effect, promote its address change engine on their own websites, customer acquisition costs have been kept down. The company spent around £600,000 promoting the brand at its launch; this compares to a £3 million average UK dot-com spend. A poster, radio and online campaign brought it 35 per cent brand awareness among its target audience.

There are also high margins associated with the service. David Anstee, director, says, 'If a customer comes onto our site and changes a lot of addresses, there's no cost of goods sold associated with the service. If companies pay us £100, we keep £98 of that because we only send a couple of letters out. It's incredibly scaleable. You have very low variable costs – just the fixed cost of the wages we pay. So though you drive more traffic through the site, your customer costs don't follow that up.'

Flexibility

In July 2000, the management team responded to demand and moved to offer clients of the Ihavemoved.com site content that can be combined with their own websites. The white label ASP has helped to solidify the customer and client relationship and means that any visitor to for example, the British Gas site, is able to change all their addresses through Ihavemoved.com. The service takes just two weeks to install and enables considerable cost savings for companies who would otherwise have to develop their own technology. Inevitably, this type of relationship with service providers has created robust barriers to entry for any future competitor sites.

The major utility companies were always viewed as a core customer-base for the site, along with banks and financial service providers. Recently, however, it has begun forging links with the letting and estate agency sector, some of whose members have become key affiliates. Ihavemoved.com contacts the organizations that agents are legally required to inform every time there is a change of tenancy, and it will adapt the offer for agents to use it.

The service has also been implemented into the offline market out of a recognition that not everyone on the move has Internet access yet. Such customers can fill out a form which the site uses to contact the various service providers.

These developments have been occurring against the backdrop of a significant sectoral change among the business's client base. Alongside deregulation in the utilities, far-reaching organizational and technological changes are taking place in banks, insurance companies and the government. And as consumers have an ever greater choice of services, their expectations are rising accordingly. As Anstee remarks, 'The slow old stupid way of doing things is just not cutting it anymore.'

Human Resources

A perceived need for the company to remain flexible so as to compete, means that its values are not fixed or static. Broadly, they centre around the need for its people to retain their enthusiasm and belief in the business, regardless of change. Indeed, it is these implicit values that are intended to serve as its identity, as the company grows and develops.

In order to retain this enthusiasm, the company regularly seeks the input of its largely twenty and thirty-something workforce. There is a weekly meeting on Friday afternoon, which as well as enabling everyone to keep up with news and developments provides a useful vehicle for social cohesion – it usually ends up in the pub! There are also monthly strategy meetings where three or four key challenges are identified.

Ownership of the company is real as well as implied. All employees have a stake, being eligible for share options to the value of 17 per cent of their salary. This compares favourably with the UK dot-com average.

Growth Markets

The company sees great scope for growth of the business; ultimately, this means forging relationships with organizations other than those who need to be contacted immediately before and after a move.

The UK government, which aims to have all its services online by 2005, is a current focus. Ihavemoved.com has been selected as one of the first private sector companies to work with the government on its electronic services delivery initiative, Government Gateway. A pilot has started which adds change of address services for the DSS, Department of Health, UK Passport Agency, DVLA, DVLNI and the Inland Revenue, to the Ihavemoved.com site. For the Passport Office this is especially attractive. The plan is to provide it with the technology to automatically contact people three months before their passport is due for renewal. This way, the renewal log-jam that occurs every summer can be prevented.

The company also sees the next logical step after capture of the residential market as that of commercial users. It plans to launch a business-to-business campaign in 2001 for small and medium-sized companies moving office and much of the second round of financing it seeks will be invested in pursuit of this aim.

There are also plans to form strategic partnerships with the site's backers. One investor, Hyundai, is willing to give the company access to markets in the Far East in exchange for Ihavemoved.com's marketing expertise.

Quality of Management

The core management team members all have their own areas of expertise: finance, IT, marketing, and sales. In a comparatively short space of time they have overseen partnerships with major blue-chip companies and received significant financial backing from investors. This, they believe, is because their proposition is fundamentally sound.

Each new recruit receives a copy of the business plan and there is an increasingly strong adherence to a business revenue model. An advisory board has been created, – foremost among whom is technology 'guru' Nicholas Negroponte, of Massachusetts Institute of Technology. The investors' acquiescence in putting back the target date for site profitability in order to establish a foothold in the German market demonstrates real faith in the methods of management. Such confidence is based on results rather than illusion. One illustration of this might be that the team of auditors appointed to investigate compliance with the Data Protection Act reported that the site was a model of best practice.

As the team has grown, so the founders have begun succession planning. They want to be able to extricate themselves from day-to-day management should the need arise, without jeopardizing the smooth functionality of operations. As to whether this is in readiness for flotation of the business, Anstee says, 'If you float, you decapitate a business for up to two months by taking out the top layer of management for investor presentations, analyst roadshows and the like, while there's a very intrusive due diligence process. So we're very cautious about the idea of going down the IPO route, though we don't rule it out.'

International Orientation

Capture of the German market is seen as a strategic priority. The country is a prime target because of its high Internet penetration and the nature of its property market. Moving is a particularly bureaucratic process and yet the population is highly mobile, with people more likely to follow where their work takes them than in the UK. As a consequence, renting rather than home ownership is the norm. The management team are all German nationals and were already known to their British counterparts. This means they share in the vision more strongly than if they were hired out there.

Yet the enthusiasm for Germany should not be read as the start of a European roll-out. The founders feel the country is a special case and are cautious about further expansion elsewhere in Europe. At the heart of any such decision, they say, will be a concern to ensure the existence of effective lines of communication.

Jobpilot was launched as Jobs and Adverts by Dr Roland Metzger in 1995 and rebranded across Europe in December 2000 as a single entity, 'jobpilot'. Founded in Germany, it operates in 15 European countries as well as in Singapore, Thailand and Malaysia, offering more than 60,000 job adverts and recruitment solutions to job seekers and personnel professionals. The UK arm was established in late 1999 and will consist of 70 staff by Easter 2001. Jobpilot.com is listed on the Neuer Markt in Germany, where in the first nine months of 2000 it turned over £17.8m, an increase of 197 per cent in revenues on 1999. It employs 1,000 people world-wide.

Scorecard:

Innovation	★★★
Flexibility	★★★★
Human resources	★★★
Growth markets	★★★
Quality of management	★★★★
International orientation	★★★★★

Biggest plus:
The ability to reap the benefits of a dot-com environment under the umbrella of an established parent company.

Biggest minus:
Staff are conscious they have to keep fighting every day to improve market share in a very competitive market.

jobpilot
Quick House
65 Clifton Street
London EC2A 4JE
Tel: 020 7684 7222
website: www.jobpilot.co.uk
e-mail: Info@jobpilot.co.uk

Jobpilot

The Business

Dr Roland Metzger holds nearly 44 per cent of stock in the group, with United Internet holding a 27.5 per cent stake and employees having 2.44 per cent in total. Established in 1995, Jobs and Adverts grew slowly for two years, then embarked on international expansion, publishing CVs world-wide and extending operations into South-East Asia. In 1998 it opened headquarters in Vienna and Zurich and in the following year the company rolled out offices across Europe.

James Sorrentino, now UK marketing manager, set up the UK arm of jobpilot and in the third quarter of 2000 the group acquired the British company Virtual Village Ltd. In the UK the company is London-focused, particularly gaining business from new media and telecoms sectors but with interest in online recruitment growing in the pharmaceutical and sales sectors. Global companies including Lucent Network Care and Nokia are among clients. 'One of our strengths is that we can recruit transnationally,' said Helen MacNamara, UK jobpilot.com's content and communications manager.

Innovation

Jobpilot.com deliberately employs staff with experience in recruitment consultancy rather than in selling, and prides itself on quality of service rather than quantity of sales. 'We hand-categorize the job advertisements that we receive, so that each job goes into the right sector. From a user's point of view, it's brilliant because it saves them from having to wade through irrelevant adverts,' said Ms Mac-Namara.

The aim is to offer a symmetrical service to job seekers and to corporate clients, with access for candidates through mobile phones and Web-cams, as well as the website and with the addition of complete back office recruitment solutions for HR professionals. These solutions increase the transparency and management of the whole recruitment process, speeding up the time to fill a post with quality candidates and reducing the administrative burden on the recruiter.

For example, via workflow software, being able to view the take-up of an advert placed, plus filtering services and other value-adding services such as pre-screening of applicants. Jobpilot.com is also talking to customers about introducing micro-sites for clients – a sub-division of a corporate website – which candidates can access to view a Web-cam presentation about the company. 'Recruitment is taking up more time and retention is increasingly important,' said Ms MacNamara.

'Our solution makes the HR manager's job easier and leaves them free to concentrate on running their department.'

In Britain, jobpilot.com finds itself in Europe's most competitive online recruitment market and has aimed to distinguish itself with a marketing campaign on sandwich bags and taxi-cabs (using the line 'Trafalgar Where?' in a speech bubble from the cab window, and the follow-on slogan 'In the wrong job?'). In 2000 it launched a banner campaign on the much-viewed *Big Brother* website, and has also put its message across by taking advantage of topical issues such as the American election race. In the next year, it is spending £5m on advertising in the UK alone.

The company has joined with brands including Freeserve, Gay.com and Handbag.com to raise its profile, and has linked up with a firm of solicitors in order to offer users legal services. Jobpilot.com is also in the process of applying for membership of the Association of Online Recruitment Consultants.

Flexibility

In the UK, the company has moved offices three times in 2000 because of rapid growth. 'The process of bringing more people on board has been managed by team building, and by keeping people informed and having good healthy internal communication,' said Ms MacNamara. When a new recruit joins the company, he or she will spend the first week with everyone in the office, a day with each department.

Jobpilot is acutely conscious of the need to work as a team, to the extent that it invested in team development by taking staff on an away-day in 2000. The employees were divided into three units and charged with the task of making a gangster movie, a spy movie or a Western. 'It was a brilliant team-building exercise. More than anything else, that really showed the kind of people we have in the company,' said Ms MacNamara.

The company is also aware of its ability to shape what is at present a malleable market. 'We're a very adaptable company because we have to be,' said Ms MacNamara. 'Part of what we are doing is to try to educate recruitment professionals into changing their habits. They are always a bit nervous about trying online recruitment, but they see that it works. Not only do they get the right people but they get them for a percentage of the cost. You buy an online advert for £250, but a similar sized advert in a newspaper would cost you £12,000. People used to advertise in newspapers and get lots of letters and CVs back in the post. We are now providing a way for clients to go out and look pro-actively. We also offer a workflow solution to help manage the responses, which can otherwise swamp the recruiter.'

Adapting to changing models on the Internet, jobpilot.com itself is becoming less reliant on publishing job adverts online, switching its focus to revenues which come from offering value-added services to HR professionals.

Human Resources

Jobpilot says it welcomes employees who are self-motivated and passionate team players. Recruits need to be flexible, equally ready to configure a laptop, give a presentation or roll up their sleeves to clear out a skip. 'There's a very open management structure, and a real sense that everyone has input and is valued,' said Helen MacNamara.

However, she cautioned: 'If you're very focused on your own thing you'll find it hard to fit in. I don't think there would be room, either, for the nakedly ambitious or someone who wasn't prepared to be patient, because things do take time and this is not a fly-by-night dot-com.'

The company has no enshrined set of values, but co-operation and consistent innovation are key features in its modus operandi. 'It requires a certain kind of culture to believe in your people and be always listening. It can be a bit of a pain when everyone likes to get their two-penn'orth in,' said Ms MacNamara. There is also a good deal of international camaraderie between offices. Every recruit visits the German headquarters, and there are opportunities within the company to be seconded abroad.

Growth Markets

In Britain about 5,000 companies have sprung up in the past five years to offer online recruitment services. Few, however, have a comprehensive spread across Europe. Jobpilot sees growth opportunities both cross-Continent and closer to home, where it is enhancing the user experience and pulling in extra traffic by developing channels on the site for various industry sectors, and offering a careers counsellor.

'On the HR professional side, time will tell, but I imagine there isn't much of their role that we can't help with,' said Ms MacNamara. 'Our remit is to offer a solution to things that are a real pain, so we're now thinking about strategic planning of recruitment campaigns.' Jobpilot has positioned itself at the top end of the market. 'We're not going to be the biggest and bounciest online recruitment service out there – it's all about quality. We're providing a better service and that's why clients will come back to us.'

Another area for focus is the undergraduate market. In Germany, jobpilot.com has launched Internet cafés on university campuses to promote its clients. In Britain, the company has launched a graduate channel catering specifically to student needs, and has plans to sponsor student events and exhibitions. 'Students are definitely a big growth area for us and we want to get them while they are young,' said the company.

Quality of Management

In Britain, Pat Elliott, formerly a marketing director at ICL, took over as managing director in autumn 2000, and the focus for management is now in three areas: staff development, process strengthening and business development. Developing staff has been intrinsic to the UK operation since it commenced: all staff receive initial and ongoing 'on the job' training, and several of the team have been supported by the company in external training, resulting in professionally recognized certification.

Each employee develops a training and development plan with his or her line manager, which is agreed during their appraisal. The company is also keen to develop a clarity of accountability and objectives, which enables every employee to have a defined role and be cognisant of how that will be measured. Remuneration then is based on merit and performance of the individual, as well as on the performance of the company.

At a time of rapid growth, the company is also intent on strengthening critical processes which underpin the business, from sales ledger processes through financial reporting to human resources processes. While these were all created along with the business, the aim is now to reinforce and clarify them, with software systems implemented to ensure they are rigorous enough to cope with continued growth. The intention is to build in controls and authority levels which will give the company sufficient flexibility, but a minimum of bureaucracy.

As the online recruitment market is rapidly developing, jobpilot.com is continually looking to develop its business capability in line with the company strategy, through alliances, partnerships and acquisitions. Working with vice-presidents in the German parent company, the UK company makes proposals for development opportunities and is then responsible for implementing and integrating new business ideas into the current business in the UK, as well as abroad.

In Germany, France and Poland, jobpilot.com has already secured the number one spot in terms of revenues and quantity of job adverts, registered users and page views. Its business model is profitable and the group has appointed top managers from organizations including FT.com and the *Wall Street Journal*. It now aims to repeat that success in Britain, where it is currently in the top eight companies in its sector.

However, it acknowledges that there is a steep learning curve to success, and is currently instituting a number of more formal evaluation procedures, such as peer group appraisal, mentoring schemes and a programme of six-monthly assessments. There is also a weekly progress meeting in the UK office.

Operations in each of the offices around Europe are monitored from jobpilot.com's headquarters in Bad Homburg, near Frankfurt in Germany, but the UK arm is a separate financial entity, expected to stand on its own two feet, but with a constant flow of ideas and support.

International Orientation

While jobpilot.com has cast its nets wide and is thinking about expansion into Africa as well as consolidation in Asia, its true focus is Europe. 'Our aim is to become Europe's leading career network on the Internet through selected acquisitions,' said the company recently. It does not plan to expand into the US at this point, but will focus on achieving and maintaining the top spot in Germany, France, Italy, Spain and the UK. It already has more than 12,500 corporate clients throughout Europe, and a presence in non-EU countries such as Hungary and Czech Republic. It has 600,000 registered users, with about 34 million page views per month.

While jobpilot has built up regional operations, it also strives for a monoculture 'in which we work together to share ideas and best practice,' said Ms MacNamara. 'One of the things we are trying to do at the moment is to bring together all the people who have similar jobs across Europe. For example, content managers at the moment have three-monthly meetings to build a communications loop. The country managers meet often and make strategic decisions,' she explained.

The company communicates globally via a weekly round-up bulletin called Hotline, and each department within the group sends round project reports fortnightly. 'We always have our eye on trying to include people and to listen,' said Ms MacNamara.

Johnson Matthey

Johnson Matthey is a world leader in advanced materials technology, applying the latest technologies to add value to precious metals and other specialized materials. The group's principal activities are the manufacture of catalysts and pollution control systems; the manufacture of pharmaceutical compounds; the refining, fabrication and marketing of precious metals; and the manufacture of decorative and specialized materials for the ceramics industry. British in origin, Johnson Matthey is unusually multinational and, of 6,500 employees world-wide, some 2,500 are in the UK. Johnson Matthey has operations in 34 countries, sells its products around the world and, in the year 2000, reported operating profits up 7 per cent to £146 million on turnover of £3,769 million.

Scorecard:

Innovation	★★★★
Flexibility	★★★★
Growth markets	★★★★★
Human resources	★★★★★
Quality of management	★★★★
International orientation	★★★★★

Biggest plus:
A friendly company – multinational, but with room for that personal touch.

Biggest minus:
A few of the traditional values still remain.

Johnson Matthey
2–4 Cockspur Street
London SW1Y 5BQ
Tel: 020 7269 8400
website: www.matthey.com

Johnson Matthey

The Business

Johnson Matthey (JM) is a highly successful British based but multi-national plc, it sells its products and services world-wide, and has its own operations in 34 countries. Founded in London's Hatton Garden by the two gentlemen whose pictures hang in the boardroom at its Trafalgar Square headquarters, the company's original forte was precious metals and its reputation for business integrity was unsurpassed. JM is still in the precious metals business, its reputation for integrity remains untarnished, but its products and the way in which the business operates are very much twenty-first century.

Innovation

According to the FTSE 100 index, Johnson Matthey is in the UK top 250, in terms of research and development spend, however, the company is firmly established in the UK's top thirty. 'Precious metals' no longer necessarily mean simply dealing in gold, platinum, or silver. There are extensive applications in the ceramics industry where JM is expanding its established business and is instrumental in the decoration of everything from porcelain to tiles: 'it is', says chief executive Chris Clark, 'a lot more than just supplying the gold line round the top of your Royal Doulton cup, although we do that too.'

It seems on first acquaintance unlikely that a Hatton Garden precious metals concern would seek entry to such apparently disparate fields as catalytic converters, fertilizers and anti-cancer drugs but the progression is a natural one: 'precious metals', says Clark, 'have catalytic properties, we've invested heavily in research on this and the result, I believe, is that our expertise is nothing less than world beating.'

As JM supplied the catalysts used for the supply of electrical power and drinking water in both the Apollo and Shuttle space programmes it is reasonable to describe the company's research and development as 'space age'. JM designs and manufactures 40 per cent of the world's catalytic converters and has partnerships with automobile giants such as Ford and General Motors. Research and development is ongoing: 'we are', says Clark, 'not far from the start in the race for environmental responsibility'. Current research involves not only improvements for conventional petrol and diesel engines but also for alternative energy supplies such as fuel cell technology which, Clark continues, 'could well lead to the long overdue replacement of the internal combustion engine – it is, after all, a pretty primitive means of propulsion and you could say it's about time the ICE age was over'.

Flexibility

The question is 'how has the company managed change in recent years including allowing for electronic commerce?' and the answer would appear to be 'very well indeed'.

'There is', says Chris Clark, 'probably no such creature as an organization or, for that matter, an individual, that never made a mistake – the real test of organizations and individuals is what they do about it. I think we've got many things right but of course JM has made mistakes – we've recognized them and done our best to put them right. That's what flexibility is about – you need it in order to survive and, to be successful, you need more and more of it. I'd still say we're prudent but that's no bad thing – if you're being adventurous about walking a tightrope sixty feet off the ground then it won't cause you any harm to be careful while you're doing it.'

JM's business strategy has deliberately been shifted from dependence on its traditional businesses to a wide range of advanced products. A sophisticated communications infrastructure is in place and JM is well positioned to take advantage of opportunities presented by electronic commerce.

JM has changed, is still changing and will continue to change. Traditional values remain; business standards and ethics are still rigorously and profitably observed, but today's Johnson Matthey is progressive, unbureaucratic, 'a lot slicker and faster in its dealings' – and very flexible.

In August 1999 the group sold its Electronic Materials Division to AlliedSignal Inc. for a profitable $655 million. JM is on the lookout for acquisition candidates.

Human Resources

JM prides itself on its ability 'to retain that all-important personal touch'. The company is highly communicative and its directors know the people in the organization – employees say 'it is easy to get noticed'.

JM today is characterized by individual leadership, by fast decision-making, by getting things done and by local responsibility. The type of person who flourishes at JM is bright, sparky, quick-thinking and action-oriented. JM employs people with character – definitely not clones – and the company's directors are said to be 'strong individual characters who value the same variety in employees'.

JM is an equal opportunities employer in fact as well as in theory – in what was a traditional male stronghold some 35 per cent of all employees are women and this includes the group's financial controller. A combination of old and new ideas has been the key to building a truly modern business for the future. This vision has been clearly communicated and subscribed to by employees; although many of the values were probably latent to the company anyway, and merely required articulating.

The group comes across strongly as an organization which, although it welcomes laurels, does not consider them resting places – the same goes for its Human Resources department.

Growth Markets

Expectations are ambitious – 'in five years' time', says Peter Garfield, 'I expect us to have doubled in size – about £250 million profit, share price doubled and I'd expect our total number of employees to have risen to more than twelve thousand'.

The catalyst business will grow – at a basic level environmental concerns over fuel emissions are in their infancy and, although the western world considers itself flooded with cars, the transport market in other parts of the globe where JM has already established itself is virtually untapped.

With more than 70 per cent of the world's power output consumed by cars, homes and offices the potential production of power 'at the point of use' is clearly attractive but the technology used must be clean, quiet and efficient. Fuel cells are clean enough for power to be generated at the point of use and can utilize a variety of fuels – when run on hydrogen, for example, the fuel cell is a true 'zero emissions' source of power, emitting only pure water. Fuel cells produce no particulates, are extremely quiet and can operate in the same room as people with almost no detrimental effect on the local environment. Johnson Matthey is committed to bringing fuel cell systems to market.

Quality of Management

Again this comes down to 'futuristic company with established traditional values' and 'it's not just the management – it's everyone involved'. It is regarded as important not only to know what's happening but personally to know the people involved and, since 1992, all high potential graduates recruited have been interviewed by the directors in an informal 'get to know you' bridge-building exercise.

JM regards its people development planning as 'excellent'. It considers senior management succession carefully, creating an impact which flows right down the organization. Graduates and other 'bright' employees go through an annual business training course. Fast-track middle managers join the management development programme, which is mirrored in the UK and US. Senior managers may find themselves on courses at INSEAD, Wharton and Harvard and high potential people have personal development interviews at appropriate intervals.

There is a real need for people who can deal with the inherent pressures and, quite simply, be better than the competition. Such people – in an average year JM takes on only about 20 of its thousand or so UK graduate applicants and admits to being 'very picky indeed' – are in short supply and it is recognized that recruitment, training and development are fundamental to having the right people for the right jobs.

JM believes strongly that far too much talent is diverted into the City or the Civil Service and away from British industry where, argues JM, it is most needed. The company has therefore established very close and personal links with leading UK universities in its quest to attract the cream of British graduates.

Employment and management policies are linked closely to business goals – Chris Clark demands a 20 per cent return on assets in all businesses and is bent on continuing to deliver the profitable growth for shareholders which has characterized the company in recent years.

International Orientation

But just how 'international' is Johnson Matthey? The answer is very. Some 4,000 of its current tally of 6,500 employees work outside the UK. The group's largest single international investment is in the US but JM's 'operations in 34 countries' encompass major investment in areas such as Africa, Australasia, China, India, Malaysia, South America. In short, the company has made its presence felt in all continents and its products are used extensively throughout the world.

Remaining in world-leading positions is often harder than getting there and, with JM competing increasingly on a global stage, 'prudent' international growth is anticipated. With serious cash reserves available it is thought likely that such growth will be approximately '75 per cent by acquisition and 25 per cent organic' but, in the words of chief executive Chris Clark, 'Johnson Matthey is flexible about this'.

Kensington Group plc

Kensington Group is one of the leading non-conforming mortgage lenders in the UK. Through its extensive relationships with financial advisers and other UK mortgage intermediaries, it identifies people who do not conform to the lending criteria of traditional mortgage providers. It then offers them a comprehensive service, including transparent processes and excellent after-sales treatment. It has achieved spectacular growth since its formation in 1995.

Scorecard:

Innovation	★★★★
Flexibility	★★★★★
Human resources	★★★★
Growth markets	★★★★
Quality of management	★★★★★
International orientation	★★★★★

Biggest plus:
Agile, dynamic, specialist operator.

Biggest minus:
Not yet a broadly based financial player.

Kensington Group
1 Derry Street
London W8 5HY
Tel: 020 7376 0110
Fax: 020 7937 4406
website: www.kmc.co.uk

Kensington Group

The Business

Kensington Group was formed in late 1994 to fill a gap in the mortgage market: offering mortgage loans to customers who fail to meet the increasingly strict lending criteria of traditional mortgage providers. Potential borrowers include temporary employees, those with credit problems, the self-employed and people needing larger loans. The company gives such borrowers a credible, reputable alternative.

It made its first mortgage loan in December 1995. Since then, Kensington Group has helped over 27,000 people to buy homes and has lent over £1.75 billion in mortgages. If the company were a building society it would rank in the top ten.

Innovation

Kensington Group is characterized by a set of principles. First, it follows industry best practice. It is a member of the Council of Mortgage Lenders, offers competitively-priced loans, and is transparent throughout its processes. Second, it focuses on parts of its business which differentiate it from other lenders – where it can add value. Administration is outsourced, allowing its 84 staff to focus on underwriting, sales and corporate finance. Third, it raises funding through mortgage 'securitization', a process of issuing bonds backed by the mortgage assets. This has brought the business a strong sense of discipline, since every loan must meet the standards of the credit agencies. And it is committed to serving its community through employing highly skilled and creative people.

The company is innovative. It seeks to match interest rates with risk. It manages customer relationships actively, including for instance calling every customer each month for three months after the sale. Its strong growth made flotation on the London Stock Exchange a natural move, and this came about on November 23, 2000.

The most obvious point about Kensington Group's culture is its strong market focus. John Maltby, chief executive: 'the size of our business, and our rapid growth, makes us very commercially focused. We are a results-driven company.' The company is also agile. In an industry traditionally more reactive than responsive, the company has made a name for itself through its rapid response and ability to maximize opportunities.

Another tenet central to the company's culture is its clear vision: to be the leader in its sector. This has made it highly information-intensive, dominated by people eager to find new ways of doing things.

Successful employees tend to be extrovert, ambitious for themselves and for the company, and equipped with strong teamworking and collaborative skills.

Inevitably, given the company's ambitious goals and the competitive market in which it operates, the work is challenging. Maltby: 'your people expect a lot of each other. We don't like passengers. Instead, we're delivery-focused. And those who deliver will flourish here. We believe in providing rewards commensurate with performance.'

Flexibility

Kensington Group is clearly initiative-driven. With such a new company, many processes and ways of doing things are not set in stone: people ambitious to take on projects can make their mark on the company's approach. Although very well controlled for a relatively youthful business, it is open in structure and the opposite of bureaucratic in nature. And though the company itself may be young, many of its employees have considerable experience gained at some of the industry's leading organizations. The skill set is widespread, and the ideas brought to the party by the staff are often taken on board rapidly.

It has to face a constantly-changing market as well, and as the first entrant it understands the need to adapt swiftly and to deliver new products to customers immediately the requirement appears to be there. This it manages by continually evaluating the market and developing relationships with the other key players in the field, such as the longer-established mortgage lenders.

Structurally the biggest change it has seen was as a result of its flotation. Although the organization had already experienced the rigours of reporting that the Stock Market required because as a financial company it was subject to similar regulations anyway, it has had to adjust to 60 per cent ownership by both institutions and private retail investors; the advantage being that it now has the capital to move even more swiftly when the market requires it.

The other area in which the group has a lot of flexibility is in customer turnover. It operates on a 'rate for risk' model, in other words its mortgages are not the cheapest, and it accepts that once someone has established a good track record in paying such an expensive mortgage they will want to move their borrowing somewhere less costly. It does everything it can to accommodate people moving their money in this way.

Human Resources

Kensington Group recognizes that its present eminence, as well as its future growth, depends on recruiting, motivating and developing the best people. As a result, good human resources has a high priority. The company is not obsessed with paper qualifications; in underwriting, for instance, it values staff experience over 'A' levels, degrees or professional certification. It is also difficult to find people, at least in Britain, with experience of 'securitization', so here it is happy to grow its own experts. As Maltby sums up: 'We don't require qualifications; we are happy to train people.'

Human resources impacts on existing staff in many ways. For instance, the company believes in open and active communication. To this end, it has invested substantially in its intranet. Communication is complicated by the company having three locations – its London headquarters and underwriting units in Skipton and Glasgow, as well as a mobile sales force. Head office management regularly travel to the other units, and an annual party helps to reinforce the company spirit.

Historically, staff turnover has been low. Above all, the company is fun to work for: energetic, stimulating, creative and problem-solving. The staff created a sports and social club in 2000 that quickly organized a whole series of events. It also put forward the suggestion of a dress-down Friday, which was quickly accepted. All vacancies are openly advertised throughout the group. Employees can earn a £500 bonus by recommending a suitable applicant to fill a vacancy.

Growth Markets

The advantage Kensington Group has over a number of other financial service players is that its market is growing sufficiently for it not to have to look too hard for its customers. Self-employment is on the increase in the UK, for example, and the demographic is shifting towards people working on short-term contracts. Such people are unable to find mortgages with traditional lenders, as are those with problems such as a bad credit history, or those who work freelance. These people may be perfectly able to pay a mortgage, but will be overlooked by usual suppliers.

A series of relationships with other companies is enabling Kensington Group to grow its market by selling on a business-to-business basis rather than by going straight to the consumer. This it does through a series of partnerships. Kensington Group has an arrangement with the Newcastle Building Society, and with many other introducers, who refer customers on when they are unable to lend them money themselves. Kensington Group then takes the trouble to find out why someone might have, say, a bad credit record – perhaps a divorcee has not received maintenance payments, and has had a problem temporarily. Kensington would be inclined to lend that person money whereas the rather black and white view of the established lenders would rule them out.

Kensington Group's business grew by 341 per cent in the year 2000 alone. Maltby says: 'In five years' time we want to be the leading financial services specialist in the UK. We believe we can extend our approach beyond our roots. If people need personal service and individual consideration, they will be able to come to us.' The way forward identified by the group is twofold: through partnership and acquisition.

Quality of Management

On a day to day basis, the group values its people above all of its other assets and makes efforts to manage them accordingly. For this reason appraisals always have three facets. First there is an evaluation and communication of company objectives and how they can be delivered; then the overall performance of an individual within the company is examined, and finally – rather more unusually – a personal effectiveness evaluation, to ensure that the individual in question is not only contributing but feels that they are. Also at this stage feedback is invited from employees.

On the corporate level, the main board contains a number of heavyweights who bring considerable experience with them. On the financial side there is representation from a former high-ranking executive at Abbey National, and one of the non-executive directors is also on the board of one of the UK's largest investment management companies. One of the other non-executive directors has experience of leading a major US merchant bank.

International Orientation

A move into the European market is not ruled out but, as Maltby says, 'the regulatory environment there is quite different, so acquisition would probably be the favoured route to the Continent'.

The challenges to the company are numerous. As well as the competition in its existing and potential markets, it faces the challenge of retaining its specialist focus, its agility, and its entrepreneurial skills while broadening into a larger organization. It also needs to continue to attract the best people. These challenges are not to be dismissed lightly. It has to be said, though, that on past form, Kensington Group looks set to enjoy continued success in the years to come.

do something **lastminute.com**

lastminute.com launched its first website in October 1998 as an online marketplace bringing together customers in search of inspiration and solutions at the last minute. The company went public in March 2000 and localized versions of the site have now been launched in seven European countries, Australia and South Africa. In August 2000 lastminute.com announced the proposed acquisition of Dégriftour, one of France's largest e-commerce companies. lastminute.com has its headquarters in London.

Scorecard:

Innovation	★★★★
Flexibility	★★★
Human resources	★★★
Growth markets	★★★★
Quality of management	★★★★
International orientation	★★★★★

Biggest plus:
You are able to take as much responsibility as you can in a dynamic entrepreneurial environment.

Biggest minus:
Not a good place to work if you like a quiet life.

Lastminute.com
4 Buckingham Gate
London SW1E 6JP
Tel: 020 7802 4200
website: www.lastminute.com

Lastminute.com

The Business

Set up in April 1998, lastminute.com is an online marketplace bringing together customers in search of inspiration and solutions at the last minute. Lastminute.com aims to provide a lifestyle solution and its range of products includes travel, leisure and shopping. With its head-quarters in London, the company was quick to expand beyond the UK and now has localized sites in seven European countries, as well as in Australia and South Africa.

The company is publicly quoted, having launched on Nasdaq and the London Stock Exchange in March 2000. In October 2000 it acquired Dégriftour, one of France's leading e-commerce companies, and now has approximately 600 staff world-wide.

Innovation

Lastminute.com is one of the few unique Internet businesses to have originated in Europe. It is an online business that does not exist in an offline world. The company leverages the power of the Internet to build a real-time last-minute marketplace.

As an early pioneer in European e-commerce lastminute.com was able to attract top quality investors such as Intel, Bass, Starwood, Sony Music, Deutsche Telekom, France Telecom and BAA plc. Furthermore the company has relationships with approximately 9,200 suppliers across its markets.

As well as developing these relationships, lastminute.com is con-tinually examining ways of using technology to reach out more effec-tively to its customers. It sees early investment in advanced technologies as serving a dual purpose: improving its own customer service and upping the stakes for the competition.

The company has invested a significant amount in redeveloping its IT architecture to provide faster response times and better scalability, plus support for personalization techniques that enable products and services to be targeted to specific customer preferences. It has estab-lished technology partnerships with several companies in the per-sonalization and search fields, including E.piphany, Ncorp and whereonearth.com. The ultimate aim is, in its own words, to be able to make the right offer to the right customer at the right time on the right device.

In terms of delivery channels, lastminute.com has already set up nine different mobile portal deals throughout Europe to make its ser-vice available over WAP and has digital TV deals in the UK and France.

It has been working with Nortel Networks, BT Syncordia and the University of Edinburgh to develop a speech recognition system that would enable customers to 'talk' to the site via a voice activated interface instead of using a screen-based interface. A pilot project was run just before Christmas 2000 in association with a specially produced Christmas Gift Catalogue.

Flexibility

Lastminute.com has already gone through a lot of changes in just over two years. First, it has grown from being a small start-up to a 600-strong public company with offices in several countries. The Dégriftour acquisition provided substantial further operations in France. In addition to integrating the two companies' different cultures, the acquisition also involves the assimilation of their two databases and business systems. In managing this expansion successfully the directors have risen to the challenge of building a strong and experienced senior management team while maintaining the company's inspirational culture.

Lastminute.com is also constantly expanding into new product areas offering cross-selling opportunities through a series of partnerships with supplier companies in the restaurant, entertainment and gift sectors. It currently has around 9,200 partnerships.

All these changes inevitably place demands on the company's business systems. Its investment in technology supports a flexible, scalable business platform that allows it to do business in many languages and currencies, through many delivery channels and across a wide variety of product lines. Lastminute.com is developing an extranet system that will reduce the cost of dealing with its many suppliers by enabling suppliers to enter their products directly into the lastminute.com database.

Human Resources

Lastminute.com prides itself on its entrepreneurial spirit and its recruitment policy, part of which, according to Hoberman, has been to take on, alongside experienced executives, 'very clever 25-year-olds' who it feels can provide the energy, enthusiasm and innovative approach that has fuelled the company thus far. In contrast with organizations where the route to the top is by toeing the company line, lastminute.com tends to reward staff for cutting through red tape and finding unconventional solutions to problems.

The merger with Dégriftour, a nine-year-old company with established business processes, is considered a perfect complement to lastminute.com's current culture.

Growth Markets

By last summer, lastminute.com had grown to be the number one travel site in Europe in terms of Internet user penetration, according to figures from media research group MMXI. However the company's products and services are not just limited to travel. Had the site been categorized in the retail section lastminute.com would have been the second most visited retail website in Europe. To demonstrate the breadth of the lastminute.com service 56 per cent of items sold through the site in the UK in the December 2000 quarter were non-travel related.

The brand has been very cost effectively marketed through an award winning ad campaign on the theme of 'making every minute count', using a mix of media that includes billboards, posters, radio and press advertising, and promotions such as its lastminute.com vouchers distributed on approximately 50 million Nestlé chocolate bars.

Its next step will be to move into last minute services such as taxis, babysitting, and hairdressing – highly customer-specific areas where the personalization support on its site will really come into its own.

Lastminute.com will use a combination of business partnerships and advanced technology to enable it to grow without having to dramatically increase its headcount.

Quality of Management

Co-founders, Martha Lane Fox and Brent Hoberman, both had previous experience in the new media sector before launching lastminute.com. Lane Fox, the company's group managing director, specialized in pay TV at Spectrum Strategy Consultants before spending a year as business development manager at Carlton Communications. Hoberman, chief executive officer, also comes from Spectrum where he was involved in setting up a number of Internet companies. Five years of strategy consulting preceded this and Hoberman was also part of founding teams at QXL.com and LineOne.

The two founders have surrounded themselves by building a team of high quality executives from the travel and entertainment worlds. In addition, they have been careful to bring to their board what Hoberman describes as 'people with more experience than us,' successfully attracting six highly respected non-executive directors. Recently appointed chairman, Allan Leighton, comes with impeccable bricks-and-mortar credentials: previously chairman and CEO of Wal-Mart Europe, he has also worked for the Mars Corporation, and Asda Group.

Lastminute.com has rapidly developed from start-up into a pan-European e-commerce company. Although the company's share price has been subject to intense scrutiny and fluctuations ever since, lastminute.com continues to execute ahead of plan and can point to solid growth in the financial year ending December 2000: transaction value is up sevenfold to £50.2 million, gross profit nearly elevenfold to £5.8 million, and gross margins up 3.9 percentage points to 11.5 per cent.

International Orientation

Lastminute.com sees penetration into global markets as bringing advantages for its customers and suppliers, offering customers a wider choice of products from around the world and bringing its suppliers a broader customer base. The company has already proved that its formula works equally well inside and outside the UK. The company's new technology platform makes it easier to generate localized versions of its basic site in different languages and different currencies and is much more scalable.

During 1999 and 2000 it launched a number of localized sites overseas and now operates in seven European countries plus Australia and South Africa through joint venture agreements.

leapingsalmon
[stress is for the other fish]

leapingsalmon is the brainchild of co-founders James Marshall and Peter Kenyon. Two years old from incorporation and trading since February 2000, its business is predicated on a blissfully simple idea; people love to eat great food and enjoy the creative parts of cooking but do not always have time to do the shopping or prepare the ingredients. So leapingsalmon delivers all the fresh ingredients the cook needs, cut, cleaned and measured, to cook a gourmet meal in 30 minutes or less. Eight staff currently work for the organization, which outsources most of its non-core functions.

Scorecard:

Innovation	★★★★★
Flexibility	★★★★★
Human resources	★★★
Growth markets	★★★★★
Quality of management	★★★★
International orientation	★★★

Biggest plus:
Innovative product with a well-understood audience served by a team with a commitment to excellence.

Biggest minus:
Share options and other benefits have yet to be formalized – they will be, however.

Leapingsalmon.com
Nightingale House
1–7 Fulham High St
London SW6 3JH
Tel: 020 7598 3077
website: www.leapingsalmon.com

Leapingsalmon.com

The Business

leapingsalmon is a service company that has achieved massive awareness in a remarkably short time by understanding the way home dining is evolving as a lifestyle option. It takes people who cannot afford the time to shop and prepare intricate recipes and offers them raw ingredients, pre-measured and sliced, so that they get all the pleasure from cooking and none of the tedium. Whilst the Internet has been used effectively to launch and promote the service, leapingsalmon is not a dot-com, rather it is a service company operating in the home meal replacement category and using different channels to distribute the product. The delivery of the ingredients is outsourced to keep overheads down; the business has succeeded in attracting two major rounds of financing and may seek a third for accelerating growth during 2001.

Innovation

The concept itself was unique at the outset: it occurred when the founders, at the time working in the corporate world, found they did not always have time to shop and prepare good food at home but at the same time were frustrated by the quality of alternatives such as takeaways or ready meals – something the company thinks of as 'Tuesday Evening syndrome'! The notion of delivering freshly prepared ingredients for a gourmet Michelin-style meal to someone's office or home in a cool bag was a natural step to take, but nobody was doing it at the time and the direct competition continues to be thin. It won a Vision 100 award for its insight into home dining trends and the future of the Home Meal Replacements category, as well as the Revolution award for 'Best Startup' in 2001.

The company was incorporated in November 1999 and the website started trading in early 2000. Take-up has been excellent with minimal spending on marketing, and word of mouth has been a valuable means of promotion. Press coverage has been overwhelmingly positive since the launch and in a survey in early 2001 the company found awareness at up to 70 per cent in London. Pricing the goods in a similar bracket to those of upmarket takeaway/delivery services has been a help.

Uptake has been helped by an increased awareness of quality food in the UK particularly over the last 5 years, and Marshall confirms that customers are less inclined to compromise than they used to be. For this reason the organization contracts recipes from experienced chefs, several of whom run Michelin-starred restaurants. Research tends to be done informally; customers are not shy of offering feedback and nor are the eight staff, all of whom are dedicated foodies. Directors and other staff regularly host 'focus groups' to test the various offerings on the menu, which is kept under constant review.

Other small innovations the company has put in place include a wine matching service in which carefully selected wines are recommended to go with specific food and then delivered in the same order.

Flexibility

A company as young as leapingsalmon has little in the way of history and has yet to demonstrate any examples of restructuring or managerial flexibility, but it has the mechanisms in place to cope when change is demanded. The founders have ensured that everything possible is outsourced, even down to hiring external chefs to develop the recipes and a serviced office so that administration spending is kept to a minimum.

The company is responsive to customer demands and introduces new menus every couple of weeks while striving to maintain innovative and modern recipes. It is constantly exploring new partnerships with which to join in promotions, and it will continue to investigate new channels by which customers can contact it as these channels emerge.

Other possibilities will include discounts for bulk orders on certain goods – for the moment, the menu is aimed at two-person dining, although numerous customers happily buy items for larger-scale entertaining.

Things that won't change are the commitment to excellence both in terms of the recipes and the quality of the ingredients; the company prides itself on presenting customers with ingredients they won't easily find in a local supermarket as well as exceptional customer service and fulfilment.

Human Resources

Most of the staff have joined the company to get away from the corporate world, and they all thrive in the start-up environment. Flexibility is therefore essential, so anybody likely to be offended by the sight of the CEO shifting furniture around should basically look elsewhere.

As a new company and a small one trying to allow staff to get away from the corporate mould, its human resources facilities might be described as basic; there are no share options as yet although these will be offered as the company matures. However, people working for leapingsalmon get a competitive salary package and the chance to work in a bonus-driven environment which will no doubt mature as the company expands, backed by managers with solid business experience as well as enthusiasm.

Growth Markets

While leapingsalmon's typical audience is the 25–45 bracket, it has a wide variety of customers ranging from students to pensioners and these are also targeted through a series of promotions and partnerships. Its typical customers are couples who, to paraphrase James Marshall, have the inclination to do the fun bits of cooking but not the time to do the tedious bits – the chopping, the shopping. He likens the experience to that of a TV chef – all the ingredients for a superb meal are delivered prepared and measured but the creative fun of cookery is still available for the customer.

As the push towards convenience food continues together with society's insistence on quality the company's core market is set to grow rapidly. Cookery programmes on television are doing much to increase the awareness of good quality food while lifestyles are allowing for less time to be taken to prepare it; the irony is that the consumer is now less inclined to compromise on quality than ever before while the time available to do something about it is diminishing. Leapingsalmon is perfectly positioned to bridge this apparent gap and the growth of its customer base suggests that it is doing so.

Quality of Management

As a company with such a short track record it's difficult to comment on leapingsalmon's management in anything other than abstract terms, since it has had no major restructures or issues to face in its first couple of years. However, both founders come from a corporate background and have MBAs, plus aggressive plans for the business to expand as quickly as possible. It has been reported in the press, for example, that the company will pull into profit in 2001; Marshall remains noncommittal on exact timing because accelerated growth through a third round of financing is also under consideration.

Ultimately the directors offer their experience, the company's trading record, excellent brand and the fact that the business has a good margin built in, as reassurance to any shareholders or potential shareholders. Repeat business is also high – customers tend to come back once they have purchased once.

International Orientation

Food delivery might sound like a localized concern but leapingsalmon already has an eye on the overseas market, although its plans of how it will address this have yet to be made public. The possibility of a franchise style of business has much to recommend it, but so does the direct presence route and although Marshall is committed to expansion he has yet to confirm which of those routes he will take. The business should certainly become international over a period of time.

Meanwhile growth in the UK continues apace with huge potential still there. The immediate priority is to increase awareness of the brand – something that appears to have gone very well indeed – keep the margins steady and build a solid business domestically.

If its performance so far can be taken as indicative of its potential, then it should be one to watch.

Set up in August 1997, Lycos UK is one of the UK's leading portal sites. It combines a search engine and a range of services including news, chat rooms, directories, maps, free Web-mail and free text messaging, and vertical channels covering sports, finance, entertainment and travel. Lycos UK is a wholly-owned subsidiary of Lycos Europe, a joint venture between Lycos Inc and German media group Bertelsmann. Lycos UK has 65 employees based at its headquarters in London.

Scorecard:

Innovation	★
Flexibility	★★
Human resources	★★★★
Growth markets	★★★
Quality of management	★★
International orientation	★★★

Biggest plus:
Lively, fast-moving environment.

Biggest minus:
Some could find the constant change unsettling.

Lycos Europe
3rd floor
Terminal House
52 Grosvenor Gardens
London SW1W 0AU
Tel: 020 7881 6505
Fax: 020 7881 6550

Lycos

The Business

Set up in August 1997, Lycos UK is one of the UK's best-known and longest-established portal sites. As well as its search engine and main directory, it also offers a range of services including news, vertical information channels, chat rooms, maps, free Web mail and free text messaging. Most of the company's revenues currently come from advertising and click-through fees, but it is planning to move further into e-commerce. It is aiming to move into profit in 2003–4. Based in London, Lycos UK is a subsidiary of Lycos Europe. It has 65 employees, based at its headquarters near London's Victoria Station.

Innovation

Lycos has invested a lot of time and money in developing a strong consumer brand identity. Its distinctive black labrador logo, reinforcing the idea of the site as a loyal companion that will fetch information for the user, has been publicized via poster and media ads and through campaigns on TV and radio. Marketing takes up about three-quarters of its total costs.

As the 'Lycos, go get it' catchline suggests, a choice of powerful search facilities is Lycos UK's main differentiator. Around 25–30 per cent of people using the site each day use the search facilities, which include the main Fast search engine, the Hotbot precision search engine, based on Inktomi search technology, or the Lycos directory, which now contains around 100,000 links and provides an alternative way to narrow down content on the Web.

The directory is the jewel in the Lycos crown. The company prides itself on using human intelligence to select the links rather than relying on automatic web crawlers. It has a team of 30 link editors whose job is to surf the Web and pick out the best links. As well as serving as a draw for visitors, the search facilities serve another purpose: the visitor's selection can be used to generate the kind of targeted ads which are preferred by advertisers and which are more likely to generate lucrative click-through revenues.

Lycos UK offers a number of information channels, with specialist information contributed by Lycos's network of over 50 partners. Within travel, for example, information on late travel deals is contributed by Thomas Cook. Other bricks-and-mortar partners include BT, Lloyds and TSB.

A distinctive Lycos feature is the Tripod homepage building and community site, launched at the end of 1998 throughout Lycos Europe.

In the UK, it supports chat rooms, forums and personal home page publication. Lycos UK plans to use Tripod as a way of enhancing its local content over the coming months.

Also available from Lycos UK is the ability to send free SMS messages from the Web to mobile phones. In contrast with its major rival Yahoo!, however, Lycos UK has so far avoided getting into WAP. It believes that SMS services are currently driving the mobile data market in the same way that e-mail has driven the Internet.

During 2001, Lycos UK will be adding a number of innovative products and services to its portal. These include the launch of its Angelfire youth community, a new Lycos Chat service, and love@lycos, an online flirting service which went live in the spring and attracted 207,000 page views on its first day live.

Flexibility

Though Lycos UK regards itself as a brand rather than a technology company, technology is its next biggest cost after marketing and provides an essential basis for responding flexibly to changes in the market. Hosting its service in-house makes it easier for the company to act fast as market needs change.

Its core technologies – the Fast search engine and Tripod community management system – provide a foundation on which Lycos UK can develop a variety of services. The company has aimed to develop its services in a technology-neutral way, enabling it to capitalize on new delivery channels such as interactive television and mobile devices as they start to take off.

Human Resources

The company's workforce divides into four groups with a fairly diverse range of skills. Marketing, sales and business development together account for about two thirds of the staff, with the rest working on content production and technical support. Content editors are generally specialists in a particular field; for example, the current news editor formerly worked in news reporting for a national newspaper. Movement within the multinational parent company means that there's a wide mix of nationalities on staff.

One common feature, however, is that most staff are in their 20s. The company is changing fast, and anyone working for Lycos needs to be comfortable with an atmosphere of high uncertainty. Because of this, it tends to recruit young, self-sufficient people who are happy to work on their own initiative and aren't bothered by the lack of a stable corporate framework.

Growth Markets

Unlike many dot-coms, Lycos UK is in the happy position of being able to draw on the resources of a large and wealthy parent company to fund its growth. Though Lycos Europe made an operating loss of around £66 million in 1999–2000, its revenues trebled and the company is cash-rich, having raised $649 million in an initial public offering last March.

At the moment, most of Lycos UK's revenue comes from banner advertising and click-through fees. Though this could be seen as a risky situation given the number of players competing for advertisers in the portal space, Lycos Europe nonetheless experienced 70 per cent growth last year and has 1800 advertising clients across Europe. Only 20 per cent of these are dot-coms, indicating that bricks-and-mortar clients are coming online.

Lycos also argues that as one of the leading portal sites, it is well placed to win what advertising business there is. According to a November 1999 study by Jupiter Research, 75 per cent of all online advertising revenue online went into the top 15 sites. Lycos derives additional revenue through white labelling and revenue share agreements.

The site already offers a limited range of online shopping opportunities via partner organizations – for example, book buying via Bol.com – but Lycos is looking to further develop its e-commerce revenues with a dedicated shopping channel due for launch in April 2001. Through the acquisition of IBO, which powers the Pangora shopping platform, Lycos Europe has gained access to an extensive product database of 2.5 million products which it can offer to Internet shoppers throughout Europe.

During 2001 Lycos UK will be expanding its finance, news, travel, sports and entertainment sections, and adding new information channels covering areas such as finance and cars, which will provide further scope for e-commerce deals with partner organizations.

Alongside this, the company plans to develop its UK content and turn itself into a focal point for local communities centred around specific interests such as football. It intends to capitalize on its Tripod community management system by increasing the number of local Tripod discussion groups, known as pods, and the company is actively trying to recruit new moderators – or poderators.

Rather than getting into WAP information services, Lycos has so far chosen to focus on SMS, which it sees as the main focus for mobile data services. The site's free SMS service has proved to be a major growth area. Visitors can use it to send free text messages from their PC to a mobile phone and the service has taken off in a big way, with up to 400,000 messages sent out daily. Though it is free to users, it can be used to generate revenue by sending out highly time-sensitive advertising at the end of messages; for example, Channel 4 used it to alert people to watch a newly-launched programme showing the same evening.

Quality of Management

'As local as possible, as central as necessary' is the management credo of Lycos Europe, Lycos UK's parent company. On one hand, the company recognizes that it can achieve huge economies of scale from centralizing resource-intensive functions such as product development. On the other, it is committed to operating on a local level, adapting its products and services to the needs of local markets.

To achieve this, it operates a matrix management structure. Alex Kovach, managing director of Lycos Europe, works with both the managing directors of the other European country operations, and with directors responsible for pan-European functions such as mobile computing, e-commerce, product development and European marketing, to plan common objectives across Europe.

But Kovach, like other country managers, is also given the autonomy to set his own objectives and strategy for the UK market. Kovach had experience of both conventional and online business before joining Lycos. He spent several years with Royal Dutch Shell followed by a stint at Price Waterhouse, and helped set up an Internet start-up company. He is supported by a team of four directors with an eclectic mix of new media and general business experience. His marketing director previously worked for Disney and On Digital; the product director comes from Yahoo!; the business development director has banking experience; and the sales director is a Lycos veteran.

International Orientation

Lycos Europe is a network of portal sites set up in May 1997 as a joint venture between Lycos Inc and German media group Bertelsmann. It claims to be the overall leading European portal network, generating 1.5 billion page views a year as of last September, up by 198 per cent on the previous year. The company recently strengthened its position in Europe by acquiring the French MultiMania online community, giving it a combined page view figure of 1.7 billion.

Lycos UK is the UK and Ireland subsidiary of Lycos Europe and as such, its strategy is extreme localization rather than globalization. Rather than looking to move into new overseas markets it will be seeking to provide more in-depth, micro coverage of its home territory, both through more highly localized content and by extending its existing community structure to encourage development of more communities centred around local interests and issues, and hosting of individual home pages.

In order to strengthen its ties with local communities it opened a northern office in Manchester in the spring of 2001.

madaboutwine.com

Madaboutwine.com is an online wine retailer that aims to 'inform and entertain' as well as supply wines to suit all tastes. Originally founded as The Rare Wine Cellar in late 1995, by Mark Bedini and Bud Cuchet, the UK-based company was launched in March 1999 as a specialist e-commerce wine merchant as a result of a joint venture between the original company and the technology company Net-Decisions.

Scorecard:

Innovation	★★★★
Flexibility	★★★★
Human resources	★★★★
Growth markets	★★★
Quality of management	★★★★
International orientation	★★★★

Biggest plus:
It is an exciting place to work with plenty of growth opportunities.

Biggest minus:
It operates in a highly competitive market.

Madaboutwine.com
Capital House
159 Hammersmith Road
London W6 8BS
Tel: 020 8762 8300
Fax: 020 8762 8301
website: madaboutwine.com

Madaboutwine.com

The Business

Madaboutwine.com was launched as a specialist e-commerce wine merchant in March 1999. It started life as The Rare Wine Cellar in late 1995. Chairman and managing director, Mark Bedini, has spent his entire adult life in various aspects of the wine business and sees the Internet as providing the opportunity to bring 'unparalleled choice and service across all aspects of premium wine and associated products to a world audience'. The company is based in West London, has a warehouse in East London, and a call centre in the north of England.

Innovation

There are several other direct selling wine companies. But Madaboutwine.com is convinced that it can succeed by becoming a large player in a highly fragmented market and by using multiple channels – including the website, a catalogue and interactive television – to reach its customers. In addition, it uses a group of wine writers to supply editorial content and so create an image or personality for the service that lives up to the company name.

The company is adamant that it can see no point in trying to compete with supermarkets at the cheap end of the market. But at the same time, it is genuinely trying to appeal to a wide audience of wine lovers. There is a deliberate attempt to abandon the somewhat stuffy image of serious wine retailing by combining being authoritative with laughing at itself. 'It stops us being a club. It stops us being elitist,' says Bedini.

It was the desire to create as robust an operating system as possible that led it to make a deal with Net Decisions. Mr Bedini's old company entered into a joint venture with the technology company because it did not have enough resources to develop the service it wanted on its own. As a result, the company combines Net Decisions' technical expertise with the 20 years' experience of the wine business gathered by Mr Bedini.

Having seen the value of partnerships, the company is now working with well-known companies to sell wines through their websites. This has the benefit of introducing the company to a wider range of customers. 'It's expanding the market. It's an opportunity to do another Amazon.com with wine,' says Mr Bedini.

Flexibility

The company's commitment to flexibility is demonstrated by its readiness to reinvent itself in order to exploit developing technology. Moreover, it has seen the value of linking up with a partner in order to make the most of that technology without threatening its expertise in the area of its core business.

Madaboutwine's management is aiming to build on this approach to develop further relationships with businesses that might have customers with shared interests. At the same time, it is developing close relationships with suppliers with the aim of giving them access to wines to which they might not normally have access. In Mr Bedini's words, 'the philosophy of the business is to work hand in glove with brand owners (chateaux or marketing companies) and co-operate.

The flexible attitude extends to its marketing strategy. Convinced that the company has a 'brilliant' brand name, Mr Bedini says the company has done direct marketing to promote it but has not rushed into online advertising. Cross-promotional activity with partners with demographically-fitting databases is the preferred approach for now – in support of the growth plan of working with established brands to develop consumer confidence in the madaboutwine name.

Human Resources

Even though it is a relatively young company, madaboutwine.com regards having a human resources policy as highly important. A particular concern is retaining the quality staff it has attracted and the company has been supported by Net Decisions in developing a clear human resources strategy.

This involves creating mentors, setting objectives, giving staff regular reviews to help them develop their careers and rewarding employees appropriately. In addition, there is a share option scheme in which the whole workforce participates.

In common with other growing companies, madaboutwine has a fast-moving, energetic environment that Mr Bedini admits might prove uncomfortable for some. Staff have come from a variety of backgrounds besides the wine trade – helping various facets of the company to develop. But they tend to be flexible and motivated individuals who are happy operating beyond the confines of their supposed roles.

'By and large, the human resources policy works,' says Mr Bedini, adding that he always thinks people should enjoy where they work.

To this end, the company's values very much echo the name – quirky, fast-paced, but passionate about wine and customer service. 'All staff have to be energized about delivering wine on time to customers,' concludes Mr Bedini.

Growth Markets

The company has always planned to establish its home market of the UK first. 'If we can't do it in our own backyard, there's no point in going abroad,' explains Mr Bedini. However, madaboutwine is interested in talking to overseas partners on the grounds that the best way of expanding into new markets is to link up with businesses that are already there and know how they operate.

Quality of Management

Pointing out that he is a shareholder as well as the chief executive, Mr Bedini says the great advantage of the boom in the dot-com economy in 2000 was the opportunity it gave a company like his to attract different sorts of recruits. The high-profile given to Internet-related businesses meant that many more people with business backgrounds in both management consultancy and established corporates had joined the company than would have been the case had it been a traditional wine business. The result was a very strong team of people. Recruits from as far afield as Australia have brought expertise in various facets of business as well as particular types of wine and direct selling.

In order to build on this, the company has instituted a management appraisal system. It has also launched a share option scheme in order to create a link between rewards and performance and locked in key management for a period of time.

International Orientation

Because madaboutwine.com relies for its stock on dealing with countries as far apart as France, Italy, Australia and the United States, the company inevitably has an international approach. Moreover, its origins in another wine business, Fine and Rare Wines, give it numerous contacts in overseas markets – the US, for example, which is a key market for some of its items.

The international aspect of the business is likely to increase in importance as the company expands its operations.

MAERSK

The Maersk Company Limited is a large shipowner and transportation operator which employs 3,400 people and has offices in London, Felixstowe, Southampton, Birmingham, Liverpool, Glasgow, Dublin, Belfast and Aberdeen. It operates over 50 British-flagged and crewed vessels, ranging from tankers to container ships, and is involved in offshore drilling for oil and gas.

Scorecard:

Innovation	★★★★★
Flexibility	★★★★
Human resources	★★★★★
Growth markets	★★★★
Quality of management	★★★★★
International orientation	★★★★★

Biggest plus:
The opportunity to work for a solid company that leads its market.

Biggest minus:
The pace of change can be unsettling for some.

The Maersk Company Limited
One Canada Square
Canary Wharf
London E14 5DP
Tel: 020 7712 5000
Fax: 020 7712 5100
website: www.maersk.co.uk

Maersk Company Limited

The Business

The Maersk Company Limited is part of the A P Møller Group, a global network of specialized companies employing 50,000 people in 325 offices and 100 countries. Founded in Copenhagen in 1904, the group's core activities are shipping and transportation. It introduced a cargo liner service in 1928 and began shipping ocean-borne containers in 1973. Today it operates more than 250 container vessels and 800,000 containers, as well as over 100 tankers. Aside from its core businesses, the group has diversified into other areas which include exploration and production of oil and gas, shipbuilding, aviation, IT solutions and retail. In 1951 operations began in the UK, where the Maersk Company is now the largest single shipowner.

Innovation

A favourite saying of A P Møller, the group's late founder, was 'If a thing is worth doing, it is worth doing well' and inherent in its business ethos is a desire to improve upon accepted methods. Maersk has long held that its employees represent a big part of its competitive edge and it invests substantial sums in its world-class training and development programme.

A similar attitude prevails in regard to research and development in its various business fields. Indeed, such is Maersk's reputation for innovation in ship construction that many of its designs have been copied by competitors. It was the first shipowner to build the largest classification of freight vessel (6,600 Twenty-foot equivalent units) currently in operation, and ten years ago built the largest ship able to navigate the Panama Canal.

Maersk's willingness to invest in new technology for its container ships also pushed it ahead of the competition. It has built up particular expertise in food transportation; for example, perfecting a system for the transportation of raw fish over long distances – which, in the process, helped contribute to the growth in popularity of Japanese food around the world.

In 1962, the A P Møller Group was awarded the concession for exploration and production of oil and gas in Denmark. Thanks to Maersk's pioneering horizontal drilling technique oil has been sourced from tight reservoirs and supply now exceeds demand for that country.

The company is also a benchmark for safety and manning standards. All seafaring employees are trained at Maersk's sea cadet colleges around the world. Trainees undertake a 3–4 year sandwich course, which combines academic study with onboard training and leads to NVQ level 3. The company spends around £30,000 per individual each year.

Flexibility

According to Ulrik Brandt, the Maersk Company's managing director, 'We're very careful in the way we invest our money, but we have the strength to invest wherever we see opportunities, and in international shipping that's all important. You must be able to act when the time is right. The most successful shipowners are the ones who are building when times are tough so that they are ready for when the market improves – for trade is very cyclical.'

At the end of 1999, Maersk bought the international business of Sea-Land, a US container ship operator, for £800 million. The acquisition increased its capacity by over 60 per cent making Maersk Sealand the world's largest ocean liner carrier – twice the size of its nearest competitor. The expansion is in line with the rising level of global trade, itself a by-product of a continuing economic growth, and has strengthened Maersk's dominant market position without breaching anti-trust laws.

Recently, Maersk's willingness to invest in new technology has helped push it further ahead of the competition. It pioneered an online booking and cargo tracking system for its customers, allowing them to track the progress of a shipment from anywhere in the world. All data is retrieved from a leading-edge global transportation system and reflects the most up-to-date and accurate information available.

Maersk has also demonstrated flexibility in regard to its people. The company is all too aware that globalization has brought with it changed customer needs; rather than restrict itself to selling cargo space aboard its vessels, it sees future business opportunity in integrated logistics and transportation service provision – that is, in moving products from factory to customer. In order to provide consistency of service across local markets, the company jettisoned its traditional policy of hiring Danes for management positions. At the start of last decade, 90 per cent of new management trainees were Danish. Today, more than three quarters are from other nationalities.

Human Resources

Maersk does not attract the type of person that likes putting down roots. Long before most companies began using transfers to foreign operations as a retention tool, it was sending its people around the world, getting them to learn foreign languages and thinking local – yet retaining throughout the Maersk way of business.

The process begins with the Maersk International Shipping Education (MISE), an international scheme developed by the A P Møller group. The two-year course combines practical education – involving placements in different departments in offices around the country – with theoretical education: this includes the study of two foreign languages and an accountancy course. In addition, modular training at the MISE academy in Copenhagen gives trainees the opportunity to meet future colleagues from around the world. Last year, 14 trainees from the UK were placed on the course.

Nowadays, the idea of a job for life is seen as outdated in many quarters. Not at Maersk. The assumption is that employees can find everything they might want from a career there and those who decide to leave are rarely welcomed back.

Growth Markets

Maersk's diversification means that it is not reliant on one area for growth. However, these are good times for its core business. International trade was estimated to be growing at around 5 per cent annually; in the last few years, however, some areas have been expanding at between 20 to 30 per cent. For Maersk, the creation of Maersk Sealand and the acquisition of a new shipyard in the Baltic have helped keep the company in the front rank of shipowners. Now carrying 1.5 million containers annually, it wants to build on its current 11 per cent share of the market.

Maersk is also involved in the onshore and offshore oil and gas industries with Maersk Contractors and Salamis (M&I) Limited. Maersk Contractors operate in drilling, floating production and environmental activities, whilst Salamis (M&I) provide fabric maintenance services.

Elsewhere, deregulation of the airline industry has created more opportunities for regional airline operators; Maersk Air is stepping up the number of its charter flights to service the growth in European tourism travel. Maersk Medical will continue to invest in the development and production of new types of single-use medical products at its sites at Redditch, Sheffield and Stamford – drawing on 250 years' expertise in this highly specialized field.

Quality of Management

The link to Maersk's founder remains strong to this day. A P Møller's son took over as leader after the former's death in 1965 and though he withdrew from day-to-day management activities last decade, is still chairman. He oversees a company that is widely recognized as a byword for excellence in the shipping industry; one that has, in recent years, been repeatedly named best shipping line in the world by trade publications. Last year the A P Møller Group was ranked second best transportation operator in the world in a *Financial Times* survey.

The company has forged close links with governments around the world. It was a major sponsor on the occasion of the visit of the Danish prime minister to China for the fiftieth anniversary of the establishment of diplomatic relations between the two countries, and when it expanded its Spanish container terminal, the inauguration was presided over by the King of Spain. 'If you have a Maersk business card, doors will open for you. We as Maersk people are very aware of that,' says Ulrik Brandt.

Almost everything the company does is the result of strategic planning. Its acquisition of Sea-Land was completed in less than a year; but the two carriers had begun vessel-sharing agreements as early as 1991 and created a formal alliance four years later.

International Orientation

Because Maersk is a shipowner and transportation operator, its very nature dictates it must have a strong international focus. Indeed, while an increasing number of companies redefine themselves as global rather than national operations, the A P Møller Group's international identity and corporate culture are inextricably linked. Despite its size and reach, there are bigger and better-known companies that may be more immediately attractive to managers of the future. Few, however, can offer the breadth of international activities to new recruits so early on in their career that Maersk does. A philosophy of rotation is made to work through the strength of its training programme; in this way, employees can be moved around every few years and acclimatize immediately to each new assignment.

Magic4 is a development company set up to provide tools and software for the mobile telephony business, aimed at extending the functions and messaging services available from handsets. This goes way beyond the capability of SMS text messaging that has become so popular. Launched in March 2000, Magic4 is in fact a spin-off from Philips. Two key people in the consumer communications group came up with the 'software for mobiles' idea, for value-added services and left to start up the company. Philips backed the move with a £2 million investment.

Scorecard:

Innovation	★★★★★
Flexibility	★★★★
Human resources	★★★
Growth markets	★★★★★
Quality of management	★★★
International orientation	★★★★

Biggest plus:
Your expertise and good ideas for advanced mobile phone technology will make a difference.

Biggest minus:
The company may never become a widely recognized brand.

Magic4
Chadwick House
Warrington WA3 6AE
Tel: 01925 286300
Fax: 01925 286 333
website: www.magic4.com

Magic4

The Business

The Magic4 founders realized that, while it would prove useful for handset providers to offer additional services, their idea for a small footprint software client to boost mobile phone services could not be developed at Philips. Luckily their former employers saw the benefits to be had from spinning off a key start-up partner and the inception of Magic4 was guaranteed. With the business plan that Magic4 devised and the backing of Philips, leading investment firm 3i also saw the potential of the company and provided £9.2 million in additional funds. Even considering the heady days when dot-coms were the vogue, the sums made available to Magic4 represent substantial seedcorn investment.

Innovation

It could be argued that Magic4 could quietly emerge as the most innovative company in this book. And this is no idle compliment. For starters, apart from the innovation inherent in its core technology, the company is a digital economy outfit with an old-style business model. Magic4 has forged agreements with leading software firms like Oracle for wireless services, as well as handset suppliers such as Motorola and Philips. There are 20 other agreements signed with a range of companies that have a stake in the burgeoning market for advanced mobile messaging solutions. The innovative nature of the Magic4 business model is that it gets a certain percentage from every handset sale where its format is included, so the company can count its revenue based on device sales figures.

Then there is the Magic4 software technology to consider. The kind of value-added service the company enables is illustrated by a football service it has helped develop. A fan of a particular football team wants to keep in touch with that club's progress on Saturday afternoon while out and about. When the team scores a familiar tune – say the *Match of The Day* theme – is played through the mobile handset and a graphic of the goal is then displayed.

Perhaps the really unique quality of Magic4 is its emphasis on the need for both a software client and back-end server development. This allows the service provider to push its offerings to end-users, as opposed to the user invoking the service. Such an approach bucks the trend set by other companies that have focused on the application of WAP as an access route to the Internet. The Magic4 formula emphasizes the server-based delivery of content.

Flexibility

As the market for the Magic4 software evolves, the company will have to increasingly show that it is flexible enough to cope with a fast moving and highly tactical customer base. For starters, Magic4 will have to keep up with the ever greater richness of content that service providers want to push to users, as well as coping with the rising inherent complexity of the services delivered. Each handset maker has a different coding structure for its products and so multiple versions of the Magic4 software have to be developed. However, the company is getting used to this syndrome and has started to predict the new advances that will emerge with each product launch.

The company has also to show great flexibility in its business planning. The lead-time for the launch of a new handset is between two and six months, so the Magic4 task is to reduce any barrier to acceptance of its software. It is imperative that Magic4 is never responsible for a delay to the planned release of a new handset.

To ensure this, Magic4 has developed an application programming interface (API) to cope with the variety of solutions its customers demand. This API is wrapped around the kernel of Magic4's software – meaning that the core of the software delivered does not need to be altered for each project undertaken. The company claims that this kernel of its product has an architecture that can cope with the varied demands placed on it.

In addition, Magic4 is operating in a highly volatile market. As we move towards the release of third generation (3G) digital and Internet-ready hand-set services – planned for release in a few years time – Magic4 has to cope with the shift to different technologies. Before the advent of 3G, there will be an interim development stage called GPRS – producing additional challenges. Yet the industry cannot wait for these advanced services to be released before getting experience with the techniques behind new services. In fact, the banks lending money to the operators that bid large amounts for 3G licences have insisted that there is no delay in development – so that 3G services will be optimized from day one. Again, this represents a challenge for Magic4.

Human Resources

Magic4 does not exhibit the classic attributes of a start-up in terms of people. The company started out with 18 engineers and this total has now risen to 30. The average age of the staff is in the 30s and many of these people can show between 5–10 years experience in the telecommunications and handset industry. These professionals left established careers at companies like Rescission, Sharp and Cymbal among others to join Magic4.

However, there is a blend of technical and business skills at the company and none of the core employees is a first-timer in this sector. Complex service challenges have to be overcome if Magic4 is to deliver compelling solutions, so mature and experienced developers are needed. It is just as important for Magic4 to consider the business angles to its projects as the enabling technology. So it is not surprising that PhD qualifications can be found in almost equal measure with MBAs – showing this balance of skills in reality.

Growth Markets

Magic4 is unlikely to become a household name to consumers, as the company is focused solely on providing advanced software solutions to large, multinational suppliers of mobile handsets and associated services. Yet, the company can look forward to healthy growth in a market that shows no signs of slowing down.

The rise in adoption of mobile communications shows little sign of abating and the market will almost certainly get an additional boost once the next generation devices become available. Wherever Magic4 can clinch deals with companies such as Motorola and Philips then revenue will follow, based on fresh sales of handsets to end-users. The issue faced by Magic4 is that, while there are relatively few handset suppliers that can be approached, they all have a global reach. Although Magic4 remains a small company, it must shadow the mobile suppliers in terms of their international operations. The opportunity for substantial growth is there for Magic4 but it must also manage its own growth without over-stretching its internal resources.

Quality of Management

Magic4 was set up by two men – Barry Jones and Simon Wilkinson – who had previously been senior people in the Philips consumer communications group. And while there are no famous names or industry celebrities among Magic4 senior management, the company is still served by professionals with deep experience of the marketplace the company is selling into.

Originally Jones and Wilkinson were head of product marketing and head of sales, respectively within their group at Philips. In addition, there are senior people who were previously responsible for strategy and development at their former companies. One person worth noting in this respect is Peter Worthy, who is head of technology services at Magic4 and who was previously employed by Sharp. So while the Magic4 senior management may not have the high profile of some other companies, all the appointees have far more valuable attributes

– such as the experience and industry knowledge to help the company fulfil its strategic business goals.

International Orientation

The need for Magic4 to follow where its key customers are located is turning the company into an international operation fairly rapidly. So Magic4 will set up and maintain a base in the Nordic countries, where several handset makers and service providers are located. France is also a key area for the company, as is Germany – which has the largest user base for information systems in Europe.

Magic4 hopes to cover Far East Asia during 2001, focusing on China, Hong Kong and Singapore – all the Magic4 locations will reflect strategic corporate needs. In particular, this is true of the Warrington setting for its corporate headquarters. The Magic4 management see this setting as key – the business park where the company has set up is close to an international airport, major motorways (such as the M4), and the founders also come from that area. This year will certainly see Magic4 moving on all fronts to supply customers with the products and support that they need.

MapInfo Ltd is the wholly-owned UK subsidiary of MapInfo Corporation of Troy, New York, founded in 1986. As a global company and acknowledged technology leader, MapInfo provides business intelligence solutions which are deployed across organizations to enable them to develop a better understanding of their markets and customers. These solutions allow customers to use location to transform information into business advantage. Turnover for fiscal 2000 was $96.2 million (33 per cent from Europe) and profits $8 million – both up on previous years. Alliances have been formed with Oracle and Lucent Technologies – and customers include Orange, BT, Marks & Spencer, Tesco, etc. The key growth market is the mobile Internet.

Scorecard:

Innovation	★★★★
Flexibility	★★★★
Human Resources	★★★★
Growth markets	★★★★
Quality of management	★★★★
International orientation	★★★★

Biggest plus:
The opportunities for career development and products that are presenting themselves.

Biggest minus:
There are not enough hours in the day to take advantage of all the opportunities.

MapInfo Ltd
Minton Place
Victoria Street
Windsor, Berks SL4 1EG
Tel: 01753 848200
website: www.mapinfo.com

MapInfo Ltd

The Business

MapInfo Ltd, the wholly-owned UK subsidiary of MapInfo Corporation, is the head office for the EMEA division (the other two divisions being the Americas and Asia-Pacific). An office is also based in Frankfurt, with representative offices in Sweden, Italy, Spain and Holland. Some 50 per cent of European revenue comes from the UK. Target markets are telcos, public sector and mobile Internet suppliers. The company provides location-based solutions and services which are deployed across organizations to help them find, serve and grow their customers. MapInfo is cash rich ($30 million in the bank), profitable ($8 million on $96.2 million revenue), with growth of 30 per cent annually.

Innovation

MapInfo designs, develops, markets, licenses and supports business mapping software products, application development tools and data products, together with a range of consulting, training and technical support services. These products are sold through multiple distribution channels, including an indirect value-added resellers and distributors, a corporate account sales force and a telemarketing sales group. The company's products are translated into 21 languages and sold in 58 countries. The company has 577 employees in total – 410 in the US, 130 in Europe (100 in the UK and 20 in Frankfurt), and 37 in Asia-Pacific. By the end of 2001, the company expects to have over 700 employees.

EMEA marketing director David Swinburne says, 'We market to three major areas – government which produces 40 per cent of our revenues and is growing at 5 to 10 per cent a year, customer relationship management which produces about 30 per cent of revenues and telephone companies (telco) which produces 30 per cent of revenues. Telco is the strongest market, showing some 50 per cent growth per annum. With the government sector, we are the market leader of geographical information systems for UK local authorities.'

IDC in a white paper 'Location in CRM: Linking virtual information to the real world' reported 'we believe MapInfo is the company to watch in location-specific CRM applications'. A major alliance has been forged with Oracle. MapInfo technology is incorporated in the company's flagship database product. The alliance covers all levels – R&D, sales and marketing. 'Wireless location-specific services represent a new and effective way to interact with customers and to support business processes,' says Swinburne. 'Mobile Internet is the future for us.' MapInfo ploughs 16 per cent of revenues into R&D.

Routes to market are 50 per cent direct, 50 per cent indirect. 'Our resellers are value-added resellers, not box shifters,' says Swinburne. 'We're solutions-focused and use a mix of advertising, PR, direct mail, seminars and new media advertising based around specific solution areas to reach target audiences.'

Flexibility

'We're helping other people to manage change,' says Swinburne. Over the past 14 years the company has moved from being a PC software vendor to become an enterprise software vendor. In the process the company established and dominated the desktop mapping market and then moved naturally to a client-server company, offering the ability to store location-specific data in a database with other applications. After this MapInfo transformed into a Web company, providing the ability to re-engineer businesses as information providers deploying information to their customers. 'Next it's the wireless Web,' says Swinburne. 'We claim to be very nimble-footed in the technology arena.'

MapInfo had set about a transformation in 1996 by positioning the company for success in the emerging and fast-growing business intelligence market. In 1999, led by its alliance with Oracle, the company transformed itself into a business that provides products and solutions for the enterprise – the alliance is a good example of MapInfo's partnering, technology and integration strategies. In 1998 IDC looked at 15 of the top analytic applications vendors. A year later all had a spatial strategy. All but two were using, or planned to use, MapInfo technology.

In 1996 the company was based in Bracknell and had 30 staff. By 2000, MapInfo had moved to Windsor and staff numbers had grown to 100. During that time, The Data Consultancy – a specialist content provider and developer – was acquired and integrated into the company. The stock price has had two splits in two years. Someone buying stock in 1999 would have done very well indeed. The $5 price tag at that time would – after record growth in 2000 – have grown to around $35.

Human Resources

'The ethos of the company is dynamic but it is also geared very much towards team working, to deliver the benefits to customers,' says Swinburne. 'The technology we're working with is fantastic, the market is exploding.' Two characteristics stand out concerning the people who flourish at MapInfo: first, people who are team players and second, those with a flexible mindset in the way they think and act. Of the 100 employees based in Windsor, 30 are in R&D, the rest are spread across the marketing team, direct sales force, channel sales team, general & admin (HR, MIS, order processing), and professional services (consulting). 'We're always recruiting aggressively,' says Swinburne. 'We find the best people with a very rigorous process. We don't take on many graduates but a first degree is essential for most roles.' While it's a young company, age is not an issue – capabilities, skills and the value added to the company are what's sought.

Growth Markets

'The mobile Internet is the growth area. It's the most phenomenal emerging market and we are the infrastructure,' says Swinburne. Wireless location-specific services represent a new and effective means of interacting with customers and supporting business processes. Companies like AOL, Microsoft, and IBM are spending billions of dollars in attempts to construct applications for access through the Internet. One of MapInfo's competitors – MapQuest – was acquired by AOL, which leaves MapInfo unfazed. 'MapQuest is burning cash and showing no returns while we are profitable and growing,' says Swinburne. 'We are attending, exhibiting and presenting at many wireless application protocol (WAP) congresses and mobile Internet events, plus we are building on our strategic relationships such as those with Lucent Technologies and Oracle.'

Meanwhile MapInfo is helping BT achieve the most effective roll-out of the high bandwidth digital link ADSL service and assisting Orange to effectively manage its relationship with each existing and prospective customer. Nortel Networks assesses customer needs with MapInfo helping it to build customer relationships and understand their needs better.

Everyone wants to become the gorilla, the known brand, in the market to have the dynamics to become the winner. MapInfo wants to be the Cisco Systems of the mobile Internet. Nothing less.

Quality of Management

For management development, MapInfo utilizes training from external consultants, 'who look at the way we manage' and use is made of Internet-based universities and e-learning at the desktop. 'Success is based on people and products,' says Swinburne. 'Fantastic products need fantastic people.' All MapInfo staff can invest in employee stock purchase plans and many will have enjoyed the recent tripling of returns in one year. Staff enjoy free personal health care and permanent health insurance. Annual leave is 20 days increasing with service to a maximum of 25. The company gives each member £100 to join a local gym and there are various company social events, such as an annual barbecue – which lasts one day and is fully paid for, including all partners. A contributory company pension scheme operates. There are no company cars, but allowances are provided to personnel should the role require the use of a vehicle.

59 per cent of the company's stock is held by institutions, 25 per cent by employees and the rest is floated on the market (Nasdaq). A shareholders' and analysts' meeting is held in February/March each year to discuss future performance and strategy. It is not uncommon to see comments voiced from the floor complimenting the style and abilities of the management.

MapInfo's transformation can be attributed to its listening to its customers. Its corporate culture is at its core, described as 'young in spirit, founded on innovation, rooted in passion, integrity and pride, and led by market vision and willingness to risk'. This is the legacy identified by the Board which 'enabled the company to combine cutting-edge technology with customer-driven marketing'. MapInfo considers it has the required resources and the combination of solutions, partnerships and management leadership to accomplish all the goals it sets. This obviously includes the mobile Internet.

International Orientation

MapInfo's traditional desktop product has been translated into 21 different languages. However Swinburne points out that 80 per cent of the company's business is handled in English-speaking parts of the world: North America, UK, Scandinavia, Benelux and Australia. 'In any international territory where we have no direct presence, we will appoint resellers and distributors,' says Swinburne. At the Sydney Olympics, MapInfo software was used to plan the route for carrying the flame across Australia so that 95 per cent of the population would have sight of the torch. This can be taken as an allegory of MapInfo's strategy with the mobile Internet, only it would be happier if the figure was 100 per cent of the population. It has the capability and drive – but it doesn't have enough hours in the day to take advantage of all the opportunities. What's truly exciting about MapInfo though are the opportunities presented to them.

MARKS & SPENCER

Renowned for its innovation in both the products it sells and how it sources and sells them, Marks & Spencer is a British institution and has repeatedly figured strongly in UK and international quality of management surveys. At the same time, Marks & Spencer has paid attention to ensuring that it has well trained, highly motivated staff and has continually set standards for others to follow in matters such as staff benefits. In early 2001 Marks & Spencer announced its intention to withdraw from wholly owned foreign operations in favour of franchise outlets.

Scorecard:

Flexibility	★★★★
Innovation	★★★★
Human resources	★★★★
Growth markets	★★★
Quality of management	★★★★
International orientation	★★

Biggest plus:
The company's commitment to developing its work force.

Biggest minus:
The incorrect perception that it may be less exciting than other retailers.

Marks and Spencer plc
Michael House
Baker Street
London W1U 8EP
Tel: 020 7935 4422
website: www.marksandspencer.com

Marks & Spencer

The Business

Marks & Spencer's origin was a Leeds market stall hired by Russian refugee Michael Marks in 1884. A decade later, Michael Marks formed a partnership with Tom Spencer – Marks and Spencer was on its way. By the time the company went public in 1926 it had adopted the then revolutionary policy of buying directly from manufacturers and, two years later, it registered the St Michael trademark. 1930 saw the opening of the flagship Marble Arch store on London's Oxford Street and, shortly afterwards, a further pennant in the Marks & Spencer reputation – the staff welfare department – came into being.

At financial year ended 1st April 2000, turnover was more than £8,195 million, pre-tax profits before exceptional items exceeded £557 million, and the company employed about 76,000 people of whom some 64,000 were based in the UK.

Flexibility

Somebody – it has been variously attributed to Bessie Smith, Tallulah Bankhead and Mae West – said 'if you want to get a future, go out and get a past'. Marks & Spencer has a splendid past and there is no reason it shouldn't have a splendid future.

As early year 2001 media coverage was not slow to emphasize, Marks & Spencer has had its problems with operations outside the UK. Whilst far from a disaster the company took the sound view that, if stores were persistently losing money, sound common sense dictated that those stores should be closed. Some stores – particularly in other EU countries – are in the process of being closed and the company's stated intention is that, in future, its foreign operations will be through franchise outlets rather than wholly-owned operations. UK performance is expected to benefit from further concentration on the domestic market.

It is fair to say the considered and sensible 'nip in the bud' action demonstrates an agility of corporate mind; nothing and nobody is perfect and the test of a company – and, for that matter, an individual – is not whether things occasionally go wrong, but how they go about putting them right. Marks & Spencer is putting things right and there is every indication that it is putting them right well.

Innovation

Marks & Spencer's record of innovation belies its twin-set and pearls image. The company has constantly sought fresh markets – expanding in recent years into home furnishings and financial services as well as increasing its long-established food sales.

The company has always worked to use the best available technology to enhance what can be offered to its customers and, since the 1930s, Marks & Spencer has been renowned for selling high-quality food – it is, indeed, widely credited with introducing ready-prepared meals to the UK. Examples of the company's innovation abound – one is pioneering the 'cold chain' which enabled food to be kept chilled throughout its journey from producer to shop. Thus Marks & Spencer was one of the influencers of Britain's eating habits: 'we were the first to sell avocado and, at the start, we had to explain how to eat it'.

In clothing, the company has also led the way, introducing machine washable lambswool knitwear and the first lambswool garments that could be tumble dried without wrecking them. Teaming up with chemical giant DuPont enabled that company's Lycra material to be used, among other purposes, to help keep the creases in M&S men's suits.

The financial services business, that effectively began with the launch of the company chargecard in 1985 and came of age a decade later – when life assurance and pension products were introduced, continues to be a profitable area for the company. Furniture was introduced to the product range and M&S has now developed a comprehensive range.

Human Resources

Marks & Spencer has long been recognized for its commitment to staff welfare, although the company is continually working to reposition itself in the recruitment market – the aim is to attract a variety of people with a range of skills.

The company has been working with the Eureka! children's museum in Halifax – on the grounds that research indicates that attitudes towards retailers are formed as early as the age of six – with a view to promoting itself as an exciting place in which to work. The 'working with education' initiative is designed to enable stores around Britain to work practically, with schoolchildren and students, in examining retail both as a business and as a possible career.

At the same time, the company is giving managers greater responsibilities, and giving that responsibility earlier than was previously the case – 'empowerment', as it is fashionably called. This is a necessary result of the enhanced training still being carried out through the organization – there is an obvious danger that people at the top level of their niche may become de-motivated – and 'to put it bluntly, a bit bored' – so, as their capabilities become 'liberated', it is in the interests of both employees and company that individuals are offered further opportunities.

Growth Markets

There is a constant drive to innovate in terms of products and service to the customer. Complacency is not a widely followed pastime in an organization which, national institution or not, has elevated continuous reinvention of itself to the level of a major art form.

M&S is well aware that 'getting there is one thing – staying there is quite another' and that it will always face 'catch up' competition. Accordingly the company continues to work on improvement – be it through merchandise presentation for customers buying sweaters, or by providing the appropriate ambience for those making financial transactions.

With a traditional sense of community and long-held commitment to the longer term, Marks & Spencer is confident that it will prosper in its intensely competitive markets.

Quality of Management

Marks & Spencer's reputation for value and honesty extends beyond the organization and helped to make a success of its launch into financial services. The company emphasises a twin focus on its customers and its people – 'it's very much attitudinal-type training, it's certainly not just learning how to work a till'. Whilst it still sets great store by ensuring that employment policies are non-discriminatory, and that people are treated fairly, M&S has moved, and is still moving, from its entrenched paternalist image – people are expected to take a predominant role in their own development.

Having won many British Quality of Management Awards M&S has quiet confidence in its ability to achieve sustainable growth. The loyalty and commitment of the staff is one of the company's most valuable assets – all staff are encouraged to develop as individuals and to make as full a contribution as possible to the success of the business.

It is also reasonably pointed out that one of the company's in depth strengths: 'decision-making devolved to the level at which it ought to be taken' – will stand it in good stead in an increasingly competitive trading environment.

International Orientation

In early 2001, announcing the results of a far-reaching strategic review, company chairman and chief executive Luc Vandevelde said:

'In order to focus all its efforts on the recovery of the UK business, Marks & Spencer intends to divest or close non-core businesses and assets, subject to consultation with its employees.'

The Company intends to close its loss-making business in Continental Europe, affecting some 3,350 jobs, subject to consultation. It also intends to dispose of its two profitable US businesses, Brooks Brothers and Kings Super Markets. These operations do not provide an appropriate platform for future international expansion by Marks & Spencer.

'The Company's ten stores in Hong Kong will be sold to become a franchise operation. Our franchise business, spanning 30 countries and operating with appropriate formats and strong local partners, continues to be successful. The Company's business in the Republic of Ireland is also growing fast and profitably. Marks & Spencer remains firmly committed to these businesses, recognizing the importance longer term of international development.'

mercator.

Mercator Software is an e-business integration company, selling a range of integration products and supporting services. Formerly known as TSI Software, it is a US public company and has been listed on Nasdaq for three years. Mercator UK is a wholly-owned subsidiary of Mercator, and as a company places emphasis on its ability to successfully integrate applications in many industry sectors. The UK operation has a strong presence in, among others, the pharmaceutical, telecoms and retail sectors, and it is the group's centre for financial services solutions, following the acquisition of UK financial middleware specialist Braid Systems eighteen months ago. It currently has around 200 employees based in offices in London and Cobham, Surrey.

Scorecard:

Innovation	★★
Flexibility	★★★
Human resources	★★★★
Growth markets	★★★
Quality of management	★★★★
International orientation	★★★★★

Biggest plus:
Lively, stimulating colleagues.

Biggest minus:
Not the place for those who want a quiet life.

Mercator
Mead Court
Thornbury
Bristol BS35 3UW
Tel: 01454 280800
website: www.mercator.co.uk

Mercator

The Business

Formerly known as TSI Software, Mercator Software is a US public company which has been listed on Nasdaq for three years. It specializes in e-business integration, and sells a range of integration products plus consulting and delivery services to support them. Mercator UK is a wholly-owned subsidiary of the company, and places emphasis on its ability to successfully integrate applications in many industry sectors. The UK operation has a strong presence in the pharmaceuticals, telecoms and retail sectors and is the group's centre for financial services solutions, following the acquisition of UK financial middleware specialist Braid Systems eighteen months ago. Mercator UK has offices in London and Cobham, Surrey and currently has around 200 employees, though this figure is set to double this year.

Innovation

Mercator's integration software has a number of innovative features, in particular its ability to create integration solutions that don't involve the need for writing code or for changes to existing applications.

However, enterprise application integration software is not an innovative concept, and neither are integration services. Mercator's unique selling point is really in offering a combination of the two: powerful integration products backed by professional services staff who have intimate knowledge of the products they are implementing. At the moment Mercator UK has around two thirds software to one third services staff, but this is changing; the company is looking to roughly double its headcount this year, most of whom will be employed on the services side.

Most of Mercator's software development is carried out in Boca Raton, Florida but the UK is unusual in having its own development centre. The acquisition of Braid Software eighteen months ago kick-started the UK operation, which until then had been very small. Braid produced middleware for integrating financial services systems and, along with the company, Mercator acquired 30 developers who now form a UK development team focused on the financial services sector. This team was responsible for producing Mercator's Global Securities Solutions (GSS), the company's new financial services product for securities transaction processing.

The UK division is seen as the leader for the company as a whole when it comes to financial applications, and is working closely with SWIFT, the global financial-messaging network operator, on its move to a new technical standard that will support developments such as straight-through processing.

Flexibility

Mercator aims to bring out one major release of its software once a year, accommodating emerging requirements for new integration products. In order to respond quickly to demand, it closely monitors relationships with its customer base.

New integration-requirements customers are often an opportunity for the company to add to its range of integration products, which now consists of three basic modules: Enterprise Broker for intra-company systems integration, Commerce Broker for business-to-business integration and Web Broker for integrating Web front-end e-commerce systems with back-end applications. To further improve its relationships with customers, the company plans to set up a Mercator user group this year.

Human Resources

Mercator has 800 employees world-wide. Around 200 of them are within Mercator UK, though this is set to double this year as the company actively recruits more services staff. The 200 UK staff are spread across a range of functions: sales, professional services, marketing and (unusually) development. Most country operations do not have development staff, since the company's software development is mainly carried out centrally in Boca Raton, Florida. However with the acquisition of Braid, Mercator also acquired a group of developers specializing in financial systems integration. These developers formed the core of a UK development team.

Mercator regards its people as its biggest asset. It aims to recruit bright, dynamic individuals with existing technological expertise or knowledge of a specific market. Once recruited, staff are offered good financial rewards plus ongoing training; Mercator invests fairly heavily in staff development. In return it expects a lot from its investment – this is not a place where people can coast along in neutral.

Growth Markets

In its former TSI persona, Mercator mainly focused on enterprise system integration. Integrating customer relationship management (CRM), supply chain management and enterprise resource planning (ERP) systems with other corporate applications have been the mainstay of its business, with particular emphasis on projects involving SAP's R/3 ERP software.

With the growth of the Web and e-business, however, it is seeing more sales coming out of business-to-business integration in its many and varied forms. As well as its Enterprise Broker integration product, it now has Commerce Broker for business-to-business integration and Web Broker for integrating Web e-commerce systems with back office systems. It is actively involved with industry initiatives such as the Universal Description, Discovery and Integration Project (UDDI), a coalition of business and technology organizations committed to the acceleration of business-to-business commerce on the Internet.

Rather than spending heavily on advertising, Mercator UK aims to raise its profile in the e-business area through direct contact with potential clients and through public events such as roadshows and appearances at management seminars and briefings.

Mercator's recent acquisition, Braid specialized in inter-bank systems integration, and the European operation is now picking up financial clients such as ABN Amro, which plans to use the Commerce Broker product as the e-business integration platform for its new online retail brokerage service, and Thomas Cook, which is using Commerce Broker as part of a project to streamline its global treasury management systems. Clients within the commercial sector include Amazon, Coca-Cola, Dell and AstraZeneca.

Quality of Management

Mercator's rapid growth, fuelled by burgeoning interest in e-commerce, presented a challenge for its former senior management team. Under new management Mercator has made massive investment in restructuring the company, so that it is now rapidly moving towards an infrastructure that can both accommodate its current growth rate and that which it foresees in the future. Like many other technology stocks, the company's share price has also suffered at the hands of an increasingly sensitive technologies market. However, the end of 2000 saw Mercator achieve a revenue growth of 40 per cent on 1999, a reassuring sign for shareholders.The company was reorganized in November 2000, and is now is steering a steadier course in the hands of Roy King, its new CEO and chairman, who joined the company in January 2001. Formerly general manager of consulting and integration services with IBM EMEA, King has twenty-eight years of business experience in manufacturing, general consulting, and the Internet. The company also has a new chief financial officer in the form of Richard Applegate, a former interim chief financial officer of two large companies and an Internet start-up, and ex-CFO of Remington Arms Company. Mark Stevens, an executive vice president with Excite@Home, joined the board, bringing to Mercator his extensive experience of the Internet market.

A key part of last year's shake up was the company's reorganization into three geographic units, covering: the Americas; Asia/Pacific and Europe, Middle East and Africa (EMEA). Each region is controlled by its own president, a move the company believes will speed up decision making, increase customer satisfaction, and maximize revenue growth. As well as setting strategy for their own regions, the three geographic presidents are responsible for setting priorities for the company's applications development group, in collaboration with the heads of marketing, global product planning and R&D.

Management of the European operation is strongly dominated by experienced ex-Oracle executives. For example Peter Jones, president of the EMEA region, was a founding manager of Oracle UK. The regional operations are given a high degree of autonomy in developing their business and exploring new markets as they see fit. This strategy seems to be working particularly well in Europe – the Northern European operation has been achieving strong revenue growth and contributing a growing percentage of the company's world-wide revenues.

International Orientation

Mercator Software is a global company with country operations around the world. Last November, the company was reorganized into three geographic units – the Americas, Asia/Pacific and Europe, Middle East and Africa – each under the control of its own president.

EMEA accounts for around 40 per cent of the company's total business, and though the company does not break its revenues down by individual country, it's prepared to say that the UK accounts for a 'significant' proportion of that 40 per cent. The UK office is the largest in the EMEA region and Peter Jones, the company's vice president for EMEA, is based in the London office.

Though Mercator UK only deals with UK-based customers, close connections with the other country subsidiaries gives it an edge when bidding for projects from large multinationals. The various local operations can work together to provide global support on multinational projects.

Merryck & Co

Merryck & Co is a highly specialist business mentoring service devoted to 'helping business leaders build successful businesses and lead fulfilling lives'. Owned one third by founder, David Carter, another third by the Faculty of Mentors and the remainder by a number of the company's major international clients, it has been running since 1997 and so far has bases in three countries; it plans to expand this to ten.

Scorecard:

Innovation	★★★★★
Flexibility	★★★★★
Human resources	★★★★★
Growth markets	★★★★
Quality of management	★★★★★
International orientation	★★★★★

Biggest plus:
The focus on the values and purpose and the far-reaching effect the service can have – if it improves profits, performance and the personal development of the CEO then the employees will benefit, as will their families and the local community – Merryck & Co gets genuine satisfaction from this trickle-down effect.

Biggest minus:
From the recruitment point of view, the applicant for partnership has to be exactly right and attuned to the company's philosophy. This leads to only around 8 per cent of applicants succeeding in joining the company.

Merryck & Co
42 Berkeley Square
London W1J 5AW
Tel: 07000 637792
website: www.merryck.com

Merryck & Co

The Business

David Carter founded Merryck & Co in 1997 after a career starting in the City, which encompassed two successful business start-ups. The company started after Carter had sold one of these businesses and he was approached by a number of entrepreneurs to be their mentor; the combination of the obvious demand and the satisfaction of helping others achieve success caused Carter to realize that this was his vocation. With the experience of building up a portfolio of his own clients he then set about assembling a team of like-minded and similarly-experienced people who could mentor business leaders through both economic upswings and downturns. The company now has bases in the UK, the US and Stockholm. The focus is equally on getting the lifestyle balance right as well as achieving business results.

Innovation

Merryck & Co has a number of unique propositions to the market, not least of which is that it specializes only in mentoring business leaders – there is no other more general business consultancy on offer. In spite of the CEO-only nature of the service, however, the company can account for a wide range of clients, each matched to the partner whose skills and preferences make them the right person to mentor that particular individual. For example, Carter himself favours the smaller company that can be turned into a more substantial concern with the right leadership, whereas other partners might prefer taking on the CEO of an established organization that has started to make a loss and needs to turn it to a profit.

Whatever the nature of the client, they all have their individual, and company, needs assessed by their mentor and have a two-day off-site retreat session as part of the service. Unusually, the agenda is dictated entirely by the client; there is no fixed curriculum or set of training 'products' into which the customer is asked to fit.

Another area in which Merryck & Co stands out is in its international scope. Most consultancies that compete with any of the elements of the business will have a solid local focus, but Carter's view is that the CEO of a multinational who wants his or her operating executives to be trained will want support throughout the international locations in which they operate. Hence the expansion plan.

Most importantly, though, the attitude of the company is vital. It has a genuine commitment to improving not just the profit-making potential but the lifestyle of its executive clients. It believes that this trickles down to the employees and their families, improving the lot of everybody in the process.

Flexibility

To understand how flexible the company can be, not simply with its mentoring offering but in its structure, it is important to understand that it operates as a virtual organization. It certainly has its UK premises in Mayfair, which is where it meets the vast majority of its clients, but this operates more as a serviced office than as a corporate headquarters. The partners are not all full-time employees of the company, in fact the only office-based full-timer will be the country manager in whichever territory is under discussion.

This means that the shape of the organization is, at any stage, likely to mirror the exact requirements of the clients. This is echoed in its choice of locations across the rest of the world – Stockholm is a Nordic financial area that compares with London, and in the US the organization is based in the financial district in San Francisco.

Such corporate flexibility is bound to reflect in the way clients are served. All of them are met both by the country manager and by a partner, following which a partner is assigned to handle their case. The assignment of the right partner is, confirms Carter, one of the most critical elements of the process, and if there isn't a good match then business will be turned away rather than done badly.

Human Resources

Merryck & Co has an unusual approach to adding to its faculty and has adopted a 'they find us' approach based on word of mouth and the company's performance with existing clients. Partners are recruited from a wide range of eclectic industries in order best to serve an array of global clients.

As might be expected, the criteria for becoming a mentor to a business leader are stringent. The company has as its stated values:

- Legendary, unequalled and uncompromising excellence
- Outstanding generosity and dedication in service to clients
- Unstoppable passion for growth and learning.

And these are more than platitudes – it believes them and has a strong ethical focus as outlined above. The commitment to this has to be total, from everyone.

Successful applicants become partners rather than employees, but the route to partnership is gruelling. There is a meeting with a country manager and then one of the existing mentors is appointed as a guide;

there follows a meeting with at least four of the mentors in the country in which the new partner will be working, and more from other countries. They are then invited to one of the company's 'First Tuesday' brainstorming events, following which up to three independent assessments and references are sought. Meanwhile there will be psychometric tests. The process normally takes up to four months.

Growth Markets

In spite of a limited number of staff, Carter and the team don't focus their marketing efforts on any particular niche. Rather they look into any potential niche and have a lot of customers coming to them as referrals from others. 50 per cent of their clients arrive in this way. 'The beauty of what we do is that whether a CEO has a turnover of £5 million or £5 billion per year, we can help improve their performance,' says Carter.

Business development is an important side of the company. Merryck & Co attends conferences for human resources personnel. It also takes note of the contents of newspapers to see who is likely to benefit from the service – if someone has a challenge in business then Merryck & Co is interested in supporting the leadership through the changes. 'Business mentoring is crucial during times of turbulence and change', says Carter.

The other area that helps the company grow is personal contact – the partners often meet people socially or in the course of their business who would find mentoring invaluable; an approach is made and if the right pitch is made, the prospect becomes a client.

Quality of Management

The management, as might be predicted in an organization with this sort of business in mind, has to be top notch otherwise the whole proposition is worthless. Carter is adamant that all of the partners need to relish continuous learning as part of their responsibility to themselves and unusually the company spends 10 per cent of its revenues (not profits) on continuous learning. This adds credibility to its stated core value of 'Unstoppable passion for growth and learning'. There will be 40 of these mentors by the end of the year 2001 and each of them will have to have some experience of running a company, typically more than one. Whether these are start-up companies as in Carter's case or sections within major corporates is flexible.

The nature of the partnership is that all of the participants are equal in terms of vote, although rewarded according to contribution. Depending on their own background and experiences, individual partners will take responsibility for finance, another for company secretarial duties and so forth.

Prior to joining the company, the vast majority of mentors will have had at least two mentoring experiences outside their own business whether formally as part of their job description or through less formal contacts. Rigorous checks are made by Merryck & Co to ensure these mentoring experiences, particularly the less formal ones, are bona fide.

International Orientation

The third of the company owned by the clients is actually owned by ten global companies in non-competing areas. Merryck & Co selected these carefully from organizations whose head offices are based in a variety of nations so that its international focus runs through every level from the shareholders down. One benefit the shareholders have is that they meet twice a year to develop thought leadership on global businesses; this allows Merryck & Co to take advantage not only of global partners but of expertise from global shareholders. These shareholders are from non-competing businesses so the quality and openness of the debates at the semi-annual forums are universally excellent. This is one of the means through which Merryck & Co aims for its 'Legendary, uncompromising and unequalled excellence.'

Merryck has a very clear aim – to have ten country subsidiaries including that in the UK, and to have each of these served by ten partners. In principle, given the virtual nature of the organization, this could happen quite quickly; in fact given the stringency of the criteria and the company philosophy it is likely to take a little while.

By the end of 2001, however, the company planned to be active in Australasia and Hong Kong, since both of these areas are centres of business activity. A European hub is also being planned, possibly in Geneva, following which Canada and possibly Brazil will open up.

What won't change is the extremely tight focus. It will remain a service for serious industry leaders and although not cheap, it will continue to aim for a tenfold return on investment for customers and to offer them a full money back guarantee if they are less than satisfied. As long as it keeps up the commitment to quality partners, it is hard to see Merryck & Co not doing well.

Microsoft ®

Microsoft is one the late twentieth century's most resounding success stories. In 1975 the company had three employees, annual revenues of $16,000 and a single software product – a version of the BASIC computer language that ran the first personal computer, the Altair 8000. A quarter of a century on, with 45,000 employees, a range of software and Internet products which includes the world's most used PC operating system, and global revenues exceeding $23 billion, Microsoft is the largest software company on the planet.

Scorecard:

Innovation	★★★★
Flexibility	★★★★★
Growth markets	★★★★
Human resources	★★★★★
Quality of management	★★★★
International orientation	★★★★★

Biggest plus:
'Being part of something that changes the ways in which people work and live.'

Biggest minus:
'The sheer volume of opportunities is huge and it's often difficult to pick the three or four on which you should focus.'

Microsoft Limited
Microsoft Campus
Thames Valley Park
Reading
Berkshire RG6 1WG
Tel: 0870 60 10 1000
Fax: 0870 60 20 1000
website: www.microsoft.com/uk/

Microsoft Limited

The Business

Twenty-five years after its foundation Microsoft has become the world's largest software company. Global revenues exceed $23 billion and Microsoft employs 45,000 people spread across 60 countries. In the company's own words 'Microsoft develops, manufactures, licenses, and supports a wide range of software products for a multitude of computing devices.' The company's rate of growth in the fiscal years 1998, 1999 and 2000 was 28, 29 and 16 per cent respectively.

Innovation

Company statement: 'in an industry that moves at lightning speed, innovation is critical to our competitiveness. Microsoft's long term approach to research and development, combined with our constant efforts to anticipate customer needs, improve quality and reduce costs will enable us to deliver the best products and technologies.' Microsoft invests heavily in research and development and, in the year 2001, the company's global research and development spend will exceed $4 billion.

Successful operations inevitably attract criticism and, fairly or not, Microsoft has come in for its share. There is a body of opinion clamouring for operating systems to be available free and Microsoft has become a regular target for vitriol as it believes that, as it has invested serious money in research and development, it is entitled to charge for its resulting products. This vitriolic response seems to be compounded by Microsoft's reference to the use of its products by those who have not paid for them as 'piracy'.

Flexibility

'Microsoft', says Steve Harvey, director of people, profit and loyalty, 'is an entrepreneurial culture. We encourage our people to speak out, to take risks and to challenge conventional wisdom. We want our employees to wake up every day with the passionate belief that their work is contributing to the evolution of technology and making a real difference to the lives of millions of people. We will always preserve the lean, competitive and entrepreneurial streak that has enabled us to grow.'

Harvey claims it is not unusual for Microsoft to be called in for a last minute 'mission impossible' rescue and that such missions are often 'accomplished in a timeframe not thought possible'. Microsoft, in short, is an organization that thinks on its feet and its published 'investments in tomorrow' include television, games, wireless and small businesses; and Microsoft.NET, which is described as 'a wide range of net experiences which will open the door to significant new benefits for consumers and business users, as well as revenue opportunities for Microsoft'.

The flexibility of the company is, perhaps, best exemplified by quoting from its year 2000 annual report:

> 'Building the future together: in partnership with thousands of other technology companies that share our visions of high-performance, affordable computing, Microsoft has helped build a high-tech industry that is thriving on innovation and competition, and driving growth in the US economy. That is one of the reasons why we believe the appellate courts will rule in Microsoft's favour in the antitrust lawsuit and uphold the well established legal precedent that US antitrust law should encourage, not discourage, firms to improve their products rapidly to meet customer needs. We also believe the appellate courts will recognize that the district court's order to break up Microsoft and impose crippling regulations reached far beyond the facts of the case, and would lead to less innovation, fewer choices, and higher prices.'

Human Resources

Microsoft sums up its values thus: 'there are two key aspects to Microsoft's past and future success – its vision of technology and the values by which we live, every day, as a company. The values are a set of principles which have evolved since our founding, and which capture the spirit, philosophy and day-to-day business practices of our company. They are not new values, but rather a reinforcement of long-held company principles that underscore our relationships with customers, partners and employees.'

Those who fit can 'have a job for life if that's what they want it to be'. A good work and life balance is recognized as vital but the environment is nevertheless demanding – 'you give blood but you get well paid in vein'. The small company mentality is emphasized as is the fact that 'you don't necessarily treat people as you would wish to be treated yourself – it's much more important to find out how they want to be treated themselves'.

Growth Markets

Microsoft's declared aim is to continue its focus on 'promising new technological advances in a number of key fields'.

Digital and enhanced television products are seen as a significant growth opportunity and the company's investment is concentrated in three main areas:

Working with TV service operators – including AT&T in the US, UPC in Europe, Rogers in Canada and Towngas/iCare in Hong Kong – to deploy enhanced TV to more than 15 million subscribers via the Microsoft platform

Joining with DIRECTV, Thomson and Sony to produce Ultimatetv – a one-box, one-service enhanced TV solution that will include two digital tuners to enable background recording, and a 40 gigabyte hard drive capable of recording 35 hours of TV programming

Continuing to grow its WebTV service whereby subscribers can use home TV sets for e-mail, up-to-the-minute news coverage, and two-way interaction.

The company is investing heavily in the PC games market and is developing its 'Xbox' which will compete with the Sony PlayStation and the games consoles produced by Sega and Nintendo. Wireless is also perceived as a growth opportunity and alliances in the market include those with AT&T, BT and the Japanese NTT DoMoCo.

Small businesses are estimated by Microsoft to represent some 60 per cent of the global economy and the company claims that, with more than one million registered users, its 'bCentral' Web-based small business portal is world number one 'in terms of reach'. The company forecasts technology spending by the small business community to rise dramatically over the next four years.

Quality of Management

The management structure is described as 'very flat – basically', states Steve Harvey, 'there are three levels and we tend to work in what I like to call superteams of eight to ten people – you could say Microsoft is a large company which has succeeded in maintaining a small company mentality.' Staff turnover is a relatively low 6 per cent.

As Harvey explains, there are four main strands to the company's overall vision: 'great hires – sometimes the best hire is no hire at all; great jobs – otherwise people will leave; great managers – we invest a lot in mentoring and training; and, in short, we want to be a great company'.

Microsoft people are encouraged to take charge of their own careers

– 'in terms of long-term development', says Steve Harvey, 'people must take control themselves. We'll give them all the help we can, even if it means that, ultimately, an individual's best interests lie elsewhere.'

There are no regulations about university education. 'What we want', says Harvey, 'is people who are smart and who speak their minds.' This, he admits, is not always best for one's self esteem – 'if you say one dumb thing you'll probably be looking at a couple of hundred e-mails in about half an hour's time' – but it's the way the company works.

International Orientation

Microsoft is an international company and, with operations in Europe, the Americas, the Pacific, the Middle East, Africa and Asia, its list of locations reads like a world atlas index. The company is openly committed to international diversity, to the active practice of equal opportunity in all hiring and promotional activities, and to meaningful contributions to local communities.

Misys is one of the world's largest applications software companies. Established in the UK in 1979, by the current chairman, it develops and licenses software for use in the banking, financial services and healthcare industries. Misys employs nearly 6,000 people in 30 countries, with over half the workforce employed in its banking division. It was the first IT company to enter the FTSE 100 index, in 1998. As well as providing industry-specific software solutions, the company also supplies key business processing – outsourcing services to a growing number of Independent Financial Advisers (IFAs) as well as electronic transaction processing services to its US physician customers.

Scorecard:

Innovation	★★★★★
Flexibility	★★★★
Human resources	★★★
Growth markets	★★★★
Quality of management	★★★★★
International orientation	★★★★

Biggest plus:
The flexible and innovative environment.

Biggest minus:
This isn't a company for those who want an easy 9 to 5 day.

Misys plc
Burleigh House
Chapel Oak
Salford Priors
Worcestershire WR11 5SH
Tel: 01386 871373
website: www.misys.co.uk

Misys

The Business

Misys started out as a supplier of computer systems to insurance brokers in the UK. Over the last 20 years, the company has grown rapidly, helped by a focused acquisition strategy. Misys was one of the early developers in the UK software industry, enabling it to make strong inroads into the global banking market. From there, it entered the US healthcare market and, later, expanded its presence in the business processing arena, outsourcing services to IFAs. Although its headquarters and a third of its workforce are based in the UK, Misys also has offices throughout the US, Europe and Asia. While not a high profile firm, Misys has enjoyed considerable growth as an independent company. For the financial year ending in August 2000 the company recorded profits of £119 million on turnover of £708 million.

Innovation

Innovation is key to Misys's long-term competitiveness, with some 12 per cent of the company's annual revenues being invested in research and development (R&D). Misys has established a network of R&D centres of excellence in Europe, the USA and Asia which will bring added value to all companies within the group. The company's commitment to R&D was reflected in its ranking in the 2000 UK R&D Scoreboard, published by the DTI. This ranked Misys as the largest independent, UK-based IT company, and sixth in the FTSE 100 index in terms of proportion of turnover invested in R&D.

Misys's own mission statement stresses the need for innovation. It says it works with customers to improve their business processes through the development, integration and delivery of industry-specific IT solutions. In essence, Misys is attempting to empower businesses and individuals so that they benefit from technology which produces more efficient ways of trading. In turn, this should lead to lower costs and, potentially, greater margins.

Across its three core divisions of banking, healthcare and financial services, Misys appears to demonstrate a flair for change.

The banking division serves some 1,600 customers in 110 countries. It provides integrated solutions that enable banks and financial institutions to increase revenues, improve customer service and reduce costs. Increasing competition in the financial services sector, and the need for financial institutions to respond through investment in technology, puts the division in a strong position for further growth.

Misys's healthcare division is benefiting from US healthcare providers' increasing requirements for flexible, information systems. IT expenditure is increasing by well over 10 per cent a year according to some independent studies, something that should help Misys win new business. Among Misys's software applications is a system which helps over 70,000 doctors run their practices more efficiently. Better information helps speedy diagnosis and more effective treatment, and in this area, Misys provides a system which enables doctors to create electronic medical records to help provide better care for their patients.

Misys's third division, financial services, is focused on life, pensions and investment product distribution as well as services for brokers and providers in the general insurance industry. Misys owns the biggest IFA network and provides systems to over 2,200 insurance brokers. Through Web-based e-commerce initiatives, Misys is also e-enabling IFAs so they can transact electronically on behalf of their clients. The process of applying for life insurance or a pension is being speeded up, leading to more efficient processes both in the IFA's office and among providers. Lower processing costs should, in turn, help consumers who will benefit from higher standards of advice and faster completion times after application.

Human Resources

Misys has a flat management structure and professes to have a company culture where employees are encouraged to offer opinions about a wide range of subjects on a regular basis. Coupled with this approach is the practice of awarding long-term incentives to both groups and individuals for positive contributions to business development. Bonuses are paid to deserving staff on either a half-yearly or annual basis and a range of share-based schemes align company performance with creating additional shareholder value. There are also regular management meetings to discuss strategy. This all suggests that the company has a positive take on staff relations. Like many companies emerging in the software industry, the employee base shows a useful mix of hard experience and youthfulness. Many of the people working in the Misys divisions are in their thirties, while management is mostly composed of fifty-somethings, an unusual profile for this market.

The company offers healthcare and pension arrangements but, by its own admission, Misys could do a lot more to retain staff, especially in an industry prone to high turnover of employees. The type of employee that wouldn't flourish in the company would be averse to new technology and new ways of thinking.

Growth Markets

Clearly Misys is expecting to make serious progress over the next few years. It seemed to be thrown off course by the Year 2000 issue, which led to many companies, particularly in the banking sector, postponing or freezing orders altogether. However, it now appears to be back on track, adopting a return to the earlier strategy of acquiring companies across its core divisions. The strategy also means Misys can return to its ambitious target of increasing earnings per share by 20 per cent a year, some would say a tough target in times of global economic uncertainty. 2001 has already seen Misys launch takeover bids in the healthcare and financial services industries, as it tries to expand its presence both in the US and UK. Its management clearly believes in reducing Misys's exposure to any one market – industry vertical or geographic – while playing a greater role in the consolidation of other areas. The company prefers to be involved in friendly takeovers rather than act as a predator on its targets.

The next few years will be crucial for Misys. They will show whether the meticulous approach the company has shown to growing its healthcare and financial services divisions will start to pay off. The internal funding is in place to support its strong development programme during volatile economic times.

Quality of Management

Misys has built a strong management team during its lifetime. Chairman, Kevin Lomax, who was a founding investor over 20 years ago, has extensive experience in the industrial sector after stints at Hanson and STC and now also sits on the board of Marks & Spencer as a non-executive director. Deputy chairman, Strone Macpherson, a former investment banker, has added his considerable expertise and experience to the group's extensive mergers and acquisitions. Managing director, John Sussens, has been at Misys for over ten years, joining the company after a career working at Ford and JCB. The company's corporate development director, Ross Graham, joined nearly 15 years ago, initially starting as finance director. The non-executive directors include Sir Dominic Cadbury, former chairman of Cadbury Schweppes.

One key point to realize about the management is the depth of experience the directors have built up in traditional bricks-and-mortar companies.

International Orientation

The seeds of Misy's growth are firmly planted in the UK but, as part of its stated aim of reducing exposure to a single market, Misys continues to develop its international operations.

Through its banking division, Misys supplies the bulk of the world's top 50 banks and is likely to go on expanding its customer base of 1,600 banking and securities firms. It is developing its Medic healthcare division, intent on retaining its position as the largest supplier of IT-related services to physicians.

Misys has clearly grown to become an important player on the world software stage. With some concern over the continued level of software spend by international firms, the company has experienced some turbulence in its development. But, it appears that strong management and extensive global operations will help it weather the storms.

MORGAN LOVELL
THE WORKPLACE SPECIALIST ®

Morgan Lovell describes itself as a 'Workplace Specialist' – in other words, it advises companies on selecting the right building for their business, then designing, fitting out or refurbishing the space and providing ongoing workplace services. Established in 1977, it has offices in London W1, Wokingham and Milton Keynes and is part of the publicly-quoted Morgan Sindall Group, a major construction company whose main activities include fitting out office spaces, regional construction and property investment.

Scorecard:

Innovation	★★★★
Flexibility	★★★★
Human resources	★★★★★
Growth markets	★★★
Quality of management	★★★★
International orientation	★★★

Biggest plus:
The quality of the people and their integrity, plus the consultative approach taken with clients.

Biggest minus:
The frustration in aiming to keep to original deadlines in cases where customers change the specification a number of times – every effort is made to keep the original date but this can make individual projects stressful at times.

Morgan Lovell
16 Noel Street
London W1F 8DA
Tel: 020 7734 4466
website: www.morganlovell.com

Morgan Lovell

The Business

Morgan Lovell is part of the publicly-quoted Morgan Sindall Group, one of the fastest-growing construction groups in the UK with four main areas of activity – fitting out office spaces, construction, affordable housing and investments.

Morgan Lovell is the workplace specialist in the fold. It identifies, designs and fits out or refurbishes workplaces and provides ongoing service and support. It offers a single point of responsibility and a one-stop-shop for all projects, providing a fast-track, cost-effective solution to workplace design and construction. The company works with their clients from the conceptual stage, through detailed design and implementation, and then, through their Workplace Services team, Morgan Lovell offers ongoing workplace maintenance where other contractors simply move on to the next project. Morgan Lovell very much has a 'client for life' philosophy.

Innovation

The first and probably most important way in which Morgan Lovell stands out from the competition is in the nature of its one-stop-shop approach. Once a client is signed up, the company seeks to build a long-term relationship, and it does this in a number of ways.

First, and quite unusually, it offers a continuing maintenance contract under which clients can have an electrician or other tradesman at their disposal for a couple of days a month to take care of any minor but important work that needs doing. This is called a Workplace Services Agreement.

At all levels the focus is 100 per cent on the client rather than on the project and the designs are tailored around the client's needs rather than produced as a preconceived 'Morgan Lovell offering'. Another fundamental element that distinguishes the company from its competition – which is a pity since it ought to be more widespread – is the approach to the client, which is strictly non-confrontational. The company aims to make the experience as pleasant as possible for the client without pulling punches when there are difficult issues surrounding impracticality of ideas to broach.

The other major area in which the company innovates is in its long-term supplier relationships under the Synergy Programme. This is a scheme by which instead of the standard short-term relationship with a sub-contractor, the company seeks to develop a long-term business relationship with a few selected contractors. These synergy partners are well briefed about the business and are steeped in the corporate culture and philosophy of Morgan Lovell.

Readers interested in innovative approaches should also read the section on Human Resources, since the participation and feedback the company encourages from its staff is notable.

Flexibility

Morgan Lovell is not afraid of change – managing director, Arie Janson, has seen a lot of it since joining the company some 15 years ago. 'It never stays still,' he comments. 'And we're always proactive in changing according to the market needs, rather than reactive.'

As an example he cites the case of the Redhill office, which closed down – not because it wasn't performing well but because its clients could be just as easily supported by the Wokingham office. It was running efficiently, but was not adding sufficient value to the business to continue operating from separate premises.

It would have been easy for customers and staff to see this as a negative move, whereas in fact the redeployment of resources along more efficient lines was extremely positive, particularly since the service to customers was uninterrupted. Janson sees the secret of managing such a change as communication – the staff and the customers all needed to know exactly what was happening and why.

As has been mentioned before, staff contact and feedback is vital.

Human Resources

The staff have share options, health plans and other benefits as appropriate to their position. New employees are handled a little unusually in that their first two weeks are spent getting to know the company and being inducted rather than at the coalface. Every employee meets Janson so that they can have a personal briefing about the company's core values.

There are 19 of those values, although in practice this boils down to a subset of four with more detailed values attached. To begin with the client always comes first and is always right – some employees have a problem with this when they join. Second the company employs only talented people; indeed when Janson was asked about the best element of the company he suggested the people without hesitation. Third that the status quo should always be challenged, and fourth that the company operates a conservative financial system.

Challenging the status quo is something the employees are asked to do in terms of the company culture itself through continuous improvement teams (CITs), each headed by an elected 'skill-base champion'. CIT meetings are held three times a year to discuss improvements within disciplines and to challenge the company's precepts. The views of the CITs are taken seriously and improvements in procedures regularly result from these forums.

Growth Markets

By definition, the company's market will be anyone who wants a workplace interior to be designed, built and managed by an expert – included in this expertise is the ability to make the space perform financially. For example, the company has enabled some organizations to cut down on the use of space and therefore pay less rent in some instances – this is a quantifiable benefit.

Typical clients include companies merging or expanding or approaching a lease break or rent review. UK companies moving into mainland Europe might ask for help, or companies that have grown to the stage at which they need to outsource their facilities management or property responsibilities in order to focus on core business issues.

To help these organizations Morgan Lovell educates through workshops and seminars. It offers strategic advice through its workplace consultancy, carries out space audits and building appraisals, designs the space and then implements the relocation or refurbishment. Finally, through its Workplace Services team it offers ongoing workplace maintenance.

Quality of Management

Before looking at the detail of Morgan Lovell's management techniques it is worth reiterating two points: that it is part of a major listed group, and the extent to which the staff are involved in change and decision-making processes. This is very much a collegiate, flat-structured organization and its openness to ideas from the staff and from clients alike informs its corporate style.

There are regular management meetings and the performance of the business is measured against set key performance indicators (KPIs). These KPIs are both financial and non-financial. Often the non-financial KPIs will be informed by customer satisfaction, as audited in surveys conducted by a director who has had no direct contact during the planning and implementation of the project. Clients assess the company on a scale of one to ten – the average score to date has been 9.25. As well as being financial and non-financial, the KPIs are both personal and departmental – everyone is assessed continuously.

Every care is taken to ensure that the business is transparent to the client, and the client-centric ethic is carried through every level of the business.

International Orientation

Morgan Lovell is an avowedly British-based company. However, for existing clients it has project-managed workplace fit outs or refurbishments in Europe.

Janson confirms that this is to do with focusing on established strengths – there is, after all, much to be said not only for knowing what you do for a living but also in understanding what you don't do. Growth plans are therefore set very firmly in the UK, where there appears to be plenty of room for expansion.

The advantage the company has is that it thrives on change and change happens in business whether times are good or bad. Should the long-threatened recession materialize in 2001 then there will be mergers and acquisitions and the companies concerned will need to operate somewhere, so the business will do well. Should the economy defy expectations and boom, there will be new companies which will need similar advice and expanding companies which will also have a use for the service.

It's a neat trick, and Morgan Lovell has a track record of pulling it off.

National Grid

National Grid is the largest independent electricity transmission company in the world. The Group has its roots in the old British CEGB (Central Electricity Generating Board) and was created following the 1990 deregulation of the UK electricity industry. Ten years on, National Grid is one of the UK's largest companies and owns and operates electricity and communications networks around the world. Massachusetts-based National Grid USA is a wholly owned subsidiary and the company's international interests spread as far afield as Argentina, Australia, Brazil, Chile, Poland and Zambia. Year 2000 turnover was in excess of £1,600 million.

Scorecard:

Innovation	★★★★
Flexibility	★★★★
Growth markets	★★★★★
Human Resources	★★★★
Quality of management	★★★★
International orientation	★★★★

Biggest plus:
'A strong feeling that the business is going places and is justifiably gaining confidence.'

Biggest minus:
'Having to adapt to jargon – there's a lot of information that needs de-mystifying.'

National Grid Group plc
15 Marylebone Road
London NW1 5JD
Tel: 020 7312 5600
Fax: 020 7312 5669
website: www.nationalgrid.com

National Grid

The Business

National Grid owns and operates the high voltage transmission system in England and Wales, taking electricity from generating companies and transmitting it through a national network of electricity lines to the companies, who then distribute electricity at progressively lower voltages to homes, businesses and industrial users.

The National Grid Company plc is responsible for UK operations, and is part of the National Grid Group, which is listed on the Stock Exchanges in London and New York with some 775,000 shareholders. In addition to its primary business the National Grid Group is developing new business opportunities in both the UK and abroad.

Innovation

Company statement:

> We have transformed National Grid from a regulated electricity utility to a dynamic business built on our skills in electricity and telecoms networks. We are able to support dividend growth through efficient operation of cash-generative electricity transmission and distribution networks and deliver significant value in the longer term through our skills in developing start up telecoms networks, gained in the creation of Energis.

Energis is a telecommunications operation which grew from the National Grid's requirement for telecoms – distributing electricity is a sophisticated business and, says director of communications, Gareth Lloyd, 'it requires sophisticated IT and communications systems'. In 1992 National Grid had the systems but lacked a reliable high-speed telecoms network; fibre optic technology was there but hadn't been used for practical networking purposes, and there wasn't a physical network.

The company hit on the simple brilliance of using what it had. An earth wire already stretched from each transmission tower to the next and, around the earth wire, National Grid engineers devised a way of wrapping a fibre optic cable. This created an instant network with stacks of bandwidth. Energis was 'cut loose' from National Grid in 1997 and has been expanding internationally since.

National Grid also claims inventiveness in the running of the electricity transmission grid itself. Electricity cannot be stored and the transmission of generated power involves cleverly planned techniques for congestion management and system operation – which, since greater efficiency was encouraged by regulation in 1994, are estimated to have saved consumers more than £450 million per annum in real terms from the 1993/94 level. In the company's own words, they have 'cut controllable costs by nearly 50 per cent in real terms, thereby reducing the transmission cost of each unit of electricity delivered by 37 per cent in real terms.'

National Grid is a capital intensive business with a spend of £316 million reported for the year to 31 March 2000.

Flexibility

National Grid has changed radically since the deregulation of the early 1990's –'quite simply', says Gareth Lloyd, 'we were in a position where we had to tear up the rules but, at the same time, retain supply availability and, most importantly, retain safety levels'. Safety is a tradition as jealously guarded as ever it was and winter peak system availability – good in 1993/4 at more than 98 per cent – is now in excess of 99 per cent.

The Group's flexibility is reflected by National Grid's operations around the world:

- Argentina and Chile: a joint electricity venture which operates 95 per cent of the 8,900 mile Argentine transmission system; and, since May 2000, 50 per cent ownership of Silica Networks, which is developing a telecoms network in Argentina with a spur to Chile – another expanding telecoms market where National Grid owns 30 per cent of the Santiago-based Manquehue net, which in turn owns 30.1 per cent of Silica Networks in Argentina.
- Australia: National Grid won the bid to build, own and operate the 220 mile Basslink power interconnector between Tasmania and the Australian transmission system.
- Poland: in joint ownership with Energis, the Polish nation railway and telecoms operator Centrala, National Grid owns 23.75 per cent of Energis Polska, which was recently selected to construct and operate a Polish national telecoms network.
- UK: the group owns the 4,500 mile high-voltage system in England and Wales where, second by second, it balances the nation's demand. There are interconnectors with Scotland, France and the Isle of Man. National Grid currently owns 33.3 per cent of Energis, which it reasonably describes as 'a telecommunications and Internet company focused on the business market and providing a full portfolio of voice, data and Internet services, which we created in 1992 and floated in 1997'.
- US: Twenty-five thousand miles of power distribution and approxi-

mately 1.7 million customers in Massachusetts, Rhode Island and New Hampshire; plus around 2,500 miles of transmission network; and wholly owned subsidiary National Grid USA owns in turn the dark-fibre telecoms business NEESCom.

• Zambia: National Grid joint venture with Copperbelt Energy Corporation which owns and operates some 500 miles of electricity transmission network supplying the mines of the Zambian Copperbelt.

• Brazil: National Grid, in a consortium with Sprint and France Telecom, in January 1999 won a telecommunications licence to operate national and international telecommunications services throughout Brazil. The company, known as Intelig, has launched both voice and data services.

Human Resources

National Grid was awarded UK Investors in People status in 2000.

In the UK, the company recruits 'fifteen to twenty potential management graduates a year' who 'tend to get moved around. It's a broad brush experience' and there are levels at which a degree is essential – 'obviously, if you want to come in as an engineer, then we'll expect you to have an engineering degree'. Most – although not all – middle managers have degrees but the lack of a university education is not necessarily a bar to other areas of the business.

The company organizes about a dozen open days a year – 'to show secondary school kids how the kit works, for example' – and it recruits at all levels 'from ads on the Internet and in the media to graduate recruitment and executive search'. There is nothing to say that those who have left the fold may not rejoin.

Results are regarded as vital: 'if we don't deliver then the lights go out', but employees are encouraged to 'think of the unthinkable – Energis was obvious five years after we invented it but anything to do with fibre optics in 1992 was regarded as pretty close to rocket science'. There are no formal rules about dress and haircuts, 'it's just common sense'. Integrity is highly regarded and those who succeed are likely to be pragmatic and intelligent – 'this not a place for people who have little substance or who are not adaptable'.

Growth Markets

National Grid plays a central role in the UK electricity industry and helps to provide a secure and stable electricity supply for individual customers and for the nation as a whole. Its high voltage electricity transmission system – consisting of a network of power lines and substations – stretches the length and breadth of England and Wales.

Outside the UK National Grid has grown, and is growing, in both the electricity and telecommunications markets. The company has established itself in Argentina, Australia, Chile, Poland, Zambia, Brazil and the US and its skills in project design, construction and commercial arrangements are valued around the world.

With a focus on emerging competitive markets the company's declared intention is to continue its expansion both organically and by acquisition.

Quality of Management

'The commitment and contribution of our staff is critical to our success. The way in which the group is fulfilling its potential is a tribute to our people, who have risen to the challenges of moving beyond our traditional borders – working internationally, integrating new business streams and taking on greater responsibility. To encourage people to see the wider context of their role, we held a staff conference in December 1999 with 900 representatives from our business in the UK with representation from North America, Europe, Latin America and Africa. We are proud of our people and proud of our record as a good employer.'

A new environmental management system for the UK operations was introduced in 1999 and received the internationally recognized ISO 14001 certification in May 2000. In the same year basic earnings per share rose 13 per cent to 78 pence and earnings per share – 'excluding exceptional items, goodwill amortization and telecoms start-up losses' – rose 15 per cent to 28.3 pence.

Total profit fell £38.8 million to a 2000 level of £538.6 million but this was largely because of expected start-up losses with the company's telecoms joint venture in Brazil.

International Orientation

In the case of National Grid, this section requires no further explanation other than to reiterate that this is an outward looking British company which has become successful in several continents. It is, as Gareth Lloyd concludes, 'an international company with the traditional British flair for innovation and an unconventional British ability and determination to make innovation work, and to make it work profitably'.

NOCHEX is an extremely new company with a simple mission in life – to make cheques redundant with the establishment of e-mail money instead. This is desirable for a number of reasons, but is of great use to individuals who want to buy items from other individuals on the Internet; they can't use credit or debit cards so they have to send a cheque. The company had 2,200 users before its formal launch and planned to have a quarter of a million by the end of 2001.

Scorecard:

Innovation	★★★★★
Flexibility	★★★
Human resources	★★★
Growth markets	★★★★★
Quality of management	★★★★
International orientation	★★★

Biggest plus:
The opportunity and the excitement of being the first in what ought to be an incredibly successful market.

Biggest minus:
The worry that someone with deeper pockets and bigger marketing budgets might come in and steal the market while the customer base is still ramping up.

NOCHEX
SecuriClickLimited
500 Chiswick High Road
London W4 5RG
Tel: 020 8956 2737
Fax: 020 8956 2234
website: www.nochex.com

NOCHEX

The Business

NOCHEX is a start-up company which had six employees as this book went to press; the plan was to increase this to nine within a few months and beyond that to 18 within a year. It should never have to be huge. Like all start-ups it is privately-owned and has yet to formulate its thinking on listings or alternatives. It managed to find 2,200 customers before any public launch, which it did by mentioning in a number of Internet chat rooms at Internet auction sites that the service was available.

Innovation

The scheme sounds incredibly simple, and from the customer's point of view it is. If an individual needs to send someone money and that person can't accept payment by credit or debit card, then they will usually send a cheque. If the rest of the transaction is taking place over the Internet, then this might be perceived as a little too slow.

So people can set up a NOCHEX account. This is a simple process which involves filling a few online forms to establish a user ID, which will be an e-mail address. The user then sets the account up to work with his or her debit card. All of the standard security precautions are taken up to this point; at this stage, however, the company goes one better and uses its trademarked scheme, called SecuriClick, which verifies that the user is who they say they are. Basically the company asks for a debit card ID and deposits a small random amount – under £1 – and only once the recipient has confirmed the amount that has been received can he or she use their account with the named card.

After this they can receive payments from people with similar accounts, which costs nothing; they can request money from other customers – by prior agreement! – and make payments themselves once there is money in their account. Uploading money from the debit card costs 99p per transaction, as does downloading money back into that card's account – but money can be left in the NOCHEX account for as long as the customer wants at no cost, so if someone waits until there is £1000 in there then the 99p charge fades into insignificance.

At the launch the service was open only to individuals, or for 'people to people' transactions. However, the potential for the trader is immense; some of the third party transaction verifiers charge a lot to organizations not registered with the banks as Internet merchants – the fees can add up to 8 or 9 per cent in some cases – so a free-to-use system that allows for 99p per download, not per item, will clearly have its part to play in that market.

The organization's approach to the market has also been unusual in that it gathered a customer base of 2200 before it launched formally. It achieved this by getting one of the staff to mention the service in chat rooms in the established Internet auction sites; the response was enormous and the company forecasts rapid growth on the strength of it now that marketing has started.

The website was not developed entirely in-house; it was partly developed by Ubik.net, which was also responsible for the Freeserve marketplace site.

Flexibility

New as the company is, it has yet to demonstrate any real corporate flexibility other than continuing to run after its formal opening. Nevertheless it is worth examining the flexibility of the offering itself in some depth.

It's not a product that needs tailoring to every individual's needs – by definition the basic offering is totally inflexible. There will be additions, however, and the company is already planning optional services for businesses which will have extra facilities – although the basic version will be available to the business community as well. It's worth glancing at *www.paypal.com*, the American alternative, which has many different forms of account for different profiles of customer; although NOCHEX feels this overcomplicates the service so there is no plan to expand the service in the same way it does demonstrate what can be done in the area.

Future flexibility will arrive as the product goes cross-currency; at the moment customers need a UK bank account in order to work it. This will change over time.

Human Resources

If a potential employee wants a steady, secure job, then this is probably not the right company to come to – or at least not yet. The atmosphere is entrepreneurial and excited, and the entire staff is thrilled at the prospect of being the first in the UK to take advantage of this market. However this has its downsides; for example, as chief executive, Philip Sheldrake, is the first to concede, someone with a bigger marketing budget might be working on the same thing! Nevertheless, the barriers to entering the market are high, and it took the company a year to set up, so the possibility is remote.

The focus is very much on the customer and making the transactions work smoothly. Staff benefits will be in place soon but at the time of writing all of the resources had been put into working towards the launch so they had yet to be formalized. The employees, whose ages range from mid-20s to early 50s, are all shareholders.

Growth Markets

The boom in Internet auction sites has clearly given NOCHEX the best start possible and it will continue to focus on that market for some time yet. It will also look towards other people who might want to transfer money around; the 19-year-old who needs money from their parents while at college, or the people who've had dinner the night before and agreed to split the bill, but put it on the one piece of plastic – all will be able to use the service.

There will also be moves into the business-to-business market, particularly for the smaller enterprise that can ill afford the percentages card-issuing companies charge for Internet transactions.

Quality of Management

Some managerial depth is essential to allow an organization like this to grow to any serious level; it is worth noting, therefore, that Rodney Potts chairs the organization. Potts was the leader of the Coda Group from 1974–1996 and as such understands the financial systems market extremely well. He oversaw the growth of the organization to the stage at which it could be sold profitably to Baan. The chief financial officer, similarly, has 19 years experience of the software industry and was financial director of Performance Software and organized its trade sale to Cyrano, and oversaw this to its IPO.

It can be gathered, then, that when the company is in a position to decide on moving to a flotation or a sale, it will have experienced management to draw on.

International Orientation

For the moment, the service can only handle one currency at a time, and has chosen pounds sterling. This is, obviously, fine for transactions taking place entirely in the UK, but it's not enough yet, even for the existing customers. They are already asking whether they can send money to, for example, family members in other countries, and the answer to date has been 'no' – so international purchasing is ruled out, which cuts off a fair chunk of the company's potential market. Cross-currency transactions are certainly on the to-do list for the company later this year, at which stage it's likely to grow substantially. The company has plans to expand into Europe and given the number of countries using the Euro as their currency this could be a lucrative niche.

Even before this happens it's going to be a company worth watching. The big drawback with e-commerce to date has been that although it's great for the companies that can trade electronically it's been lousy for mere mortals. This company addresses that basic need in the absence of competition for the moment; this gives it the chance to build up a solid group of loyal customers before anybody else gets a chance. It should do extremely well.

oyster

Oyster Partners is a rapidly-growing Internet consultancy based near London's King's Cross. Its revenues grew 168 per cent last year, from £4 million to £11 million, and the company believes it is on track to make £69 million by 2003. Its headcount has grown from 100 people a year ago to 210 today. Nearly three-quarters of the company is owned by its founders and employees, with the remainder held by its external investors Omnicom and ComVergIT, who last year injected £10 million into Oyster to fund growth and international expansion.

Scorecard:

Innovation	★★
Flexibility	★★★
Human resources	★★★★
Growth markets	★★★
Quality of management	★★★★★
International orientation	★

Biggest plus:
Being a part of leading-edge creative projects.

Biggest minus:
Culture shock resulting from moving to a new, more structured corporate regime.

Oyster Partners
Holford Yard
Cruickshank Street
London WC1X 9HD
Tel: 020 7446 7500
website: www.oyster.com

Oyster Partners

The Business

Oyster Partners is an Internet consultancy formed in July 1998 by the merger of services company Oyster Systems and software house KBW Consulting. The merged organization combines Oyster's strengths in strategy and client management with KBW's strong cross-platform technology skills – a combination which, the company believes, enables it to stand out from the competition.

Both Oyster's revenues and its headcount have been growing rapidly over the past couple of years. In April 2000 the company received its first external investment in the form of £10 million from Omnicom Group and ComVergIT, to fund growth and European expansion. Omnicom now owns 22 per cent of the company and ComVergIT 5 per cent, with the founders holding 60 per cent and the remainder held by non-executive directors and management.

Based in London, the company sells e-business consultancy, design and engineering services to a range of corporate clients, nearly half its business coming from the telecoms and media sector. Past and present customers include Carphone Warehouse, Accessorize, Flemings, British Airways, BBC, Channel 4, the Victoria and Albert Museum and Unilever.

Innovation

Innovation has always been Oyster's lifeblood. It quickly built up a reputation as a trail-blazer in the Internet space, winning 13 major awards during the second half of 2000 alone, for adventurous sites such as the site it built for computer gaming company Rockstar Games. This high-profile achievement has made it easier for the company to attract creative and innovative people. In October 2000, for example, it took on David Warner, former creative director of leading Web company Razorfish, as its new creative director.

Now, while retaining all its creative assets, the company is trying to emphasize its ability to take on industrial-strength projects for big blue-chip companies and to reinforce its capabilities in traditional areas such as the ability to deliver on time and to budget. These capabilities could, in fact, be regarded as genuinely innovative in an industry that until recently has been characterized by style rather than substance.

Marketing still accounts for less than 10 per cent of its total costs. Until recently most of its business has come about by word of mouth or from existing clients. Its strategic consulting work often leads to further implementation work, and it is increasingly carrying out strategy clinics with clients.

But as Internet projects have become bigger and more complex, the company is now having to take on marketing staff and learn to pitch for contracts. Development partnerships with vendors such as Sun, IBM and Epiphany also bring in significant amounts of new business, and Oyster undertakes joint marketing projects with partners.

Flexibility

Rapid expansion of the e-business market has brought big changes for Oyster. From its beginnings two years ago as a small, creative company taking on relatively small-scale Web design and development jobs, it is now having to deal with all the issues arising from a maturing market: larger and more complex projects, the need to form solid industry partnerships, and all the management problems resulting from its own exponential growth.

Other creative young companies have not been flexible enough to adapt to the changes taking place in the Internet market and have already gone under, while others are struggling. But Oyster is in for the long haul; people are its most important resource and it has realized that to deal with the changes it needs the right structures and business processes to enable those people to work effectively.

During 2000, it had risen to the challenge by strengthening its original board, made up of its five founders, with four new senior managers. They have helped introduce new working practices to complement the creativity of Oyster's design and development teams and build a strong foundation for future growth.

Human Resources

Oyster has always believed that a non-hierarchical structure and an open, relaxed and fun working environment will pay off by enabling its people to produce the most innovative ideas. Staff work in self-governing groups and are encouraged to feel responsible for their work and their own destiny. The main King's Cross offices feature a café and a pool table which staff are free to use as the mood takes them.

Latterly however the company has had to modify this laid-back philosophy in response to both a more rigorous economic climate and to the changing nature of its business. As it has taken on larger, more complex projects, a more disciplined approach is becoming essential to delivering on time and to budget.

As a result its young team of, predominantly, creative and technical staff has been faced with the need to work within tighter management guidelines, a change that has not been universally welcomed. Offsetting this, however, the high-profile collapse of several Internet firms has underlined the consequences of an over-relaxed way of working and staff turnover, which had got as high as 35 per cent in the heady days of the dot-com boom, is now down to 10 per cent.

Growth Markets

With the new network economy fuelling continuing demand for e-business services, Oyster does not have far to look for sources of revenue growth. Nor does it have to look far afield; the company points out that as Europe has so far trailed behind the US in terms of Internet usage, more rapid growth can be expected here over the next few years.

As well as conventional Web technology, it is exploring emerging potential delivery channels such as interactive TV and wireless, for serving the needs of its customer base. In response to customer demand, it is also taking on more ambitious and higher-value projects that often incorporate a number of components: consultancy, design, development, and increasingly systems integration. In February it was awarded Sun Microsystems' E-Integrator of the Year 2000 award.

To maintain and build its share of the maturing Internet market, the company is having to work on approaches to demand creation. Until now, it has mainly relied on recommendation and repeat business to bring in the work, but Internet projects are becoming too costly to award on the basis of word of mouth; average project value has grown from $30-$100,000 in the days when Web development meant little more than online brochures to $2-$10 million for a large project involving a range of services and extensive integration. As a result the company is strengthening its sales and marketing team to enable it to pitch more effectively for large contracts.

Quality of Management

Oyster started out as a young, creative company that was very much its five founders' baby. Its management now faces the challenge of retaining its initial energy and creativity while introducing the structure needed to support a growing business.

The original founders recognized the problem and responded by appointing a new chief executive officer, Alan Bell, who has 33 years experience in the IT industry with big-name companies including IBM and Amdahl, where he was president of the services operation.

In addition to Bell, a number of other new arrivals have strengthened the Oyster management team. Its new chief financial officer, Paul Kingsley, joins the company from Omnicom Group; and its head of human resources, Maxine Sutton, comes from Merrill Lynch. On their advice, the company has introduced stronger financial controls and a more structured management process whereby the company still has a flat team-based structure but each team is under the firm leadership of a project manager.

Dr Richard Rolfe, Oyster's recently-appointed head of projects, brings extensive project management experience acquired at Carpe Diem Innovations and PricewaterhouseCoopers Kinesis, where he managed several major e-business programmes. Further professional experience and connections come from Oyster's two new client partners. Mark Otway, an ex-Andersen Consulting senior global partner of 30 years, now advises the company on best practice; and Peter Rawlins, ex-CEO of the London Stock Exchange provides a special focus on strategy.

Working practices at Oyster may have sometimes been a little laissez faire, but strong cash management has been a principle from the start. Set up with the founders' own money, Oyster has been profitable from the word go, and has no debt. Revenue growth is accelerating, up from £4 million in 1999 to £11 million in 2000. The company is projecting this will increase more than sixfold to £69 million by 2003. Its financial performance and business plan have been sufficiently convincing to persuade Omnicom to take on Oyster as its only European investment to date.

Though Oyster is currently expanding fast, it acknowledges the need for quality rather than quantity in the projects it takes on to ensure that its growth is sustainable. In following up sales leads from its partners, for example, it is careful to take on only as much work as it can comfortably handle in order to maintain its reputation for delivering a quality result on time and within budget.

International Orientation

Oyster's investors have suggested that the company needs to 'think global' in order to move towards a successful IPO. For the next few years, at least, the major growth in Internet services is likely to be in Europe rather than the US, and the company has considered setting up an office in France. However the management's current thinking is that globalization of an essentially client-facing service business is something to be undertaken only with extreme care. Oyster's board has taken the view that rather than rushing to set up operations overseas for the sake of it, with all the costs and management overheads that this would entail, it makes more sense to follow its clients.

Its current strategy is to expand globally as and when client projects require it – which to date they have not – while, at the same time, continuing to explore the considerable growth potential emerging in the UK through the growth of e-commerce and the development of new media. In support of this decision, it points to the dearth of successful pan-European services companies, and the fact that many UK new media firms have had to close their overseas operations.

Parcel2go.com is part of FAM Logistics, a family-owned firm which since its inception in 1997 has specialized in packaging, distribution and storage. Its turnover is now around £1.25m. FAM Logistics was founded by Fil Adams-Mercer, an entrepreneur who previously built up and sold a chain of video stores and a publishing business, now owned respectively by Blockbuster Video and Haymarket. Parcel2go-.com is the e-commerce arm of the company and employs ten people in the UK, all based at its Bolton office.

Scorecard:

Innovation	★★★
Flexibility	★★★★
Human resources	★★
Growth markets	★★★
Quality of management	★★
International orientation	★★★

Biggest plus:
Opportunities to show initiative and the chance to become expert in a quickly-expanding sector.

Biggest minus:
Requires sensitive dealing with customers and suppliers to maintain a reputation for high quality service.

Parcel2go.com
Albion Mill
St Marks Street
Bolton
Tel: 01204 384426
website: www.parcel2go.com
e-mail: info@parcel2go.com

Parcel2go.com

The Business

Parcel2go is a relatively young company, established in April 2000 to expand FAM Logistics' reach via the Internet. It is privately owned, with its founder Fil Adams-Mercer holding the majority stake.

The company competes in the UK parcel delivery market, offering a cheap, next-day one-off service to consumers through its website, and account services for parcels weighing under 25 kilos to small and medium-sized enterprises such as Moben Kitchens.

Parcel2go has dozens of pick-up points throughout the UK and is growing its customer base at a rate of about 20 per cent per month. It plans to expand operations in the UK and extend them to the US within the next three years.

However, as yet FAM has made only a marginal investment in the company, preferring to wait and see how demand develops for Web-based parcel delivery and storage in the UK and overseas. 'The advantage is that we're not a dot-com brimming with staff and waiting for things to happen,' said Mr Adams-Mercer.

Innovation

The company is seeking to develop both a new consumer mindset and fresh capacities for parcel delivery. As a wholesaler of parcel space from two of the world's largest carriers, Omega Securicor and UPS, it already stands to benefit over the next twelve to twenty-four months from the sizeable investments made by those carriers in Web-based tracking systems around the globe.

'We want to educate our users to look at our website for information and to encourage a self-manage mindset. Our customers can log on to the Web and find out what has happened to their parcel, what time it was delivered and who signed for it. Within twelve months, we will be able to send a text message to your mobile phone to let you know that your parcel has been delivered,' said Mr Adams-Mercer.

The company offers a £50 cashback guarantee to customers that parcels will arrive on time. Meanwhile, it is keen to pioneer improvements in delivery. 'We are becoming the experts, and it's very simple things that make a person an expert,' said Mr Adams-Mercer. 'For example, I noticed that in another operation, the postcodes on the parcels being processed were very small. All they needed to do was to make the postcodes larger to reduce the risk of them going astray.'

Other examples of innovation include time-saving features on its website, saving the user from having to fill in multiple address details.

The system allows customers to simply enter credit card details for a one-off delivery, rather than having to open an account.

At present the bulk of the company's business comes from SMEs but Parcel2go is working with the logistics group Christian Salvesen to develop a pallet-service for larger deliveries, and is looking at offering its own retail content in the way of personalized gifts and toys.

Two of the company's employees are detailed to concentrate solely on developing the business abroad and developing marketing initiatives, although to date it has focused on local, rather than national advertising campaigns. A main thrust for the company at this point in time is to build up repeat business.

Flexibility

As the company was only established in early 2000 it has yet to undergo any extensive restructuring although growth over the last months has led to an expansion in its warehouse capacity at its headquarters in Lancashire. Parcel2go has positioned itself as a troubleshooter with a reputation for customer service, and as it grows further, the challenge will be for it to maintain those standards.

At present, the company manages growth simply by putting a lid on its seasonal activities and declining orders after it has reached a certain capacity. 'Our Christmas period is very tight and deliveries increase by about 30 per cent in November and December, so there will be no expansion until the New Year,' explained Mr Adams-Mercer. 'This way, we may not be making much money but neither are we losing money.'

However, he and his team are looking to grow the company quite rapidly now that they have established the success of the business model. All profits are reinvested into the parcels business. 'The beauty of the model is that we don't lose any money if we don't do business. I don't buy a product – that is, the parcel space from the carrier – until I have already got the money from the customer. That said, we will probably look to raise equity for expansion in the near future,' he said.

Being so close to the ground, the company is uniquely adaptable to changing markets and customer needs. Recently, for instance, after many e-mail requests from abroad, it has been considering an extension to its warehouse space to offer a customized storage and delivery package to small US e-retailers who want to cater for UK customers without the expense of establishing a full-blown delivery operation.

'When a parcel goes missing, Moben Kitchens don't ring Securicor for details, they ring us. A customer doesn't want to end up talking to a machine. We say "Give us ten minutes and we will trace the parcel for you". We're the problem-solvers,' said Mr Adams-Mercer.

Human Resources

Parcel2go may be small, but it has a lively, energetic culture according to its founder. Employees are taken abroad to locations such as Belgium or Dublin for Christmas parties and habitually gather in the local pub on Friday nights to debrief on the week.

'My attitude to the company and to my employees is: if you're not happy, don't do it. Life is too short. We don't have clocking in and clocking off. We have "Let's come in and get stuck in",' said Mr Adams-Mercer.

He conceded that while the hours for most employees are regular (9.30am to 5.30pm), working in such an intense 'hotline' environment can sometimes be aggravating. 'We might get an ear-bashing but we must ring the customer and tell them "I know where your parcel is" because it's all about quality of customer service.'

The office and adjoining 60,000 sq ft of warehouse space in Bolton are together the nerve-centre of the business, and all new employees are given six months of intensive one-to-one training in areas of expertise such as customer service, warehousing and routing systems.

Growth Markets

Parcel2go sees its growth occurring simultaneously abroad and in the UK. It is presently in talks with several companies based overseas with a view to offering a customized pick, pack, storage and distribution package, and it is actively marketing the initiative among smaller retailers in the US and elsewhere, with customers already established in South-East Asia. 15 per cent of the company's customers find the Parcel2go site simply by surfing the Net. However, it has yet to decide where to concentrate the bulk of future investment, whether in developing its Web-based parcel delivery operations or in expanding its warehousing facilities.

One of the company's strongest points is its accumulation of e-commerce expertise, still very much an emerging medium, in the SME arena. 'I don't know of any direct competitors. I haven't found a website yet that will take your credit card details, your pick-up point and your delivery address, and it's a done deal,' said Mr Adams-Mercer.

He is looking for a growth rate for the company of 25 per cent this financial year, and is open to UK initiatives and partnerships as well as global deals. For example, Parcel2go is presently in talks to co-operate with an operator that specializes in offering logistics products and services to UK charities, this could double the business overnight.

Quality of Management

One of the strengths of the company is Mr Adams-Mercer's own long-established links with major carriers such as Securicor Omega. 'My loyalties lie firmly with them and we try to accommodate each other,' he said. 'The benefits for Parcel2go lie in the understanding we have been able to achieve for both sides. Working in close conjunction with these large carriers, we have seen that the further north you go in the UK, the more the services given by some carriers deteriorate. We have been able to develop an understanding of their limitations as well as their strengths.'

The company is also aiming to develop relationships with various other strategic partners and to recruit associates and franchisees overseas. It is currently in talks with a number of Web-based companies to develop customized Internet delivery services.

In the coming years, Mr Adams-Mercer is looking to hand on the company management baton to younger recruits, including his own son Richard and Stephen Kramer, who are presently new accounts manager and Internet relations manager, respectively.

'I see the future lying very much with people such as Richard and Stephen. As we become more and more Internet-focused, they are the ones who are most at home dealing with the evolution of technology and the business models which are growing out of it. It's a new company and it's a place where at the moment, you can very quickly become a senior person, so it's a quick way to the top.'

The company is currently completing procedures to win its ISO 9002 accreditation. It has also just won an award for excellence from the Institute of Transport Management. 'It's very busy here and very tight in terms of time,' said Mr Adams-Mercer. 'However, it's also become a close-knit family of employees and because of that, we don't tend to have people leaving.'

Parcel2go is at the moment 90 per cent owned by Mr Adams-Mercer, with the other 10 per cent held by his personal assistant. However, in the near future he aims to restructure and dilute the equity stakes in the company, giving other investors a chance to back the company. The long-term intention is to float, sell or merge the parcels business.

International Orientation

With the parcel industry set to grow at an estimated 35 per cent per year world-wide, and as more people buy from Internet sites and the security of e-transactions tightens, Parcel2go potentially has the world at its feet. With this in mind, the company is considering setting up franchises overseas, particularly in the US where the concept of a one-stop mail-shop is more established. 'My relationships with carriers, and with UPS in particular, enable me to bring a lot to the party,' said Mr Adams-Mercer.

However, as yet operations are confined to the British Isles. The Post Office is currently pre-eminent in the delivery of small items in the UK, but fast-moving, Web-based companies such as Parcel2go could soon steal a march on the status quo by developing customer-facing initiatives, such as drop boxes for parcels located at nearby petrol stations. 'Home deliveries are the future and you can't ignore that. Everyone wants to sell over the Internet, but someone has got to deliver it so it's going to be a challenge to keep up with the industry and to help to direct it,' said Mr Adams-Mercer.

PLEXIAN

Plexian has become a major player in the booming IT recruitment market as a result of the merger late last year of two high-flying agencies, Plexus and Olympian. The merged company is a £40m business with 200,000 candidates on its database, 114 staff, six UK locations, an Australian arm, and plans for more international offices. As well as its recruitment operations, Plexian operates a training division; it also has a minority stake in a contract human resources and psychometric testing company.

Scorecard:

Innovation	★★★★
Flexibility	★★★★
Human resources	★★★★
Growth markets	★★★★
Quality of management	★★★★★
International orientation	★★★★

Biggest plus:
Plexian values the relationships it has with its clients, and in turn that means it values the people who build and maintain those relationships.

Biggest minus:
As in any sales-oriented organization, however, there is constant pressure to sustain growth and meet targets.

Plexian
Plexian plc
40 Craven Street
London WC2N 5NG
Tel: 020 7839 7799
Fax: 020 7766 7601
website: www.plexian.com

Plexian

The Business

Plexian is one of the newest names in the Top UK Companies list – but only because it represents the merger (on 1 November 2000) of two high-flying recruitment agencies, either of which might have made the grade on their own account.

Both Plexus (founded in 1990 by Howard Butterfield) and Olympian Consultancy (established by UK hockey international Richard Leman in 1993 – he is a non-executive director of Plexian) operate in the high-profile fast-growing IT sector. A merger always seemed good sense, given the neat fit between the two – a similarity of cultures, the complementary service range and geographical spread and the obvious empathy of the two managing directors.

Plexus contributed sales of around £11.5m and some 44 staff; it also had a central London base. Olympian, with its headquarters in Weybridge, had 100 employees and in 1999 a turnover of £26m. Howard Butterfield is now Plexian's executive chairman, Olympian's Mark Taylor is managing director.

Currently Plexian is a £40m organization with headquarters in central London. It has 200,000 candidates on its jobseekers' database and receives between 4,000 and 5,000 new registrations each month. The company employs a total of 114 staff; they are spread around six regional offices in the UK, plus an active overseas subsidiary in Australia.

As well as its recruitment operations, which include several specialist teams (for Oracle, e-business, new media, control systems, Lotus Notes, and Open Systems) Plexian operates a training division and has a stake in an external training company.

Innovation

Plexian has a sophisticated internal IT system based on Lotus Notes, a major investment that has provided a competitive advantage – extra automation in internal record keeping and candidate matching means faster, more accurate and more resilient systems with the flexibility to adapt quickly to business changes.

Plexian also has a mature Web presence for external access. The website features a variety of imaginative functions for candidates and recruiters. They include Metamail, a Web-based e-mail service that allows job hunters an e-mail account which doesn't go through their current employer's systems. Metajobs is another interesting idea, a cost-saving job advertising service for employers that provides a custom-made Web page for them to add or edit vacancies themselves; candidates respond to the jobs on offer but are screened by Plexian staff before being passed on.

Plexian does not regard itself as a high-turnover labour exchange so much as a human resource consultancy, and this represents an imaginative yet entirely logical development of the core business. Current management services include skills audits and salary rate recommendations, advice on personnel issues and employment law, and trend analyses.

As part of the emphasis on building long-term relationships, key clients are invited to contribute to 'customer advisory boards' where innovations can be discussed and feedback offered.

Plexian is a member of the industry body Association of Technology Staffing Companies (ATSCo), which runs a strict Code of Practice and represents about half of the IT recruitment industry in the UK.

Flexibility

Plexian already has the resources and the imagination to adapt quickly and to seize market opportunities. Specialist divisions have been added for particular types of vacancy, for instance in e-business and new media; this approach will obviously continue. And international expansion will provide clients with round-the-clock access from anywhere in the world to a common set of services, including the candidate database. The investment in internal and external IT systems is a key factor here.

Plexian is also approaching the stage where its size and reputation will enable it to lead the market. Its plans to become more of a human resources consultancy will enable Plexian to offer clients a portfolio of new services – some of which they may not yet realize that they need or want.

Human Resources

Plexian sees its core business technique as 'relationship marketing' rather than sales. Clients are given a single point of contact, so staff retention is a key issue – the company argues that the full fruits of the client relationship will be seen only after twelve-eighteen months, so longevity is very important in a business that is conventionally known for its very high staff turnover.

So Plexian works hard to attract the right people and keep them happy. Pay rates are good; consultants work to targets, but management appears sympathetic to temporary hiccups. The culture also emphasizes teamwork alongside personal responsibility; it would certainly suit someone who worked well under moderate pressure and who could see a career future beyond the simple job-placement round.

Plexian operates a share option scheme for employees with at least three years service, and 10 per cent of the company's equity is reserved for this in trust.

Growth Markets

The core business remains IT recruitment, and at a time of skills shortages and increasing outsourcing this is growing strongly. The respected Holway Report for 2000 valued the IT recruitment market last year at £4.1bn. Though the rate of increase was just 9 per cent – a dramatic slowdown from the late 1990s, caused presumably by the loss of Y2K demand – Holway anticipates that things will pick up quickly with a return to double-digit growth for the next few years.

Both Plexus and Olympian had been expanding year-on-year, beating the industry averages and slowing only slightly when everyone else in IT recruitment was feeling the pinch. The merger came about partly because the two companies felt they were reaching the limits of organic growth, however. Plexian is aiming to be a £100m company in the near future, and feels the merger will provide the critical mass it needs to service clients on a global scale and with an enhanced portfolio.

There's scope in the recruitment market for this level of activity – Holway forecasts a £6bn market for 2003. Training for industry-standard IT qualifications is already part of the portfolio, too. Plexian's recently established professional training operation is doing well and expanding with all-in packaged courses on offer to individuals and to corporate clients. The company also has a 22 per cent interest in Academy Limited, a specialist human resources and psychometric testing operation.

In general terms the business plan includes more and closer contact with the clients, continuing the existing strategy that will enable Plexian to offer better services in recruitment, employment, and personnel development – to anticipate demand from the client and to contribute creative proposals. The mid-term aim is to position Plexian as a global provider of IT human capital management (HCM) services in the IT sector.

HCM is a fairly new management tool, but one that has great potential as an extension of conventional human resources' services like recruitment and professional development. The principle behind HCM is that organizations have traditionally focused on their use of capital and technology, neglecting the third key element – people, and especially the impact they can have on the success of the business. In theory HCM shows businesses how to distribute resources more effectively among capital, technology, and people.

Plexian is working to build the in-house knowledge that will be required, and it already has the client contacts to make a commercial success of HCM.

Quality of Management

Plexian's progenitors Plexus and Olympian were both recording substantial year-on-year sales increases before the merger, and in neither case was there any sign that normal management controls were lost in the dash for growth. Indeed, it's worth noting that Plexian's board has recently added Ian Smith, a specialist in corporate strategy development whose published works include the prescient *Growing a Private Company*.

International Orientation

Plexian is looking to build an international network. Before the merger, Olympian already had an office in Sydney (the Australian arm will effectively provide 24-hour access to Plexian for clients and contractors). Expansion this year will see a Continental presence, probably in the Netherlands, and a US office in Boston.

IT recruitment continues to expand in most developed parts of the world, and Plexian's association with big-name transnational clients can help the company establish itself outside Britain.

There is also a strategic issue. Apart from the local business, international operations are seen as reducing Plexian's dependence on the UK economy – not a major issue at present, but one that represents a prudent management policy for the future.

POWERGEN

Powergen plc has the vision to create one of the world's leading integrated energy businesses. Powergen seeks to grow by generating, distributing and supplying power, gas and telecom facilities in the UK and the US. In December 2000 the company completed its $3.2bn acquisition of LG&E Energy Corp of Kentucky, which has given the company a strong platform for growth in the deregulating US energy market. The successful integration of East Midlands Electricity into the UK business has helped to push the company into a leading position as well as raising the quality and stability of its earnings. An integrated international future beckons.

Scorecard:

Innovation	★★★★
Flexibility	★★★★
Human resources	★★★★
Growth markets	★★★★
Quality of management	★★★★
International orientation	★★★★

Biggest plus:
The strength of the Powergen brand in the UK and the company's track record in world-class asset management.

Biggest minus:
The company needs to be bigger to give it access to the capital investment needed to be able to realize its strategy more quickly.

Powergen plc
53 New Broad Street
London EC2M 1SL
Tel: 020 7826 2826
Fax: 020 7826 2890
website: www.powergenplc.com

Powergen plc

The Business

Powergen is one of the UK's leading names in electricity and gas. With the $3.2bn dollar acquisition of LG&E Energy Corp of Kentucky in late 2000, and the sale of most of its international portfolio Powergen has essentially become an Anglo-American company. The vision is to be the leading essential services provider in all the markets in which it operates. The successful integration of East Midlands Electricity consolidated Powergen's position in UK gas and electricity markets, while mobile phone, Internet and financial services were also initiated and are now under further development. Reducing the debt incurred by the US acquisition is being handled by selling interests in facilities in Australia and India, as well as Asia. The focus now is on the US: the largest global energy market and the UK: the most deregulated energy market in the world.

Innovation

Powergen made history a decade ago with its sponsorship of the national weather bulletins on independent television, which is now the longest running TV sponsorship in UK history. Research has shown that Powergen has the best-known national brand name in the electricity sector as one of just two nationally recognized energy brands. This provides a significant competitive advantage in the deregulated domestic energy market. The energy market is fast-moving and it is only through innovation and new ideas that Powergen can maintain its competitive edge. In October, 1999, Powergen was the first company in its sector to become an Internet service provider. It was also the first major energy company to allow customers to switch suppliers online.

'There are cash incentives to switch online,' says Nick Baldwin, Powergen's chief executive. 'Buy gas, telephone and electricity services from us and we offer them at highly competitive rates plus if customers switch to us online we give them £50 cash.' The Internet is seen as a major revenue source for sales and marketing in the future. Small and medium enterprises can access Web-enabling services through Alto Digital and Powergen also offers websites with online payment services.

As a mobile phone provider, the company started as a 'reseller' offering packages to small-to-medium sized companies. Later in 2001 Powergen mobile telecom services will be rolled out more widely. 'We recognize that everyone has different needs and requirements so we strive to create products and service packages to suit each individual,' says Baldwin. 'We have developed a multi-product billing system that allows customers to mix-and-match payment details and a range of products so we can provide a clearly-itemized single bill for a range of products and services.'

Two Nottingham-based business units handle research and development. Powergen Power Technology is a £27 million pound business with experts in all aspects of power production technology. Powergen Energy Solutions is a service provider which focuses on helping companies manage energy usage more successfully.

Flexibility

'Powergen has an excellent track record in industrial relations,' says Baldwin. 'Our policy has always been not to make compulsory redundancies.' A strong statement given the UK workforce is less than half what it was when the business was privatized ten years ago. In the last two years alone the company has reduced its distribution business workforce by over 1,000 staff with no strikes. That this was done is attributed to Powergen's good industrial relations policies, its excellent track record and the fact it provides an attractive voluntary redundancy package. Relations between management, unions and workforce are good. 'There has been a great deal of structural change in our business, driven by fundamental changes in the industry and the diversity of our business compared with when we started' says Baldwin. 'We have evolved and the management structure has changed dramatically over the years.'

Powergen's UK business splits into five businesses: retail (further divided into large business, small-to-medium enterprises, and residential); distribution; energy trading; European asset management; and combined heat and power (CHP). There is now also a substantial business in the US in the form of LG&E Energy Corp. of Kentucky as well as the remainder of Powergen International.

'The energy trading business is ahead of the game,' says Baldwin. 'Until recently, everything was handled separately – electricity trading, gas trading, coal and oil trading. By moving to an integrated trading group, we are maximising our return in a market where wholesale electricity prices have been falling. It works because when market rates are low for electricity and high for gas we sell gas instead of burning it in our power stations. By the same logic we increase the proportion of our generation delivered by our coal-fired plant and turn down the gas plant. The market is getting increasingly dynamic. Centralizing it into the energy trading business has enabled us to squeeze the best returns possible for the company.'

A key strength is asset management – take power stations, running more efficiently and reliably than ever with fewer than half the workforce at privatization.

Human Resources

Due to the diversity of the different types of business within Powergen, there's a mix of personnel. The retail business is fast-moving and consumer-focused which demands a certain type of person to do the job successfully. Energy trading people are a 'different breed', more akin to City traders. The European asset management business is focused on engineering excellence and deal making, while the distribution business is centred around the management of geographically-spread fixed assets – 'do the wires work properly?' The CHP business calls for corporate relationship management and deal making and those who can understand other business's problems.

Hay evaluations, adjusted to take account of market rates are paid to employees to reflect the true value of the role they play. Generous holiday allowances are offered, plus share save schemes, profit sharing (payable in cash or shares), and bonus and share options for a significant number of managers. A final salary contributory pension plan operates. However staff do not enjoy reductions on utility bills, for regulatory reasons.

Growth Markets

'The UK retail business is a significant growth area,' says Baldwin. 'But our focus is on organic growth rather than acquisition. During 2000, the domestic customer base grew at over 1 per cent a month while the small-to-medium enterprise customer base is showing 4 per cent per month growth. We are still the market leader in the large business sector. There is tremendous growth in the fixed-line phone markets where we acquired 130,000 customer accounts in 2000 and beat our main rival to market by over six months. The UK distribution business has been a real success too and we would seriously consider buying/ managing another distribution operation if a suitable opportunity presented itself at the right price and terms.'

'The mid-West market in the US, where we acquired LG&E Energy Corp, is growing at 5 per cent per annum, so there we will be looking for organic growth,' says Baldwin. Kentucky, where LG&E Energy is based, sits at the crossroads of the major gas and electricity transmission lines feeding the mid-West area, which itself constitutes 25 per cent of the US's electricity demand. This is bigger than the demand for the whole of France and Germany combined. In the mid-West there are 25 similarly-sized companies to LG&E Energy. In France and Germany there are eight – soon to be six. 'Increasing the scale of the US operation through a further acquisition is a distinct future possibility.'

Quality of Management

Powergen has the driven aim – as a low-cost, innovative and environmentally-responsible operator – to deliver value and quality to its customers, shareholders, employees, partners and the communities in which it operates throughout the world. Powergen is a FTSE 100 company with some 750,000 small shareholders with significant numbers of shares held by big institutions and pensions companies.

A flat management structure operates, where managers are given scope to make decisions. It's common to find a cross-section of management levels in a meeting – board level director, operating director, business unit head and operational manager for example.

There's a corporate development programme to spot and nurture those with potential. Responsibility for human resources is devolved to individual business unit heads, who are given responsibility for identifying appropriate training needs and nurturing rising stars. MBA training is offered where it is deemed useful for high-potential individuals.

'We have avoided the trap some companies have fallen into where people are repeatedly promoted and promoted until they're in a job for which they are incompetent,' says Baldwin. 'You get optimal performance from staff when it's recognized they've reached the peak of their ability at a particular level of responsibility and they are valued and rewarded for it or trained in preparation for the next step.

'We have a graduate management training programme, and we also recruit staff as needed,' says Baldwin who himself started with the company when it was part of the CEGB and worked his way up through various parts of the business. Four of the five UK business managing directors are from outside the company, brought in to add the expertise and depth of management experience deemed necessary for long-term success.

The Board comprises Nick Baldwin as chief executive, an executive finance director, the chief executive of the US operation and five non-executive directors including Ed Wallis as chairman.

International Orientation

Following the LG&E acquisition, Powergen's earnings are split roughly 55 per cent UK and 45 per cent US business. With the LG&E deal 'not the end of the road', Powergen is well-placed to make a follow-on acquisition to increase the scale of its US operations. Five years from now Baldwin says if a follow-on acquisition has been made, the balance of Powergen's business will be in the US.

Europe is a different issue. Most UK utility companies are too small to muscle into Europe, which is characterized by huge consolidated firms. Consequently, several UK companies, including Powergen, have turned to US markets to seek growth by acquisition

Powergen's expansion in the US and the development of its LG&E subsidiary will be based on applying the lessons learnt from the deregulation of the UK market and its unique ability to manage assets at minimum cost and maximum efficiency and reliability.

It's these same competencies which underpin Powergen's intention to develop service businesses in Europe which will offer incumbents in the deregulating European markets the opportunity to benefit from Powergen's ability to cut costs and improve efficiency.

QSA Limited (UK) is a British firm that specializes in building software solutions for manufacturers and retailers in the food and drinks industry. The software enables users to manage production data such as the nutritional content of ingredients, the geographical source of raw materials, allergen contents, hygiene, quality control and product testing. The company is based in St Albans, but has a wholly-owned subsidiary called ProductVine Inc, in Delaware, USA. It has also formed a partnership with Fort Worth-based Marketing Management Inc to represent its products and services in the US.

Scorecard:

Innovation	★★★★★
Flexibility	★★★★★
Human resources	★★★★
Growth markets	★★★★
Quality of management	★★★★★
International orientation	★★★★

Biggest plus:
The company has targeted a market that is only awakening to the benefits of using software to boost production techniques.

Biggest minus:
QSA Limited (UK) doesn't really have any minus points.

QSA Limited (UK)
Wellington House
273/275 High Street
London Colney
St Albans
Hertfordshire AL2 1HA
Tel: 01727 744700
website: www.qsa.co.uk

QSA Limited

The Business

QSA Limited (UK) was set up in 1995 by Tim Winfield and Paul Byfleet, both of whom were food technologists. Based on their experiences at J Sainsbury's the pair spotted the potential benefits from the computerization of the technical specifications for food and drink products' ingredients. The company has recently secured £2 million in second round funding and has laid plans for an initial public offering (possibly within the next 36 months) which have included appointing Simon Shepherd as managing director. The company began as a team of seven, but now has a staff of 38. Its list of clients includes Asda Stores PLC, Budgens Stores and Iceland Foods PLC.

Innovation

According to business development director Paul Byfleet, it's speed to market and production control that are the key areas affecting profitability in the food and drink industry, and QSA Limited (UK) software enables users to dictate both. Its main product is QSA Specifications, which is a software database package accessible to retailers and manufacturers, allowing them to work together collaboratively during the production process.

QSA Limited (UK)'s other products include HACCP, which is designed to assesses the risk attributes of food products during their life cycle and QSA Exchange, which gives retailers information from their suppliers on a diskette system. There are two new products in development right now, and they are called Enterprise NPD and ProductVine. Enterprise NPD is an intranet version of the Specifications software, targeted at large multi-site and multinational organizations in the food and drink industry. ProductVine is an online version of the Specifications software, enabling greater collaboration during the production process and reducing the time it takes to bring a product to market. Demand for the software has been driven by the numerous press related scares that have appeared regularly. Mr Byfleet believes QSA Limited (UK) is distinguishable from its competitors through its products' depth of functionality and relevance to its users. He says that unlike rivals' products his firm's packages are applicable across the board so whether it's dairy products or meat, for example, the software can be used.

The firm's products are marketed directly to retailers, with the belief that user endorsement is the most effective way of building business. A website *www.qsa.co.uk* gives visitors a rundown of the different software packages on offer and the companies that are using the products. In order to boost its status the company went for, and obtained, Microsoft Business Partner status. It is also on the Oracle Partner Programme. So far up to 60 per cent of annual turnover has been spent on software development, which the company says accounts for its losses to date.

Flexibility

The take up of the Internet has prompted the company to develop its online application ProductVine, which takes advantage of the Net's ability to distribute information quickly; they have applied it to an industry that, in the words of Mr Byfleet, 'is underdeveloped in the use of technological applications'.

However, wary of cannibalizing existing business, the company is not rushing to market with its latest development, but launching it during the second quarter of this year with the announcement of its first users among the firm's high-profile clients. In order to meet the needs of these users, QSA Limited (UK) has made changes to its delivery engine infrastructure so that customers get standardized service level agreements. This has resulted in its bosses investing heavily in the development of the sales and support functions of the business.

'The Internet has given us another way of delivering our software,' says Mr Byfleet, 'but it would have been no good introducing new products which made use of the medium if we didn't invest in the back-up systems to ensure everything ran smoothly'.

At present, with the market for QSA Limited (UK) software growing at a considerable rate especially over the last eighteen months, the business has not so much had to adapt to a changing market but evolve at such a rate as to keep up with demand. Hence, as Mr Byfleet explains, the drive is to continue successfully delivering its products to a market late in embracing technology rather than assessing its core business.

'We really feel we have stolen a march on our competitors, giving us first-mover advantage,' he says. 'Through our products, clients are discovering just how much money can be saved on bringing a product to market that much earlier. Their enthusiasm for our products is reflected by how fast we have grown since our launch.'

Human Resources

QSA Limited (UK) achieved the Government-sponsored Investors in People national standard during 2000. This recognition was in part due to the firm's keenness to provide training for staff so that they were kept up-to-date with the changing technologies fundamental to its core business. The company puts the word empowerment at the centre of its employee philosophy, and has started a share option scheme to allow staff the opportunity to have a stake in the business's fortunes.

The company's belief in its staff is hammered home when Mr Byfleet describes how the workers most likely to succeed in the firm are the ones who reflect a pioneering approach, while the ones least likely to do well will be those who avoid challenges.

Growth Markets

The firm has been funding a US expansion initiative over the past 12 months and has set up the wholly owned subsidiary ProductVine Inc, in Delaware. On top of this the business has signed a partnership agreement with Fort Worth-based Marketing Management Inc, to represent QSA Limited (UK), and become the reseller of its products in the US. Both moves indicate how much the firm wants to tap into the US market. As Mr Byfleet explains the rewards are there: 'its potential market is five times as big as the one in the UK, plus there is very little competition in the space we are operating in, right now'.

Apart from expanding into the US, the company also plans to create a presence in the European grocery market, where like in the US, it will look to win over multinational retailers and manufacturers.

It believes by investing so much of its revenues into research and development, the company will continue to be at the cutting-edge of technology, thus making it the key player for inventory systems in the grocery industry across each market it enters.

'We will ensure existing and potential customers will receive the best of breed e-products from us, always,' says Mr Byfleet.

Quality of Management

Despite its rapid growth, QSA Limited still only employs 38 people in the UK. Its management has, therefore, not reached the level of complexity experienced by a large corporation with hundreds of workers on its payroll. However, the firm has looked seriously at its management structure and recently expanded its middle management sector. This expanded tier allows the directors to avoid getting bogged down in the day-to-day running of the firm and concentrate on the company's development. The increase in worker numbers and management tiers has made employee appraisal more important to the company, which now uses systems devised by the Investors in People organization.

'The senior management team is currently assessed by using 360 degree appraisal, as well as self assessment using psychometric testing,' says Mr Byfleet.

The appraisers are a mix of peers and members of the managed team. Appraisals are conducted annually and the results collated centrally by the managing director. Results are fed back individually via the consultant conducting the psychometric tests and the managing director, and collectively as a senior management team. Mr Byfleet believes this helps to identify any skills gaps and to decide how to fill those gaps.

The whole process is currently under review, and changes will be the responsibility of the human resource manager.

International Orientation

It's fair to say the company is very internationally focused, with this reflected in its entrance into the US market through its partnering agreement and launch of ProductVine Inc. The first US sale of QSA Limited (UK) software was made in December 2000, and Mr Byfleet is currently a frequent visitor to the US, where the company now has its own permanently based employee. Mr Byfleet says the company's international growth is fundamental to its business strategy, as the firm sees opportunities for its software in grocery industries across the globe. By targeting multinationals in both the US and Europe, where it is now keen to make in-roads, it is hoped the businesses will fit the applications across their whole networks from country to country. As Mr Byfleet says, the company intends to remain as focused on existing markets as new ones. 'It's important that going forward we provide the right level of customer care and service for existing customers as we do for new clients. It's the way to be successful.'

Razorfish is a specialist in digital media and in enabling other companies to participate in the digital revolution. It uses communication tools such as TVs, PCs, mobile phones and personal digital organizers to solve problems such as how to buy and sell products electronically, deliver digital information and entertainment, and enable geographically-dispersed workers to collaborate. Established in 1995, the company has been a key consolidator, pulling together the diverse skills needed to work effectively in the digital business. It employs around 1500 people in offices across Europe, North America and Asia.

Scorecard:

Flexibility	★★★★
Innovation	★★★★★
Human resources	★★★★★
Growth markets	★★★
Quality of management	★★★
International orientation	★★★★

Biggest plus:
The use of digital media will continue to grow by leaps and bounds.

Biggest minus:
The 'pure digital' approach faces strong competition from existing full-spectrum consultancies.

Razorfish
2 East Poultry Avenue
Smithfield
London EC1A 9PT
Tel: 020 7549 4200
Fax: 020 7236 2605
website: www.razorfish.com

Razorfish

The Business

Razorfish started six years ago as a digital services provider. It began largely as a developer of websites, helping its clients exploit the World Wide Web to reach an increasingly computer-literate market. Since then it has acquired the skills to handle more complex projects, address bigger customers and operate as a consultancy.

It has now evolved into a provider of all sorts of digital systems, enabling client companies to use digital technology to reach employees, business partners and customers, whether they are mobile or static. The one common thread to the projects that Razorfish undertakes is that they are based on digital technology.

The company had a positive net income during its 99/00 financial year, which suggests that its long-term prospects should be good, although during 2001 it reported its first ever quarterly loss, and implemented cost reduction measures (including redundancies) as a result.

Innovation

Razorfish's primary innovation has been to organize its staff, which it calls Fish, into four interconnecting global networks. It calls these Strategy, Experience, Technology and Value, and each project will involve a team built up from each of these networks, and, of course, a project manager. The aim is a holistic approach to projects, with all members of the team involved at all stages. Razorfish sees this as a key point, differentiating it from competitors who may keep the key disciplines separate.

Strategy is the consulting group, whose aim is to develop a plan or roadmap based on the client's market and the business opportunities it contains. The Experience network supplies the creative skills needed to create useful and useable products and services based on those opportunities, and Technology then builds the systems required to deliver those products and services, as well as researching new and emerging technology for future use. Value is the group that brings all of this together, managing the project, ensuring that it has the necessary resources and information, and that it lines up with the client's objectives.

Razorfish also organizes its staff into practices aimed at specific industries or vertical markets, such as media and entertainment, mobile solutions and broadband solutions. Each of these areas requires different questions to be asked and a different mixture of skills and knowledge from the project team.

'Our view is that digital technology in particular is merciless if you don't deliver on your promises. Expectations are set by promises, and if you don't deliver you have broken a trust', says Glenn Cornett, Razorfish's vice-president of Strategy, Europe.

'We still have a functional structure,' he adds. 'The genesis was an explosion in the number of skills required to complete a job, for example e-commerce would need a strategic understanding of retail, then you have to define the proposition to solve the needs, build it as a business and as technology, explain it in terms the user understands, test it with users, and translate the branding into design. You could end up with 50 people all having a claim on the project.'

Flexibility

During 2000, Razorfish faced greater competition, as the big consultancy firms also saw the digital opportunity and created in-house teams to address this market. In addition, dot-com failures and the market downturn prompted businesses and the stock market to begin questioning the commercial benefits of digital technology.

Glenn Cornett said that this encouraged the entire digital industry, including Razorfish, to take a long hard look at how they were operating and take steps to fix the problems they found.

'The questions were right to be asked,' he said. 'Instead of just diving in, the market began to look at proper business planning, return on investment, project management and delivery. The market is growing up. The industry was not very business-facing – market demand was so strong that it didn't have to be. It is now very business-facing.'

The European market for digital services began slowing in May 2000 but Razorfish did not adjust immediately, expecting the slow-down to be temporary and knowing that this is a business where retaining skilled staff is crucial. Unfortunately, it delayed too long and left itself with a cash gap as the revenues from existing projects ended and as at least one client closed down.

It then had to make staffing cuts in order to reduce expenditure and follow this up with a voluntary severance programme aimed at reducing its consultant numbers to better match the reduced level of new business. It has also instituted a corporate improvement plan to set global and individual objectives.

'Although the situation has bottomed out, growth is not as good as we'd wish,' said Glenn Cornett. 'There is a slow return to health with a substantial core of growth. Digital has been questioned but inherently it is right. Our business is well founded.'

Human Resources

Razorfish has a strong focus on people, and its unwillingness to cut staff numbers except when absolutely necessary has made it unpopular in the past with finance-driven market analysts. It recognizes that the people are the company's most valuable resource, indeed that they are the company, and much of its behaviour has therefore been aimed at keeping them.

'You know the market is returning and that your clients will need skilled people. The lack of recovery speed was the problem,' explained Glenn Cornett. 'During the growth period there was no problem with business development, so the focus was internal, on getting people in and onto projects. Now the focus is outwards towards the clients.'

The company is continuing to upgrade its capabilities and seek experience. The average age of its staff is 31, and the staff are drawn from a range of backgrounds including strategy consulting, systems integration, branding, TV, print media, advertising media and marketing.

The London office contributes to a charity project every year. For example, in 1999 it used its skills in designing systems for use by the visually-impaired and learning-impaired to create an accessibility site for the Millennium Dome. In 2000 it worked with the medical charity Médecins Sans Frontières and with Peach, a parent-led charity organization for autistic children.

Growth Markets

Razorfish remains convinced that digital media is a growth market, but now recognizes that it must obey the same rules of good business practice as any other commercial organization. It has instituted a global improvement plan to ensure everyone within the company has clear and measurable objectives regarding individual and group performance.

'The sector has to do something, and that is to regain the agenda,' said Glenn Cornett. 'The danger is not lack of growth, it is not articulating the unique benefits that we bring. We need to fill the vacuum with a clear analysis of what our sector can deliver that is uniquely different from any other.

'Digital enables our clients to realize more value from their relationships with customers and suppliers. Our sector needs to articulate its skills more proactively. Our response is to be forward-looking so we are part of the market change.'

In particular, Razorfish sees future market growth in business-to-business e-commerce, from looking at how businesses can benefit from making their operations more transparent through to cost savings from supply chain management.

Quality of Management

Most of Razorfish's managers have a digital media background, but they also have experience in well established businesses in other areas of the media. Of the two founders, CEO and chairman Jeffrey Dachis was vice-president of corporate marketing for Game Financial Corporation, and chief strategic officer and chairman, Craig Kanarick, was a digital media consultant and a designer for Bolt, Beranek and Newman.

European vice-president Michael Moore joined Razorfish when it acquired I-Cube and has a background in strategic consultancy, and European vice-president of strategy, Glenn Cornett, joined with a background in neuroscience, the pharmaceutical industry and management consulting.

The company's loyalty to its staff caused it problems as the market slowed down, leaving it with surplus staff. It has since acted to cut its headcount, including merging the management of its offices in London and Amsterdam.

The company has so far been a consolidator, and its management has consistently pushed back against being acquired. While this could change in the future, the nature of this market means that any take-over would have to carry the staff with it.

International Orientation

Razorfish acts like a holding company, providing direction, operational parameters and support for the national offices. The European, American and Tokyo groups each have an executive who is responsible to the overall company. In the case of Europe, for example, there is no head office, with nine offices instead reporting to the European vice-president who then reports to the board.

At the operational level, the company is assessed on client and staff satisfaction and operational metrics. There is a fluidity between offices, so that different offices may work together on projects or on projects nominally in other countries. The operational targets are for the company as a network.

For example, there are around six to eight pan-European projects, each has one client-facing project manager but the team can extend across multiple offices and include specialists from different countries.

Reality

The Reality Group is a total business solutions company offering electronic enablement, customer relations management (CRM), and logistics for a range of traditional and e-commerce third party organizations. It sees itself as being in line with the needs of business, allowing companies to concentrate on their core skills while Reality employees provide commerce and e-commerce solutions. It has 20,000 staff in the UK, and has a turnover of £400 million. Outside the UK, it has a staff of 1,700 spread around Europe.

Reality is part of the Great Universal Stores (GUS), which also owns retailer Argos and information solutions company Experian.

Scorecard:

Innovation	★★★★★
Flexibility	★★★★
Human resources	★★★★★
Growth markets	★★★★★
Quality of management	★★★★
International orientation	★★★★

Biggest plus:
It is the leading European provider of commerce and e-commerce solutions.

Biggest minus:
Operating in a continually innovating business that requires a high degree of flexibility.

Reality Group
Universal House
Devonshire Street
Manchester M60 6EL
Tel: 0161 273 8282
website: www.reality.co.uk

Reality Group

The Business

The company evolved in May 2000 from the merger of a web development company with GUS. It is a clicks-and-mortar company, meaning
it combines its Internet presence with powerful offline logistics and
support services. Its vehicle services are made up of the White Arrow
delivery business, owned by GUS. Reality can do everything for an
e-commerce company – from designing its website to dealing with its
customers through its call centre facilities, to making the delivery of
a item. In its first 90 days of trading Reality generated £119 million in
new business. France, Germany, Austria, Holland, Switzerland and
Sweden represent its international locations.

Innovation

Though dot-com mania brought with it talk of the ability of e-commerce businesses to undercut their high street rivals by massively
reducing their costs, it soon became apparent that having a great looking website wasn't enough. To back up the offering companies found
they also needed a well-developed infrastructure consisting of an order
fulfilment system, millions of square feet of warehousing and fleets of
delivery vans. Many of the start-ups just couldn't deliver their
promises, quite literally. That's where Reality stepped in. Its cradle-to-
grave service provided the design and e-fulfilment service lacking in
so much of the dot-com market. Acting as a third party, the business
quickly won clients as it ensured that by using its know-how and the
facilities it inherited from GUS (such as call centre facilities and fleets
of vehicles) it could deliver what it promised.

Steve Johnson, marketing director of Reality says: 'It's very difficult
to put the infrastructure needed for e-commerce in place, giving the
skills and capabilities needed when you have no experience of doing
it, but Reality has those skills and capabilities. . .This is still an area of
business that is very embryonic.'

The company is in a position where through its standing as a commerce and e-commerce solutions provider it is approached by potential
clients to help with their businesses. But, on top of this, it also uses
conferences on the topic of e-commerce and associated exhibitions to
deliver the message of what Reality can do for your company. In
pushing ahead with its bid to continually improve its service, the company has signed a deal with Cable & Wireless, which works with Reality
to provide unique global end-to-end e-commerce services to online
retail clients. Johnson says the company is looking to form partnerships

with other businesses that would provide a natural synergy with Reality in terms of their ability to offer an aspect of an e-commerce solution.

Flexibility

Despite being such a new company – it was only launched in May of last year – Reality has focused on cutting costs and operating more efficiently. This isn't really surprising considering the fast-moving nature of the e-commerce industry.

Johnson says: 'We have brought in a number of people from outside GUS as more companies have begun to understand the principles of e-commerce, impacting on the service they wanted, and the technology for providing commerce and e-commerce solutions has developed.

'We are determined to make all the elements of our operation as good as market leading.'

An example of where Reality has had to make changes in its business since its creation is in logistics, the delivery of purchases to customers' doors.

Johnson explains: 'The logistics business that we inherited from GUS when we were created was designed to service GUS's home shopping service which meant an item would be delivered in three to five days.

'The market has now moved on, and people expect delivery either next day or in 48 hours. We had to invest in our physical capabilities in this area, but also redesign the way that it worked, which meant investing in the systems we used to organize our deliveries to increase the number that we could make.'

Reflecting on the requirements of clients nowadays, Johnson says the focus on web design has been tempered by the realization that e-fulfilment was as important.

'At one time there were lots of dot-coms around all wanting you to design a website for them. But it's a different environment now, and our involvement in these companies e-commerce strategies has become deeper.'

The emphasis may have changed, but Reality still has to offer a complete service so it has steadily invested in technology and personnel.

Human Resources

The company describes its business as exciting, citing it as one of the reasons why people want to work for Reality in the first place. It is keen for employees to feel they are in a position where they can affect the success of the company and shape its development in the future.

Johnson describes the difference between working for Reality against other organizations.

'At Reality we aim to give our employees a feeling that they can make a significant contribution to the business.'

This attitude is highlighted by the fact that all staff are able to take out share options in the company, thus enabling them to directly benefit from Reality's achievements.

Johnson adds: 'People who do well here, realize they are in a fast moving environment, and want to have an impact on how the company performs.'

Growth Markets

The development of e-commerce, even over such a relatively short period, has seen the evolution of a number of business channels. Not only is the Internet available through your PC, but you can now log-on via your television and through mobile technologies such as WAP. These channels represent major growth markets for Reality.

'More and more companies are wanting to deal with their customers through multiple channels, and therefore we are finding there is a greater need for multiple e-commerce solutions. These businesses have no experience of new technologies to fall back on.'

As a result of this firms want companies such as Reality to come onboard earlier and earlier in their e-commerce development.

The company is ensuring it gets a good share of these new opportunities by investing in the technology and the people to build multi-channel offerings for its clients.

Johnson also points out that increasingly smaller companies want e-commerce solutions, so Reality is having to develop its service to take into account the needs of all sizes of business. One thing they have in common is that they all want flexibility built into their e-commerce operation enabling them to cross over to different platforms easily.

Quality of Management

The company's management structure is flat, which it believes is the only way a business such as Reality, where its service is continually evolving, can operate successfully.

'You couldn't develop a business like ours if you have lots of layers of management,' explains Johnson.

'More important, though, is that everyone in the business is customer facing – if you are not serving a customer, you are serving someone who is.'

The human resources department is an example of where Reality has overhauled the system formerly used by GUS, before the company was created.

'We inherited a very large human resources function and all the decisions and activities around employees had to go through this monolithic structure. But now it's been structured to support our business at the operational level such as logistics,' he says.

'It means the human resources decisions are being made by and with the people best placed to make them.'

The company is keen that everyone in Reality shares a common objective and that good performance is recognized and rewarded. Each manager has an overall set of objectives and through face-to-face meetings the progress of these objectives is measured.

But management is not just measured against these objectives quantitatively, but also qualitatively, with emphasis put on the way these objectives are achieved.

Feedback from employees on how the company could improve its service is highly valued. The company encourages employee involvement in the firm's development in two ways. It has empowered frontline managers to make improvements to their work practices at a local level. It has also launched a programme called Speak Up! where anybody in the company can send in ideas about the business and how it can be improved. Each suggestion is looked at by a board director, with the aim of delivering a reply to senders within five working days.

International Orientation

Reality has a logistics operation and call centre facilities on the Continent, reflecting the business's plan to exploit its service offering in Europe. Johnson says it is important to the company to be able to give a complete service to its clients, and increasingly these clients are looking to develop their companies in Europe.

'We obviously have the e-commerce system design capabilities and these capabilities enable a client to do business across borders and more and more want to,' he says.

'We are developing our call centre facilities and logistics on the Continent through partnering so to fulfil our clients' e-commerce strategies.'

The focus is Europe right now as the company sees it as unlikely a company would want a global solution, pointing to the likes of Amazon.com, which instead of extending the US-based operation world-wide set up separate companies such as Amazon.co.uk to operate its business model abroad.

MESSAGE

Red Message is one of the leading suppliers in the fast-growing mobile messaging and mobile commerce market. Based in Sweden, with offices in several European countries, it has developed some innovative applications, and is building up a solid base of established corporate clients.

Scorecard:

Innovation	★★★★
Flexibility	★★★
Human resources	★★★
Growth markets	★★★★★
Quality of management	★★★
International orientation	★★★★★

Biggest plus:

A leading supplier in a fast-growing field, well placed to cash in on new technologies and increasing demand.

Biggest minus:

The mobile messaging and commerce sector is still small, so the success of the company is largely dependent on the success of its market.

Red Message
1st Floor, suites 17–21
181–183 Warwick Road
London W14 8PU
Tel: 020 7373 7475
Fax: 020 7373 9757
website: www.redmessage.com

Red Message

The Business

Red Message is a business-to-business mobile service provider, building solutions which enable companies to interact and transact with their customers or staff. It operates like a giant switch, taking information from its clients in a variety of formats, and converting this for transmission to mobile phones, generally using short message service (SMS).

The company has several products, including secure text messaging, two-way messaging, direct marketing, mobile shopping, and charging for information. Its customers are as diverse as Reed Employment, Chancellors the estate agents, and Arsenal FC.

Red Message was founded in Sweden, in February 1999. The company raised $3.5m in September 1999 from six venture capital firms, and a further $20m in April 2000, from Goldman Sachs and Reuters. This has placed it on a firm financial footing for at least two years, before it needs to consider going public.

Innovation

Red Message was founded to take advantage of the opportunities offered by mobile data services, and has several firsts to its name.

'We are perceived as being a leader in applications,' says Steven Yurisich, co-founder and chief marketing officer. 'We built the first mobile job alert service in the world for Reed Employment, which allows them to notify job seekers as soon as a suitable job is advertised.' Another first is a system for a music retailer, which can send a message when a new album is released and let customers hear a sample over their mobile phones.

The mobile messaging market is so new that there are few existing components from which to build a system, so technological innovation is essential. Red Message's technology platform is essentially self-built, by the firm's technical team in Gothenburg; Unix-based, it makes extensive use of tried-and-tested technologies such as Oracle databases and the Internet standards XML and TCP/IP. Development and research account for about half the company's staff.

A key element of Red Message's business model is the ability to incorporate new mobile phone technologies, such GPRS and UMTS, as they are adopted. But the company will wait until the market is ready for them. 'We are innovative, but in a pragmatic sense,' says Yurisich. 'We innovate within the framework of what works, and what the customer wants.'

Flexibility

Like many young, high-tech companies, Red Message had to trim its sails after the downturn in high-tech stocks and investment during 2000. The company's original plan was to expand into Asia and the USA by the end of that year, but this had to be shelved, while the company focused on becoming profitable.

'We've got to reach breakeven point much more quickly now,' says Yurisich. 'You can't assume that you can go on raising more money, and the market doesn't value having 20 different flags on your map.' Instead of reaching breakeven point in 2003, the target date is now late 2001 or early 2002.

The company's routes to market are changing, too. At first it mostly sold direct to customers, or via partners such as Hewlett-Packard and Ericsson. But now it is establishing an indirect channel, consisting of a number of systems integrators, software developers and value-added resellers, which will be an essential ingredient in the company's future growth.

Operating as it does in a young and fast-moving market, Red Message has to be quick on its feet. 'We try to hire people who are broad and flexible, and create a culture of flexibility within the company,' says Yurisich. 'And we've tried to decentralize decision-making, because we don't want to become a bureaucracy.' This will become increasingly important as more international offices are opened.

Human Resources

'This is a fun place to work, but hard-working and with very committed people,' says Yurisich. 'The people who flourish here are fast moving, with an ability to learn quickly. They are very adaptive and results-focused. Anyone who expected to receive a lot of direction would not fit in.'

Most of Red Message's staff are graduates, but experience and ability count for more than paper qualifications. The company is still too young to be able to take on trainees, so all recruits must be experienced, although a lot of training is provided on the company's own products and relevant technologies.

The average age is youngish, around 30, and the gender balance is about 60/40 in favour of men – quite typical for a high-tech firm. Remuneration is competitive but no more, since the business is too young to be overly generous. Everyone gets stock options, and 20 days' holiday.

Growth Markets

The future success of Red Message will depend largely on how fast mobile messaging and mobile commerce grow. The company has put itself in a strong position to grow with the market – as long the predicted demand materializes. 'It's not a mass market yet,' says Yurisich. 'It's where the Internet was two or three years ago.'

There were undeniable setbacks during 2000. The downturn in the dot-com economy made people wary of new technologies, and WAP (Internet access on mobile phones) failed to deliver on its over-hyped promise. Moreover, the unexpectedly high price of the G3 (third generation) mobile phone licences has left the major operators with less cash to spend on marketing and R&D, which could put a brake on development in the whole sector.

But analysts are still predicting that the global market for mobile messaging and mobile commerce – which barely topped $100m in 2000 – could exceed 50bn dollars by 2005, which would put Red Message seriously in the money. Yurisich thinks the sector is too specialized to attract the big mobile operators, so the main competition will come from other start-up companies like Goyada, Minick and Wireless Interactive Networks. 'But we have a broader range of customer experience than them, and we're faster at implementation,' says Yurisich.

The advent this year of GPRS mobile services will give messaging a boost, Yurisich believes. 'It will clearly drive usage, particularly because the fact that it's always on will make it much more attractive to use the phone,' he says.

Yurisich expects Red Message's main growth markets to be in established businesses, not struggling dot-coms – retailers sending details of special offers, recruitment consultants wiring job vacancies, and all manner of content providers, from sports results to financial information.

'Greatly improved personalization will be a bigger driver than just higher bandwidth,' says Yurisich. 'It's all about getting the information that's important to you.'

Quality of Management

Red Message was founded by three engineers: chief executive, Fredrik Landahl, and chief technology officer, Michael Walenius, both formerly worked for Telia, the leading Scandinavian mobile phone operator; and chief marketing officer, Steven Yurisich, had a background in media and entertainment with Andersen Consulting, after which he was a partner at Real Venture Group, a business creation company focusing on the mobile space. These three form the main board of the company, along with chief operating officer Pieter Djuist, formerly European head of Silicon Graphics. The non-executive directors are drawn from the various investors.

The board's attitude is best summed up as forward-looking but realistic. Yurisich says: 'We want to offer the most appropriate technology, but we're not going to try to be ahead of the curve. That's a very lonely place to be.' For example the company has refused to be swayed by the hype about WAP, preferring to wait until WAP can demonstrate real benefits for customers.

Yurisich encapsulates the firm's values in four words: trust, delivery, innovation and fun. He says the management style is 'collaborative but open'. The directors believe in involving staff in decisions, and devolving responsibility wherever possible. Basically people are set clear goals and then left to get on with their job. Allied to this is a strong culture of accountability and responsibility, which is essential in dealing with the established, corporate businesses which form the bulk of the company's clientele.

The next stage, believes Yurisich, must be to develop a more formal management methodology for the firm. 'We should be faster to market, although we're fast already,' he says. 'It can vary a lot, so we need to be more systematized.'

The company must also be wary of letting its engineering strengths overshadow its marketing efforts, which have been fairly low-key to date. As competition increases, building and maintaining the Red Message brand will become critical – hopefully the company's new channel strategy will help it gain a high profile.

International Orientation

Red Message already operates in five countries – Sweden, the UK, Italy, Germany and France – and deliberately chose financial backers in several countries in order to gain wider international influence. In 2001 the company plans to expand into Spain.

Its technology works seamlessly with mobile networks in many countries. This puts it in a strong position to service international clients who wish to send messages to multiple countries. 'It enables us to target big international companies and be a one-stop shop,' says Yurisich, 'although it means we have to spread ourselves more thinly.'

Sweden and the UK are Red Message's biggest markets, with Italy growing strongly. Further afield, Asia beckons. Currently there is little or no indigenous competition there, but the mobile commerce market is even less mature than in Europe, so Red Message will have to time its entry with precision. The US also offers possibilities.

'In five years' time, we want to be the leading player in this space in Europe, and ideally in the world,' says Yurisich.

REUTERS

Reuters has become both an institution and an international byword for impartiality. Inevitably at the forefront of technology the company pioneered many facets of electronic information usage and, in a considerable number of ways, successfully anticipated the coming of the Internet. The company floated on the London Stock Exchange in 1984 and its subsequent performance has rarely been less than impressive.

Scorecard:

Innovation	★★★★★
Flexibility	★★★★★
Growth markets	★★★★★
Human resources	★★★★★
Quality of management	★★★★★
International orientation	★★★★★

Biggest plus:
'It's international, it's very well managed and it's a market leader that gets its timing right.'

Biggest minus:
'It's full of clever people so there's a lot of competition.'

Reuters
85 Fleet Street
London EC4P 4AJ
Tel: 020 7250 1122
website: www.reuters.com

Reuters

The Business

Reuters describes itself as 'the world news, information and technology organization'. Founded in London in 1851 to take advantage of the newly installed cross channel cable, Reuters has become both an institution and an international byword for impartiality. Inevitably at the forefront of technology the company pioneered many facets of electronic information usage and, in a considerable number of ways, successfully anticipated the coming of the Internet with its use of what were then considered 'private' networks.

The company floated on the London Stock Exchange in 1984 and its subsequent performance has been impressive. In the year ending December 2000 Reuters reported turnover of £3.59 billion, with pre-tax profits at £657 million and earnings per ordinary share of 37.9 pence.

Innovation

It is fair to say that Reuters has exhibited a history of innovation from its earliest days, when one service on offer was the telegraphic delivery of stock and share information from the Paris Bourse. There was, however, no telegraph system between Aachen and Brussels – a problem solved by the simple brilliance of bridging the gap with carrier pigeons.

Reuters has traditionally identified and exploited the best technology available but, if the best isn't considered up to scratch, the company has displayed little compunction about providing its own. Reuters has been known to produce its own computer software and, on occasion, its own computers but, as the company's declared intention and usual modus operandi is to use the best available wherever possible, its 7 per cent of turnover invested in research and development is particularly impressive.

In the 1980s foreign exchange dealing – and, indeed, almost all electronic communication – was done by telephone or telex. To say that Reuters invented the Internet would be to exaggerate but the company was at the forefront of network development and, to quote one example, the money dealing network developed by Reuters was, to all intents and purposes, a 'private Internet'.

In the recent words of Reuters' chairman, Sir Christopher Hogg: 'The view opening in front of us now is Internet-dominated and it is good to be able to get to grips with it as a total priority, having plotted our course towards it for many years.'

Flexibility

Reuters' reputation for flexibility is widely recognized but, says director of corporate relations, Geoff Wicks, there are some things on which the company is immovable.

Integrity is Reuters' lifeblood and the company's values are enshrined in the statement: 'Customers in all parts of the world depend on Reuters to provide them with reliable and objective news and information. Reuters therefore has a special need to safeguard its independence and integrity and avoid any bias which may stem from control by any particular individuals or interests. Reuters' share structure includes two mechanisms specifically designed to prevent this happening.'

The company is now focused on three business areas: Reuters financial, which includes Reuters information and Reuters trading solutions divisions; Instinet, the electronic equities and fixed income brokerage; and Reuterspace, (formerly called Reuters Ventures), the vehicle for developing new businesses outside the core financial markets. The company believes 'all of these business areas are well positioned to exploit the opportunities of the Internet and e-commerce'.

An example of this is the company's 'Dealing 3000 Forwards' which provides an electronic matching and global conversational dealing service for Forwards foreign exchange traders. Key features are described as 'extended functionality with broken dates, split amounts and depth of book' and the flexibility for traders to tailor their screens to individual trading needs – along with the ability to integrate core Reuters' information services and run other applications in conjunction with a Dealing 3000 keystation, whilst ensuring performance and security are maintained via a secure private network.

Human Resources

There is no simple description for the kind of person who would flourish at Reuters. 'The company is truly international and it has always operated on the principle that its employees are to be trusted,' says Geoff Wicks.

'There is', he continues, 'a broad mix with journalists, technologists and marketers working together. We've always had an open attitude, we encourage risk-taking and original thought. There are those who say Reuters is lucky; you might also consider that we've got a lot of things right.' Working arrangements are flexible, there are no specific rules about appearance, and there is nothing to stop those who have left the fold from rejoining.

Growth Markets

The largest growth market will be 'new media' which, says Geoff
Wicks, 'is growing very rapidly'.

This is highlighted in a company statement:

> Reuters' vision is to make financial markets really work on the
> Internet. The company plays an important role in the functioning
> of the world's financial markets. The Internet is prompting dramatic
> shifts in the financial landscape, giving Reuters the opportunity to
> deliver products in a different way, to many more people needing
> to manage their interests more dynamically.
>
> In today's world, Reuters is already present across all major parts
> of the electronic-value-trading chain inside its customers' organiza-
> tions. The process starts with tailored information in front of an
> individual trader in a dealing room and feeding seamlessly into
> spreadsheets to facilitate analysis. Analysis generates the knowledge
> for buying, or selling, successfully. Positions are adjusted and, at the
> touch of a button, the user can transact, settle and clear.
>
> E-commerce is about making money by going from 'knowing' to
> 'doing' in minutes or seconds. Reuters, with its indivisible combi-
> nation of content and technology, is well positioned to extend to
> each link of the information and technology value chain and to
> offer integrated solutions to a broader range of financial customers.
>
> The Internet recognizes no frontiers and enables Reuters to serve
> this new, wider audience of financial activists. The new Internet
> age requires fast decisions, an appetite for risks, and an ability to
> adapt organizations quickly. The new structure Reuters adopted
> in 1999 moved the company from a country-based outlook to a
> business-line structure and continues to evolve. Further changes
> will make Reuters more customer-focused, more e-enabled, and
> lock into wider audiences to exploit the opportunities of the
> Internet.

Quality of Management

'Reuters', says Geoff Wicks, 'is in the knowledge business – it's as
simple as that and it's pretty obvious our people are our key asset.
You need to be good to work for Reuters and you need to be very
good to manage Reuters' people – in quite a few cases you're managing
millionaires.'

Reuters takes its responsibilities seriously and its combination of
paternalism, altruism, sharp business sense and sheer common decency
is well encapsulated by a description of the Reuters Foundation, which
supports a global range of educational and humanitarian causes.

Reuters established the Foundation in 1982 as a charitable trust to implement its corporate support policy.

The first cause was international journalism – the Foundation began offering grants for journalists from the developing world to study at universities in Europe and the United States. Its aims today have expanded to cover a broad spread of corporate support – reflecting the diverse interests of Reuters and the concerns of its employees around the world. Reuters Foundation is independent of Reuters' business interests, but its guidelines 'are based on its founder's principles of accuracy, impartiality, reliability and technical innovation. The Foundation aims to safeguard this tradition and pass it on to others.'

The Foundation tries to use information techniques, and communication skills, to add value to its work and to give its assistance a practical and professional edge.

Causes supported include:

- Journalism – practical training and academic study, with special emphasis on economic and financial news and assistance for parts of the world most in need
- Education – co-operation with schools and universities, technical training and research
- Humanitarian and relief aid – community projects, health care, environmental issues, the arts – an international programme backing the initiatives of Reuters' staff with cash or with services in kind.

International Orientation

Reuters is in every country in the world and has offices in more than 200 cities. Further comment would be superfluous.

TM

Based in West London, Rivals Europe is a fan-based media group. Its main focus is currently Rivals.net, a network of 250 independent – read unofficial – sports websites produced by fan editors. Most sites are currently UK-based, but the company recently started operating in France and is looking for partners to take it into Germany, Spain and Italy. Rivals Europe also took over Puremix, the Chrysalis Internet radio station, and plans to relaunch it as a network of music fan sites later in 2001. Launched in August 2000, Rivals Europe now employs 42 people. It is 90.1 per cent owned by UK media company Chrysalis Group, the rest being held by US online sports network Rivals.com.

Scorecard:

Innovation	★★★★
Flexibility	★★★★
Human resources	★★★
Growth markets	★★★
Quality of management	★★★★
International orientation	★★★

Biggest plus:
Lots of responsibility, and inside information on a range of sports from football to cycling.

Biggest minus:
Being based in the remote part of Notting Hill – hang on to your wallet on the walk back to Latimer Road tube.

Rivals.net
151 Freston Road
London W10 6TH
Tel: 020 8692 1300
Fax: 020 8692 1301
website: www.rivals.net

Rivals.net

The Business

Rivals Europe is a fan-based media group currently centred on Rivals.net, a network of 250 unofficial sports fan sites covering a growing range of sports. The network is broadly based on the model of US sports network Rivals.com, from which it derives its content management system.

The company was first set up in 1999 by Rivals Europe CEO Marcus Leaver, formerly of Chrysalis Group, and the site went live in August 2000. Originally rivals.net was 75per cent owned by rivals.com, but Chrysalis took a majority stake in September 2000.

Like most dot-coms, the company generates revenues from banner ads and sponsorship, and also makes money through online betting and by charging a commission on online sales. Other revenue comes from content syndication and distribution to ISPs and portals. The company is considering a range of future revenue sources, including content licensing, premium content, subscriptions and micro-payments with plans well advanced to exploit database marketing and offline publishing.

Rivals.net has 42 staff based at its West London office, but material for the sites comes from its network of fan editors. A content management system developed by rivals.com helps streamline site production. Most of the fan sites are currently UK-based, but the company recently expanded into France and has plans to open sites in Germany, Italy, Spain, the Netherlands and Scandinavia once it has signed up partners there.

In February 2001 Rivals Europe took over Puremix, the Chrysalis Internet radio station, along with four of its staff. Rivals Europe plans to apply the same model used for the sports network and re-launch the company later this year as a network of music fan sites.

Innovation

Unofficial sports sites are nothing new, but where rivals.net really scores is in its innovative use of technology, to enable a network of fan editors to generate unique content. These amateur enthusiasts, supported by staff at rivals.net's head office and armed with its easy to use content management system, help it to offer fan's-eye content that stands out from the standard sports news feeds, build effective communities through inside knowledge of the local fan scene, and attract local sponsorship. The payment scheme for editors, based on a combination of the number of page impressions and amount of revenue their site attracts, is designed to motivate them in all these areas.

In contrast with the more flamboyant dot-coms, rivals.net also displays a radical approach to cost control. Effective use of automation means that staff levels will not, Leaver claims, ever rise beyond 65 even as the company expands into Europe. Its offices could be politely described as minimalist, and it spends a tiny 1 per cent of revenues on sales and marketing. Nearly everything is done in-house, including design work and software support. Exceptions are specialist areas such as online betting, which is done through an alliance with sportingodds.com.

Lateral thinking is enabling the company to keep its marketing costs to a minimum, and it makes creative use of paper media to complement its online activities. A recent marketing initiative, for example, involved distributing fanzines covering football divisions 1–3, and featuring a page on each league club, at local matches. Using content from the online site to produce the fanzines helped keep production costs to a minimum. In future, rivals.net plans to produce further paper publications by reusing content originally generated for online use.

Flexibility

Rivals.net is aiming to add new sites that reflect consumer demand – plans are advanced to add more motorsports sites. Another priority is expanding into Europe – but this will only happen as and when partners are found within target territories to absorb the costs. The company has invested heavily in technology and this investment will pay off, Leaver says, by giving rivals.net the flexibility to expand rapidly. Its technical infrastructure has been designed to support rapid growth without the need to increase overheads by adding large numbers of staff or moving to larger premises.

Its content management technology, licensed from rivals.com, makes it easy for fan editors to produce pages that conform to the house brand with minimal central supervision. It also makes it possible to support editors across Europe, and ultimately in other continents, from a small office in London.

But the long-term goal is to become a broad-based media company focusing on fans of any passion; the Puremix takeover, for example, will move Rivals Europe into the music sector. It is also looking beyond the Web to other media; rivals.net plans to bring out several sports-related books in the autumn and move into magazine publishing, either by acquiring an existing sports magazine or by launching its own. Again, technology will provide the flexibility to do this quickly and inexpensively, exploiting both the content and the brand rivals.net has developed online. Its ability to reuse content effectively has already been demonstrated in the series of promotional fanzines.

Human Resources

Nearly half the 42 staff based at rivals.net's small, informal offices in the less salubrious area of London's Notting Hill are concerned with content management: finding new fan editors, liasing with them, and ensuring that their contributions come up to standard. The company's unseen workforce and hidden asset is its network of fan editors, and keeping in regular contact with them is a high priority for the editorial team.

Rivals.net's company slogan is 'Powered by Passion'. Passion for sport is the company's main ethos, and on the content side particularly, sport-haters would not flourish here. Nor would those who put a high priority on a flashy working environment!

Few of rivals.net's operations are contracted out: even creative and design work and website hosting are carried out in-house. Both in-house staff and fan editors carry a lot of responsibility for the company's success. The company is built on self-reliant, entrepreneurial, innovative people who can take new ideas and run with them.

Growth Markets

Rivals.net has four main directions for expansion: within its existing markets, and into new sports, territories and media. Key to its success in all of these areas is the ability to offer more compelling original content than the opposition, and to establish a recognizable and well-respected brand.

Quality of the content is largely down to its network of editors. Finding and attracting the right people is crucial and is the responsibility of the central team. So far rivals.com has succeeded in building up a network of 200 enthusiasts, some of whom are becoming established as sports commentators in other media.

So far football dominates up to 70 per cent of the traffic. Other sports are increasingly balancing the overall mix of traffic thanks to a major push into Formula 1, rugby and cricket. The recently launched F1babes.com site generated a million page impressions the day after its launch. 6nations.com proved similarly popular, becoming one of the company's top ten sites almost overnight.

Leaver argues that since sport is an international language, international expansion should not be a problem. It's still early days for its French site and only time will tell how effectively the rivals.net formula will work outside the UK.

Rivals.net is working hard to establish brand recognition through carefully targeted activity such as its sponsorship of Channel 4's *Football Italia* season and a recent Big Ticket promotion carried out with sports radio channel TalkSPORT. In February it secured sponsorship of Futbol

Argentina on cable and satellite channel Bravo, and sponsorship of *Real Football* – a docu-soap on the Discovery Channel. A promotional tie-up with Express newspapers led to co-branded national radio and TV advertising. It recently signed up to sponsor Sky One's primetime drama *Dream Team* from August 2001.

Early figures are encouraging. By January 2001 the network had doubled its traffic with ABC figures showing it to be the fastest growing online sports property in Europe. Many individual sites are fast approaching one million a month page impressions.

Quality of Management

Rivals Europe can point to an experienced management team with a solid track record in both established and emerging business sectors.

CEO Marcus Leaver worked in corporate development for Chrysalis and was responsible for formulating its Internet strategy. His chief operating and financial officer, Steve Lewis, is a certified accountant who previously worked in the oil and gas industry, for DHL, and most recently as finance and business development director for Megalomedia. Chief technology officer, Colin Davies, was production manager for the *Financial Times'* successful FT.com website, and commercial director Rob Avis was formerly sales director of TheStreet.co.uk, where he helped generate around 20 per cent of all online financial advertising. Marketing director, Christopher Reed, joined the company from News International, where he was marketing and promotions manager for *The Times* and the *Sunday Times*.

One of the keynotes of Rivals Europe's management style is tight cost control and a sharp focus on delivering shareholder value. Leaver says that unless the company makes any major investments, it's on track to become profitable in three years.

Certainly no-one could accuse rivals.net's management of profligacy: the company has cut out all frills: its offices are low-cost and functional, its headcount is low, and its sales and marketing spend is carefully designed to achieve the maximum impact with the minimum outlay. Its fanzine promotion, for example, cost all of £20,000 – about the price of one billboard.

International Orientation

Rivals Europe was set up as a European version of its US cousin Rivals.com, so has no plans to enter the US market in its own right. It does, however, see scope for a network of sites throughout Europe, and later Asia, Africa and the Middle East. Rivals.fr in France has already been launched. Once partners have been found, Germany, Italy, Spain, the Netherlands and Scandinavia will follow in late 2001 or early 2002. The company believes that its strategy of using local fan editors will serve it well as it expands beyond the UK, since foreign editors can add their regional knowledge to rivals.net's technology and branding. It is also looking towards setting up sites in Commonwealth countries that share the same language and similar sporting tastes to the UK.

Rivals Europe aims to set up partnerships in each country to cost effectively grow the businesses. By partnering with relevant media groups and other online properties it hopes to keep costs low and margins high.

Safeway

Safeway plc is one of the leading grocery retailers in the UK, with annual sales of more than £8 billion, and with more than 480 stores nation-wide, attracting more than six million shoppers every week. Among those 480 stores are 183 superstores (stores with more than 25,000 sq ft sales area), and these bring in half of the company's sales. The arrival of Carlos Criado-Perez as chief operating officer in August 2000, and his subsequent promotion to chief executive in November of the same year, reflects a company that has adopted a new trading strategy.

Scorecard:

Innovation	★★★★
Flexibility	★★★★
Human resources	★★★★
Growth markets	★★★★★
Quality of management	★★★★
International orientation	★★★

Biggest plus:
The drive within the company, right up to board level, is already paying off.

Biggest minus:
Has little faith in e-tailing possibilities.

Safeway plc
6 Millington Road
Hayes
Middlesex UB3 4AY
Tel: 020 8848 8744
website: www.safeway.co.uk

Safeway plc

The Business

Safeway plc was originally a US-owned company called Safeway Food Stores Ltd, and saw its first British store built in Bedford in 1962. By1986 it had become the sixth largest UK food retailer. In 1987 Argyll bought the UK arm of Safeway Food Stores Ltd for £681 million. Right now, it purchases more than 20,000 product lines for its stores from all over the world, and this includes its own label products. It has 18 regional distribution centres, employing around 5,600 staff, and these centres manage the distribution of food to its stores. Some of its stores offer dry cleaning, coffee shops and pharmacies and banking services.

Innovation

The company is going through a process of reinventing itself, accelerated by the appointment of Carlos Criado-Perez, and is quite literally attempting to bring a freshness to grocery retailing in the UK. Over a two-year period up to 1999, the business lost its price competitiveness, according to Dr Kevin Hawkins, director of communications, and with it, its customers. But it's reversing this trend by refocusing on what it believes shoppers want, and that's fresh food. The company's trading performance over Christmas 2000 reflected how customers have been coming back to its stores with figures revealing that the 12 weeks up to 6 January 2001 saw a sales increase of 7.7 per cent. To highlight its new outlook, the store points to its latest development at St Katharine's Dock, in London, which is its first outlet to be remodelled around the 'Fresh To Go' methodology with an international food hall offering everything from Thai noodles to roast chickens. Unlike rivals such as Tesco, it is not embracing the Internet as a medium for boosting sales. Having said that it plans to offer wine on the Web, a move that it predicts will bring sufficient returns. It is also a member of the Worldwide Retail Exchange, which claims to be the leading retail-focused business-to-business exchange in the world. It has no plans to use the Internet as a significant marketing tool though and has in fact completely overhauled its marketing strategy. Gone are the television advertisements, they have been replaced by more localized marketing such as leaflet drops. The logic behind this, says Hawkins, is that people shop locally, so if they are made aware of the great prices at a Safeway nearby they are more likely to act on this information than if they saw a generic TV advert that promised the company's offering on a national basis.

Flexibility

The grocery industry in the UK has seen a sharp rise in price competitiveness, in part driven by consumer campaigns with titles such as 'Rip off Britain', where retailers took a hammering for supposedly over-pricing goods. Tying in with this increased price awareness was Safeway plc's refocus on competitive pricing and freshness, which in turn saw staffing changes throughout the company. The number of staff at its headquarters was cut from 2,000 to 1,500, and in stores, a new tier of management was created specifically to deal with the expanded areas of fresh fruit, vegetables and bakery products. This tier was created by promoting staff who showed an interest in taking on the new responsibilities. Safeway has 84,000 employees in the UK. 'Traditionally food retailing like most retailing was centrally controlled,' says Hawkins, 'but over the last eighteen months we have pushed more responsibility out to the stores.'

He explains this makes perfect sense when you consider that competitiveness is seen locally by shoppers who, on average, travel no more than ten minutes from their homes to reach a store. Local managers know the needs of their customers better than those that are miles away in head offices.

Of course, this re-emphasis on local stores has produced a number of casualties right up to board level.

According to Hawkins, a degree of intransigence to the Internet is supported by figures that value grocery sales on the Internet at barely £600 million, out of a total market of more than £100 billion a year. Bearing this in mind there are no plans to offer doorstep delivery from Internet orders, instead the firm is putting plans together for selling wine online.

Human Resources

Reflecting the company's bid to reverse its fortunes and the appointment of former Wal-Mart executive Carlos Criado-Perez, the firm has become a lot more aggressive and this can be seen in the drive of its employees. 'Our core values are based around taking the fight to our competitors, and everyone being much more deterministic in the company's fortunes,' explains Hawkins. 'We want staff to take more responsibility and come forward with their ideas, though we recognize that this can lead to mistakes being made. That's part of the new drive here, which is attracting interest among people in retailing – many of whom have recently joined the company, when a couple of years ago they wouldn't have even thought of us.' People that prosper at Safeways plc are people who first and foremost 'think sales, and think customers'.

Growth Markets

The company has fallen behind its competitors in the area of sales per sq ft of store space, managing only £16/£17 per sq ft compared to Sainsbury's which manages £21 per sq ft. So this is an area that the company needs to improve. How it intends to do that is through its 'Fresh To Go' strategy, which has been a great success in the St Katharine's Dock store with many of the city's financial types descending on the store for lunchtime bites such as you'd find in a top New York delicatessen. In keeping with the new ranges of foods on the shelves, as seen at St Katharine's Dock and planned for further stores, the company is investing in the development of the stores' look and feel. Considering it forked out £2.5 million on refurbishing the store near Tower Bridge, overhauling many of its stores in this way will represent a major investment. As well as growing its 'Fresh To Go' offering, the company plans to convert 70 of its supermarkets into hypermarkets, boosting the sales areas up to 60,000 sq ft plus. This will see the stores retailing non-food lines such as household products, health and beauty products.

Quality of Management

As a result of the company's determination to catch-up with its competitors, it expects a lot more from its management. Sales and profit targets are tough but managers can double their salaries if these targets are exceeded. Hawkins describes the atmosphere among managers as being very 'incentivized'. However, managers are not expected to shine without any support from the company, which has invested in boosting training facilities, building a Safeway school at its head office. Apart from a formal assessment programme, which you would expect from any major company, Safeways plc, through its newfound drive, carries out regular management assessments on an informal basis. These are through regular store visits by area sales managers. The bottom line of management assessment is meeting sales and profit targets, for which bonuses are available to all staff. Store managers and their teams should be well rewarded if they perform well.

This hardnosed approach is tempered somewhat by the inclusion of forward-thinking management assessments in the company such as 360° assessments. These have been introduced in the last couple of years – so managers can get feedback on their performance based on the interaction of all colleagues whatever rank. This is all part of the company's nod to more interactive assessments. These assessments go right the way up to board level, with weekly video conferences involving board members such as Carlos Criado-Perez, where staff can put questions to the board on company issues.

International Orientation

At this stage in the company's bid to regain lost ground in the UK grocery retailing industry, business opportunities abroad are not a high priority. Right now, it is keen to boost profits and customer numbers at its stores. But this doesn't mean it has no intentions of pursuing profit in foreign stores. Grocery retailing is becoming a more global marketplace, with US retailers such as Wal-Mart expanding aggressively in Europe. 'Our priority is to grow the UK business and to get better returns from our stores here, but that is not to say our eyes are closed on what's going on in this business around the world, particularly in Europe with companies like Wal-Mart.' Equally, while the company keeps tabs on the industry, it also looks out for the high fliers.

Sage has for a long time been the leading accounting system software supplier in the UK, with upwards of 400,000 customers. It has grown internationally and at home both organically and through acquisition. Perhaps uniquely it can supply products to allow customers to grow from sole trader through to a medium-sized company with a clean upgrade path throughout. It turns over £400 million per annum and has over 1500 employees.

Scorecard:

Innovation	★★★★★
Flexibility	★★★★★
Human resources	★★★★★
Growth markets	★★★★★
Quality of management	★★★★★
International orientation	★★★★★

Biggest plus:
The absolute commitment to the customer and to market leadership.

Biggest minus:
There is never enough time in the day!

Sage House
Benton Park Road
Newcastle upon Tyne NE7 7LZ
Tel: 0191 255 3000
Fax: 0191 255 0308
website: www.sage.com

Sage

The Business

Sage began in 1981, making it one of the earliest examples of a company making 'shrinkwrapped' accounting system software. The norm before this was to have software designed specifically for a particular organization to run its accounts. David Goldman realized there would be money to be made selling the software as well as the stationery to support the financial function. He founded Sage before the PC or Windows were heard of and sold his software to early adopters of computer technology. The end result is that the company has over 190,000 support contracts, more than 400,000 customers and over 2,500 resellers in the UK and has expanded into Europe and the US.

Innovation

Sage started and continues as an innovative company. Its first innovation was to recognize that there would be a considerable market for a standard software system for the small to medium enterprise – before the development of computers on which these systems would run had truly matured. The second innovation came from the background of the late chairman, David Goldman, who was a printer – and as such understood that the real revenue to be made from business systems would be in selling consumables such as stationery, and in forging ongoing relationships with customers by selling upgrades and matching their business requirements as the technology allowed.

The other area in which the company scored was in its early decision to focus on the needs of the small/medium enterprise (SME). It's easy to forget that in the 1980s computer companies simply weren't interested in the SME; during the late 1990s and early 2000s the majority of companies have been pushing themselves at this market sector but when Sage started up, the perception was that the market would be too small and its participants insufficiently knowledgeable to handle the technology. It was this that spurred Sage to forge solid relationships with its resellers and avoid selling direct to the customer. This has resulted in a lively customer and reseller base, including an Accountants Club. The company clearly realized early on that the best argument for buying an accounting suite was that 'your accountant uses it'.

Other areas in which Sage has scored firsts include the fact that its product range covers all small to medium businesses from the start-up sole trader with Sage Instant Accounting to the medium-sized company, with Sage Enterprise (formerly Tetra, an acquisition the company made). As this book went to press it was still the only company offering this facility. More recently it has acquired competitor TAS Software to consolidate its lead with smaller businesses.

Flexibility

The company has undergone many changes since its inception and City analysts often comment that it is well-run. This denotes an ability to manage change, but what is often overlooked about the organization is its consistent track record in, for example, corporate objectives, target market and a total commitment to the indirect sales channel.

It does change, though, and as is the case with any IT company, one of the major areas of alteration in recent times has been the focus on e-commerce. Sage has paid this a great deal more than lip-service, setting up a separate business division to focus on it and providing the facility for every registered customer to build their own website, which the company will host. Specialists have been hired specifically to spearhead the e-commerce division as well as to organize the re-alignment of existing staff.

The other major upheavals that Sage has undergone occur when it acquires another company, which is not an infrequent occurrence. Normally the target business, if in the UK, is brought within the Sage branded family, so, for example, companies such as Multisoft and Tetra have both been incorporated into Sage. The management of bought-out companies also tend to move on, although many of the field and support staff are retained. The products, too, are then redeveloped so that over a period of time they will fit into Sage's range and the upgrade path will be completely smooth for the end customer. It manages its acquisitions entirely differently overseas.

The work that goes into the frequent acquisition of new products should not be underestimated. It involves not only integrating the new company, but also retraining its sales force and indirect sales channels, and re-educating the existing Sage dealers.

Human Resources

Employees of Sage get all the benefits that might be expected from a respected company that has been listed on the London Stock Exchange since the 1980s: competitive salary, share options and car loans, are all in place as are regular supervision and evaluation sessions.

The style of the organization is resolutely informal, however, as long as targets are met and the customers served. There is a healthy emphasis on fun and enjoying the job, and chief operating officer Paul Stobart appears proud of the fact that when the company was due to have its Christmas party one year the local press carried a story about it in advance! 'Local' is a good word to bear in mind when discussing

Sage. For a business that is effectively a multinational it keeps its eyes resolutely on its Newcastle roots. It supports local charities and initiatives and is never likely to desert its native town.

Growth Markets

Sage is growing in a number of directions but its focus remains completely on the small to medium enterprise area. There are a number of reasons for this. First, the figures: there are approx. 2.7 million VAT registered businesses in the UK alone and only 55 per cent of them have so far computerized their accounts, so the room for growth is considerable. Second, it is a matter of company policy to grow only in the areas with which it is familiar.

This doesn't make the company static, however. It is investigating means of delivering at least some of its services through WAP and PDA interfaces and has people developing for Application Service Provider (ASP) delivery, the set-up in which a third party company handles all of the computer requirements of a small business. The small business arena appeared unwilling to accept the model at the time of writing, but Stobart believes it will within a very few years.

The other area the company wants to evaluate, after a semi-successful stab at it in the 1990s, is what is now known as customer relationship management (CRM). Nowhere in a company's database is there as much detail about a customer's individual transactions as in the accounting system, and extending that information so that it serves more than the accounts department is a potentially lucrative way forward for the company.

Quality of Management

Sage has a decentralized management approach and encourages people to come forward with ideas. It accepts that the failure of certain ideas should be regarded as a learning process and as such fosters an entrepreneurial spirit; everyone who comes forward with an idea will be taken seriously. At the top of the company is only a handful of directors, who see it as their job to guide initially and then to consult. This ethic is underpinned by a solid IT infrastructure so that ideas can be put forward and shared over the company intranet.

The other thing the management insists upon is consistency. With a handful of exceptions such as Nestlé, with which the account is so substantial the company refuses to deal with a third party, the rule about selling only through indirect channels is otherwise absolute.

Finally the directors themselves are willing to take risks and answer their critics or their representatives in public. For two years in a row, managing director Graham Wylie has subjected himself to a public grilling by the BBC's John Humphrys in front of an audience of dealers in a sales conference, and Humphrys is not known for taking prisoners . . .

International Orientation

Sage has moved into a number of territories very successfully, with the acquisition of Peachtree in America and Ciel and Saari in France. These products are not re-branded as Sage products because the company believes the local market will have accepted the products best suited to its accounting regulations and will therefore not welcome being told what to do by a newcomer. The international policy is therefore to acquire the market leader wherever possible and grow it as an independent concern.

The company is currently looking at Eastern Europe as a possible new market; a full listing of the countries in which it operates is on its website at www.sage.com.

Selftrade UK

The Business

Selftrade UK is an execution-only stockbroker. This means it offers no advice and anyone who doesn't already know what they want to buy need not apply – this means the cost to the customer plummets. Founded in 1997 it overcame a number of practical and regulatory hurdles to launch in 1998 and grew to become the third largest trader in France by 1999 (and the largest by number of trades). In 1999 it embarked upon expansion plans in the UK, Germany, Italy and Spain, beginning with the UK in August 1999. It employs 100 people over here, having started as a single person with a laptop in a hotel lobby! After undergoing regulatory procedures it started trading in May 2000.

Innovation

Given the amount of online share trading companies currently in existence it's easy to forget just how recently they have appeared. The founders saw the colossal opportunity that was there for anyone able to sell shares but more than that, they saw that it cost them no more to set up a transaction worth £100,000 than one worth £10. The company therefore introduced the notion of an egalitarian flat fee of £12.50 per transaction regardless of its size.

The company's UK chief executive, Haakon Overli, sees the main innovation as the straightforwardness of the trades that can happen: 'no gobbledegook', as he puts it. There was no pre-launch PR and there has been no dot-com hype. People – including potential customers – hardly knew the company existed because it just wanted to get the basic site functions right and start trading properly at the start. It has a 24-hour helpline for customers in difficulty and the site itself is noticeably jargon-free. Every new customer gets a 40-page share guide and the company endeavours to anticipate any difficulty the customers might experience.

These trimmings are underpinned by a solid commitment to the technology, and to date the company has spent some $80 million on computer equipment – a third of all of the money raised for the business so far. This should not sound over the top in any way; the organization is well aware that its stock would fall dramatically if share transactions were to stop happening at any time for any reason.

It has picked up a number of awards on the way; Datamonitor has accorded it its number one for customer service and number two out of all of the financial institutions, Blue Sky has rated it number one, and Lafferty has named it the number one European share trading company.

Flexibility

Any organization that started with a man and a laptop in a hotel lobby and has grown to gain the above awards plus the approval of the City's regulators has seen a lot of changes in a very short time. It has primarily managed these changes by avoiding the common 'dot-com' failing of trying to survive on ideas – instead the company has focused on old-fashioned concepts like turnover and solid management practice.

Undoubtedly its small company status has helped it to continue trading throughout the changes it has put in place, and there is no problem with the chief executive taking a hands-on approach whenever this is deemed necessary. By the same token every member of staff is encouraged to have some input into the management of the business.

The most interesting changes with which the company has had to deal, however, have come from outside and consist largely of changing attitudes to share ownership in the UK. It's easy to forget that buying and selling shares was perceived as an activity for the elite in this country until so many people became shareholders when the building societies demutualized. The end result is a market full of both long- and short-term investors, both of whom need a lot of reassurance before they commit their money. This prompted Selftrade in the UK to move slightly away from the Internet-only model of trading it had adopted elsewhere and to set up a set of premises in the UK. The trades will still happen on screen in these centres but there will be someone there in case customers have questions or problems.

In terms of what happens next to the business plan, the UK is still about eighteen months behind Germany in terms of share trading so the company has some precedents and experience to follow.

Human Resources

Understandably the company sees its values as customer-facing; the typical profile of employee is someone who has initiative. A balance between a clear sense of priority and a lot of flexibility will be essential as will an understanding that Selftrade operates in a market it is helping to create, not one that already exists by default.

Ideas and the willingness to come forward with them are therefore welcomed. The team as it stands is small so anyone too attached to a particular role and hierarchy will be uncomfortable as they may come to work one day to find the chief executive officer helping to shift furniture. In return candidates for employment can expect a good basic salary and a generous benefits package.

Growth Markets

The UK itself represents a substantial market for the company. What should be even more interesting is the change in the sort of investor that uses the service as the market matures. For the moment the typical customer is cautious in the extreme – they are often people who want to put some money away and build a nest-egg for their retirement. This attitude will change and it is instructive to look at other markets such as the US, where there are professional 'day traders' who earn a living buying and selling shares at their computer, increasing the value of their holdings and retaining some of the spoils for living expenses.

Such business carries a lot of risk and should only be carried out by experts; however, the Internet-based, low-cost, transaction-only model adopted by Selftrade would lend itself to this sort of trading should it ever take off in the UK, and the possibility illustrates some of the potential growth the company could enjoy as the market develops.

Quality of Management

Selftrade's management philosophy is a relatively simple matter of looking after its people and ensuring that they stay motivated and fulfilled. This is achieved by communicating the company's strategy (and reasons for it) clearly, and by ensuring that the right people are in the right jobs. Overli regards the staff as a community that needs to be motivated rather than as a set of individuals.

People are expected to do a good job and are told when they are doing so. Training is regarded as very important for people at all levels since as a new company, Selftrade already has an eye on the likely identities of the next generation of managers. Titles are less important than tasks and staff retention is high – by the time the research for this book took place (in late 2000) nobody had left the company since its UK inception.

International Orientation

Selftrade is a European company and for the moment it appears happy to continue growing in this area. Although the market is further developed in the US, the American market is already filled by a number of good quality competitors, many of whom are trying to set up in the UK at the moment.

The company therefore remains avowedly European in scope as well as origin, and is concentrating on tailoring its message for each of the markets it serves. In the UK we get simplicity, a good price and some off-beat advertising to attract customers – elsewhere they take a different tack.

The change in attitudes towards the accessibility of investment in the UK suggests that in the medium and long-term, the company should be able to do well.

Share plc

The Share Centre, a subsidiary of Share plc, is a low-cost share-dealing service aimed at individual investors on a modest budget and at companies looking to introduce employee investment schemes. Set up in 1991 by chief executive officer Gavin Oldham, it offers a range of services including share accounts, ISAs, PEPs and pension plans. In December 1999 it launched its Internet service, www.share.com, which enables customers to place orders and access their account online. During 2000, in an innovative move, The Share Centre account customers were issued with free shares in Share plc. The Share Centre has 125 employees and recently moved into new offices in Aylesbury.

Scorecard:

Innovation	★★★
Flexibility	★★★
Human resources	★★★★
Growth markets	★★★
Quality of management	★★★★
International orientation	★

Biggest plus:
The chance to have a real stake in the business.

Biggest minus:
Could be too low-key for those who like their Internet companies glitzy.

The Share Centre
Oxford House
Oxford Road
Aylesbury
Bucks HP21 8SX
Tel: 01296 414141
website: www.share.com

The Share Centre

The Business

The Share Centre was set up in 1991 by CEO, Gavin Oldham, to cater for the customers other retail stockbrokers didn't want to know about: investors on a low budget, with a small portfolio. As well as individual investors it is also increasingly catering for companies who want to introduce employee investment schemes. The company offers a range of services including share accounts, ISAs and pension plans. In December 1999 it launched its Internet service, www.share.com, which enables customers to place orders and access their account online.

At present Oldham and his family have a 77 per cent stake in Share plc, The Share Centre's parent company, with a further 10 per cent held by employees and 12.5 per cent held by customers. However the company's policy of issuing free shares to customers, initiated in 2000, will dilute this stakeholding over time. The Share Centre has 125 employees and recently moved into new offices in Aylesbury.

Innovation

The Share Centre is strongly committed to the principle of wider popular share ownership and its unique selling point is its extremely low-cost share dealing service for the small investor on a limited budget. Its average investor portfolio value is £4,000 – considerably lower than Web share dealing services from competitors such as NatWest, Barclays and Charles Schwab – and since 1996 its minimum purchase commission has been just £2.50.

This service is backed up by investment advice in the form of a monthly customer advice bulletin, and a premium-rate telephone advice line. The company also sends out a fortnightly advice sheet to the media via PR Newswire.

One of The Share Centre's most striking innovations has been its introduction, during 2000, of a free share scheme for existing account holders and new ISA customers. This involved the issue of 6.7 million shares in Share plc, The Share Centre's holding company, and this brought the number of shareholders in the company to over 90,000. The company sees the share issue as a way of attracting new customers while upholding its core belief in wider share ownership. It has created its own internal market, known as ShareMark, to allow trading in Share plc shares.

Clearly, in order to run a cost-effective service while also making a respectable profit The Share Centre has to exert strict cost control. The company has done this partly by simplifying its business. It offers a straightforward service with no complex financial instruments, and it has only recently started to offer immediate dealing. It has also taken the unusual step of keeping most of its business functions in-house, giving it maximum control. Having its own settlement system (an unusual move for a stockbroker) has played an important part in both controlling costs and enabling it to bring out new services quickly.

In promoting its service, the company has steered away from using expensive advertising. It gets a lot of business through gateway sites, through traditional routes such as Yellow Pages, and through word of mouth. The investment schemes it operates for corporates and its acquisition of Bradford & Bingley's corporate PEPs have also helped to raise its profile with investors.

Flexibility

A key element of The Share Centre's strategy is to outsource as little as possible, partly in order to ensure a good and cost-effective service for its members, but partly also to be able to move quickly in response to market changes. It has consciously avoided being dependent on third parties for dealing, settlement, IT and accounting, feeling that the extra capital investment required has been outweighed by the resulting freedom of movement. Its directors believe that this commitment to self-determination is what has enabled The Share Centre to be first with innovations such as its direct transfer to PEP for building society demutualization shares and its All-Employee Share Ownership Plan.

Moving its business on to the Internet in 1999 has provided The Share Centre with a way to reach a wider customer base and do a much greater volume of business without having to greatly beef up its headcount and therefore its costs. The Web now accounts for 40 per cent of its business, and click-throughs from other sites also help to bring in new customers. It started to offer immediate dealing and confirmation in January 2001. Investment in its IT infrastructure, to support these changes, was one of its major costs in 2000.

Human Resources

Though The Share Centre has a Net presence, it is not a typical Internet company from several points of view. One is its profitability; another is its emphasis on building up a stable and long-serving workforce. Whereas most emerging Internet companies are staffed mainly by men in their twenties, The Share Centre's staff is 63 per cent female, and the average age is 34.

The company aims to foster teamwork and a sense of involvement in the business among its 125 employees. One of the most obvious ways it does this is through its employee share schemes which enable staff to have a real financial stake in the business. So far, 90 per cent of its employees are involved in these schemes. The company is applying for Investors in People accreditation.

Until recently staff were split between three sites in Tring, creating problems with intra-company communication and co-ordination. This April the company moved to new premises in Aylesbury where the entire workforce are under one roof.

Growth Markets

During the 1990s, individual share ownership got a boost from a spate of privatizations and demutualizations. The Share Centre believes that this trend is now slowing down, to be replaced with growth in employee share services, fuelled by the emergence of new, more tax-efficient share schemes such as ISAs, stakeholder pensions and employee share schemes. While continuing to provide its low-cost share dealing service to individual investors, The Share Centre is building on its existing corporate business, and moving more strongly towards providing employee services for small and medium businesses who have been largely ignored by traditional financial services companies.

It sees the SME sector as a large and mostly untapped market where there is relatively little competition. To cater for corporate customers it has brought out new products such as ShareMark, and its All-Employee Share Ownership Plan, which includes free shares in The Share Centre.

In bidding for SME business, the company's credibility is boosted by its established track record in administering corporate schemes. Since 1993 it has operated the UBS Warburg corporate share service, which offers low-cost share dealing services for employees and shareholders of their corporate clients. In 1999 it acquired Bradford & Bingley's corporate PEP business, through which it operates PEP schemes for employees and shareholders of a range of public companies. Largely as a result of the Bradford & Bingley acquisition, The Share Centre now has over 100 corporate share service relationships.

Quality of Management

The Share Centre's financial performance is the best testimonial to the quality of its management: it is a profitable company which can point to consistent growth in its revenues, profits and customer base. Revenue growth, in fact, has been not just consistent, but consistently high: 44 per cent, 53 per cent and 42 per cent over the past three years.

Given this above-average performance, it's perhaps not surprising that its directors are older and more experienced than average too, with over 40 years of experience in retail stockbroking between them. Its founder, chairman and chief executive Gavin Oldham was a partner in Wedd Durlacher Mordaunt before becoming founder and chief executive of Barclayshare, the Barclays retail share service. The company's group business development director, Peter Forster, and group operations director, Jeremy Helliwell, also came from Barclayshare. Roger Wilson, its group finance director, has been finance director of various private companies and financial controller of Abacus Electronics, and Iain Wallace, group compliance and legal services director, was previously a surveillance inspector at the Securities & Futures Authority.

Careful management has been essential to enable The Share Centre to offer a cost-effective service to its investors. The company is run on very simple lines, keeping overheads to a minimum, and avoiding complex financial instruments such as futures and options. Its heaviest investment has been in technology and customer service.

The company has been built up comparatively slowly since it was set up in 1991, thereby avoiding heavy start-up losses, the need for major external investment, and the constraints that external investors would inevitably impose. It has got by with just a small amount of external funding and has been in profit since 1997. Characteristically however it does not intend to rush into flotation, according to Oldham, until it has a 'seriously good' market capitalization. Instead it is focusing on trading its shares through its own ShareMark scheme.

International Orientation

The Share Centre started dealing in overseas stock this spring following changes to London Stock Exchange systems, adding the top 300 European and US securities to its portfolio.

It is, however, in no hurry to take on customers outside the UK. In the short term at least, it takes the view that the need to comply with the varying regulations governing share dealing in different European countries would complicate its business, add to its costs and conflict with its aim of providing a highly cost-effective service. Dealing with customers beyond the reach of European Union red tape – for example in India – is a possible option for the future. For the time being though, the company has its hands full dealing with new growth opportunities in the UK.

silicon.com

In spite of its name, Silicon doesn't regard itself as a classic 'dot-com' – for one thing its financing is solid and it makes actual money rather than promises. Founded in 1998, the British company is Network Multimedia Television (NMTV) and publishes silicon.com, a Web-based IT news and recruitment service for IT and business decision makers. The site includes real-time news, analysis and comment in a text and TV format. It also operates in contract publishing on the Net, making programmes for corporate clients and as the various elements of the business grow it will be re-branding as the Silicon Media Group during 2001.

Scorecard:

Innovation	★★★★
Flexibility	★★★★
Human resources	★★★★
Growth markets	★★★★
Quality of management	★★★★
International orientation	★★★

Biggest plus:
Being the first to market with an innovative product.

Biggest minus:
The comparatively slow introduction of broadband in the UK has distorted the potential market for the TV service.

Silicon.com
Anchor House
15–19 Britten Street
London SW3 3TY
Tel: 020 7761 8000
websites: www.silicon.com
www.atscojobs.com

silicon.com

The Business

Silicon Media Group, as it will shortly be known, formed in 1998 as NMTV – Network Multimedia Television – with the then peculiar idea of broadcasting television programmes with IT news on the Internet, and delivering a motivated, precisely-targeted user group to advertisers as a result. It was backed entirely by private investors and remains in private hands. It has enjoyed rapid growth both in the UK and internationally, with offices in France and Germany and plans for offices in other major European countries. By the time this growth phase is finished, which will take about two years, it should employ around 500 people.

Innovation

Much of Silicon's innovation comes from the simple fact that nobody was making TV programming for the Internet when it started. More than that, though, it demonstrated an early understanding that the corporate customer would wish to receive all content, whether text or video, through the one channel and from one source. The *www.silicon.com* site therefore contains much well-written comment as well as taped interviews.

The TV element is only the start, however. Since the first day the company has worked on marketing itself to a high quality premium customer base and providing them with personalized information based on their individual needs. It combines this with serious investment in technology that tracks what the user does on the site so the company knows exactly who its users actually are.

The knock-on effect of this is that advertisers get offered a lot more than the standard offer of a banner ad on a website; they get to display their wares to exactly the right people who have a track record of interest in their area. This adds up to lead generation, branding, zero wastage and a platform that effectively guarantees a return on investment to the paying advertiser.

Underpinning this is Silicon's commitment to quality content. It employs experienced journalists as its broadcasters and owns its own studios in London, Paris and Munich. This does two things: it reduces potential overheads from hiring facilities and demonstrates that the company is serious about making programmes rather than simply being an Internet company.

Several of the advantages it believes it has over its competitors can be found by checking the identities of the original investors. Philip

Knatchbull was one of the original founders of Sky while Peter Ogden was the founder of Computacenter, one of the leading corporate IT dealers in the UK and itself listed on the Stock Exchange. The calibre of these individuals plus the offering itself led to a successful private equity round in October 1999 and a further round in October 2000 which included a lot of European money and the latter cash from Bank of America.

What appealed to the investors was undoubtedly the clarity of vision, and the focus on the target market, which is the corporate computer user and manager – for the moment there is little content aimed at the smaller trader. There remains a massive opportunity for the company once broadband Internet becomes widespread, and it is looking into ways of making its presence felt by building up partnerships with broadband players. In terms of other partnerships it has worked alongside the British Computer Society and the Computing Software and Services Association and content distribution deals through MSN, Yahoo! and others.

Flexibility

In spite of its relatively short history, Silicon has had to face up to the need for change and will continue to do so if its growth continues according to plan. Over the past 2 years the company has grown from approximately 40 people to an organization employing more than 120 people operating in three European countries. The company has needed to put in place a new corporate and management structure to ensure smooth and managed growth.

As we went to press the company was therefore evaluating its managerial strengths and weaknesses with a view to filling gaps as necessary. A renewed focus on training was also very much in evidence so that the existing staff could move upwards and fill the requisite gaps wherever possible. The resulting organization is likely to differ from the current one in a number of respects: there will be cleaner lines of accountability and reporting and more formalized forums for discussion; personnel strategies will be more formalized than they have been to date, to include the rolling out of Key Performance Indicators for both individuals and the company.

None of this should suggest that the organization has taken any of these areas less than seriously before; it simply reflects the difference between managing a medium-sized organization as compared to the small start-up that was. Content and marketing director, Anna Russell, admits that the transformation process is likely to be painful but stresses that it will be essential, and believes the staff will buy into it as long as it is communicated properly.

Human Resources

The company aims to be very open and honest – it seeks to employ the best people to do the job and pay them the going rate. Self-starters and team players are more welcome than nine to fivers. Training is therefore regarded as very important and the development of a proper career path and formal appraisal are prioritized. People who want a career in television should probably look elsewhere since there are already enough people manning that area – however people with skills in contract publishing who wish to expand into broadcasting will be much in demand as that area of the company grows.

Demographically it is a young company, at least in the UK; the German operation employs more people in their late thirties. The company also operates an Associate Share scheme so that the majority of the people working for the company are shareholders.

Growth Markets

From being the brand leader for Internet television in the UK, Silicon now has its eye firmly on Europe. The company launched its German site, silicon.de, in November 2000 and silicon.fr in April 2001.

Much of the company's domestic growth will inevitably be dictated by the increase in demand for broadband Internet services, and it has content partnerships in place with BT and others to take advantage of this when it arrives. This will happen gradually and care will be taken to ensure a non-broadband version of the site is available as long as the corporate customers want it.

The other area that is likely to grow is the mobile Internet, particularly once the next generation of faster mobile phones emerges. At the moment the company is examining the short message service (SMS) space, using which people can have headlines delivered to their mobile phones. WAP will also be evaluated as more companies and individuals start to find it desirable.

The availability of the Internet more cheaply will also open up another market – the small-to-medium enterprise, which initially would have found the cost of a constant Internet connection prohibitive.

Quality of Management

As discussed above, the company is currently evaluating its management and identifying gaps in preparation for rapid growth. Structures will become more formal without becoming stuffy and the straightforward air of reporting changes to the staff will continue as a central ethic.

It's difficult to say too much more about the quality of management as it stands. The existing management has identified its need to change, but succeeded in taking the company from a standing start to a success-ful round of financing within two years so should not be written off.

International Orientation

As established earlier on, the international focus of the company is something that will be growing in the coming couple of years. The pace of this growth is likely to be dictated by the growth of the Internet itself in the target countries; France and Germany's Internet use is on a par with that of the UK which made them the natural territories into which to expand in Europe, and Silicon.de was a matter of months old as this book went to press. France launched almost as we were publishing, although the structures had been in place for some months in readiness.

The other country that will prove a major challenge is, of course, the US. The funding from Bank of America demonstrates that serious investors believe Silicon can pull this off, but the US is a notoriously difficult market for foreign companies to crack.

Other territories in the future are likely to include Scandinavia, Italy, Spain and Benelux, and these along with the US might happen through partnership instead of through a direct presence.

skillvest

Skillvest is an organization that helps large corporates to manage people more effectively at very high levels. Set up in late summer 1999, Skillvest commands the backing of several big-league venture capitalists and operates using a high quality pedigree of managers. The company eschews the traditional human resources training model and offers instead a fresh dynamic approach that begins with the individual, fundamentally integrating the development of employee capabilities with a client's business model, processes and objectives. Getting results from staff becomes faster, better and easier, so maximizing the value of the clients' greatest assets – their people. Full international coverage is underway.

Scorecard:

Innovation	★★★★
Flexibility	★★★★
Human resources	★★★★
Growth markets	★★★★
Quality of management	★★★★
International orientation	★★★★

Biggest plus:
People with determination and vision, and who bring the required energy and emotional commitment to the team will thrive.

Biggest minus:
People who lack the necessary drive and emotional commitment will not fit in.

Skillvest
100 Grays Inn Road
London WC1X 8AL
Tel: 020 7421 9900
Fax: 020 7421 9901
website: www.skillvest.com

Skillvest

The Business

Skillvest enables businesses to manage people more effectively, aligning individual performance and development with corporate objectives. Set up by CEO Jac Peeris in late summer 1999, Skillvest currently services pan-European clients from three on-the-ground locations in the UK, France and Germany. The company intends to be a global player, and already has global clients. Offices are soon to be opened in the US and Asia. Skillvest has 150 client-facing people and offers a set of tailored Internet/intranet-based tools to support its five-step process (that is, to assess needs; source development and training; deliver development and training; evaluate performance; and to manage). Skillvest works with big prestigious multinationals to get the best out of their people.

Innovation

Skillvest offers a revolutionary solution for corporate management. Using Web-enabled technology, the company aligns individual development to business objectives and processes, all under customers' control. It's a business problem that various companies (including consultants, human resources advisers and IT players, training organizations and e-learning companies) have tried to solve. 'But nobody has created an integrated commercial solution,' says Jac Peeris. 'We take a mix of technology, Internet, customer service, data and information and combine it in the best possible way to solve problems for our customers. It's based on a premise of serving a customer need.'

As Skillvest's customers tend to be large corporates, the marketing approach is discreet, intimate, targeted and by word of mouth. 'You don't place advertisements in diverse magazines in this business,' says Peeris. 'We are dealing with CEOs of large prestigious multinational corporations. The approach is a personal one. You not only have to be adept, but also professional, confident and successful. We have the track record. We've built our company from scratch to approach corporates in this way, and during that time we've seen the dot-com phenomenon mushroom for a few in the right way but for most in the wrong business direction.'

The company has watched business and technology market moves, and 'architected' its own technology solution in-house, investing several million pounds into R&D. Some 30 per cent of the money invested in Skillvest has gone into its products. Critically, Skillvest forms alliances with 'the big boys' – the best training and development consultancies and companies around the world. 'The turning point was the arrival of the Internet,' says Peeris. 'There's universal communication and the ability to put Web pages in front of people, with multiple self-service opportunities. The Internet enables the exchange of rich data globally and has terrific potential.' Skillvest uses Internet technology innovatively, as a business tool.

Flexibility

'We're very cautious not to fall prey to circumstances that have afflicted so many other businesses over the last decade,' says Peeris. 'We are determined and organized. We build from the ground up.' For illustration, Peeris draws on an analogy. 'We built a strong oak boat. Certain key people chose to embark, we pulled up the anchor. We knew where we were going, but how to get there? We're on an uncharted ocean, which was sometimes choppy, calm or rocky. A line over the side might produce a catch. What does it mean? It's the brave new world. Many armadas are sailing, each with a 1-in-10,000 chance of getting there. We have the best crew, and we will get there. That's the premise on which Skillvest was built.'

Pods of people are dotted around the offices. Pods can be combined to form a team, then split up and reformed into other teams. The approach is central to the overall objectives of the business. There are few titles within Skillvest. The titles that do exist are switched regularly, it could be product development for a while, then recruitment. But the customers' needs always come first. Everyone moves around, constantly gaining experience, and everyone also 'bales if water comes on board, irrespective of job responsibility'. This is endemic to the culture of the organization. It's about building an organization fully equipped to deal with a future the staff cannot command. 'We're structured to move the organization very quickly,' says Peeris. 'Nobody gets away with not being able to help or not knowing our strategy.'

Skillvest's tools are 'very powerful within the marketplace', which is communicated to the market so 'everyone knows what we do'. Peeris has ensured flexibility is built into the organization at a deep level. Vision and strategy are shared regularly with the whole company. Most of the staff – 90 per cent – own stock in the company. 'They're on an adventure. That's why they joined.'

Human Resources

'There is no Human Resources department,' says Peeris. 'We have empowered line managers.' There are people who help the company recruit, and this can be by word-of-mouth, Internet, creative means, or alumni boards. But Skillvest 'knows who we are looking for'. Everyone on board has a blue-chip background, is highly educated and comes with experience (eg, from Merrill Lynch, American Express, Microsoft, Andersen Consulting, Bain & Co, Gemini Consulting). 'All of our staff experience what we sell and come with a passion for driving companies to become more effective and getting the most effort out of their people.'

All starters are asked: 1. What are you better at than 90 per cent of the population? That's what you're going to do here. 2. What do you want to contribute to the bottom line of the organization? 3. You should enjoy the feeling of being with people while doing 1 & 2. There are no strict 'working hours', it's very personal. You're in or out – there's nowhere to hide.

Growth Markets

What's driving Skillvest is passion. This is needed in the quest for growth and is part of the group adventure. The basic perspective is 'the boat is going to reach the brave new worlds'. That the right course has been plotted so far can be gauged from the fact that the first five employees on board at the start are still with the company. Some staff have left – they saw the ship, saw the crew and got the 'buzz', but were not willing to make the necessary emotional commitment. It's this that's powering Skillvest. Already it's trading in 15 countries which has brought a multi-cultural environment.

'Run hard and fast sums up our approach to where we see ourselves going,' says Peeris. 'Our growth markets are defined as where we create value.' Peeris wants to see the money spent on customer employees doubled. The market comprises the spend on developing and managing people – which is a massive global market. Skillvest believes it has the unique solution and that growth will come through the arrival of technology which brings in its wake new, and more efficient, ways of doing things. The company believes it is ahead of the curve. As well as having customers in the US, discussions are underway in Asia. It's these regions which are expected to be part of growth plans.

Quality of Management

Skillvest is backed by leading venture capitalists. These include Carlyle Internet Partners, the largest venture capital company in the US; Bain-lab, the Internet investment arm of Bain & Co; global player AMP; and leading European Internet investors NewMedia Spark and Zouk Ventures. All these companies play an active role in company strategy and development. The eight-strong board includes investors hand-picked for their global experience. The pedigree of the companies that are backing Skillvest, shows that it should be taken seriously.

The company's management team brings together expertise from a range of business backgrounds. 'Our quality of management comes down to the fact we brought in people with the right experience at very high levels,' says Peeris. The team combines international, blue-chip management experience in marketing, sales, operations and finance, expertise in leading-edge technology, in-depth knowledge of human resources practices and considerable experience in managing fast-growing companies. As well as the companies mentioned earlier, team members come from the Bank of England, BT, Procter & Gamble, Glaxo Wellcome and PepsiCo. The experience the team brings to customers includes launching and managing global businesses, building state-of-the-art multi-million dollar systems, and handling global marketing and deal-closing exercises.

The *Sunday Times*, in its ranking of new Internet companies, found that the quality of management at Skillvest was far better than in any other company in its class. Skillvest is an entrepreneurial success story.

International Orientation

There is a clear and demonstrable correlation between the effectiveness of a corporate's management and development of its people and its ability to increase shareholder value. The ongoing skill development cycle required, that links the performance of the individual to the performance of the business as a whole, constitutes the space Skillvest plays in. Skillvest considers it has a global offering with a global target audience, and already possesses cross-border skills in English, French, Spanish, German and Italian. Already strong in Europe with inroads into the US, Skillvest sees itself within five years as being well-established across the world.

'We want to be on every desktop in every major corporate in the world helping people and managers to channel their contributions to the business,' says Peeris. 'We expect to be like the Microsoft Word of people management.' Definitely one to watch.

smart 421

Smart solutions for the 21st Century

Smart421 aims to provide a one-stop-shop covering strategy, design, development and deployment for end-to-end online business solutions, working with a number of strategic partners to provide a full service. It has developed specialities in hot areas like portal design, m-commerce and online financial transactions. Smart421 has yet to report its first year's trading, following a de-merger in June 2000 from a successful IT project developer, but at that time a turnover of £12 million was forecast. The company is 100 per cent owned by its founder and CEO. Currently it employs nearly 200 people.

Scorecard:

Innovation	★★★★
Flexibility	★★★★
Human resources	★★★★
Growth markets	★★★★
Quality of management	★★★★
International orientation	★★★

Biggest plus:
Smart421 specializes in imaginative business solutions at the sharp end of the high-tech industry.

Biggest minus:
The split company location suggests that the localized departmental teams might not always share a common culture.

Smart421 Limited
The Gate House
Fretherne Road
Welwyn Garden City
Hertfordshire AL8 6NS
Tel: 07004 421421
Fax: 07004 124421
website: www.smart421.com

Smart421 Limited

The Business

Smart421 (the name comes from 'Smart solutions for the twenty-first century') specializes in the delivery of e-business solutions, from strategic consultancy to the design and implementation of integrated systems for online business. Mobile commerce – delivered via WAP phones and GPRS – and online financial transactions have become areas of particular expertise.

Smart421 also has its own R&D activities, some of which involve blue-sky projects; and it has investments in a number of companies that own key technologies or have novel applications.

Smart421 is a very young company, so young in fact that its auditors have yet to release its first year's accounts. But IT entrepreneur Julian Harris, the sole shareholder in Smart421, was formerly co-owner and joint MD of Salmon Ltd – formed in 1989, providing leading edge IT and business solutions, and turning over nearly £22 million in 1999. In June 2000 Harris effectively de-merged the Smart421 operation from Salmon, at which time each business was projected to have an annual turnover in excess of £12 million.

Major clients – some for Smart421's previous incarnation under the Salmon brand – have included BT (various projects over five years) and BTCellnet (including development of a Web portal and integrating back-end and Web-based systems with WAP and GPRS technologies), Chubb and Pickfords (consultancy) and Phones 4U and Shell (extranets). Around 80 per cent of its sales are repeat business.

Smart421 has UK centres in Cambridge, Ipswich and Welwyn Garden City, with a small overseas presence in Phoenix and San Francisco. It currently has 195 staff.

Innovation

Smart421 operates at the leading edge of some important technologies, notably in mCommerce (delivery of services via WAP and GPRS) and eCash (online purchasing solutions). Equally important is the holistic approach it brings to these issues. For some users the arrival of new-technology delivery mechanisms has resulted in parallel systems for different technologies when it comes to marketing, merchandising and delivering products and services: Smart421 generally aims to provide a single view of the client's customer, integrating and co-ordinating systems to avoid duplications.

Smart421 is organized into three principal operating divisions: SmartSolutions handles client projects, but there are also two non-client operations – SmartStars for investments and start-ups, and SmartStart for R&D and product development.

SmartSolutions provides the revenue, of course, but the development activity is important. It's unusual for a project-based IT consultancy to run an R&D division. Smart421 encourages its staff to come up with innovative ideas, and the research work is done by line production people rather than by a dedicated R&D department.

The results will probably be seen in new ventures but will primarily appear as new technologies for use on client projects – one of the keys for profitability in the consultancy business is repeatability, being able to reuse techniques and technologies in different circumstances.

Flexibility

The apparently amicable split from Salmon Ltd happened primarily because the operations that became Smart421 were showing their own clear lines of development, focussing particularly on providing new channels to the consumer – Web portals, WAP systems, and the like. Within that structure Smart421 has shown itself willing to adopt interesting solutions to issues like the development of its own tools and procedures and support for in-house entrepreneurs.

The split location isn't the handicap it might be. Indeed, it represents a flexible solution to some pressing practical problems. A high-tech business corridor that is emerging in the area North and East of London allows high-speed communication between the offices, avoiding the overheads and people problems of central London or the Thames Valley while at the same time keeping Smart421 close to a nucleus of project work and a core of qualified staff.

Human Resources

Staff can move easily between the operating divisions as required, and the management structure is pretty flat with heads of divisions all reporting directly to CEO Julian Harris. In fact reporting lines are generally informal; like all the best new-technology companies, Smart421 is prepared to back the competence and responsibility of its people. As a result, there is a marked lack of internal politics.

Smart421 also encourages entrepreneurship within the company, and it is prepared to act effectively as an incubator for good ideas. This has happened with GiveUsTheScore, a real-time sports news delivery service that delivers SMS messages about goals and final scores for the customer's favourite soccer teams. This product was devised by a Smart421 staff member, and it was funded and developed in-house.

Smart421 employs 195 people, 85 of whom are permanent; the rest are on long-term consulting contracts, a common situation with new-technology companies. Of that total, 165 work in production (including research and development).

There is a share option scheme for permanent staff, and for all staff Smart421 is also continuing a profit-share annual bonus scheme similar to that which applies at Salmon – this has ranged from £500 to £5,000 per employee in the Salmon days.

Growth Markets

The willingness to invest in related areas has seen Smart421 take a 50 per cent stake in Active421, a strategic consulting company that has just started trading. It also has a 20 per cent share of Oakington (this is shortly to increase to 51 per cent); Oakington has a proprietary digital cash solution under the name Amadigi which is analogous to the pre-pay model for mobile phones. Smart421 sees successful start-ups like these as building the valuation of the company.

More fundamental, of course, is the core business. Smart421 has become a leader in some high-growth areas of technology, notably mobile commerce including WAP phones and the forthcoming GPRS delivery systems. And Smart421 is well positioned in some of the key markets for IT today – the client list has particular bias to telecommunications, utilities and financial services, all sectors that are prepared to invest immediately in high-tech solutions.

The company is able to match this presence with a concern for long-term client relationships, as evidenced by a high level of repeat business. Its reputation obviously counts for a lot here. New business is brought in by a sales team of just five people.

Quality of Management

Smart421 is structured into five operating divisions: SmartSolutions in both the UK and the US; SmartStars for start-ups and investments; SmartStart for development; and a group functions arm for marketing and administration.

Although the SmartSolutions operation is clearly the major activity and the principal money-earner, the divisional split effectively summarizes Smart421's view of itself; as well as designing and implementing systems for clients, the company is prepared to invest in projects and people for its middle-term future.

The company is still too young to make judgements about its progress as an independent operation. However, the management team which established Smart421 had a proven track record from ten years at the pre-split Salmon Limited.

International Orientation

It's still early days yet for Smart421 as an independent company, and to date the international activity consists of a small-scale presence in the States; but Smart421 has targeted Scandinavia and the US as obvious markets for its specialities in new-technology delivery mechanisms, especially in terms of clients for its mCommerce skills and tools. Some of the existing clients also have multinational operations. It is likely that the next eighteen months will see more international action at Smart421.

smashed**atom**

Founded in October 2000, Smashed Atom is a products and services company specializing in interactive TV. It offers business consultancy, creative and technical development services to clients including television channels, advertisers, retailers and government. In addition, it has products which provide interactive synchronization across all major technical broadcast platforms. It is 60 per cent owned by digital communications group Telewest, with the remainder of its stock held by technology transfer firm AtomicTangerine. The company has 45 employees based at its headquarters in London. It is also planning to set up a European office before the end of 2001.

Scorecard:

Innovation	★★★
Flexibility	★★★★
Human resources	★★★★
Growth markets	★★★
Quality of management	★★★★
International orientation	★★★

Biggest plus:
Plenty of opportunity for career development and learning new skills.

Biggest minus:
No grand job title to put on your business card.

Smashed Atom
2 Stephen Street
London W1T 1AN
Tel: 020 7504 7700
Fax: 020 7504 7777
website: www.smashedatom.com

Smashed Atom

The Business

Smashed Atom offers business consultancy, creative and technical development services to clients looking to enter or develop their presence in the interactive TV market. Current clients include the Department of Health, Kirsh Media, Energis/Bright Blue and Scene One. The company was launched in October 2000 as a joint venture between digital communications group Telewest, the UK's second-largest cable operator, and technology transfer firm AtomicTangerine, an offshoot of SRI. Telewest has a 60 per cent stake, with AtomicTangerine holding the remainder. The company has 45 employees based at its London headquarters, and is also planning to set up a European office, probably in Germany, before the end of 2001.

Innovation

Despite its wacky name and new-media image, SmashedAtom can boast a long pedigree and it has rock-solid resources of technological and commercial expertise to draw on. AtomicTangerine is the venture consulting offshoot of SRI, founded in 1946 as Stanford Research Institute. SRI and its sister company Sarnoff have a distinguished history of IT and broadcast innovation (including the mouse, colour TV, LCD screens and High Definition TV), and now have 2,500 research scientists on their payroll.

SmashedAtom's other parent company, Telewest division Flextech Interactive, had already built up commercial experience of the interactive TV market. Importantly, it had also developed two pieces of intellectual property which were transferred over to SmashedAtom: a triggering and scheduling system which can be used to trigger interactive content, and a system that enables centrally-stored content to be published across a number of different platforms.

SmashedAtom plans to use these two software products as components that will complement its consulting activities by enabling it to deliver interactive TV solutions for clients faster and more effectively. It plans to add further software building bricks to its portfolio. Fifteen of its 45 staff are specialists who work on developing a leading-edge technical architecture for digital TV applications.

SmashedAtom has moved quickly to establish itself as an innovator and thought leader in the digital TV market. In January 2001 it announced it was setting up a cross-industry interactive design forum, open to all design professionals, which will issue best-practice guidance for creative design on TV. The impetus for setting up the forum came from original research it commissioned towards the end of 2000 from consultancy Shelley Taylor & Associates which indicated that poor design and lack of understanding of human factors issues was resulting in digital TV services that viewers found difficult to use.

Flexibility

After just a few months of trading, SmashedAtom has not had much opportunity to demonstrate its ability or otherwise to cope with change. However its human resources strategy is designed to give it flexibility to adapt to the changing demands of a fast-paced and volatile market. Apart from the directors, nobody has a job title – the aim is to create a flexible resource pool.

SmashedAtom reinvests 5 per cent of its revenues in staff training. Its aim is to have multi-skilled people capable of taking on a variety of different roles according to the requirements of a given project; the same individual might be expected to act as a consultant, account manager or developer depending on the situation.

Human Resources

Five months after launch, SmashedAtom's staff had already grown from 27 to 45, and the company is actively recruiting. It prides itself on its human relations policy, which involves investing in its employees' personal growth and development in order to create a flexible and multi-skilled workforce.

As outlined above, only the directors have specific job titles because staff are expected to be able to act in a variety of different roles according to the demands of the business. To enable them to do this, the company offers them access to plenty of high-quality training.

The risk, of course, is that they will improve their skills and then go off to the competition; but SmashedAtom is gambling that the opportunities it offers for skill development, plus the leading-edge projects it is involved in, will help it to keep its existing staff as well as to attract talented new employees. As an added incentive for staff to stay, it offers good salaries and a stock option plan.

The company has a non-hierarchical, team-based structure designed to foster creativity and initiative among its staff. Employees are encouraged to research and implement new technologies, and also to contribute to setting company policy. Management places a high priority on good intra-company communication; a weekly company meeting is held to update everyone on latest developments in the company.

Growth Markets

With interactive TV still in its early days, SmashedAtom is in at the start of what looks set to be a huge and rapidly-growing market. The founders had expected that for the company's first year, parent company Telewest would provide up to 70 per cent of its business, with other customers building up gradually; they have been gratified to find that work for Telewest already accounts for less than 50 per cent of its revenues.

In this accelerating market, the challenge is not so much in finding growth opportunities but in deciding which ones to pursue. Smashed-Atom has identified three main markets that it will focus on. One is TV companies, for which interactivity will provide a way of differentiating themselves to viewers in the face of burgeoning numbers of channels. The second is retailers who, as new technologies enable viewers to filter out TV ads, will increasingly be turning to sponsorship of interactive TV to get their brand in front of the public. Thirdly is central and local government, which hopes that interactive TV will make public services more widely accessible. For example, the company is working with the Department of Health on a prototype for NHS Digital, which will build on the existing NHS Direct initiative and make healthcare information available on interactive TV.

In addressing these markets SmashedAtom will be offering clients what it believes is a unique combination of vibrant creativity and a solid Big Five commercial mindset, derived both from its management team's experience and from its parent company SRI. It offers a range of services including strategy planning, creative work and brand development, technical development and project management.

To kick-start its growth the company has been spending 15–20 per cent of its revenues on marketing, mainly in the form of ads in key business, creative and IT publications. But it expects this percentage to decline as its client base and reputation grows and the need to raise its profile decreases.

Quality of Management

As they strive to build a dynamic, creative team that can generate genuinely innovative solutions for clients, SmashedAtom's directors are experienced enough to ensure that the company also steers a hard-headed commercial course. Co-founders Jonathan Peachey, the chief executive officer, and chief operating officer, Phil Fearnley, both started their careers in the traditional business environment of Coopers & Lybrand before joining Flextech Interactive and AtomicTangerine respectively.

Peachey knows his way around the interactive TV market, having been in charge of Flextech's interactive services production unit, where he led the launch of the company's first interactive services on digital TV and mobile phones and developed its Electronic Programme Guide information supply business.

Fearnley worked in business transformation consultancy with Ernst & Young before founding AtomicTangerine's European practice. Other members of the management team have also contributed consulting, TV and general business experience.

SmashedAtom started life with a healthy investment from its parent companies, but under the guidance of its directors it has made an operating profit from the start, and generated £1.75 million of business in its first five months. However the management team recognizes that to fund overseas expansion and development of new intellectual property the company will need to raise additional finance. They are looking for a strategic investor, possibly a media company, to take a stake in the business.

International Orientation

As the world's most advanced interactive market, the UK already provides SmashedAtom with plenty of growth opportunity. However the company already has one major non-UK client, the giant German media group Kirsh Media, which has aspirations to sell its products in 32 countries world-wide.

To further develop its international business, the company intends to open its first European office by the end of the year, either in Germany or Scandinavia – both regions where the interactive TV market is fairly well developed. This is likely to be a new venture rather than an acquisition of a local company, but the management team recognizes the importance of finding good local staff to run it.

SmashedAtom already has a foothold in the US market through its parent company Sarnoff, and is also considering opening a US office around the first half of 2002. However it is notoriously difficult for European services companies to penetrate the US, and any moves across the Atlantic would be likely to be in partnership with an existing US company.

Set up in May 1999 and launched in August 1999, Sports.com is a dedicated portal service for European sports fans, both over the fixed and mobile Internet. Crucially, the company received financial support from Sportsline, a US pioneer in online portals for followers of different sports, leading IT company Intel, Reuters and Media One. These four organizations have supplied Sports.com with $10 million of investment. Sportsline was founded in 1995 moving towards profit, while Sports.com has still to reach profitability, although its precursor's success augurs well for the future of this UK-based company.

Scorecard:

Innovation	★★★★
Flexibility	★★★★
Human resources	★★★★
Growth markets	★★★★
Quality of management	★★★★
International orientation	★★★★

Biggest plus:
The sheer enthusiasm of the fans and the staff.

Biggest minus:
Tarred with the 'dot-com' brush when it actually has a solid business plan behind it.

Sports.com
23 Eyot Gardens
London W6 9TR
Tel: 020 8233 7642
Fax: 020 8233 7428
website: www.sports.com

Sports.com

The Business

Sports.com started its first operation in the UK, adding Germany, Italy and Spain in 2000.

The company received $52.5 million in second round funding, with much of this total coming from high profile investment firms such as Goldman Sachs. Up until February 2001, Sports.com found its revenue from three main sources – advertising, content sales and e-commerce.

Of the company's gross income, 75 per cent came from advertising, significantly, 23 per cent of its revenue from original content sold to the media. This is one of the advantages claimed by Sports.com, as it owns the vast majority of content carried on its service, including crucially live scores.

Other sports portal services cannot syndicate all of their content, as in most cases, sports sites buy agency feeds as opposed to doing it themselves.

In February, Sports.com launched its own gambling service, which it expects to provide a significant fourth revenue stream.

Sports.com has 2.7 million users each month on its site (Source ABC Electronic). Over 200 people work for the company full time, staff numbers are augmented by a pool of freelancers brought in according to need.

Innovation

Within the Internet sports service sector, Sports.com claims a lead in terms of innovation due to its WAP service for mobile phone users. WAP has been a cause célèbre for some time, but Sports.com claims it is not just providing a so-called 'website on WAP'. It has focused specifically on providing dedicated content for this medium and the company is planning to deliver a portal for mobile users. One issue faced here by Sports.com is the fact that a great deal of the content delivered over WAP phones is free. So building up revenues from this source is going to be a challenge.

Sports.com offers more than just a straight news and feature service to its users.

One interesting claim to innovation made by Sports.com is its success in terms of marketing and brand awareness compared to many other dot-com operations. The two and a half million-user base clicking on each month is testimony to this fact. And the key factor here is that Sports.com refused to follow the beaten track many other Internet start-ups went down, often to their loss. Instead of taking an expensive and high-risk strategy based on television advertising, Sports.com used radio to develop awareness of its brand.

However, this almost philosophical approach at the company must largely stem from the profile of the Sports.com senior management team – as we shall see later in this chapter. The bottom line is that, for Sports.com at least, it is essential to build up a brand name first before getting into TV advertising. In particular, this seems to be true of Europe as a whole where cultural and media related differences hardly indicate an easy and homogenous market for an expensive TV campaign.

Flexibility

Like all the dot-coms, Sports.com has had to deal with the issue of ongoing change as the online markets start to take shape. This has reached down to the departmental level, where groups have shifted or moved on from designated tasks as the business has evolved. Economic pressure points have needed to be controlled, with staff being the highest cost factor in any workplace.

Yet the company reckons that only a couple of people have had to be relocated. Many of those who have come and gone at Sports.com have been freelancers, which the company uses to cope with heavy workloads on an as-needed basis.

Sports.com has also been able to show flexibility in its business goal setting, due to its strong financial backing. Apart from running its own branded service, Sports.com has been able to provide a website development service for third parties, typically official sporting organizations. The company also provides content to several major telecommunications companies for their online services. These include BT Internet, France Telecom, a subsidiary of Deutsche Telecom and AOL, a leading Internet service provider.

Such arrangements with third parties have allowed Sports.com to evolve into a content provider – a role that promises to bring the company significant advantages over time. The company also has a flexible approach to the possibility of an IPO, which would change Sports.com into a public company from its present status as a privately owned enterprise. Sports.com sees itself as unlike many other dot-coms, in that it treats its financial status with the same kind of seriousness that bricks and mortar companies do. Arthur Andersen is used to keep an eye on the financial side of things.

Despite facing the typically changeable market conditions for dot-com start-ups, Sports.com claims to have remained relatively stable since its formation and evidence of this comes from the fact that the company has been capable of expanding its European operations. Then again, few start-ups could claim to have investors Sports.com has attracted – a situation that promises that a longer-term view prevails.

Human Resources

Sports.com is staffed by professionals who left jobs at sizeable organizations, in the media and elsewhere, to join the company. In many ways, such a move might be seen as risky – in particular since the ongoing decline in fortunes for dot-coms. However, these people are highly focused, enthusiastic, knowledgeable and straight talking. Managers at Sports.com say that the staff does not include any prima donnas – allegedly common in many dot-coms.

The company describes the atmosphere prevalent among the employees as one of 'quiet confidence'. The people are bright, thoughtful and dynamic, according to the senior management. A highly commercial vibe permeates Sports.com, but the mentality is based on forward looking, but down-to-earth principles. All activity at the company is gauged by the effects it has on the business and, necessarily, the bottom line.

Sports.com in the UK is a cosmopolitan workplace, with a mixture of British and continental staff. People put in extra time where necessary, but Sports.com claims to ensure that staff get a 'life outside work'. The employees seem to get along well enough together to socialize fairly extensively after work.

Growth Markets

Sports.com is looking to expand within its existing markets for the immediate future. This means exploiting the opportunities within the European countries where the company already operates. Yet Sports.com is also looking further over the horizon at additional expansion for the business into new markets. However, this longer-term planning is weighted with a pragmatic attitude. If steady progress is made and current operations show expansion, then Sports.com could easily evolve into a fully pan-European and even global company.

For instance, a lot of TV companies have already outsourced the supply of content, but still want to get their unique angles on stories and reports. This is clearly a direction that Sports.com could move in and on an international basis as well. However, like all young companies enough critical mass will have to be achieved before Sports.com can expand to reach its full potential.

Quality of Management

Due to the close support it has received from its US sponsor Sportsline, Sports.com has benefited from the extensive quality and management experience. In fact, the chief executive officer of Sports.com came from Sportsline.

In addition to this high standard of management in the background, Sports.com has also attracted top managers to its UK operation. Directors come from companies in television including Sky, or Internet companies such as Yahoo! and AOL as well as from other business sectors. The chief financial officer is in his forties and previously worked for the Trust House Forte chain. Managers have been hired from across Europe.

It seems as if the Sports.com management are not merely riding an opportunistic wave – they seem to have no plans to get share option payback from the company in the short term. The boardroom wants to lead Sports.com to attain clearly defined business goals and strategies.

International Orientation

With a strong European presence already established, Sports.com can claim to have successfully expanded from its primary market in the UK. As mentioned earlier in this profile, Sports.com intends to grow in the international context according to its capacity to do this over time. Over-eager expansion can be highly damaging to any start-up and it will eventually dilute the potential of the enterprise. Yet any company keen to succeed on the Internet has to go global. While this ultimate goal has been tempered in the case of Sports.com by a pragmatic approach to the future, it is clear that Sports.com quietly wants to be the premier sports portal in the world.

ST. JAMES'S PLACE

The St. James's Place Group provides a range of financial products and solutions in areas such as life assurance, pensions, investment planning and banking. Its salesforce (the St. James's Place Partnership) has grown to over 1000 self-employed advisers, called partners. The company began life in 1991 under the name of J. Rothschild Assurance. Its parent company, St. James's Place Capital plc, was originally established by Lord Rothschild and was listed on the London Stock Exchange. In 1997, St. James's Place Capital and the J. Rothschild Assurance Group were merged. Last year, the Halifax acquired a majority stake in the company, and the Group was renamed St. James's Place to match its holding company.

Scorecard:

Innovation	★★★★
Flexibility	★★★
Human resources	★★★★
Growth markets	★★★★
Quality of management	★★★★★
International orientation	★★★

Biggest plus:
The quality and experience of the St. James's Place Partnership.

Biggest minus:
Disintermediation threatens the whole industry.

St. James's Place
J. Rothschild House
Dollar Street
Cirencester
Gloucestershire GL7 2AQ
Tel: 01285 640302
Fax: 01285 640436

St. James's Place

The Business

Having built a solid reputation in the UK life assurance and personal investment market, the St. James's Place Partnership is now broadening the range of financial services it offers, with the aim of providing a complete service for what is sometimes called wealth management. The company was created by senior managers who already had a strong track record in the financial industry and it has grown steadily ever since, now having over £5bn of funds under management and a market capitalization of £1.7bn.

The company's clients come from two extremes. At one end there were over thirty clients last year alone who invested over £1 million in the company, and at the other are young professionals who might only be investing modest amounts at present and who have other financial commitments today such as a mortgage, but who are on the fast track to much greater earnings.

Innovation

The success of St. James's Place derives, to some extent, from its partnership concept. Instead of direct sales, the company's founders came up with the idea of working with top-class self-employed advisers who would each have their own client base, built up through personal recommendations and seminars, and would distribute the company's products to those clients.

St. James's Place is actually a limited company with the St. James's Place Partnership as its lead brand: the partners operate as separate autonomous businesses. Their clients have widely differing circumstances, resources and needs, but all are successful individuals and companies in their own right.

It was decided when the company was originally created that it would subcontract many of the activities which life assurance companies traditionally perform in-house. 'We asked ourselves where we could add value, for example we didn't have the necessary skills or resource to run the back office or do investment management so we contracted these out,' explains the company's chief executive, Michael Wilson.

The back office was outsourced to Scottish Amicable. Similarly, investment management was subcontracted to top investment houses with specialist fund managers selected for specific market sectors.

'Top investment managers don't want to work for a life company, they want to work for an investment house, so we contract investment management to top investment houses,' says Michael Wilson.

The way this works is that St. James's Place designs an investment product such as a managed fund or a specialist fund, and then pays an investment manager say, 0.25 per cent to manage the money. The client can choose their investment manager and swap from one to another, if desired. If an investment house under-performs significantly, then the company's Investment Monitoring Committee can transfer all the money managed by that house to a new manager.

Flexibility

The investment business has seen a number of major changes in recent years, especially in the regulatory environment, and also a number of scandals. St. James's Place has managed to weather all these storms, thanks in part to the skills of its partners at following changing customer needs, and in part to a deliberate policy of adapting to a new competitive environment, however it may evolve.

For example, the pensions business generally was badly hit during 2000 by the imminent launch of stakeholder pensions. The company's partners reacted by switching their business and selling more investment policies instead, to compensate for the fall in pension business. As a result the company considerably exceeded its own predictions for new business growth.

The company has also taken up the challenge of increased regulation of the financial industry and turned it to an advantage, using it to strengthen its operations and the service it provides.

'Companies that had a bad year all say it's the regulator's fault,' says Michael Wilson. 'My attitude is if those are the new rules, then play by them and be a winner by them. Sure, some of them are bureaucratic and petty but there's no point sulking about it.

'I ban talk about "the good old days" in the office. Bluntly, the quality of the business is far higher now than it was then, and far more in tune with what the customer wants.'

The changes in the financial industry mean new services, but they also mean more competition, especially from companies who start with a banking proposition and aim to grow from there. But while St. James's Place needs banking services to enhance its product range, its partners have the trust and personal relationship with clients that those rivals currently lack.

Human Resources

'We view our partners as our clients, and the policyholders are then their clients,' says Michael Wilson. He believes that traditional life assurance companies delude themselves if they regard policyholders as clients of the company. His view is that policyholders tend to stay loyal to an adviser rather than a company, so it is those salespeople that the company must work to keep.

The advisers are cherry-picked on their record of past performance and persistency, and have an average of 12 years sales experience. Persistency measures products which are maintained by their purchasers instead of being allowed to lapse, and signifies a long-term relationship with a satisfied customer rather than the short-term pursuit of new business that fails to stick.

This focus on working with the partners is reflected in the salesforce's low turnover. Some companies may lose and replace up to 50 per cent of their sales staff each year, but St. James's Place claims a 90 per cent annual retention rate. Partners have an average of 400 clients each, and it is then their job to retain and build this client base.

An interesting demonstration of the company's ability to retain staff is that it will celebrate its tenth anniversary with a Founders Dinner, and Michael Wilson says that all of the 200 people invited will have worked for the company since it started.

St. James's Place also operates a charity called the St. James's Place Foundation, for the benefit of others less fortunate. It helps build a sense of belonging to the organization. 'I believe the fortunate should give to the less fortunate,' says Wilson. '70 per cent of our partners and employees give regularly to the Foundation, and we have a committee that decides which charities to support each year.'

Growth Markets

The company aims to reposition itself as a wealth management organization and to lose the unfashionable 'life assurance' tag. It continues to recruit more partners, subject to their meeting its strict criteria, and sees them as the ideal way to gain customer feedback and respond to changing needs in the marketplace.

The St. James's Place Partnership name change derives from its desire to broaden its financial services coverage. It had used the J. Rothschild name under licence to great effect, but one condition had been that it would not compete directly with the bank N M Rothschild. However, with its desire to move into banking, the decision was taken to rename it to match its parent holding company.

'The Rothschild name was incredibly valuable when we were starting the company,' says Michael Wilson. 'But nine years on our business hasn't suffered from the change. And the salespeople like the way that "Assurance" has been dropped from the name, because life assurance companies don't have a great reputation at present.'

St. James's Place will offer banking services through a relationship with its majority shareholder the Halifax, using the engine of its Internet bank, Intelligent Finance, which it will licence and rebrand.

Quality of Management

A flat and informal management structure is an essential part of the
St. James's Place operation, as defined by its highly experienced founders Sir Mark Weinberg and Michael Wilson, Chairman and Chief
Executive respectively. The Directors regularly and willingly attend
social evenings, and when a partner joins the company, he or she
receives a 'No Hiding Place' sheet, listing the Directors' office, home
and mobile phone numbers and other contact details. They are encouraged to call if they need advice or assistance, or if they have feedback
from clients.

'People shudder at that, but in nine years I've only had two calls
from it that were dubious,' says Michael Wilson. 'There is psychology
involved – there is great kudos when someone can call the chief executive and even put their client on the line.'

The company has 21 offices around the country, each run by a
head of location and a management team. Approximately half of the
partners work from those offices, the remainder have their own offices
but are attached to one of the regional offices. Its marketing and support functions are located in Cirencester.

The advantage of this management style is that it is scaleable. The
company directly employs very few people compared to others with
a similar market capitalization, yet it has been able to maintain steady
and strong growth without needing to change the way it is run.

International Orientation

The company's main operations are UK-based. It does, however, have
an international company based in Dublin whose products are sold by
the partnership in the UK. In addition, St. James's Place has a joint
venture in Italy with Securitas Capital.

STANDARD LIFE

Founded in Edinburgh in 1825, Standard Life is one of the world's leading mutual financial services companies, with its activities ranging from the provision of traditional life assurance and savings, pensions and mortgage repayment plans to investment, the management of pension funds, unit trusts, mortgages, banking products and health insurance.

Scorecard:

Innovation	★★★★
Flexibility	★★★★
Human resources	★★★★
Growth markets	★★★
Quality of management	★★★★
International orientation	★★★

Biggest plus:
Standard Life continues to do things which surprise and please the market.

Biggest minus:
The spectre of enforced demutualization still hangs over it.

Standard Life House,
30 Lothian Road,
Edinburgh EH1 2DH
Tel: 0131 225 2552
website: standardlife.com

Standard Life

The Business

Standard Life is one of the largest investors in the UK equity market. It invests over £35 million each week and manages the equivalent of 2 per cent of the All Share Index. It is one of only a handful of life assurance groups in the world to hold Triple A ratings for financial strength from the international rating agencies, Standard & Poor and Moody's.

It is a company with no shareholders – it is owned by its with-profit policyholders. Not all are happy with this – the company had a long, costly battle with a group of policyholders seeking to demutualize. The company won, but it took a few punches and might have to fight again those who see a listing as the way to advance.

Jim Stretton, chief executive, UK operations, states: 'we will continue to keep an open mind but at the moment there is nothing better open to us – we believe mutuality is a superb concept and we believe we are big enough and strong enough to survive as a mutual'.

Innovation

The company constantly shows that size and age are not a bar to innovation, and Standard Life has a list of award-winning products which please the independent financial advisers who bring in a substantial part of the company's business.

It has moved successfully into medical insurance with an astute acquisition, it has launched the hugely successful Standard Life Bank and set up Standard Life Investments as an independent company, selling the company's investment expertise. It has moved into with-profit bonds, with-profit annuities and it drew a lot of plaudits for its innovative Futureperfect mortgage product.

The business philosophy is simple: Standard Life is there for the major financial events in people's lives, such as taking out a mortgage, investing money, arranging a pension and banking.

These are increasingly competitive areas and the company is alive to the changing demands of the marketplace. It has a determination to be ahead of the game and not to be seen trying to catch up.

According to Jim Stretton: 'big monolithic companies are not well equipped to deal with things which are thrust upon them but we have many more people thinking about how the company works and how we can do more than adapt to change but take advantage of it and even anticipate it. The challenge is to make sure that the change is channelled into where it is seen as progress for the company.'

Flexibility

Standard Life is a cautious mover, studying its markets carefully before moving in.

Its formation of the Standard Life Bank, focusing on savings and mortgages, demonstrated a flexibility and ingenuity which surprised its rivals. The bank maintains costs which are lower than those of its rivals and it is continuing to pull in the business.

It has produced a stream of products which consistently gain the approval of the market and win loyalty. More are on the way as the Edinburgh-based Standard Life office continues to show that big does not mean cumbersome.

It is operating in a sector of low margins and it predicts that there will be a smaller number of players in the business in five years' time. It believes that to survive it has to continue to grow and that will be through organic growth and entry into new markets and not by acquisition. At the heart of that growth will be the cautious flexibility which is the company's hallmark.

Human Resources

The five-month fight against 'carpetbaggers' seeking demutualization tested staff loyalty to the limit. A vigorous campaign by a leading Edinburgh newspaper in favour of the carpetbaggers added to the pressures on the workforce. They all passed with flying colours, demonstrating team spirit and loyalty by the barrowload. While fighting to preserve the way the company successfully operates – street marches and protests were not unusual – the staff rolled up their sleeves and still brought the business in and continued to create award-winning products with a dedication and pride which money can't buy.

Well, maybe it can – the company pays by performance, has a development plan for each member of staff and believes that the prudent investment in staff is at the top of its list of priorities. The training ethic runs through the company, from top to bottom. Jim Stretton again: 'we have always believed that companies have to be led from the top. There is no point in telling young people to go away and educate themselves if they see the people they work for doing absolutely nothing about it for themselves.'

Growth Markets

India has been identified as the company's big growth market to the extent that it has been dubbed the jewel in Standard Life's crown. The company believes that by the year 2006 it will have more customers in India than in the UK and it intends to be the sub-continent's leading life insurer. To this end it has set up a joint venture with India's largest home loan company and opened the venture's headquarters near Bombay. This represents a return to the India market which the company gave up in the last days of the Raj.

Another new market in the company's sights is Hong Kong where the company is now operating through a joint venture, Standard Life Asia. It is also active in Spain, where it has made a small acquisition, and in Germany. It sells products in Austria from its German base and it has two representative offices in China. In the past year there has been a 25 per cent increase in world-wide new business – a good indication that the company has recognized its growth markets and is going after them.

Quality of Management

The management was undoubtedly under the spotlight as never before when fighting the long campaign against the enforced demutualization of the company. It was a true test of management ability and determination and the carpetbaggers were eventually sent packing – but not until they had exposed some weaknesses in the management and some apparent weaknesses in the case for remaining a mutual company.

Standard Life's management at first appeared to be caught off guard, despite the warnings of the battle ahead. But they stuck to their guns and the important thing is that they have learned from the experience. They realize that they have not managed to get across to policyholders the full benefits and advantages of being a mutual company and they are now addressing this. They also understand that their handling of the press, and public relations, could have been a lot better and they are also addressing this.

They accept that there might be a perception that Standard Life is rather old and stuffy, but the company has a tremendous ability to move into new but compatible areas of business, making cutting-edge decisions and competing with the best while remaining true to policyholders and the company's mutual status.

International Orientation

Around 70 per cent of the company's income comes from the UK, a quarter comes from Canada and the rest from Germany, Ireland and Spain.

It has other overseas operations, has moved into India and has Hong Kong as part of the game plan. But big and bold though it might be in Britain and Europe the company could hardly claim to be an international organization.

In its early life it had more of an international outlook but after the Second World War it cut back on its international activities to concentrate on the home market. It is now back on the international trail again. There is so much potential and the company is looking at many overseas markets in the knowledge that it has a brand-building job to do beyond Europe. It has shown that it is patient and determined when it spots its market. It has, for example, launched a joint venture in India to a market where its research shows that 200 million people have the capacity to buy life assurance. For a full year in advance of the launch it had twenty-two staff based in India preparing for the launch. It will be sure-footed in its overseas expansion but it will not be rushed.

streets online

Streets Online started life as an online bookshop; it then became an online audio shop, raising more than a few eyebrows with its prices – then a DVD shop, game shop and most recently (at the time of going to press anyway) a VHS video shop. Now owned by the Kingfisher group, probably best known as the parent company of Woolworths, it started with private finance and has earned its place as the top UK online entertainment supplier. Less well known is its business as an application service provider (ASP), developing and hosting e-commerce for other companies.

Scorecard:

Innovation	★★★★★
Flexibility	★★★★★
Human resources	★★★★
Growth markets	★★★★★
Quality of management	★★★★
International orientation	★★

Biggest plus:
Reaching profitability with a solid business in such a new market – in spite of the bad press earned by so many dot-coms the company has traded profitably from the outset without compromising on customer service or value for money.

Biggest minus:
Rapid growth has meant the size of the team that needs managing has increased uncomfortably quickly!

Streets Online
Overline House
Station Way
Crawley RH10 1JA
Tel: 01293 402040
website: www.infront.co.uk

Streets Online

The Business

Streets Online started life in 1996, when managing director, Stephen Cole, realized that there was a market to be exploited in building software systems that allowed for financial transactions to take place electronically. Towards the end of 1997 he put Alphabetstreet together – as much to demonstrate that it could be done as anything – and rapidly found that customers rather liked the idea of ordering a book and not paying any postage costs (the competition almost invariably offers a discount of £1 on a paperback then charges £2.75 for delivery). Corporate business for companies like Exco Securities and Legal and General followed, meanwhile Audiostreet launched in 1998 and became the number one UK music retailer within three months; a slew of other sites followed and the company was bought by Kingfisher in 2000.

Innovation

The essential thing to understand about Streets Online is that it is more than just an online retailer – its commitment to the entertainment market goes much further than that. It owns its own record label called Labrador records, and it plans to move into digital/Internet radio and possibly video when broadband Internet is fully in place in the UK. The clue to this is in Cole's background as a software engineer rather than as a retailer.

All the same, it is the company's retail operations at Alphabetstreet, DVDstreet, Audiostreet, Videostreet and no doubt other forthcoming variations, that have established it as a brand. This has been due to a number of factors. The aforementioned absence of postage costs helps a great deal – the price that is quoted is the one the customer pays and there are no hidden surprises. The prices themselves can therefore look less keen than those of some of the competition but the experienced buyer soon realizes that there are real savings to be made. The company also takes the market by surprise occasionally as well; in 1998 it launched Audiostreet with the then-revolutionary offer of chart CD albums for £9.99.

Something the Streets Online brand has that its competitors don't offer in the same way is the sense of community. Customers are invited to subscribe to newsletters on the various specialist areas on the sites, and these are written by journalists – and proper journalists, too, the music area has its jazz enthusiasts who live for the music, and the film sites are catered for by real movie buffs. Unlike some of the competition, if they don't like a release they'll say so. Even more importantly there are the customer reviews – people can submit their views on anything available on the site, and they are rewarded with points for doing so. Given that 25 points is worth £5, it can be gathered that this is a loyalty scheme worth having.

Other areas that serve customer interests include the Xchange, in which customers can put their goods up for sale. Cole sees this as an ideal venue for record companies, book publishers, music groups, theatre groups and other entertainers to showcase and distribute their goods without paying a fortune for a professional e-commerce site that has the essential ingredient of traffic. To this end there is also an area on the site from which customers can download MP3 music files from new and unsigned bands.

The end result is a business that looks completely focused on its customer and their needs, and which won't hide costs that in fact make it more expensive to buy from than the high street competition.

Flexibility

There are two sides to the company's flexibility: that which applies to the customer and that which applies to the organization itself. From the customers' point of view the ease with which elements can be added and subtracted from Streets Online is almost comical. It was in the year 2001 that customers said much as they liked being able to buy DVDs from DVDstreet they would also like VHS videos; the company used the same basic template to spin off Videostreet almost overnight and with no publicity other than e-mails to existing customers it had another success on its hands. In theory it could add another site equally easily. Staff are always informed of developments well in advance so there are no surprises for anyone.

In terms of corporate structure, it has had to remain flexible because of increasing staff numbers from six people to 160 in just under three years. The change of ownership has made comparatively little difference; except that it has enabled an influx of funds so that development work can happen more quickly but apart from the fact that the board of directors now needs to report back to a parent company there have been few day-to-day changes.

Human Resources

One of Cole's firmly-held beliefs is that anyone can be good at a job as long as they are doing a job that they enjoy. For this reason he hires people who are passionate about their position; if you want to work for Streets Online and write about film, then fine, but you'd better know your Walter Huston from your John Huston and preferably love them both. The music people feel that they own their site, and the published authors working on the book site feel the same about their area.

Remuneration is good. All of the staff had stock options and a range of benefits, but the real driver for anyone considering applying for a job with the company must be customer service and the excellence of the site. Promotion prospects are excellent for the right people.

Staff retention has been exceptional since 1996 – only 4 per cent of the people have moved on. This presumably says something about what the company is getting right.

Growth Markets

As this profile was being researched, the buzz at the company was about the video site – it was very new and doing very well without any advanced publicity at all – equalling many high street brands for numbers of orders. However, the company won't lie still and is already looking into other entertainment areas it could exploit, first in terms of expanding its existing sites and spinning off separate sites around niche products (a 'classic pop' site for thirtysomethings, for example). Tickets for entertainment events are already sold online by a number of companies, but if they can be added on to an album sale then it increases the value of the whole transaction.

Expect to see increased personalization and more products aimed at the same audience for the moment, then. Also in terms of emerging markets, the 'broadcast' and 'digital' sections of the site will be interesting to watch as broadband hits the UK properly; these will allow music to be broadcast to PCs at will. What you're unlikely to find is TV to the PC from Streets Online; Cole just doesn't believe people want to sit in front of the computer and watch it, they're more likely to watch television in their living rooms.

The company will also continue to market itself as a service organization to other corporate clients – the nature of the business dictates that this will never be as high-profile as the retail operation but it will remain an important element of the company.

Quality of Management

The staff retention rate speaks a lot about the quality of the management at the company's admittedly unlovely headquarters in Crawley. Quarterly and annual appraisals are carried out for all of the staff on a one-to-one basis and are used for feedback on how the company is progressing overall. As has been established, Streets values its staff and tries to enable them to manage their careers as far as possible. Objectives are negotiated and agreed on the basis of their being achievable and believable.

The shareholders (who numbered 130 prior to the Kingfisher acqui-sition) have little say in the day-to-day management of the company since it doesn't need any obvious fixing. However, Cole and the team have nothing against using Kingfisher in particular as a resource for business advice where necessary, particularly as the company grows beyond the stage at which the management can be completely hands-on the whole time. There are now some non-executive directors representing shareholders, who are extremely supportive.

International Orientation

Although the scope of the Internet is such that the company can – and does – sell its products overseas (to over 160 countries, at which point it starts charging for postage and packing), it has no plans to market itself overseas or set up a separate subsidiary in another country. The reason is simple: there would be nowhere to go. There are 20 million people in the UK who have the funds to buy items from the Internet and as at early 2001, only 20 per cent of them had done so. Marketing to the rest is enough of a challenge and provides plenty of room for growth.

Add to this that there are 400,000 books in print at any one time and that no bookshop can carry them all and you can see the value of a well-stocked online outlet that can locate any of them within 24 hours. Given the customer participation and the increase in business due to the constant addition of new sites, plus the corporate services, it is clear that Streets Online has enormous potential to grow on its home turf for a good while yet.

microsystems

Sun Microsystems designs, manufactures and sells computer systems with the declared aim of 'creating a seamless computing infrastructure that's so reliable and easy to use you don't have to think about it any more that you think about electricity'. The company was founded in 1982, is based in Palo Alto, California, employs 42,500 people world-wide and reported year 2000 revenues of $15.7 billion. Annual growth has exceeded 20 per cent for the past ten years and was 33 per cent in 2000.

Scorecard:

Innovation	★★★★★
Flexibility	★★★★★
Growth markets	★★★★★
Human resources	★★★★★
Quality of management	★★★★★
International orientation	★★★★★

Biggest plus:
'You're in the right place at the right time – if you enjoy taking responsibility then there's plenty available.'

Biggest minus:
'It's great fun but it can be hectic.'

Sun Microsystems
Java House
Guillemont Park
Minley Road
Blackwater
Camberley
Surrey GU17 9QG
Tel: 01252 420000
Fax: 01252 420001
website: www.sun.com

Sun Microsystems

The Business

Sun Microsystems designs, manufactures and sells computer systems. The company was founded in 1982, is based in California, and employs 42,500 people world-wide. Annual growth has exceeded 20 per cent for the past ten years and was 33 per cent in 2000. Sun manufactures in two countries, has research and development in eight, has sales, service and support in 53 countries and operates throughout 180.

Innovation

Sun Microsystems is a company based upon innovation and whose continued innovation has generated continued success. Founded with the declared notion that 'individual computers should be built with something more than the individual computer in mind – the real value of any system is how it connects with others', Sun has prospered and has grown – in 1995 it reported a net income per share of 22 cents which, by the year 2000, had escalated to $2.20.

The company's approach has been to acquire brains rather than to try to buy finished products. A significant Sun investment was its embrace of the Unix operating system – mooted in the late 1960s as the open computing operating platform to come but not seriously taken up at the time by the major manufacturers and said for some time to be headed for obscurity. The investment delivered and competitors are now falling over themselves to claim Unix compatibility. Sun's recent acquisition of California-based Cobalt is said to be another such investment.

Sun ploughs back over 10 per cent of its revenues into research and development, in which the company is one of the world's top ten investors. Research and development spend has grown steadily from its 1991 level of $356 million to $3.381 billion in 2000. This was invested primarily in the areas of network storage, system design and the company's SPARC microprocessors, Solaris software and Java technologies.

Flexibility

Sun chief executive officer, Scott McNealy, quotes Canadian ice hockey legend Wayne Gretzky – 'don't skate to the puck – skate to where it's going'. Sun's ten-year history has witnessed many instances of being in the right place at the right time and this has happened too often for it to have been the result of happy accident. As McNealy emphasizes when he says:

As we grow, we intend to stay focused on a winning formula that has always emphasized three things, and to take each to an entirely new level.

The first is scalability – being able to add capacity without degrading performance; to grow quickly without adding undue complexity. We see this as imperative. The continued growth of the Internet and e-commerce depends on the ability to accommodate computing on a massive scale.

Next is what we call continuous real-time access. We want to make 'Webtone' more reliable than dialtone – more available, and more useful. And we're getting there. We're getting there, with remote monitoring and load balancing capabilities, with built-in redundancy and fault tolerance, with everything we can think of so you never get a busy signal on the Net.

Finally, we're focusing more than ever on integration. The name of our company is Sun Microsystems, with the emphasis on 'systems' – combining all the hardware components and all the necessary software programs into a cohesive unit. Call it the Webtone switch. As tightly integrated as a telephone switch, it will be the key to building a never-say-die network.

Here at Sun we have always been passionate about the possibilities of open network computing, and it's gratifying to see our ideas play out in the marketplace – boosting productivity, strengthening the economy, and improving people's lives. Our future is to go on doing that.

Human Resources

Sun human resources sees its role as driving 'people strategy' by supporting the managers who own the company's relationship with its employees; it seeks to be approachable rather than remote. Sun is proud of its Investors in People status, its recent awards for Best Recruitment Strategy in the KPMG-sponsored HR Excellence Awards, and the Employer of Choice and Business of the Year awards at the year 2000 Thames Valley Business Awards.

Those prepared to seek and take responsibility will flourish – an unofficial motto is 'to seek permission is to ask for denial' – and Sun openly states that no-one demands that their way is the only or best methodology: 'our people feel empowered to challenge the way we operate, shaping their own careers and introducing new ideas to the business'. Team players will succeed but loners who want a predictable, structured existence probably won't.

Growth Markets

That Sun Microsystems has established itself as a major player in the fastest growing market in the world is beyond question but having the right vision and the right focus can only take a company so far. You must then deliver the goods and you have to produce the real-world products and services that transform vision into reality.

Scott McNealy:

Growth is just a single metric of our success. At Sun, we have a long history of making the right decisions at just the right time, positioning ourselves to set the agenda for our industry, grow market share more quickly, and become the thought leaders that others look to in a fast-changing world. The decisions we've made have clearly paid off for us, for our partners, for our customers, and for our stockholders.

Some companies change directions more often than I change the oil in my car. Sun's focus is right where it's always been: the Net.

Quality of Management

'We create an environment in which everyone can excel. We expect a lot from our people but give them the tools and resources they need to do their best work. It's a no limits environment and the performance of our people is the most important component in making our business successful.'

McNealy has gone on record with the remark 'if you're not having fun, tell your manager' and the most important facets of life at Sun are said by the company to be 'technology; training and development; and fun'. Sun subscribes strongly to the 'work hard, play hard' ethic but it is fair to say this does not comprise the whole story.

Facilities at Sun's Surrey campus include a subsidized restaurant and café, gym, well-being centre and, interestingly and originally (this arrangement is claimed to be the first outside the US) a concierge, who is: 'a bit like a hotel concierge – they'll arrange things like last minute present buying and so on'.

Strongly led organizations tend to adopt the personalities of their makers and McNealy's reputation is long on go-getting charisma but short on compromise – the company's ethical stance is absolute and it is 'hard on people who cross the line'; or, as McNealy puts it, 'character matters'.

Sun has a low staff turnover – consistently less than 10 per cent per annum which compares well with the industry average of 24 per cent – and the company's attitude is well summarized by another McNealy quote: 'I want to hire really, really bright people wherever they happen to be, and I don't care who they report to and where their bosses are. We'll use telecommuting and tele-everything. We'll use planes if we have to. These days we have to bring work to people, as opposed to taking them to work. We think if we can get better at doing that than any other company, then we'll win.'

International Orientation

Sun, both by its nature and by definition, is an international organiz-ation. Its manufacturing plants are in San Francisco and Scotland's Linlithgow. Its engineering operates globally throughout the US, Europe and Asia; and a list of the countries in which the company operates reads like a majority portion of a world atlas index.

The international orientation of Sun Microsystems, however, goes beyond mere geography; it is an attitude.

'We believe that one day every man, woman and child on the planet will be connected to a high-speed network at all times – and even that is only a small part of the story currently unfolding.'

Scott G. McNealy
Chairman of the board and chief executive officer
Sun Microsystems

symbian

Symbian's vision is to locate itself at the heart of the mobile industry by creating operating systems for mobile devices of the future and licensing its own technology as a de facto standard. Spun off in 1998 from Psion, it is now also part-owned by handset manufacturers Ericsson, Nokia, Motorola and Matsushita. The company employs 750 people, three-quarters of whom are based in London; it also has offices in the US, Sweden and Japan.

Scorecard

Innovation	★★★★★
Flexibility	★★★★
Human resources	★★★★
Growth markets	★★★★★
Quality of management	★★★★
International orientation	★★★★★

Biggest plus:
Working in a company at the heart of a growth market, and the excitement of seeing the product in the hands of customers.

Biggest minus:
The intensity of the environment, which can sometimes be all-consuming, and a working culture which fosters long hours.

Symbian Ltd
2–6 Boundary Row
Southwark
London SE1 8HP
Tel: 020 7563 2000
Fax: 020 7563 2140
website: www.symbian.com

Symbian

The Business

The DNA of the company can be traced to the year 1985, when its parent Psion decided that there was a compelling business case for the development of handheld devices. In the early 1990s the company identified a market beyond its own handheld organizers and saw that it needed to license software in order to develop a standard for a larger emerging market.

Psion realized that it should separate its software activities from its hardware activities. This ultimately led to the formation of an independent joint venture called Symbian in 1998 – bringing together as shareholders Ericsson, Nokia and Motorola. Matsushita – better known under its brand name Panasonic – became the fifth shareholder in Symbian in 1999.

Innovation

By the time Symbian emerged as a company in its own right under the leadership of its chief executive Colly Myers, it had already evolved a robust 32-bit operating system, which it aimed to plant at the heart of the mobile industry by licensing the platform to handset manufacturers and others.

Crucially, it also brought in major shareholders who had an interest in developing the technology to be an industry standard. Mark Edwards, executive vice president of marketing and sales, said: 'bringing in those shareholders at an early stage was an innovation that paralleled our technology. It required a lot of foresight by the mobile industry to see that they needed a standard.

'The requirements of mobile devices are quite specific and separate from others in the computing environment. Within the mobile arena we considered it important that we made our charter very clear: to provide an operating system for devices, rather than compete in other parts of the value chain.'

Symbian has a design and technology department, plus several think-tanks, but as Mr Edwards points out: 'a large proportion of our staff are focused on software development – delivering the right technologies for our customers'. There is little room for 'a rigid silo mentality'. Teams gather from across the company to collaborate on projects which have included developing Europe's first smartphones.

One major marketing aim this year and next is to create an identity which is recognizable to consumers in the same way as, for example, the Intel Pentium chip. 'People will be touching our "chip" directly for many hours a day. It's a very present and intense engagement, and therefore the opportunity to create that brand relationship is very much here,' said Mr Edwards. As yet Symbian has released few details about planned advertising and marketing, but said branding will be 'a key focus'.

The profile of the company is set to rise with the release of devices based upon version 6 of its software platform. 'The Internet is central to what we are doing, and is probably our core conduit for marketing, to develop a community of users and licensees and to disseminate information and communicate with them,' said Mr Edwards. Symbian is continuing to build up its portfolio of licensees, who already include Nokia, Ericsson, Motorola, Panasonic, Psion, Sony, Sanyo, Kenwood and Philips.

Flexibility

The company has positioned itself at the leading edge of an emerging market and since it split from Psion, has grown from 150 to 750 staff. Human resources structures and others within the company are 'continually evolving', said Mr Edwards. The key attribute for its employees is therefore the ability to adapt to rapidly changing circumstances.

'Flexibility in employees is almost a mandatory requirement for any software company because the market is morphing very quickly. Our company reflects the developments of the market, and by the very nature of what we are doing, Symbian has to be flexible.'

However, this degree of pliancy may lessen as the company grows and becomes a standard-setter. 'So far, we have responded to current market needs but probably over time that flexibility will start to lessen as we take more of a market leading position versus a customer-led approach. Over the last few years Symbian has had a unique insight into the market. We can now start to take more of an overall view and influence the licensees.'

Analysts believe that by the year 2005, there will be more data traffic than voice traffic on mobile networks, a change which opens the door to a myriad of possibilities. 'We are allowing our licensees to bring to market different kinds of devices, different shapes and sizes. It's a bit like Darwinian determinism as to what goes forward,' said Mr Edwards.

With the shelf life of a piece of software lasting an average of six months, Symbian must remain constantly alert if it is to stay ahead. At the same time, the company emphasizes that flexibility stems from well-defined parameters. 'We innovate from having a clear strategy and a plan, and that underlines what we are trying to do. While the way to get to that end goal might change, the vision of being the company that licenses and creates the standard is the same.'

Human Resources

The company holds regular monthly meetings within departments and teams, and hosts an annual company-wide meeting which may include team presentations, outside speakers, exhibitions and workshops.

On a day-to-day basis, its culture revolves around innovation and challenge. 'One of the things I feel here is that it's a humbling experience to be working around so many bright people,' said Mr Edwards. 'It's a very passionate environment, and inspirational; we have big ideas and a big vision – to become a leader and define this market, and this constantly raises everyone's game and broadens their horizons and what they need to contribute.'

Symbian is on the lookout for thoughtful individuals, who demonstrate openness and a willingness to work in a team. 'We also look for a kind of hunger to really excel, to have an impact, to have responsibility and be empowered with a high level of responsibility and autonomy.'

Growth Markets

The company and the market are looking to embark on a phase of rapid growth over the coming years, with expansion rates 'at the multi-100 per cent level,' according to Mark Edwards. 'There's a huge vested interest in the industry to make this happen. The handset companies need to be able to invest in and develop these new markets and the network operators have just shelled out on licence fees for third generation telephony, so they need to promote the idea and gain traction.'

The forecast is for a billion users of mobile phones and devices by the end of 2003. At the moment, Symbian's platform is the standard in 90 per cent of smartphone handsets sold. A number of waves of technology are set to break in Europe, Asia and the US, and by the end of the decade, it is projected that a billion new phones will be sold per year.

'We are geared up to ride those waves and we believe that we have a couple of years' lead from a technical perspective,' said Mr Edwards. 'Our way of maintaining that lead is to continually innovate. With the licences we've already signed, we have a quorum of the market and we have the first-mover advantage. That's a very strong position to be in. Our first-to-market position is a reflection in part of the speed and focus of the company, but it's also about when we started – which was early.'

Quality of Management

Symbian has considerably strengthened its management team this year, with appointments of senior personnel from companies including Hewlett-Packard, Microsoft and First Telecom, but it also firmly believes in grooming its own staff from graduate level upward.

All employees enrol on a leadership programme, which is run by an outside consultancy, and Symbian is currently developing higher-level management courses. In addition, employees undergo a 360° appraisal twice a year.

The company's operational board is accountable to a board of shareholders and consults it on matters of strategy. Symbian is headed by Colly Myers, who was originally a software engineer and had primary involvement in developing the operating system which Symbian licenses. Symbian's operational board also includes a number of other executives, all with considerable experience and expertise in the technology sector. Mr Edwards is a prime example of the depth of this experience, having been responsible for the UK launches of Windows 3.1 and Windows for Workgroups during his time at Microsoft.

'Given the fact that this is a very thoughtful, intelligent, democratic business, there's a high level of visibility in all parts of the company,' said Mr Edwards. 'Managers and project leaders are visible, and their contributions are transparent, so a self-regulating meritocracy has evolved.'

International Orientation

Although development is concentrated in central London, the company is international at its hub, with its shareholders based in the US, Europe and Japan.

Outside the UK Symbian employs nationals as regional managers and supplies software to businesses and industries around the world in local language formats. There are also active social communities in each office and the company itself sponsors social events.

Employees who wish to transfer to an overseas office, or from overseas to the UK, may do so at the discretion of management. As the company expands along the growth curve, opportunities look likely to emerge for employees who wish to work and develop operations abroad.

Thomson Intermedia was established in April 1997 and is a media monitoring service with a difference. Formed by two ex-staffers from market research organization Mintel International, it offers all of the standard press monitoring services to track marketing and media spending as well as positive or negative coverage for clients, but also examines spending on Internet and other media advertising.

Scorecard:

Innovation	★★★★
Flexibility	★★★★★
Human resources	★★★
Growth markets	★★★★
Quality of management	★★★★
International orientation	★★★

Biggest plus:
The company's confidence in its future. Fast growth and an expanding market augur well for growth to come.

Biggest minus:
Chief executive, Sarah Jane Thomson, cheerfully admits that the 'sheer bloody hard work' in setting up a new company would not be to everybody's taste!

Thomson Intermedia
58 Farringdon Road
London EC1R 3BP
Tel: 020 7549 4343
Fax: 020 7549 4333
website: www.thomson-intermedia.com

Thomson Intermedia

The Business

Thomson Intermedia is in the area of media monitoring, and examines press coverage in terms of both advertising and editorial for a number of corporate clients who want information on what their competition is doing. It takes account of the Internet as well – both as an advertising medium and as a delivery mechanism – thus allowing its customers access to what's being spent in every area of the media. Although a very young company it has floated successfully on the Alternative Investments market, with the directors retaining more than 50 per cent of the organization. There were 160 employees as this book went to press in early 2001, with more expected.

Innovation

Thomson likes to think its first area of innovation was in detecting that the Internet was at all relevant in media monitoring as early as 1996 when Steve and Sarah Jane Thomson thought of the idea. The two of them shared the vision and were able to produce the technology to back it up. The products they developed were and are syndicated rather than bespoke.

They started the service with a product, still available today, called ART, a product which, for the first time, brought together press advertising creative data together with expenditure and offered it directly to companies. This product started by monitoring the financial services industry covering 30 UK publications and quickly moved to cover all industries and over 400 publications, providing companies with personal alerts of relevant data and is available as an analysis of the day's papers by 9.30am.

The product portfolio has expanded over the years to encompass a number of other offerings. Also on offer is Dart, an analysis tool for the direct mail market; TV Live offers streamed TV to the desktop coupled with expenditure data, while Radio and Outdoor offers monitoring of radio and outdoor advertisements.

Coupled with advertising monitoring comes a News Monitoring Service, Newsmetrics offering precise service-evaluation and on-line clippings. Another facet of the Newsmetrics service is the National News Index (NNI). This is a more analytical service giving a detailed evaluation of the coverage of all companies in the press in a given market. Each mention of a client company is graded so that the customer gets not simply a picture of whether they have been mentioned and where but in what context and how favourably. It also includes journalist profiles and tickertape news services.

The key to understanding all of the above products and precisely why they are innovative is that they can all be delivered through the Internet or to someone's corporate intranet – they can even be delivered to a specific person's desk, within minutes of publication.

Flexibility

The most obvious change to happen to the company so far is, of course, its listing and the preparation for it. It was a six-month process and in terms of operating a small company, Sarah Jane Thomson agrees it took a little time to get back to the basics of day-to-day trading once it was done.

Thomson feels very strongly that the company's best asset is its people, and therefore the priority whenever there is any sort of change is to achieve staff buy-in as swiftly as possible. This has been particularly important when managing growth for the company, both in terms of product offerings and people. Internet systems can be produced very quickly with the right expertise, and the first was fully operational within a couple of months of its inception; growing from three people to 160 is less straightforward and involved recruiting managers immediately.

The other key thing to have changed in the half-decade since the company launched is the calibre of the competition. As has been said already, in 1996 the Internet was a minority interest. In the early twenty-first century well established media monitoring companies saw the success and the power of coupling creative and expenditure data and using the Internet so they started to compete. However, the success of the Internet brought about a consolidation of companies within the industry and Thomson find themselves now with only one main competitor. The result has been increased emphasis on research and development; the side effect is that Thomson feels the market has become legitimized by the emergence of other players.

Human Resources

In spite of its flotation and established success, Thomson Intermedia has the feel of a new, young company and it looks for people passionate about working in both media monitoring and an Internet environment. The profile of the technical staff, certainly, is young, although the age balance is slowly shifting upwards as the company grows and needs more people with managerial experience – for example the company now has a Human Resources manager who has put appraisals and other personnel structures in place.

The company is spread across three sites. Farringdon is sales and marketing across all products, the head office in Bromley houses the technical team and developers as well as human resources, finance and training. The other big site is in Bromley where production is based, they do the inputting and scanning across all products and work 24 hours for seven days a week.

The atmosphere is very much one that will appeal to those who want to participate in something – shrinking violets and slouches need not apply. The benefits and salary package are competitive and were under review as this book went to press as the human resources team was only just being recruited.

Growth Markets

Thomson Intermedia is growing in a number of areas, each of which is associated with its core product – information, and in particular market information. Its second website, www.free2look.co.uk, is a prime example of this. Consumers can log on and check prices on various categories of product from personal finance offerings to DVDs and videos; the site acts as a shopping portal and searches the Internet for the best price on a given product. This is not to be confused with the various portals around the Internet that compare prices and take a percentage of any purchase as an affiliate site; this offers completely independent assessments. The company then sells information on consumer buying habits to the marketing staff of their clients. Thomson is also, due to demand developing the software to enable e-commerce across many of its 21,000 companies – starting with the large retailers where it will be receiving about 5 per cent commission for all products sold.

By the time this book sees print, the company will also be monitoring television advertising alongside its other services. This will allow it to compete with other monitoring services that cater for all media, such as AC Neilsen – but using the Internet and customers' intranets as a means to deliver the information.

Quality of Management

As the company has grown, its demand for management skills has increased dramatically. It has addressed this need in a number of ways, first by hiring an external company to offer the existing managers training.

Sarah Jane Thomson confirms that the culture when the company started up was very much that of a group of like-minded equals putting a business together, which is different from the current state of the company – managing 150 young creative people requires an entirely different set of skills. Her response, and that of joint CEO Steve Thomson, is to be very hands-on – Steve is responsible for the IT side and has close links with the technical team. Both were experienced at managerial level in their previous employer, Mintel.

As has been mentioned already, the human resources team was recently in place as this book went to press. The sales team was similarly getting training and extra personnel with more experience in management areas.

International Orientation

Managed growth is going to be important as the organization comes to realize one of the company's major ambitions – expanding its operations overseas.

Initially at least, Thomson Intermedia had the advantage of being unique so it was no surprise when companies from other nations started approaching it for information about its service. It is left in the luxurious position of being able to decide how it will proceed on growing its business abroad; it could license the technology, which is an idea that appeals in particular when it comes to American markets; the other possibility is to set up separately from anyone else. The sales and marketing director is fluent in six languages so consolidating initial contacts would not be problematic.

Whichever means it chooses, Thomson Intermedia has established itself as the first of its kind in terms of monitoring and utilizing the Internet to its fullest advantage. It has kept delivering new products in a bid to keep even the most demanding market satisfied, and its successful flotation indicates that the serious money is on its continued success.

TNT United Kingdom is part of the Amsterdam-based multinational giant TPG (TNT Post Group NV) and is the UK market leader in time-certain express delivery and logistics. Since TNT entered the UK market in 1978, the company has contributed many innovations to these sectors. TNT distributes a multitude of goods ranging from clothing and computers, through to car parts, cement, baby food, donor organs, cheques and magazines. It is also responsible for delivering 90 per cent of the country's national newspapers.

Scorecard:

Innovation	★★★★★
Flexibility	★★★★★
Growth markets	★★★★
Human resources	★★★★★
Quality of management	★★★★★
International orientation	★★★★★

Biggest plus:
'The opportunities – it's fast moving, it's fast changing, and it's a great place to be.'

Biggest minus:
'Getting to where you want to be is one thing; staying there brings its own pressures.'

TNT United Kingdom
TNT Express House
Holly Lane
Atherstone
Warwickshire CV9 2RY
Tel: 01827 303030
Fax: 01827 714925
website: www.tnt.co.uk

TNT United Kingdom

The Business

Founded in 1978, TNT UK Limited is a subsidiary of the Dutch TNT Post Group (TPG) and describes itself as 'a dynamic international transport organization operating within a fast-moving, highly competitive marketplace and with a strong focus on quality'. TNT UK has three principal business units – TNT Express Services, TNT Logistics and TNT Newsfast – and employs some 12,000 people at over 400 locations. The company's annual turnover exceeds £725 million and it is established as leader in its market. Growth – the company has doubled both revenue and profits over the last five years – is impressive.

Innovation

This is a company with a history of 'getting there first'. In the pre-TNT era there was no UK parcel carrier providing nationwide on-demand next-day-delivery services, and real time communication with drivers on the road was almost unknown. TNT changed all that and – using a fleet of radio equipped vehicles when its 'Overnite' service was launched in 1980 – offered both. TNT Sameday – the first nationwide door to door immediate delivery service started in 1982 and was followed by a range of new services through the eighties and nineties while the company collected record numbers of industry, excellence and European quality awards plus a Queen's Award for Innovation.

Customer satisfaction is writ large and, in addition to its long running six monthly satisfaction surveys, TNT has taken the unusual step of conducting 'customer dissatisfaction surveys' – it is, says managing director, Tom Bell, 'amazing what you discover when, instead of asking people if everything's OK and waiting for them to say "yes", you ask if there's anything you do that really irritates them.'

There is no aversion to technology which is used to its fullest extent where and whenever it is perceived to have a genuine use. This does not include the call centre which is operated by 'real people rather than machines that contribute nothing apart from annoying nearly everybody'. Everyone gets customer care training once a year and any ringing phone is answered within three rings. There is a 'no screening' policy which means telephone callers get connected to their requested destination with no interrogation as to their identities. TNT is the only organization of its kind with a Freephone number 'for everything – and that includes complaints'; and *Which?* magazine famously remarked that 'if you want to know how to answer the telephone, call TNT'.

Flexibility

TNT provides services for almost all FTSE 100 index companies and, says Tom Bell, TNT Logistics 'has more vehicles in other companies' livery than in its own; each of these operations is a unique contract and we are able to offer tailor made solutions by understanding our customers' needs and by giving them a better service than they could provide if they did it themselves. This sort of flexibility is crucial to our customers' success, and it's crucial to ours'.

What sort of people will flourish at TNT? 'Those who are entrepreneurial, fly by the seat of their pants, not afraid to roll their sleeves up – it's a make it happen culture'. What sort of people won't? 'The opposite'. Is there a place for shrinking violets? 'No'. TNT does not employ external consultants – but the company is decidedly keen on the notion of 'home grown timber'.

'What we want', says Tom Bell, 'is the best people – we look for attitude first and then we look for skills. Anyone can get hold of trucks, aircraft, warehouses and bar coders – they're tools of the trade but they're just things you buy or rent. It's people who give you the edge and, if you want to become the best and stay the best, then you need the best. Our training programmes have brought us national awards – all our departments have collected a major industry award of some kind – and our investment in training is huge. So it should be, our payroll adds up to well over £200 million a year and we'll do everything we can to get TNT the best value for that money.'

Human Resources

Suzie Theobald, group personnel director, sees no need to label the department 'human resources', and believes 'a personnel department should be transparent – if people keep being made aware you exist then you're not doing your job properly. The cornerstone is nothing more nor less than good, basic people management.'

TNT has been accredited to Investors in People UK since making its first application in 1993 and the following is extracted from the Investors in People re-assessment made in November 2000:

> The assessment revealed extremely sound people management procedures that have been overhauled, updated and adequately applied. The interviews revealed very positive staff perceptions of the organization's commitment to, and application of, training and development. The assessors interviewed a representative sample of the staff, and these interviews gave a high affirmative response rate, limited qualified answers, and very few negative responses.

In short, the staff like it and it seems like a good place to be.

Growth Markets

The company's objective – to be the best player and the market leader in every field in which it operates – is simple and straightforward and there are specific aims which mirror its determination to achieve that objective.

First is an absolute focus on customers and the provision of outstanding levels of customer satisfaction – TNT goes out of its way to offer better quality service than its competition and the organization thereby wins and retains the loyalty of its customers.

The second strand is to involve everyone in the company. Tom Bell: 'We want all our staff to take part in setting the policy for the business – which means empowering people to do their jobs. I firmly believe the role of managers should be to give people the tools and the training to do their jobs and thus create a climate of enthusiasm and success in which everyone can flourish.'

Continuous improvement is a third element – the aim is to inspire everyone to beat their previous best performance as, in addition to overall company improvement, this produces considerable personal satisfaction. The company approach to improvement is also bound up with continually identifying the changing needs of TNT's customers and finding ever more effective ways to meet those needs.

Quality of Management

It is not uncommon for strongly led organizations to exhibit some of the characteristics of those at the helm. Managing director, Tom Bell, has been with TNT since 1977 and comes across as charismatic, relaxed, straight and blunt.

TNT is messianic about measuring key outcomes for improvement and its on-time delivery performance is monitored relentlessly. Underlying this activity is the belief that 'the quality of service provided for our customers has always been our main concern, and it always will be,' says Bell.

> Our future is about continuing to provide an outstanding service, it's about growing organically and it's about continuing to innovate so that we stay at the leading edge of our markets. At the moment we're a very good company – I want us to be a great company and I want our employee satisfaction levels to be so high that people will be begging to join.
>
> Complacency is taboo. It's easy to say we're the market leader and there's only weak opposition – rather than strong competition, but weak opposition can become strong competition tomorrow if you start to believe your laurels are things on which you just loll around.

With the right mentality, you can do anything. Faced with unusually demanding problems, our people make extraordinary efforts. The 'must get through' TNT attitude is famous enough to have helped us win a competitive advantage, and I want it to stand us in equally good stead in the years to come . . .

In ten years time? What I'd really like is to see my job being done by home grown timber.

International Orientation

TNT is part of a thriving global group and its international orientation is strong. Employees may move in order to gain promotion but TNT's policy on families is strong and its preference is to avoid uprooting people needlessly – 'you can', says Bell, 'carve out just as successful a niche by helping the company expand in the area where you're working now'.

For those keen to move there is no shortage of opportunity. World-wide vacancies are on the increase, anyone may apply, and recent examples of relocation from the UK under the company's international assignment policy included Australia, Asia and America – as Tom Bell sanguinely points out, 'with our parent company TNT Post Group, we actually operate in more countries than the United Nations represents'.

tradebasics.com

Trade Basics was set up to provide no-nonsense investment education to businesses and consumers across Europe. It has two sites – Tradebasics.com and Wealthbasics.com – which act as shop windows for the more tailored content and applications service it sells to corporate clients. The company employs ten permanent staff plus several freelance specialists. It has headquarters in London but is looking to expand into Europe. Set up with private funding, it is now looking for further investment to fund product development and European expansion.

Scorecard:

Innovation	★★
Flexibility	★★★
Human resources	★★
Growth markets	★★★
Quality of management	★★★★
International orientation	★★★★

Biggest plus:
Friendly, informal atmosphere.

Biggest minus:
Lack of security.

Trade Basics
52–54 Rosebery Avenue
London EC1R 4RP
Tel: 020 7837 8400
Fax: 020 7837 8411
website: www.tradebasics.com

Trade Basics

The Business

Trade Basics was set up in 1999 by an ex-Euromoney Publications manager and a digital media entrepreneur, to provide investment education to businesses and consumers across Europe. Its public website, Tradebasics.com, and a restricted access site, Wealthbasics.com, act as shop windows for the tailored service it sells to corporate clients, and which forms its main source of revenue.

The company employs ten permanent staff plus a number of freelance specialist writers and translators. It has headquarters in London but is looking to expand into Europe. Further funding is now being sought to help accelerate international expansion and new product development.

Innovation

With over 5,000 finance-related sites in the UK alone, Trade Basics is clearly going to have its work cut out to ensure it stands out from the crowd. To meet this challenge, the company has set itself the ambitious goal of providing the best content, presented in a down-to-earth way that makes the most of the Web's full interactive potential.

Trade Basics is well placed to do this; several of its full-time staff have experience of financial training and education, and it also draws on freelance contributors with specialist expertise in banking and finance. The company believes that it can offer unrivalled depth and breadth of coverage, including comprehensive coverage of more complex trading and investment products such as derivatives and alternative investments, which are often ignored by other financial information sites.

Unlike information sites which aim to make money purely through advertising and sponsorship, Trade Basics does not expect its public site, tradebasics.com, to generate significant advertising revenue. In the short-term the public site works as a shop window helping to draw in the company's main revenue source: corporate clients who want alternative financial information services to offer to their own customers.

It claims to offer its clients best-in-class educational content that has broad appeal not only in the UK but across Western Europe, with localized versions of its service being made available to investors in France, Germany, Spain, Italy, the Netherlands and Scandinavia.

As well as building its brand and reputation for high-quality content, the company is trying to differentiate itself and build barriers against the competition by forming strong partnerships for channel, content and distribution.

In order to hold down costs, the company has developed its own unique publishing and content management system which enables it to rapidly generate content in a variety of formats for different clients and update it dynamically. Other companies have shown interest in this system, sales of which could potentially form another revenue stream for Trade Basics.

Flexibility

Having a largely freelance editorial and advisory team gives Trade Basics considerable flexibility in how it runs its business. The team can be scaled up or down comparatively quickly, and new skills brought on board as demand for them arises, without the need to incur heavy fixed costs.

Supporting this flexible workforce, the company's content creation and management system provides additional flexibility by enabling it to generate a range of content and rapidly repurpose it for clients in different European markets. In the longer term, it provides scope for the company to move beyond the financial sector and provides learning solutions for other vertical markets – and next generation broadband platforms.

Human Resources

Trade Basics has only a small team of ten permanent employees, covering a wide range of functions: editorial, creative, programming and sales. Though integrating these different functions into a single team could potentially be a problem, the company is helped by its small size and the founders' emphasis on building an informal working environment in which everyone lends a hand – even to the extent of helping to paint the office.

As well as the core team, Trade Basics has a network of part-time freelance associates based in several European countries, providing services including content creation, translation, and strategic advice. A couple of these freelances, though part-time, have a stake in the business, which helps to create a stronger team. Having a large freelance workforce does create management issues however, and in the longer term the company would like to bring more of its staff in-house.

Growth Markets

Despite the reported slowing in the growth of online trading towards the end of 2000 (a key indicator for the relative health of online finance), Trade Basics points to the fact that the number of European online share dealing accounts still rose by 13 per cent in the last quarter of that year. It believes that over the next five years Europe is set to become the world's largest emerging stock market.

Faced with increasing competition, online trading firms and information providers in Europe are having to find original ways of attracting new clients and keeping old ones. Adding educational content, tools and games to their sites, thereby helping their investors make informed decisions, is one way they can add value to their client relationships.

Trade Basics is meeting this growing demand by licencing business learning solutions to financial institutions and online partners, who want to offer their clients high quality educational and training material. It has two basic solutions aimed at different sectors of the financial market, Tradebasics.com and Wealthbasics.com. Tradebasics.com is aimed at online brokers, financial information providers, ISPs and portals, independent financial advisers and private investors.

Current clients include multinational banking, insurance and investment group Fortis; online spread betting firm IG Index; private investor site Interactive Investor International; and Comdirect, the largest European online broker. It has also agreed content deals with companies that include Gomez, Rainbow Network and Global Investor.

The second service, Wealthbasics.com, has been created to cater for affluent investors with assets of over £50,000, and is being sold to customers including private banks, financial services firms, stockbrokers and wealth management aggregators. Wealthbasics launched with its first client, major Swiss private bank UBP, earlier this year.

Catering to these two markets gives Trade Basics plenty of room for growth in the short-to-medium term, especially given the opportunities to exploit emerging media such as interactive TV as well as the Internet. It has already been approached by Freeserve to provide content for Web TV.

In the longer term, the company sees scope for building on its strengths in financial education solutions and providing other related financial services, such as broking and financial advice.

A number of external companies have shown interest in Trade Basics' proprietary publishing and content management system and its investment tools and financial games. Developing and licensing these applications to third parties using an Application Service Provider model gives Trade Basics access to yet another potentially lucrative revenue stream.

Quality of Management

Between them, Trade Basics' management team can claim a wide range of senior management, financial training, banking industry and digital media production experience. Co-founder and operations director Roger Thornham started his career at Economist Books and as managing director for IMC Digital Media, developed multimedia financial education products for some of the world's largest companies. Managing director Charlie Warburton, the other founder, worked for Euromoney Publications before launching DCG Private Banking, a wealth management training service.

As well as the two founders, Kate Lossius, the sales director, has 14 years of international banking experience with Lloyds Bank Group, and speaks seven languages. Rod Kohler, the marketing director, has eight years marketing experience for blue-chip companies.

The founders have also assembled a team of three non-executive directors with extensive banking and business experience, who provide considerable strategic assistance and management advice.

The founders successfully raised start-up funding of over half a million pounds, and four months after the tradebasics.com site was launched had already generated revenues of £150,000. They are predicting positive cashflow by 2002 and net profits of over £2.5 million by 2003. They have a carefully-thought-through business plan including detailed milestones which potential investors can use to judge the company's performance.

International Orientation

Trade Basics believes that to achieve its strategic goals it needs to grow revenue from opportunities in continental Europe, particularly in the more mature online investment markets such as France and Germany, which by itself now accounts for 55 per cent of all online trading accounts in Europe. Part of the company's strategy is to create localized versions of its material for a number of European countries. UBP, one of its major clients, already takes its service in French and English and the Fortis Group in four languages, including Dutch.

Selected content is already available in both French and German, and fully localized services will be ready for these markets later this year. Services for Scandinavia, Italy and Spain will then follow.

The company is well aware of the pitfalls of translation. As well as having native speakers check the translation itself, it uses high-calibre financial specialists to check the translated content, helping to ensure it makes sense from a financial point of view. One of its advisers, for example, was assistant managing director for ABB, based at its World Treasury Centre, and speaks seven languages.

Translation is not an issue in the US, another overseas market which Trade Basics is eyeing. Localization, however, is, and given the difficulty that non-US firms have had in penetrating the American market the company recognizes that it will need to find a US partner if it is to succeed there.

unmissable *Promotions Incentives Prizes*

Unmissable Ltd is an online information service for the hundreds of amazing experiences in the world that you either didn't know existed or cannot find a supplier for. It has researched and aggregated an extraordinary range of unique events, activities and holidays characterized by their exclusivity, desirability and scarcity; it doesn't sell these directly, instead acting as a commission agent for bookings received via its website. The company, which is owned by its directors and investors, sees great potential in the luxury market, especially for corporate and incentive sales. It recently acquired the theatre listings service Whatsonstage.com, the country's biggest performing arts website.

Scorecard:

Innovation	★★★★★
Flexibility	★★★★
Human resources	★★★
Growth markets	★★★★
Quality of management	★★★★
International orientation	★★★

Biggest plus:
Unmissable has prime-mover advantage in a potentially lucrative market; it's in for a fun ride.

Biggest minus:
The danger is that it may also be a bumpy ride, if bigger players decide to move in.

Unmissable
4th Floor
57–59 Neal Street
London WC2H 9PP
Tel: 020 7240 9841
Fax: 020 7379 4785
website: www.unmissable.com

Unmissable

The Business

Unmissable.com is a unique travel and ticketing agent, dealing in over 1,500 'difficult-to-find, extraordinary and unmissable lifetime experiences' – unusual holidays, exciting activities and sought-after events, sourced from more than 150 suppliers. Unmissable.com's 'ready-to-go' experiences include Storm chasing, MiG fighter flights, archaeological digs with British Museum curators, classic car luxury weekends, trips to the wreck of the Titanic, horse riding across the Mongolian steppes, Space Shuttle launches at NASA, kayaking alongside killer whales, the world's best hotels and spas, celebrity meetings, private islands, and suites at Wimbledon.

The company, which plans a family of 'experiences' websites, is aiming at high-worth individual consumers who want extraordinary experiences and business customers who are looking for unique ways to reward and entertain valued staff and clients.

In October 2000 Unmissable acquired the award-winning performing arts website Whatsonstage.com from EMAP Online; arts-related travel is the most obvious synergy, but Whatsonstage is a business with some potential in its own right.

Unmissable has also just launched the first of a series of alliances, a joint venture travel club with leading Internet sports content provider Sports.com. *New Media Age* magazine has commented, 'Partnerships like this are onto a winner'.

Unmissable Ltd was formed in autumn 1999 with £0.5 million backing from a venture capital fund and a group of private investors, all of whom are represented on the board. The company's two founders are actively involved, David Dobson as CEO and Terri Paddock as editorial director. The website went live in September 2000 following an intensive three-month pilot phase during which over £30,000 in bookings was generated by word of mouth alone.

Unmissable's business plan forecasts profitability in mid 2002.

Innovation

The Web is full of suppliers for cut-price flights and package holidays; Unmissable is aiming for the other end of the market, targeting the high value, high-margin niches of the travel, entertainment and corporate hospitality sectors.

The theoretical basis for this is what some analysts have termed the 'experience economy' – a trend away from stockpiling material goods and investing instead in experiences and memories. The commercial argument is that people with time and money often fail to take advantage of what's on offer, typically because they don't know how to access the experience in the first place. Specialist travel and ticketing is an ideal application for the Internet, allowing users an experience that is tailored to them – very difficult to find in an offline world dominated by the mass-market high-volume high street travel agents.

Unmissable.com provides an online service that appears to be unique. It also combines the best the Web can offer – detailed information, extensive research and aggregation, helpful links – with a person-to-person service. Unmissable doesn't actually sell anything directly, instead it refers site visitors either to the specific supplier or the call centre at its partner Page & Moy.

The website is loaded with content. As well as the pre-packaged offerings on the site, Unmissable offers a customizing service that might involve adapting an existing product or building one from scratch. Unmissable promises a 48-hour response to such requests, with full details and costed suggestions.

The site also has some useful extras. In addition to the wide range of product offerings, there is a good selection of high quality content created by an experienced in-house team working with more than two dozen regular contributors and travel experts. There are summaries of condensed travel reports in newspapers and magazines, for example, plus reports from travel-specific surveys and awards.

Unmissable's weekly e-mail newsletter, which includes information on new products, promotions and editorial features, provides a means of capturing basic user information – which is strictly confidential and will not be available to third parties. Unmissable wants to keep its community to itself.

Unmissable recognizes the potential drawbacks to an online-only operation, particularly for high-value products. The call centre is open seven days a week for telephone or e-mail enquiries; and with some of the more specialized holidays, the would-be customer can speak directly to the relevant supplier.

Flexibility

Unmissable has all the right attributes for a start-up in a vibrant sector – it is small enough to move fast, and has adapted quickly to changing circumstances. The increased emphasis on the corporate hospitality market, for instance, resulted from customer requests rather than from original business research; Unmissable has been able to develop appropriate products and services swiftly for this burgeoning commercial opportunity.

Human Resources

Unmissable Ltd is a small company, albeit one with big ambitions and a large-scale view of its role in the market, and it has many of the employment characteristics you would expect in that environment. There are no rigid lines of demarcation, though personal responsibility and job commitment are prerequisites; and with a total full-time staff of just eight, there are no formal staff development systems in place. Unmissable's management expects that staff will grow with the company, and confidently expects to share the benefits of future commercial success with employees.

The company's offices are in London's Covent Garden.

Growth Markets

With the number of UK millionaires increasing at a rate of 40 per cent each year, the luxury travel market is booming – in Britain its current value is around £1 billion. The corporate hospitality market is about the same size, with activity-based entertainment its fastest growing segment. New markets for the company also include the burgeoning sales promotion industry which is currently worth approximately £10 billion.

Whatsonstage.com was acquired early in 2001 from EMAP Online, which set up the service in 1996. This is the only comprehensive UK theatre listings guide on the Web, with a database of 5,500-plus performances nation-wide, as well as unrivalled theatre news, reviews and lively discussion boards. The site, which provides online ticketing through FirstCall, has won a string of awards. Over the past three months, the site has been totally rebuilt with a new look, new features and greatly expanded content.

Quality of Management

Unmissable has so far conducted itself with a commendable conservatism – the company launched with a modest £500,000 in personal and corporate investment, it has worked assiduously to develop product offerings and content on the website in preference to any marketing extravagance, the infrastructure has featured outsourcing and public domain software wherever feasible. This is a tightly run ship.

The commercial decisions also look sound. Interestingly, you can't actually book online. This decision was based on customer research, which suggested that users are not yet comfortable buying specialized and often high-value products without talking to someone in person. Unmissable has partnered with Page & Moy, the award-winning Leicester-based travel agent, to provide its call centre support. Most of the bookings are also handled by Page & Moy, which is both ABTA and ATOL bonded; in other cases the booking will go direct to the supplier, and Unmissable guarantees that all its suppliers carry full customer protection.

Unmissable's partnerships – with ISPs and portals, but also in joint ventures such as the Sports.com link-up – is an equally important move, increasing its exposure without significant risk. The purchase of Whatsonstage cost very little and promises much.

Most of the Unmissable team are travel industry and media veterans: Chief executive officer, David Dobson, was formerly responsible for the launch of community website and cashback shopping portal, Blue-Carrots.com, and previously held senior editorial and management positions in leading publishing houses. Editorial director, Terri Paddock, has a background in PR, journalism and marketing.

Unmissable is part-funded by leading UK incubator, Cube8.com. Cube8.com has invested substantial seed capital into Unmissable Ltd and also provides management and financial services to the company.

International Orientation

At present the focus is on the British or European market, and Unmissable's initial commercial relationships have been with UK-based partners. Given the luxury niche it occupies, however, Unmissable regards geography as less of a market restriction than the wealth of the consumer. As a pure online operation, the company does not yet see a need for local offices outside the UK; for most of Unmissable's products there is no problem about selling to clients who do not have a UK address, and of course the majority of the services it sells actually take place outside the UK.

The obvious potential for overseas expansion, notably into the US and Australasia, will necessitate local relationships; at present Unmissable is happy to develop the existing business and build the brand before it risks any international adventures of its own.

Virgin is the largest group of private companies in the UK, employing 24,000 people. Its global business interests encompass planes, trains, finance, soft drinks, music, mobile phones, holidays, cars, wines, publishing and bridal wear. Total world-wide revenues in 2001 were in excess of £3.5 billion.

Scorecard:

Innovation	★★★★★
Flexibility	★★★★★
Human resources	★★★★
Growth markets	★★★★★
Quality of management	★★★★★
International orientation	★★★★

Biggest plus:
The sheer strength of the brand.

Biggest minus:
A pressurised area, and one that refuses to stay still.

Virgin Management Limited
120 Campden Hill Road
London W8 7AR
Tel: 020 7313 2000
Fax: 020 7727 8200
website: www.virgin.com

Virgin Management Limited

The Business

'The important thing about Virgin is that we are not a company as such,' explains Will Whitehorn, Virgin's brand development and corporate affairs director, 'Virgin is a brand name shared by a lot of different holding companies in which Richard Branson is an investor, and almost every one of them has a partner.'

Accordingly, Virgin resembles a branded venture capital organization, behind which values such as innovation and flexibility are key. The businesses in which it invests vary widely, though they tend to be people-oriented. The rationale behind any decision to invest is always a belief that Virgin can improve on existing standards and in turn meet the public's own high expectation of what the brand can deliver. Because Virgin is in private hands it must often raise capital to run new ventures through its strategic partnerships.

Innovation

Virgin has an excellent track record in improving on existing distribution channels – indeed, it can justifiably lay claim to being one of the UK's leading direct sellers. Its innovation in this area has inspired more than one competitor and revolutionized industry practice. For example, in 1995 the Virgin Direct business model was greeted with considerable scepticism by the financial services industry. Experts argued that customers would be reluctant to buy financial products over the telephone. But in bypassing IFAs, the company was able to significantly reduce commission charges across its product portfolio. Today, the company manages funds in excess of £3 billion and Virgin Direct is ranked in the top five industry performers.

Its success heralded the creation of other such business concepts, like the Virgin One account – a unique mortgage-based account run as a joint venture with the Royal Bank of Scotland. Now with nearly 100,000 customers, the product has proved an attractive model for at least one other bank. The same principle has been extended to the rail industry. Together with Stagecoach, Virgin operates Thetrainline.com – a website which has so far sold over 2 million tickets online for all train companies.

Flexibility

Though the Virgin brand can seem ubiquitous to the British consumer, the group nonetheless has several core business areas that direct most strategic decision-making. And it has proved it can capitalize on opportunities as they arise in pursuit of wider corporate objectives.

For example, by acquiring the MGM cinema chain for £195 million, Virgin gained the target customer base to which it could sell its cola drink. It retained and developed the multiplex cinemas it took over and sold off the remaining smaller high street venues to a French operator for £65 million. Though the multiplexes thereafter became a healthy revenue-generating business for the group, soon afterwards it needed to establish a retail presence for its mobile product line – yet was reluctant to use an existing distributor. So when, in 1999, another French operator signalled an interest, it sold the multiplex chain for £250 million. Taken with the earlier sale, Virgin was able to finance a roll-out of its V Shop concept.

In structural terms, flexibility is intrinsic to Virgin's corporate identity. But it is the case more so now than ever before. Whitehorn says, 'This is a branded venture capital organization. Things change all the time. What's changed in the management structure is that we've realized we've got a strategic set of businesses now. We've got one of the top three brands in the UK and one of the top 50 brands in the world. We've got to capitalize on this.'

Human Resources

Virgin has rarely had problems recruiting. For its leaders, the real challenge is to meet the expectations of those who come to work there. In part due to the public image of its founder, the brand is associated with entrepreneurism and the chance to quickly realize creative ideas. Though such opportunities do exist, each business requires a variety of skill-sets and not everyone can expect to follow in the footsteps of Richard Branson.

Now into its fourth decade, Virgin's continued expansion is prompting organizational change. Traditional informality is giving way to more clearly-defined processes – for example, in regard to career development. One of the primary objectives of a newly-created human resources function will be to develop a structured career path for managers across the various individual holding companies. In doing so, it will strengthen the relationships between different businesses.

There are also plans to introduce a formal graduate training programme. A past preference for hiring post-graduates with industry experience had to be rethought given the sheer level of demand from graduates keen to begin their career at Virgin.

Growth Markets

Virgin's flexible approach to venture capital means that the number of potential growth markets is very large indeed. The acquisition, in 1997, of South West trains – what was then Britain's most underperforming train operator – proved that it was not afraid to enter markets where returns require considerable capital outlay.

Wherever it does go Virgin will continue to harness the power of the Web to enhance the business model. Branson in fact was initially cautious about the e-revolution and five years ago Virgin intended to do no more than develop branded versions of its core businesses on the Internet. That attitude has greatly changed. Virtual enterprises such as Thetrainline.com are intended not only to be revenue-generating in themselves but to benefit other areas of the group. For in taking ownership of online ticket-selling and making it easier to book seats on trains, Virgin hopes it will encourage more people into rail travel and improve the profitability of its own train operations.

Having rebranded the loss-making Our Price retail chain as V Shop, Virgin cut inventory costs and pushed its mobile products to the forefront of that distribution channel. With Virgin Mobile acting as a portal, the technology has brought all the group's products and services much closer to its customers, and the introduction of 3G wireless technology will further enhance the offering. Whether booking a holiday or buying wine, as a single provider Virgin can make the process easier and add value with a range of discounts and special offers. 'The convergence of all these ideas and technologies into a single entity we believe will serve to completely blur the line between product and brand in the next five to ten years,' says Whitehorn.

Quality of Management

More than any other UK business, Virgin's high brand visibility can be attributed to its founder. According to its own most recent survey (at the end of 2000), 97 per cent of people had heard of Virgin, while 96 per cent could name Richard Branson.

Will Whitehorn says, 'Marketers often wonder why we have such a diverse range of products and yet the public don't believe we're stretching the brand. It's because Virgin is not perceived in relation to products – the public thinks of the brand in relation to personality and that closely mirrors the perception of Richard Branson.'

The size of the group obviously precludes Branson's day-to-day involvement everywhere. Currently, most of his energies are devoted to the airline, train and mobile companies. In order to formulate a coherent strategy, the managers of all the businesses meet weekly to report on progress. Global developments are also closely monitored, often via the Internet, and a detailed strategic performance report is drawn up every month.

Under Branson's leadership the group has come a long way, but over the next five years changes will occur to enable extra capitalization. Many of the companies launched in the mid-1990s are nearing profitability and are likely to be either fully or partially floated. The process of looking for non-strategic investors began in December 2000 with a fund-raising round for Virgin Mobile that raised £150 million on the London stock market.

International Orientation

Already ranked in the top 30 brands in the US, Virgin aims to be a leading global brand by the year 2010. It hopes to achieve this through the roll-out of its mobile products around the world, acting as a virtual network operator in joint ventures with telco operators in local markets – as it does with One-2-One in the UK. The other means of spreading the brand will be the continuing expansion of its flagship airline business, primarily to locations in North and South America, and the Asia-Pacific region.

The US is obviously a key market. Virgin already has a strong presence in major cities via its Megastores and along the coasts through Virgin Atlantic destinations. But though visibility elsewhere is low, the growing awareness of Richard Branson (his autobiography was a financial bestseller) is expected to help in launching its mobile product – scheduled for Spring 2002 at the latest. With a highly fragmented mobile network, Virgin has genuine ambitions to grab the largest share of the American market.

whereonearth

Whereonearth is a privately owned company employing over 50 people in North America and Western Europe. It provides localization infrastructure for Internet, wireless Internet and enterprise applications. Companies that have licensed its technology include new media businesses such as Yahoo! and lastminute.com as well as corporate clients like Shell and Royal & Sun Alliance.

Scorecard:

Innovation	★★★★★
Flexibility	★★★
Human resources	★★★
Growth markets	★★★★★
Quality of management	★★★★
International orientation	★★★★

Biggest plus:
Its proprietary technology makes whereonearth well-placed to benefit from a wireless revolution.

Biggest minus:
Corporate visibility remains comparitively low.

Whereonearth.com Limited
Royex House
Aldermanbury Square
London E2V 7HR
Tel: 020 7246 1400
Fax: 020 7246 1401
website: www.whereonearth.com

Whereonearth.com Limited

The Business

While Internet activity was still in its infancy, whereonearth's founder and CEO Steve Packard anticipated that spatial information would, in time, provide a key dimension to the Web, so he acquired the technology to develop localization software. In August 1995, he set up InferNet as a vehicle for this product.

As a demonstrator of its functionality, he launched a UK hotel-finder website called Leisurehunt. However, the business grew strongly as an independent venture in its own right and Packard acquired digitized map data in order to extend the capability to cover international territories. In doing so, he turned to Graphical Data Capture (GDC), whose founder, Mike Klein, had been more than 25 years in that business.

In 1998, Packard and Klein decided to integrate their operations and take the proposition to market. InferNet acquired GDC and whereonearth was born. The venture attracted seed investment of £2.1 million and secured second round funding worth £5m. Subsequently the success of Leisurehunt led to it being spun off.

Innovation

Whereonearth.com provides location infrastructure for companies on the Internet. Rather than providing content this means whereonearth delivers the ability to index content using geography. In essence, it is the spatial equivalent of a text-based search engine, using the equivalent of an atlas to locate information as opposed to a dictionary.

The benefit to consumers is obvious. Just as a keyword will prompt a list of options arranged according to relevancy, whereonearth's technology gives you the exact location of a product or service. Feeling hungry? Whereonearth can help tell you where to find the nearest restaurants.

Businesses can use the infrastructure to make site content more relevant to divergent markets and help build up information on user profiles. As a growing number of organizations establish global networks, cost and logistical reasons dictate the need to use local suppliers. And while text searches are an important aid to information-gathering, location assumes primary significance in e-commerce.

The infrastructure is comprised of three main components. The first is a global data set, or intelligent map of the world, called GeoPlanet. Created at GDC, it is based on a truly spherical model of the world. This has allowed for additional layers of information to be laid one on top of another: postcodes first, then dialling codes, administrative boundaries, road networks and so on.

GeoZip is a powerful software tool developed at InferNet which processes different types of geographic data and assigns latitude and longitude co-ordinates. This means it can distinguish between information relating to two places that share the same name but are in different parts of the world. Given that fewer than two thirds of all place names are unique, this facility is crucial. GeoZip makes use of the underlying GeoPlanet data and so remains up to date. Last year alone, for example, 9 per cent of UK postcodes were changed.

The third element is a proximity search engine called GeoLocata. It makes stored information useful to a user and enables responses to the question: 'Where is my nearest . . . ?'.

Understandably, research and development has accounted for the bulk of investment to date. But although comparatively little has been spent on advertising, client wins such as Yahoo!, lastminute.com, Emap, Royal & Sun Alliance and VirginNet are enhancing the product's credibility. ISPs and e-tailers represent the first of two key markets being targeted by whereonearth. For the second see growth markets.

Flexibility

The logistical and cultural challenge of integrating the two companies, InferNet and GDC, has been successfully overcome. It was felt early on that cross-fertilization of the respective businesses was important and this could only be achieved by bringing them together under one roof. Whereonearth could have found a cheaper home but its offices were chosen to best suit both sets of employees (previously based in Ipswich and Finchley).

The company's key strategic decision-making so far has focused on whether to grow organically, or acquire functionality and get to market quicker. One such 'buy versus build' decision came with regard to very precise street-level information that is used for in-car navigation. Rather than 'reinvent the wheel' and develop the technology themselves, the company struck a deal with TeleAtlas which holds a vast amount of street-level information for North America and western Europe. Under the lengthy deal, whereonearth can access those parts of the topography that will be of practical use to its customers – for example, in major urban areas. This is the kind of barrier to entry upon which whereonearth's future profitability is also presaged.

Human Resources

Appropriately enough for a company that provides spatial information, Whereonearth is finally getting airborne. Speaking at the start of this year, Keith Dixon, COO, said, 'It's an exceptionally exciting time in the sense that we're at take-off point. We've been pounding down the runway and the aeroplane's now getting into the air. The question now is how high, how fast and which direction will we go?'

No doubt about it, whereonearth offers its employees the adrenaline rush of a genuine start-up. This means there is unbridled enthusiasm and belief in the product. But a sense of realism also prevails in the company: witness the decision to pull its IPO at the eleventh hour due to the depressed state of the technology market.

According to Dixon, self-starters who do not require a high level of guidance in their roles flourish there. This ability to manage without supervision applies right through to the top of the organization. Because of the need to take the product to foreign markets – particularly the US – its founder is more removed from the day-to-day running of business than in previous years.

All employees are eligible for share options and there is a pension scheme for those who want it. A corporate membership deal with a nearby gym is also in the offing.

Growth Markets

The importance of location in e-commerce is set to grow with the introduction of wireless Internet services. As mobility and Internet use are linked, those companies that do not tie content to end-user locations are likely to lose out. Whereonearth's infrastructure will enable content providers to target local markets and integrate online promotional activity with offline events. Direct marketing will be taken to its logical conclusion, alerting consenting consumers to products and services that may be of interest or use within a given radius.

Targeting network operators and content providers directly, whereonearth is also set to use the manufacturers as a channel for its technology and is currently putting together partnership agreements. It has also joined the newly-formed Location Interchange Forum, which brings together manufacturers and operators of wireless services to co-ordinate effective communication across the different systems.

Business-to-business exchanges represent another future revenue stream. Again, rather than sell direct to suppliers, the company has decided to partner with the software providers in the various marketplaces.

Quality of Management

Whereonearth's founder and the creator of GeoZip is an entrepreneur with over 20 years' experience in direct marketing and fulfilment. He successfully grew his first business, Portica Ltd, before turning it into a public company, and later raised further capital by selling off San Serif Print Promotions, the exclusive world-wide producer of the Trivial

Pursuit and Pictionary board games. Through his foresight and vision, Packard has successfully raised two rounds of financing from investors including Reuters Venture Capital and Amadeus Capital Partners.

Around him he has assembled a high-calibre management team. Research and development director Mike Klein created GeoPlanet, while CFO David Baynes is also a start-up entrepreneur, having helped achieve a full listing for Toad plc, from where he joined. He and Devesh Patel, director of business development, both have considerable experience in mergers and acquisitions.

Though its business plan had to be revised after the IPO was pulled, the company still has funds for most of this year and the experience is in no way viewed as a failure. After the share prices of comparable companies dropped to half their value at the time of the initial announcement, the company felt to delay flotation was the only sensible course of action. With profitability confidently in sight, the company appointed ex-Merrill Lynch MD Steven Licht as non-executive chairman, to help drum up interest from investors.

International Orientation

Development of the database is ongoing. Early resources were naturally targeted at those areas of the globe where Internet penetration is highest: Western Europe and the US. However, the company has recently begun adding several layers of spatial information for cities in South America and the Asia Pacific Region. It will aim to cover other key emerging markets, such as India, and by necessity employs language experts to interpret different character sets used around the world. Mapping information for eastern Europe is sourced from a facility in Russia.

Whereonearth has a global product in the truest sense of the word and intends to sell it on a global basis. Whether it does so directly or through channels is likely to vary according to the market. Ultimately a regional presence in each continent is envisaged.

Workthing.com is an online recruitment site that is part of the Guardian Media Group – owner not only of the *Guardian* newspaper but also of the *Observer, Money Observer* and a number of other businesses. This in turn is owned by the Scott Trust, an unusual business in that it doesn't have profit as its brief, it needs simply not to make a loss on the money CP Scott put in in the first place with the following objective:

To secure the financial and editorial independence of the *Guardian* in perpetuity: as a quality national newspaper without party affiliation; remaining faithful to liberal tradition.

Workthing positions itself as much as a lifestyle offering as a recruitment dot-com; it launched in 2000.

Scorecard:

Innovation	★★★★
Flexibility	★★★★★
Human resources	★★★★
Growth markets	★★★★
Quality of management	★★★★★
International orientation	★★★

Biggest plus:
The buzz about the company and the lively atmosphere.

Biggest minus:
People need resilience to work there – a start-up, and an Internet start-up at that, won't suit everyone.

Workthing.com
107–111 Fleet Street
London EC4A 2AB
Tel: 020 7669 5144
Fax: 020 7669 5195
website: www.workthing.com

workthing.com

The Business

Workthing was less than a year old as this book went to press. Owned by the Guardian Media Group it is nonetheless a commercial organization that needs to make a profit in its own right; its working practices and culture are also quite distinct from those of the parent company. It is essentially an online recruitment site, which addresses a number of niche areas in recruitment but which also offers its members more value than just jobs. It employs 76 full-time staff.

Innovation

At first glance the company appears to be a perfectly ordinary if better designed than the average recruitment website. It has a number of extras that are worth mentioning, however.

First it carries a lot of news about the industries for which it recruits candidates – so as well as finding the right job, candidates can research news items that are likely to impress at the interview stage. There are also areas for training and re-skilling for individuals whose aspirations outstrip their existing potential.

Building up an individual's potential is an important facet of what the company does, explains managing director, Andy Baker. 'What we do is work-life fulfilment, we're not just a job board,' he says. 'We do a lot of things that others try to do but they make a poor job of it.' Some of the basics he considers the other sites get wrong include the search facilities and the ability to drill down into details on the various positions on offer. For example, a lot of sites will have a generic group of jobs called 'sales manager' which, while accurate, tells the job seeker nothing; on workthing.com you can specify a job in sales, then move to specify a salary, location, industry and other requirements – leading to a much narrower selection of jobs to investigate. The site is written as a relational database as are most repositories of information on the Internet; the unusual thing about workthing.com is that it allows the user to manipulate the data with ease.

Another area in which it does things slightly differently from the competition is in private labelling. This is the process by which other companies can take workthing's basic product, this being the search technology, and put their own brand on it – so another business could present it to its clients as an added value service.

In addition every job is tagged so the advertiser can get reports on how many people have looked at it, and an e-mail service is available so candidates for jobs can have vacancy details delivered to them.

Workthing is a member of the Association of Online Recruiters.

Flexibility

Since the company had been running for less than a year as this book went to press there had been no major reorganizations or corporate refocuses as yet – other than managing rapid growth; however, planning ahead for any changes that might have to take place is very much in Baker's mind. He and the other directors have a strict policy of continuing development for themselves as well as for the staff.

The other area in which workthing.com has demonstrated an ability to adapt is in the way it gets to the prospective worker not only through its own website and those branded sites using the private labelling scheme but also through a network of affiliates. These are administered through the TradeDoubler affiliate scheme so the company pays other companies 20p for each individual that gets delivered to its site.

Human Resources

The strategy to allow the company to trade through any organizational changes is to attend to the basics and ensure the people management side of the business runs smoothly. As Baker says, 'everyone has regular appraisals, everyone has personal development plans'. Staff events are organized so that people can communicate any difficulties and contribute to the business and as a result the staff retention rate has been good.

Essentially the idea is to carry the same work/life fulfilment ethic within the company as the organization seeks to engender on its website. In addition to this every member of staff is a shareholder and the salaries are competitive; there is, however, no pension or health plan – the quid pro quo is in the company's total commitment to the personal development of all of its staff.

Growth Markets

The UK recruitment market is worth around £6-£7 billion per annum, half of which is accounted for in fees and the other half in advertising revenue. It's a well-established business and the great thing about workthing.com's way of doing business is that it takes a lot of the administrative hassle out of a human resources manager's day because people can be reading about a vacancy within minutes of the notification being placed.

There is therefore a lot of scope for workthing and companies like it to change the way in which the relatively technophobic human resources directors recruit; however Baker isn't among those who think the online revolution will subsume everything else: 'There are some poor quality vehicles both on and offline for recruitment, and those are the ones from whom we'll take market share.' Clearly, though, he believes the scope for online recruitment is increasing – and the numbers of both applicants and companies using it as a means of finding people bears him out.

Quality of Management

Workthing is predominantly a young company but it does have managerial depth, not only in the shape of two non-executive directors from the Scott Trust but also from some of the people it has hired. Former senior executives from BBC Worldwide rub shoulders with those who were their counterparts at Reed Business Information to build one of the strongest teams you're likely to find in a start-up environment.

It's not just a question of bodies in the right place either; the company seeks feedback from its consumers and customers, and therefore conducts the largest annual piece of market research in its field in which BMRB (the British Market Research Board) interviews some 3000 people. In addition to this there is an ongoing user and customer panel.

In addition to this the company uses 26 key performance indicators to monitor its progress and it also has a series of milestones, by which it means set objectives and times in which it must achieve them. All of the milestones had been reached on time as this book went to press.

International Orientation

One of the aforementioned milestones the company has set and hopes to achieve during 2001 is its expansion outside the UK. It will be moving into new territories by the end of the year, and plans to grow by taking people on within the countries it will service rather than by sending its UK staff out to work in its new territories.

Workthing is a new company but it comes from an old established pedigree, one of the most respected private trusts in the UK. It has grown incredibly quickly and has captured a slice of the market partly through its associations with key media players; its next task will be to justify its presence in the Guardian Media Group by establishing itself as an independent company in the long-term.

It has clearly made a solid start and there is every reason to anticipate a successful future.

WPP Group plc

WPP describes its business as: 'advertising, media investment management, information, consultancy, public relations, public affairs, branding, identity, healthcare and specialist communications'. It became, following the $4.7 billion merger with Young & Rubicam in mid 2000, the world's second largest marketing services group. WPP employs some 55,000 people working in 1,300 offices in 92 countries. The company is ranked in the top half of the FTSE 100 index, is listed in the *BusinessWeek* Global 1000 and, were it based in the US, in terms both of revenue and market capitalization, WPP would also be in the Fortune 500.

Scorecard:

Innovation	★★★★★
Flexibility	★★★★★
Human resources	★★★★
Growth markets	★★★★
Quality of management	★★★★
International orientation	★★★★★

Biggest plus:
'It's a very exciting business to be in.'

Biggest minus:
'It can be a frustrating and time consuming business.'

WPP Group plc
27 Farm Street
London W1J 5RJ
Tel: 020 7408 2204
Fax: 020 7493 6819
website: www.wpp.com

WPP Group plc

The Business

WPP is a public company based in the UK which started in 1985. It is the parent company of a group comprising some 80 individual operating businesses including household names such as Ogilvy & Mather, J. Walter Thompson and Young & Rubicam. The client list also reads like a Who's Who and contains more than 300 of the Fortune Global 500, more than a third of the US Nasdaq 100 and two thirds of the FTSE 100 index.

Innovation

WPP is big – world-wide revenues have grown to around £4 billion – but the company is quick to point out that it uses 'brain as well as brawn' and its mission statement reads 'to develop and manage talent; to apply that talent, throughout the world, for the benefit of clients; to do so in partnership; to do so with profit.'

WPP sees itself as a thoughtful parent which plays an active role in adding value to clients' businesses and the careers of its people across the group and across the globe and, whilst centralization of some functions is clearly advantageous, 'if centralizing an activity threatens the autonomy or identity of an individual operating company, then that activity stays de-centralized'.

In short, WPP set out to create a global organization which used the obvious advantages of sheer size but where individual flair is nourished rather than stifled – a highly ambitious target but the company clearly believes it has been successful in capturing the best from disparate worlds.

The company's culture and style can best be described by the apparent contradiction 'collective individuality' – WPP is crammed with talented people and intends to stay that way – making its various companies more attractive to more talented people throughout the world. Creativity is regarded as crucial and is not solely the preserve of art directors and copywriters whose work is tangibly creative – everyone in WPP companies is encouraged to take a positive approach to problem solving.

Flexibility

In a business which is about reflecting what its customers think, diversity is almost an end in itself. 'You could', says chief human resources officer, Brian Brooks, 'reasonably say our common themes are that we all have a belief in creativity and diversity of ideas'.

There are no rules as to the size of the companies within WPP –
'many', says Brooks, 'are small but about a quarter of them are seriously big and global' and culture differs not only from one company
to another but, often, within one company:

> there are even differences between, say, Ogilvy & Mather in Cali-
> fornia and Ogilvy & Mather in New York so you'd expect to find
> quite a few between a PR company in Belgium and a media buying
> agency in China. Obviously, the ways in which we operate reflect
> local customs and with an operation of this size and diversity it's
> impossible to make concrete rules and regulations – I also believe
> it would be both counter productive and highly undesirable.

In so far as generalization is possible WPP encourages openness; style
and hours of working are flexible; and risk taking – so often the cause
of an instant organizational reversion to conservatism – is valued.
Women make up 55 per cent of the group's workforce and the percentage of women in management positions – currently 'about a third' –
is growing.

WPP is an unusual organization and every cultural approach has
its problems. 'Ours', says Brian Brooks, 'has many advantages and I
believe they outweigh any disadvantages – it works brilliantly for us.'

Human Resources

The mission of WPP human resources is to help WPP managers develop
remuneration plans and, more importantly, to develop talent. 'Without
a strategic perspective', says Brooks, 'talented people can easily fall
through the cracks – you can't just rely on instinct and hope for the
best. What it really comes down to is a policy for facilitating learning
and development and you've got to have that in place if you're going
to help your people exploit their full potential.'

There is no official legislation about university or advanced degrees
but Brooks points out that, 'as most of the company's clients have
degrees, getting through the WPP door initially may well be harder
without one'. Competing as it does with investment banks and management consultancies for the cream of university, business school and
creative talent WPP works at recruiting those with strong creative
instincts and interests: 'these are the people most likely to be comfortable with the inevitable ambiguity and lack of structure that typifies
all marketing services consultancies.'

WPP has spent more than five years developing its Fellowship Program which recruits first degree graduates and MBAs who spend three
years in different companies or functions and 'preferably, in three
different geographies'. An employee could, for example, 'spend one

year in London with J. Walter Thompson in advertising; one year in Chicago with Hill and Knowlton in public relations and public affairs; and a final year in direct and interactive marketing with OgilvyOne in France'. The rotation programme is followed by a permanent assignment to a group company, the objective being 'not just to attract the brightest and the best but to develop people who understand and can co-ordinate and integrate communications service disciplines.'

WPP is publicly committed to internal share ownership and various programs have been developed to allow its people actively to participate in the company's growing value. Pensions, health insurance, company cars, holidays and remuneration itself are all influenced by local conditions, but stock ownership and financial incentives are emphasized.

Growth Markets

Ever faster and more widely available technology presents a global opportunity which is also a challenge – particularly to creative businesses which have traditionally been more comfortable with 'soft' creative information rather than with 'hard' data.

WPP is committed to using technology to its advantage and its Space Programme is focused on restructuring the workplace and transforming organizational structures: 'basically', says Brian Brooks, 'we want to deliver the best client service available – better work, done faster. That's what our clients want too.'

'It is', he continues, 'a matter of indisputable fact that WPP is now one of the biggest marketing services companies in the world. I believe we're the best as well but, in five years' time, we want that to be undisputed too.'

Quality of Management

The company's website offers a listing of its board of directors, whose combined experience includes managerial posts at Saatchi & Saatchi, Hanson, PepsiCo and numerous others. There are no lightweights around.

The non-execs also include some extremely well-known names. Jeremy Bullimore is a non-executive director of the Guardian Media Group, while Esther Dyson has been hailed as editor and founder of one of the most influential newsletters in the whole of the IT world. Numerous others include representatives from the Japan Advertising Agencies Association, the chair and ex-chair of the TI Group and an academic from the London Business School.

Shareholders and potential shareholders who need to know more about exactly who does what at the company can find up to date details at www.wppinvestor.com/commentary/management.jsp.

International Orientation

WPP's focus has been entirely global for a number of years. Many of its virtual companies have been international from the outset, starting with the acquisition of some marketing service companies in the US as long ago as 1985. In 1987 it acquired MRB Group, the sixth largest world-wide market research group, and in 1990 it was named the top agency group in the world.

In spite of restructures since that time its outlook remains resolutely global; in 1997 for instance, it introduced its world-wide share option scheme for WPP professionals, and in the same year it was investing in market research in Latin America as well as media planning in Europe and an advertising network in Asia.

The company is a genuinely international, diverse organization, and is showing no signs of slowing down.

Xbridge adds services to a client company's website, which enables visitors to purchase a broad array of complementary products and services there. Once integrated into websites, Xbridge's software enables the end user to request quotes for, and procure a variety of, goods and services. Such goods and services can include Xbridge's customers' own products, its partners' products and any of the products and services of a growing number of pre-integrated vendors. Xbridge produces the relevant Web pages and integrates them seamlessly into the existing website.

Scorecard:

Innovation	★★★★★
Flexibility	★★★★
Human resources	★★★
Growth markets	★★★★
Quality of management	★★★★★
International orientation	★★

Biggest plus:
Xbridge has all the positive attributes of a young company – no rigid hierarchies, a pleasant working environment, amiable atmosphere, and opportunities to share in the company's success.

Biggest minus:
The downsides also apply: there are no big-company perks, remuneration is based in part on jam tomorrow rather than rewards today, and commitment is a prerequisite.

Xbridge Limited
94 Maltings Place
169 Tower Bridge Road
London SE1 3LJ
Tel: 020 7378 9800
website: www.xbridge.com

Xbridge Limited

The Business

Xbridge provides Web-based software that enhances the online offering of its customers' products by adding a suite of complementary products and services to a customer's website. The customer selects which of these syndicated offerings, services and products best fits their site (over 30 are so far on offer, with more to follow), and Xbridge produces the relevant Web pages in an appropriate style. Each individual 'marketplace area' is highly customized to reinforce the customer's brand. Xbridge actually hosts the extra pages too, though the integration is seamless as far as the site visitor is concerned, and Xbridge supports the customer with marketing advice. This approach enables a business to offer a broad array of products and services from well-recognized vendors in various industries from any website powered by the company without the otherwise necessary business and technology integration efforts. It would be entirely possible for the website owner to develop such relationships themselves; but Xbridge provides a quicker, simpler and less risky way to do it. The customer also pays less than the equivalent in-house solution – up to a few hundred thousand pounds plus periodic maintenance fees – and receives a royalty on any sales of syndicated products from their website.

Xbridge has identified a definite business need, its solution is demonstrable, and there are no direct competitors in sight – Xbridge believes it has the only fully out-sourced solution available in its market.

Xbridge is a start-up that is only just hitting its stride; it has just 20 staff, 20 syndicated product offerings from over 30 suppliers, and a handful of early customers (who do include some impressive names, such as LineOne, LibertySurf, Reed Elsevier – for *Computer Weekly*'s site at www.cwbiz.co.uk – and the VerticalNet group with www.biopharmaweb.com/bsc, www.eurochemweb.com/bsc and more).

The company was established in April 2000 by Brad Liebmann and three co-founding partners (Ralph Arnold, Deno Fischer and Jim Nelson). The four provided the initial funding and all have full-time operational responsibilities. In December 2000 a second round of financing was concluded – £5 million from strategic investors, primarily Prudential plc, which now has a non-executive board member and is a supplier of syndicated products. The company is also backed by The Boston Consulting Group.

Innovation

At base, the Xbridge idea is simple but imaginative: website owners want to give visitors more reasons for coming to the site, vendors of business products and services want additional sales, both parties can see the merit in being associated with complementary non-competing brands. But designing a marketplace area for a website and developing all the necessary business relationships is time-consuming and expensive. Xbridge offers a speedy and relatively inexpensive alternative, utilizing state-of-the-art XML-based integration technology. This is an imaginative yet proven solution.

Flexibility

As a young and still small company Xbridge is able to react quickly to seize opportunities and deflect threats. It appears to have the cash reserves to cope with some variation in the business plan, though none is anticipated. Xbridge does not yet have the financial muscle or the track record to influence trends or determine the shape of the market, but that may well come – it does have a solid product offering with a core of satisfied early-adopter customers, and the business proposition appears very attractive.

Human Resources

Xbridge recognizes that it cannot compete with the human relations infrastructure of a large company, the environment from which all of its key staff have come. Career paths, remuneration plans and professional development programmes will have to come later. For now Xbridge has concentrated on making its staff physically comfortable – the high-quality ergonomically approved work chairs are the only obvious signs of luxury in the offices, which themselves are a spacious loft-style development with balcony and shower room. Staff salaries are below industry norms for such highly qualified people in Central London, but all staff do have share options that represent significant value on the basis of the December investment round.

Growth Markets

Xbridge describes its market as larger enterprises looking to transform a single-purpose website into a full-service procurement enabler. Put that way, there's a huge and largely untapped market in Britain – virtually every website owner is keen to provide additional reasons for a visitor to stay on the site, especially when such services support the site's own branding. The basic business model can of course be applied to any geographical area with a well-developed Internet community, and the range of syndicated services on offer can be expanded considerably before Xbridge runs out of appropriate candidates or runs into branding conflicts.

Quality of Management

It's early days yet for any evidence of a track record in management decisions, but Xbridge directors have a good deal of practical experience in management and the company clearly runs a tight ship. Xbridge's four working directors come from Lehman Brothers, Bain & Co, Aventis and Barclays Capital, a relatively conservative environment that is evident from the company's relatively low cash burn rate during its early development. Salaries are comparatively modest, with compensation coming from the working environment and the generous share options – yet Xbridge has been able to attract some top-class people, including an experienced development team that had a successful track record working on systems for a major European investment bank.

Similarly, investment has obviously gone into product development and targeted customer relationship building; Xbridge has spent virtually nothing on its own corporate image. The intention is to build a portfolio of successful case studies and use them as the basis for expansion, rather than go for marketing-led growth from the start. Management responsibilities are defined, but at this stage the company runs on a project-by-project basis and there is a deliberate policy of eschewing job titles wherever possible.

International Orientation

There is no particular reason why Xbridge should not take its message to other countries, and clearly the company sees its immediate future within Europe. Of the four working directors, three speak at least three languages fluently, the company already prefers to use the Euro in its financial statements, and two of the early clients (VerticalNet and LibertySurf) have parent companies outside the UK. It is likely that the first international expansion will take Xbridge to Germany and France, though the company emphasizes that this will be driven by customer demand rather than speculative marketing.

WORLDWIDE **XCEED** GROUP, INC.

Xceed is a Web services company that handles everything from Web design to electronic strategy and e-commerce. An emphasis on solid methodology has underpinned an excellent delivery record while strong focus on profitability positions Xceed well to take advantage of a rapidly maturing marketplace. The UK branch of an American company, it set up as methodfive in August 1999 and was bought by Xceed in February 2000. Nasdaq listed, the company now employs 45 people and turns over £5 million in the UK.

Scorecard:

Innovation	★★★★
Flexibility	★★★★
Human resources	★★★
Growth markets	★★★
Quality of management	★★★★
International orientation	★★★★

Biggest plus:
The solid focus on profitability of the company and its relationships internationally.

Biggest minus:
The company gets tarred with the 'dot-com' brush and asked whether it is losing money when this is not an appropriate way to regard its business.

Worldwide Xceed Group Inc.
7th Floor
Corn Exchange
55 Mark Lane
London EC3R 7NE
Tel: 020 7767 0700
website: www.xceed.com

Worldwide Xceed Group Inc.

The Business

Xceed has existed in the UK for only a year and rapidly gained considerable ground. It specializes in Web technologies and will help customers to implement Internet, extranet and intranet systems. It is avowedly not a dot-com, however, but a service company placing the emphasis on understanding the client's needs and making recommendations in order to deliver a solid Web-based solution, rather than suggesting 'website' as the knee-jerk solution to everything. Its client list includes BT, MTV Europe, News Corporation and Hilton Hotels International, the latter being run from the American office.

Innovation

The company perceives its main innovation as the fact that it delivers on the promises it makes. In the Web sector, suggests UK managing director Michael Walls, delivering to deadline and to brief is the exception rather than the rule. As a result, Xceed spends as much on its infrastructure as it does on research and development so that it can offer a genuine 24 hour, 7 days a week service using its international network of developers.

It is a technology services company, however, and everybody involved in the process has to have a flair, and liking, for the technology involved. The company prides itself on pushing technology as far as it will go, working with a new generation of Web development tools. For example, ATG Dynamo offers the opportunity to build a relationship between the viewer's preferences and what gets viewed on first opening a website, to encourage them to stay on the same site. The objective is always to deliver a business benefit to the client rather than to make a showy website.

It also develops and innovates in its own right. A company called Spherion, which is big in recruitment, has invested in Xceed and is developing the organization's ability to develop technical solutions for its market.

Something the company does less of is the business advice side of Internet consultancy. It's true that there is a certain inevitability about telling someone their Net business must be at the centre of their strategy and advice is available for people wanting to know how to manage rather than just look at their website; however, full-blown business process re-engineering is not something that the company offers. It stands by its methodology, however, as a major factor in its ability to deliver.

Flexibility

As an extremely young company, even prior to its acquisition by Xceed, the business has had precious little time to devote to organizational change. The management altered when the American company became the owner, and certain elements of the company are still controlled from the US, this being an area in which Walls is looking for some flexibility (for example the UK office doesn't get a lot of space on the parent company's website, so controlling this from the UK is something that will hopefully happen in the near future).

The company has successfully traded through a change of ownership and gone from being a start-up with a handful of employees to an employer of some 45 people in a very short time. It has had to demonstrate an adaptability to changes not so much in its market, although the potential for website development has ballooned since it started up, but in the perceptions of its market. As a result it spends more time than would be ideal explaining to customers and prospects that it is a service company rather than a 'dot-com'.

One area in which it has been forced to change its management style has been in the use of freelancers. Changes to the UK laws have meant that 'freelance' is now more rigidly defined than ever before, so a lot of former contractors are now on the staff instead.

Human Resources

In spite of the commonly-held perception that the computing sector has gone through a hard time, jobs for people with the right skills are still relatively easy to come by and as a result the terms and conditions of companies like Xceed have to be very competitive indeed. It therefore has a good offering in terms of remuneration, healthcare and insurance. The company has a very low staff attrition rate and few people have left; in fact several of the contractors (see above) took a pay cut in order to continue working for the company.

The people who respond well to the company's environment will be able to work to objectives rather than specific tasks. Managers set personal goals for people and everyone takes responsibility for the accounts on which they are working at any time. That said, the company is trying to put a more formal process in place to cover the usual human resource functions ; the low attrition rate suggests they have succeeded while the company is at its current size, but as it continues to grow this will need to alter.

Growth Markets

Although Xceed could apply its services to more or less any market, it chooses to grow by focusing on a handful of business areas and doing them well. It therefore specializes in media/publishing and financial services, which it anticipates will grow considerably as the transactional side of e-commerce becomes more sophisticated. In 2000 the UK passed the law required to recognize electronic signatures as legally binding and this will push financial applications more to the fore.

There are also signs that credit card companies are starting to accept the Internet more than they did. Until now the default position for credit card issuers has been to treat the Net like another form of 'card-holder not present' transaction. The other factor affecting this will be the increasing trust people have in Internet security. There has been a lot of research to demonstrate that people are wary of handing their credit card details over online but that they are less so than they were a year ago. Walls believes that many people have a tendency to use the Internet only for research on prices, and that Xceed's job will be to help companies convert those people comparing prices to solid online sales prospects.

Quality of Management

Aside from minor elements, such as the lack of UK reference material on the corporate website as this book went to press, the UK operation has full autonomy from the US. Clearly it doesn't do anything against the company's global interests but as long as it reaches its targets it has total freedom to achieve them in whatever manner it considers appropriate.

It is a very figure-driven business, and management appraisals happen periodically as appropriate; the fact of remaining profitable in the Internet market of the early twentieth century and the low staff turnover tells its own story.

International Orientation

There are numerous justifiable suggestions that the Internet was hyped to death in the late 1990s. One claim that was totally justified, however, was that it would help diminish the relevance of geographical borders for people who were trading. It is therefore no surprise to hear that in a distributed company like Xceed, the UK does a lot of work for clients located in other countries. A lot of the work on Fortune in New York actually happens in London, as does a lot of the work on sites for CBS, Fox and MTV. This is because the people with the most appropriate skills happen to be located in London.

There is a temptation to look at a company like Xceed and dismiss it as another Web design company – something the staff themselves admit is an attitude they come across all too frequently. However, its global nature and consequent 24x7 service offering, plus the insistence on basing itself in the service and consultancy area rather than the dot-com arena has led it to solid profits based on reliable service delivery. If it can perform this way when the sector is in decline then there must be every reason for optimism about its future.

xtempus
natural mobile thinking

Xtempus is a pioneer in developing software and solutions for mobile marketing (m-marketing). Its key products are a 'marketing toolkit', the 'glue' which sticks business-to-business m-marketing applications together, and allows them to be accessed for marketing purposes using a variety of technologies. Based in London, the company is backed by some big names in corporate finance, and already has several major international clients.

Scorecard:

Innovation	★★★★★
Flexibility	★★★★
Human resources	★★★★
Growth markets	★★★★
Quality of management	★★★★
International orientation	★★★

Biggest plus:
Xtempus has developed a unique set of solutions that enable advertisers and marketing professionals to utilize the mobile medium as a marketing channel.

Biggest minus:
The company's success depends on the growth of what is currently an immature market.

Xtempus
New London House
172 Drury Lane
London
WC2B 5QR
Tel: 020 7665 5999
Fax: 020 7665 5998
website: www.xtempus.com

X tempus

The Business

Xtempus creates software and solutions which enable marketing professionals to reach their customers and employees over mobile channels. 'Our marketing toolkit enables companies to drive efficiencies in their marketing effort,' says Richard England, Xtempus's commercial director.

'We're aiming to provide a simple and intuitive mobile marketing platform that enables the utilization of mobile as a marketing channel, says England. 'The Xtempus platform will facilitate the planning, execution and evaluation of m-marketing campaigns.'

Innovation

We have a unique vision of how broad-ranging and important the mobile channel will become as a way for companies to reach customers. This is really driven by our belief in the interactive opportunities afforded by mobile communications.

Xtempus was set up, in December 1999, precisely to exploit these opportunities. Most of its expenditure to date has been on research and development, which occupies two-thirds of the company's staff. The intention is to build software components which are not tied to one device or technology, but could be applied across the board, and this gives Xtempus one of its key differentiators.

'Even if a customer only wants one technology today, such as SMS, our broader vision is tremendously attractive to them, because the future direction of this market is so exciting,' says England.

The original plan was to produce software components which really could be bolted together and made to work first time. These components include SMS messaging, rendering (displaying data), provisioning (setting up users' mobile phones), and advertising. Xtempus has shown, for clients like Reed Exhibitions, that working solutions really can be assembled in a few days.

But because of the immaturity of the market, Xtempus has found it necessary to focus specifically on components required by marketing professionals and to prove the value of its components by building them into complete solutions. These solutions include the Game Engine, supporting solo and interactive games played via mobile devices, successfully employed in 2000 by News International.

The next round of innovations is likely to include location-sensitive marketing, voice and data integration, and stronger integration with back-end systems like core customer relationship management (CRM).

Flexibility

The 'm-marketing' business sector is so young and fluid that no company could survive if it was not flexible – this applies to both the products themselves and the way they are developed. As well as switching its focus from pure components to mobile marketing solutions, Xtempus has had to change the underlying technology on which its software is built. Originally developed in C++ on Microsoft NT, the platform was changed to Java 2 Enterprise Edition to broaden its appeal to corporate companies and systems integrators.

To cope with rapid change, Xtempus is experimenting with 'extreme programming', an American technique where programmers work in pairs, sharing a single terminal. This is a radical departure for many programmers, but it seems to make them more productive, and results in shorter development cycles and more re-usable code – exactly right for a component-based approach in a fast-moving market.

The component approach will also stand Xtempus in good stead in the future, as new and emerging technologies like interactive TV and GPRS (high-bandwidth mobile) become popular. A key factor will be the ability to separate the process logic (what you are trying to do) from the end user interaction (how you are trying to do it), so that new technologies can be introduced at one end of the link without affecting the other – which is exactly what the component approach enables.

Human Resources

As you would expect from a marketing company one of Xtempus's key aims is to enjoy life. 'We got a lot of people out of comfortable, corporate jobs, who were very frustrated with the bureaucracy and lack of creativity and wanted some fun,' says the company's head of human resources, Melanie Wheatley.

'We respect the individual but we also work hard at the team spirit – and for us, the team means the whole company. People are expected to contribute ideas outside their own space.

Anyone who wants a structured, bureaucratic environment with fixed processes wouldn't fit in.'

For a high-tech start-up, Xtempus offers good training opportunities, pay and flexible benefits, including share options for all staff, six-monthly performance-related bonuses, and 25 days' holiday.

Growth Markets

Xtempus is entirely predicated on significant growth in the 'm-marketing' area. 'Our business model is ready today for the stellar adoption of mobile as an additional marketing channel' says England. 'It's such an immature sector that people don't yet realize that technology will play an essential part.'

Initially, therefore, the company had to sell its solutions direct. But it is now developing an indirect sales channel, especially among mobile network operators and major marketing services networks such as Ogilvy & Mather.

It does not matter which technologies become popular, since Xtempus's software can interface with them all. 'We haven't bet the farm on any single technology, like WAP (wireless application protocol), or on any one vertical market,' says England. 'The only bet we've made is that mobile data use will significantly increase over the next few years.'

The advent of new mobile technologies, such as GPRS this year and UMTS in 2002, will doubtless help inspire demand. Xtempus expects sales to be modest in 2001 (six figures), but hopes for a steep increase in 2002 (well into seven figures), and over £7 million by 2003. Competition will doubtless grow with the market, but Xtempus believes it is already ahead of potential direct competitors, and hopes to partner with existing vendors before they develop their own solutions.

Quality of Management

Xtempus was founded by a group of marketing and mobile technology enthusiasts, and for its first few months the company rather lacked direction. But in February 2001 it merged with Talkcast Wireless (a privately held m-marketing business), who brought with it Mark Opzoomer (formerly deputy CEO Hodder Headline, Virgin Interactive) and Toby Constantine (previously marketing director of *The Times* and *Sunday Times*). Since February the company has recruited CTO, Paul Schulz (ex Nokia) and managing director, Kate Walker (ex News Corporation).

The company has a strong and experienced management team. 'We have a very open management style, which is set from the top,' says. Constantine 'We try to avoid bureaucracy, and nobody has a private office.'

Xtempus's first round of funding came from small investors who put up about £2 million. In August, 2000 it raised £10 million from a fund led by Morgan Stanley and Anschutz, who have been extremely helpful opening a lot of doors for the company.

There are no firm plans for more fund-raising.

International Orientation

By the end of 2000, Xtempus had not made any sales outside the UK, although it has pan-European carrier relationships. However, the company's business plan predicts that international sales could outstrip UK sales within two years.

yourautochoice.com
An Avis Europe plc company

No.1 in Nearly New Cars.

Yourautochoice.com is the classic model of a business success story – it detected a long-standing need in its market, addressed it and took a lot of the pain out of what had previously been a laborious process and looks set to do very well as a result. Put simply, it takes nearly new cars, that is cars between 3–18 months old with less than 15,000 miles on the clock, from fleets, refurbishes them to a high standard and delivers them to customers who specify what they want on the Web, typically priced at 20–40 per cent less than new cars.

Scorecard:

Innovation	★★★★★
Flexibility	★★★★
Human resources	★★★★
Growth markets	★★★★★
Quality of management	★★★★
International orientation	★★★★

Biggest plus:
The simplicity and execution of the idea.

Biggest minus:
The state of the market for 'dot-coms' – although yourautochoice is clearly a service company, the Web-based nature of its business may downgrade its value disproportionately in a way that does not equate with the value of its transactions.

Yourautochoice
10 Barley Mow Passage
Chiswick, London W4 4PH
Tel: 020 8580 4701
website: www.yourautochoice.com

Yourautochoice.com

The Business

Yourautochoice.com is designed to change the way fleets dispose of and the way consumers buy nearly new cars.

Today, fleet owners have to use inefficient channels for the disposal of their cars. They suffer from high transaction costs, extended delays in customer fulfilment and severe pressure on margins (intermediaries take 10–25 per cent out of the value chain). Meanwhile end consumers find nearly new cars economically more attractive than brand new or older cars. Consumers tend to worry about the quality and history of older used cars, with a nearly new car they can enjoy the most up-to-date models and a nearly new car with a warranty has great appeal.

Yourautochoice's solution works from two angles. For fleet owners yourautochoice.com re-markets cars while they are still on fleet based on projected car availability dates. This means that the minute a car is 'defleeted' it has an identified purchaser. For consumers, yourauto-choice.com provides the largest supply of nearly new cars on the Internet, and offers an unrivalled level of customer service and support. It quite literally puts the consumer in the driving seat.

Innovation

The company's clearly designed website outlines the individual benefits of selling and buying in this way. A number of areas are worth highlighting, however: the hassle-free nature of buying without salespeople intervening; the choice and value, the guaranteed quality – every car will have an 111-point mechanical and electrical check before it's sent to the buyer, the non-commissioned customer service centre and the fast delivery.

Whether selling fleet cars off to individuals is innovative is open to question; historically they have been disposed of somehow, and there is certainly nothing new about pre-owned car dealers displaying their wares online.

Nevertheless, it is fair to say that yourautochoice innovates in its field – it scores five stars out of five for innovation for a number of reasons. First, the whole concept of upstream re-marketing (that is, marketing a vehicle before it is physically available for sale) is a radical re-think of traditional car distribution – it often takes many months before a car is even presented to an end consumer. Then there is the website itself, which is constantly packed with up-to-date details of which cars are available and for what price at any given time and in a manner fully searchable by the customer. For example, if someone wanted a one-year-old Renault Laguna, they can search Renault Lagunas; if they wanted a hatchback or a 4x4 they can enter that as a criterion; searching by budget or looking for a trade-in value on an existing car is also possible.

After entering details, the customer can log on again after one hour to be presented with carefully selected cars that match their criteria. They can then opt to buy one and it will be delivered within a fortnight. Anyone who has ever bought a second-hand car will confirm that the simplicity and ease of this process are a blessed relief if nothing else!

Another area in which the company is starting to do things slightly differently from the competition is in its approach to the market. As well as members of the public and indeed businesses logging on to the site to buy cars, it is active in setting up deals to push its cars to corporate intranets – so a company could offer its employees early warning of cars in which they might be interested as a cost-free staff support service. This unique business-to-employee marketing programme is facilitated by Avis Europe's corporate partnerships with 75 per cent of the top 500 companies in Europe, including British Airways, SNCF and Diageo.

Yourautochoice is also building white labels for companies or associations with established brand equities and large customer bases to avoid incurring the huge costs involved in building a new brand from scratch and to accelerate customer acquisition. In April 2001, it launched the first of these with the RAC which has a base of more than 5 million members, called RACCarPartner.co.uk. The RAC have undertaken to do all the marketing whilst yourautochoice looks after fulfilling the demand generated on the new site.

Flexibility

The beauty of yourautochoice's business is clearly its simplicity; however, this does not mean it takes a regimented, inflexible approach to how it does its business. The aforementioned corporate intranet scheme, for example, has meant a completely different style of sales pitch, since the company is selling into the corporate arena rather than directly to the consumer, and this requires a suited and booted approach rather than the consumer-ish tone of the website.

The company also found fairly quickly once it had set itself up that customers wanted more than just a website to support them, they needed a helpline to reassure them of the quality of the vehicles and, of course, to arrange for delivery and other practical elements of the sale. The small size of the company meant that it could respond to these and other requests very swiftly. It has also been energetic in pursuing industry alliances with people like the RAC, which effectively underwrites all of the vehicle warranties, or the Bank of Scotland which will arrange financing while a customer is still online, and the company is constantly looking for other ways of improving its service.

Yourautochoice benefits from a stable, sizeable and secure source of vehicles from its relationship with Avis Europe plc, the largest fleet purchaser in Europe. However, given yourautochoice's ambition to become the industry standard for the re-marketing of nearly new vehicles, supply is not restricted to ex-Avis cars: yourautochoice has augmented its supply by targeting other large fleet owners (for example, major lease companies and other rental companies), as well as individual OEMs and franchise dealers.

Human Resources

Although the so-called dot-com sector has suffered in terms of its profile lately, the skills that underpin it are still much in demand. The policy at yourautochoice is therefore to offer competitive remuneration and share options in the company to the people who will be able to take the business forward. Health insurance and other benefits are on offer as a matter of course.

The office is busy but resolutely informal; the hierarchy is flat and the entire staff is welcome to approach chief executive, Saad Hammad, with creative ideas on promoting the company and building on the service – and then they are encouraged to run with those ideas. Hammad is understandably proud of the entrepreneurial and supportive atmosphere this engenders – if you have an idea, great; if it doesn't work, fine, as long as you and the company can learn from it. A problem-solving attitude is a pre-requisite in this predominantly young team, which is being honed to fall back on its own resources as often as it can.

Growth Markets

There are two sorts of car purchase of interest to yourautochoice.com – the individual purchaser and the company looking for a fleet replacement solution. New sales have been up in the UK in recent years so it follows that the pre-owned market will follow this trend, and the company plans to take a fair chunk of the nearly-new section of this area. It has high hopes of its intranet and white-label strategies in taking it further.

Given the complexities involved in dealer buying from fleet owners, yourautochoice plans to develop a fleet to dealer transaction capability in the coming months.

There are also areas it won't touch. Cars older than 36 months are of no interest at the moment, and there are no plans to alter this; it also won't look at any areas that might involve a drop in standards.

Quality of Management

For companies like the Bank of Scotland and the RAC to be interested in sinking money into what could have looked on the drawing board like yet another dot-com, proves that its management is made up of serious people. Some of them are ex-Avis and therefore know the car market extremely well. They were also aware that the quality of the cars from Avis was not reflected in the reputation of the pre-owned car market.

Hammad himself offers a lot of leadership and energy to the company, taking very much a hands-on approach. He is receptive to ideas from more or less anywhere; a question from the Corporate Research Foundation about whether a certain professional organization had been approached about the possibility of offering refurbished nearly-new cars met with a negative answer at the time, but the speed at which he wrote the details down suggested that the answer might well be positive by the time this book comes out!

The flat company structure allows the staff to come forward with ideas at any time, and the company appears to consider its staff and its motivation above all other factors in ensuring the customer receives good service.

International Orientation

Selling pre-owned cars is normally a somewhat parochial process; the presence of the Internet element of yourautochoice means that there is no reason not to build a global element into the business without increasing the development costs dramatically.

The costs that will need to be addressed are of course the logistics; partnerships with the equivalents of the RAC, local support staff and delivery operatives will need to be set up in order for the international operation to work properly. There is every reason to believe this will happen, and successfully; although the company has yet to publicize any international ambitions, it doesn't take any energetic deduction to work out that Avis Europe's presence suggests that branching out into Avis's international territories is in the planning stages somewhere.

zeus

Zeus is one of the companies of which people very rarely hear but whose products are used by a great many people. This is because it supplies Web-server infrastructure products, selling to people in e-business including Internet service providers and other 'under the bonnet' types. It offers a combination of consultancy support and technology solutions and has numbered Cable and Wireless, Lycos, UUNet, Comic Relief and others among its customers. Almost 100 people work for the company, which is privately owned and was founded in 1995.

Scorecard:

Innovation	★★★★
Flexibility	★★★★
Human resources	★★★★
Growth markets	★★★★★
Quality of management	★★★★★
International orientation	★★★★

Biggest plus:
The calibre of the team.

Biggest minus:
Different sections of the company have grown at different rates, which means that it's not always in synch and some departments have a little catching up to do.

Zeus Technology Ltd
Newton House
Cambridge Business Park
Cowley Road
Cambridge CB4 0WZ
Tel: 01223 525000
website: www.zeus.com

Zeus Technology Ltd

The Business:

Zeus is one of the de facto companies of choice for anyone wanting server-side Web infrastructure products, whether because they are an ISP or a company with its own e-commerce website or indeed anyone with mission-critical content on a corporate intranet. *Red Herring* magazine named it one of the 50 most important privately held companies in the year 2000 and it serves some of the world's most demanding websites. The founders were still at college when they set the company up; its mission statement is to provide a fully-supported framework of Web-server infrastructure technologies that reduce the burden of support and maintenance for enterprise customers.

Innovation

Zeus' innovations for its customers lie in the technology and what it enables them to do. Essentially it makes Web services more reliable and scalable. A few years ago when someone needed a more robust presence on the Internet the best option would have been to go and buy another Web server; the scale of the projects involved now means this isn't practical and the complex inter-relation of the various websites means it wouldn't be desirable either. So Zeus has developed software that enables the same server to be pushed further.

The company's flagship product is Zeus Web Server, which has been rated highly by the Standard Performance Evaluation Corporation (SPEC) as the fastest Web server in the world. The architecture uses a number of single-threaded I/O multiplexing processes, each of which can handle ten-thousands of simultaneous connections.

Founders Adam Twiss and Damian Reeves came up with the basic concept while studying computer science at Cambridge in 1995. They made their own website but became aware that the software at the time, which had been designed years before with non-profit making, small audiences in mind, was not equal to the job of mass-market Internet connections. They developed their own software and soon found demand for it started to ramp up once they made it available on the Internet.

The company has scored a number of technical firsts. In October 2000 it set the world record for the fastest Web server by getting to 2.6 gigabytes per second at a sustained rate – the speed of an average modem is 56K. Much of the company's resources go into research and development and it has recognition from a number of companies for its products, including Hewlett-Packard, IBM and Sun.

Flexibility

Although the company has had a solid five years to build up to its current size, the main part of the growth happened in the year 2000. At the end of 1999 the business employed 25 people and managing the growth has been a major task. Twiss explains that the culture of the company as an open and fun place to work has helped but some serious restructuring effort has happened as well. 'We restructured the reporting lines and made each team more autonomous with its own manager,' he says. Attention was then paid to the structure and manpower within each of the teams.

The calibre of the people recruited during this period of rapid growth was also felt to be important. For this reason any visitors to the company's Cambridge offices will find managers who are ex-Oracle, ex-Peoplesoft – in other words people who are used to working in a fast, substantial environment serving enterprise-sized customers.

This should not, incidentally, be taken as any indication that the company is any less than 100 per cent committed to developing its own staff through training and continuing development programmes; rather it foresaw the speed of the growth that was about to happen and took a sensible decision on how quickly the existing staff could be brought p to speed.

In terms of product flexibility, the company's software is all designed with absolute flexibility and scalability in mind – it is well aware that what looks like an extraordinary demand for bandwidth and internet power today can be commonplace tomorrow. Its existing products are therefore more than capable of transferring streaming media such as video in real time; they should also handle whatever new applications are developed over the next few years.

Human Resources

In spite of having imported a tranche of external managers, the company is completely committed to the personal development of all of its staff as far as it can help. The offices are open plan and the atmosphere informal and open. 'We believe in playing hard and playing to win,' comments Twiss. Remuneration is competitive but not excessively so; the assumption, sensibly, is that people who come to a company attracted by only a high salary will be looking for a higher one within a couple of months. Zeus is more interested in people who are excited and motivated by the potential of Internet technology and ready to buy into the ethos of making it run faster and better for the customer.

Growth Markets

There are a number of geographical territories into which Zeus plans to expand (see International Orientation, below), and it already has offices outside the UK. Its main growth area will be dictated by the growth of the Internet itself, which in spite of negative coverage in the media is still building up at a phenomenal rate, to the extent that ISPs and other customers simply can't keep adding new machines to compensate for increasing demand. Software such as Zeus' offering expands their existing systems and should therefore save a lot of money. Use of Internet technology internally in companies with intranets is also increasing.

Basically, Zeus will continue to grow as long as companies need to make their Web systems run better and faster. So far customers including Telefonica, BT and UUNet have adopted the technology, which is an endorsement of some sort.

Quality of Management

As has already been stated, Zeus spent a lot of 2000 building up its management capacity so that it was ready to sustain its new-found size. This has been a success. The current management team has various backgrounds including Twiss and Reeves' own college-to-multi-million-dollar-organization route, an executive chairman who has managed branches of the Whitbread Group and the entire Jeyes Group, a sales vice-president with management experience at Primus Knowledge and Smallworld, and team leaders from Atlantic Systems.

In terms of the day-to-day running of the place, clearly it's different from the way it was when a quarter of its current size. Nonetheless Twiss remains fond of 'management by walking about', believing there is no substitute for the people in charge being able to see what is actually happening in an organization rather than delegating absolutely everything. He also remains committed to being accessible to the staff.

International Orientation

Zeus has a number of international offices already; its head office is in Cambridge, UK, and it has an office in Silicon Valley. It has a support network for sales operations in the Pacific Rim based in Tokyo and sees more business coming from what might be called the developing economies, at least in Internet terms – South America, Eastern Europe and the Middle East are all becoming interested in the electronic communications world but are not yet as advanced as the UK and the US, for example.

The Internet itself is making this development possible by changing slowly from an English-speaking enclave to an internationally-accepted standard. More and more Japanese sites are becoming established, and indeed Zeus has an area for Japanese speakers on its own site. Continental Europe is also becoming more interesting to companies selling this sort of technology, because the French are moving away from their non-standard Minitel system and onto more mainstream Net technologies while countries including Italy are looking more and more at Internet connection.

All of the above points to a lucrative market for Zeus for a long time to come. Its sudden expansion might have become a cause for concern at one point but the increased strength of its management ensured that it worked through this without much of a hitch. It should be a fascinating company to watch as it continues its quiet domination of an area that so many other businesses find so important.

zygon

Zygon Systems provides enterprise software for catalogue management. Its product is a £200,000-plus automated solution to the problems of publishing product information in different media (paper catalogues, websites, WAP phones and so on) and for different purposes (internally for different company departments, externally for customers and suppliers). Based in London, it opened a US office in Spring 2001. The company was formed in 1996 but started serious development of its product in 1999; it has $15 million funding from a group of four investment funds.

Scorecard:

Innovation	★★★★
Flexibility	★★★★
Human resources	★★★
Growth markets	★★★★
Quality of management	★★★★
International orientation	★★★★

Biggest plus:
Zygon is an exciting place to work – operating at the leading edge of its technology in a high-potential market, working with more than adequate funding, full of optimism and opportunity.

Biggest minus:
It's a tight, team-oriented environment, however, and maximum commitment will often be required of staff.

Zygon Systems Limited
Jessica House
191 Wandsworth High Street
London SW18 4LS
Tel: 020 8877 7400
Fax: 020 8877 7401
website: www.zygon.com

Zygon Systems Limited

The Business

Zygon is a privately held software company that provides enterprise catalogue management solutions. The basic principle is that many organizations will need a central repository of product information that can be packaged in different ways for different purposes – for physical catalogues, websites, business-to-business marketplaces, mobile platforms, digital television, and even internal departments (engineering, marketing, sales and support) and trading partners. Zygon was incorporated in 1996 but ran at a very modest level of activity until mid 1999, when it first attracted significant external capital. The version of the Zygon software that was launched in March 2000 has set the style for subsequent developments. Additional funding was secured late in 2000 and the current version of the core product, Zygon 4 Enterprise Catalogue Management (ECM), was launched in Spring 2001. Zygon has now attracted a total of $15 million in two rounds of venture capital funding (June 1999 and November 2000) from prominent investors, Intel Capital, 3i, Bamboo and Taylor Young Investments.

The company currently employs 70 people, mostly at its London headquarters with a small team in a recently established San Francisco office.

Innovation

As e-commerce matures, consumers and trading partners are demanding more product information, richer multimedia content, and the ability to obtain that information from varied sources with delivery in various forms. Zygon's software effectively automates and controls any or all of this. The technology is quite advanced, but it is the application itself that represents a real imaginative leap.

The effective management of product information – for alternative retail channels, within the enterprise, and to an enterprise's customers and suppliers – is also a critical issue in the development of 'collaborative commerce'. Zygon sees this as the third phase of online business, evolving from a first generation that consisted of simple, static HTML pages which were basically online brochures and a second stage that featured some interaction and primitive online transactions. Zygon's third generation extends the transaction capabilities, enables the addition of rich multimedia content, gives users the ability to ask for specific product information, and allows the organization to transact business online with suppliers, partners and employees.

Zygon's vision for e-business is a flow of product information within the value chains from manufacturers through distributors and retailers to consumers. There should be no human intervention unless it is to add incremental value.

This is the philosophical basis for Zygon 4 ECM, but it is also a practical proposition that appeals to many larger enterprises. Zygon's software offers the promise of coherence, and compatibility, it gives organizations an option on the type and quantity of product information, and it supplies an automated environment that speeds up the whole process and minimizes costs.

Zygon has become a member of RosettaNet, a non-profit organization of more than 400 companies that seeks to implement standards for supply-chain transactions on the Internet – particularly in relation to key elements such as product descriptions, part numbers, pricing data, and inventory status. Zygon has demonstrated compatibility with RosettaNet's current standards.

Flexibility

The origins of the company lie in the practicalities of managing library information, and the early prototype products grew out of the need to integrate and publish information in the simplest possible way. But the then management made a significant change in direction during the late 1990s, as the relevance of this technology to the burgeoning e-commerce field became increasingly obvious. In 1999 the product's specification was significantly extended to include multi-channel publishing of multimedia information about a user's products, and this has coincided with the growth in demand for automated catalogue management software.

The founders recognized that they needed both a qualified CEO and a significant tranche of investment capital; both had arrived by summer 1999.

Human Resources

Zygon manages to combine much of the energy and enthusiasm of a start-up with the infrastructure and perks of an established company. As with many companies in this position, the working atmosphere appears casual but is actually committed – tight schedules are the norm, long hours are often required, and a passion for enterprise software technology in general and Zygon's activities in particular would probably be a prerequisite for employment.

There is a strong team ethic, too, particularly among the product developers (half of Zygon's 70 employees work in R&D). Peer review is the norm for professional analysis, an open and supportive approach that avoids a lot of finger-pointing. This is an environment for the team player.

Growth Markets

Typically Zygon partners with big-name IT organizations such as Unipower, Intershop, IBM, and Oracle. Through such relationships the company aims to deliver complete, integrated e-business solutions to its customers. Zygon sells into the manufacturing, distribution and retail sectors generally, and early customers include the electronics components distributor Electrospeed and the generalized retailer *Electrospeed.com* Argos. Pricing for Zygon 4 starts at around £200,000.

The market for Zygon and its products is potentially huge; leading analysts Goldman Sachs and the Yankee Group, have forecast that the product content management business will be worth $4 billion by 2004. The company is an early player in a fast-growing market, and while it does have competitors – mostly US-based – no one company yet has dominance. Zygon's product and the company's vision are both well developed, and Zygon Systems could well become a market leader. Certainly it is alive to specific user requirements, for instance by launching a 'publishing module' for WAP that would allow a user to 'publish' catalogue information to mobile phones.

Quality of Management

Zygon has assembled a high-calibre management team most of whom have particular skills in enterprise database products, a sector that is particularly relevant for Zygon. James Dobree, CEO and President, was formerly VP for sales and business development at network software company RedBox Technologies Inc and before that he was head of strategy and operations for Oracle Europe. The VP for sales came from a top sales role at Informix Software and the VP of marketing joined from a strategic planning position at BT. Sajeeve Bahl, VP of operations and one of the longest standing members of the management team, has had several key IT industry jobs, most recently at The Baan Company and Oracle Europe.

International Orientation

Zygon 4 Enterprise Catalogue Management is designed for international use; it includes multiple language and currency capabilities, for instance, and can be used with geographic modelling tools. Zygon's target markets obviously include the developed world.

The US represents a particularly promising field, of course: e-commerce is better developed on that side of the Atlantic, and there is a willingness to analyse and theorize about the operation of systems which suits the ECM concept. Accordingly, Zygon Systems Inc. opened for business in February 2001 with a US office in San Francisco and a fast-growing pool of employees (primarily for marketing and business development). Zygon is actively looking to form partnerships in the US with system integrators and others; it already has such a deal with Sema plc in Europe, and will expand internationally as customers and opportunities dictate.